W9-DCJ-669

# CONTEMPORARY JUDAISM
## *Patterns of Survival*

# CONTEMPORARY JUDAISM
## Patterns of Survival
### Second Edition

# GILBERT S. ROSENTHAL

HUMAN SCIENCES PRESS, INC.
72 FIFTH AVENUE
NEW YORK, N.Y. 10011

Copyright © 1986 by Human Sciences Press, Inc.
72 Fifth Avenue, New York, New York 10011

Printed in the United States of America
987654321

**Library of Congress Cataloging in Publication Data**

Rosenthal, Gilbert S.
  Contemporary Judaism.

    Updated ed. of: Four paths to one God. 1973.
    Includes bibliographies and index.
    1. Judaism—United States—History. 2. Orthodox
Judaism—United States—History. 3. Reform Judaism—
United States—History. 4. Conservative Judaism—
United States—History. 5. Reconstructionist Judaism—
History. I. Rosenthal, Gilbert S. Four paths to one
God. II. Title.
BM205.R59  1986      296.8'3'0973      85-7659
ISBN 0-89885-260-9
ISBN 0-89885-277-3 (pbk.)

*For Ann*
*He who has found a wife*
*has found goodness.*

# Contents

# *Foreword to the Second Edition*

The first edition of this work, previously entitled *Four Paths to One God: Today's Jew and His Religion*, is no longer in print and I have been encouraged to produce a new and updated version. Evidently the book has filled a need both on the college campuses and in adult education classes in synagogues throughout the country.

Moreover, Jewish life has never been static and the last few years have been no exception to that rule. There have been some interesting changes, and trends have shifted noticeably. For example, the demography of American Jewry has followed new and perhaps unexpected courses. The Jewish population has declined alarmingly so that we never did reach the expected 6 million mark. Additionally, the intermarriage rate has soared beyond expectation and is approaching 40 percent of couples involving a Jewish mate.

I was also unprepared for some of the new developments in religious life. I had not expected Reconstructionism to solidify so quickly into a separate religious movement, although it is still unclear whether it can survive the loss of its incomparable founder, Mordecai M. Kaplan. Nor did I anticipate the unusual resurgence of Orthodoxy, especially in its fundamentalistic, right-wing version. And I could cite other examples.

Consequently, I considered it important to update the earlier version of this study, to incorporate and assimilate new data and facts, and present the latest developments and trends in American Jewish religious life for the consideration of the reader and student. American Jewry is, after all, no monolith or stagnant pool; it is, rather, fluid, organismic, and dynamic. I trust that this new edition will help the reader to fathom the often enigmatic and frequently puzzling phenomenon we call American Jewry.

In preparing this newly revised study, I was fortunate in having the benefit of my supportive and encouraging wife, Ann, to whom I am ever in debt. My colleague, Rabbi Joel Zion of Temple Israel, Lawrence, New York, furnished me with crucial volumes. My dear students and congregants at Temple Beth El in Cedarhurst, New York, inspired me to write and study and for that I am most appreciative. My dedicated secretary, Andrea Gomez, typed the manuscript with care and concern. To them all I offer my profound gratitude.

Gilbert S. Rosenthal

January, 1985
Tevet 5745

# Foreword to the First Edition

It is a strange and perplexing fact that American Judaism, which in its more than three hundred years of existence has produced innumerable volumes and countless periodicals, is still so much of an unknown quantity. American Jews do not seem to understand properly the history of their own community; even less do they grasp the theological trends and religious patterns of the various schools of thought in American Judaism. American Christians are even more in the dark about the history, ideologies, and practices of their Jewish neighbors. Obviously there is a need to present the story of the religious life of American Jewry in an intelligible, lucid, and objective fashion so that all may learn and know.

Such is the purpose of this volume. I have tried to depict the religious life of American Jews in an objective and accurate way so that Jews and non-Jews, collegians and intelligent adults, may understand somewhat better how Jewry in America has built its religious and cultural institutions, how its ideologies and ritual patterns differ, and how the religious trends are evolving in

xi

Jewish life in North America. I have attempted to clear up common misconceptions about variations in theory and practice between the Orthodox, Reform, Conservative, and Reconstructionist versions of Judaism. My hope is that this book will serve the function for which it was intended.

It is my pleasure to express my appreciation to several people who helped me in the conception and execution of this volume. My friend, Mr. Charles E. Bloch, president of Bloch Publishing Company, invited me to undertake the project and has watched its development closely. Mr. Samuel Gross, editor at Bloch Publishing Company, read the manuscript and offered many important suggestions and corrections. My friend Mr. David Gross, executive vice president of the Jewish Publication Society of America, was helpful in improving the style. Rabbis Benjamin L. Teller and Philmore Berger provided me with much of the bibliographical items vital for the extensive research involved. My devoted secretary, Mrs. Dorothy Bernbaum, typed the manuscript.

And lastly and most preciously: my wife, Ann, encouraged me, as always, in my scholarly efforts and enabled me to bring forth the present volume from the realm of thought into that of the printed word. "Give her of the fruit of her hands; wherever people gather, her deeds speak her praise."

G. S. R.

June, 1973
Sivan, 5733

# Introduction

Perhaps the old saw that the only constant factor in life is change is still valid. Certainly there have been many changes in the past decade or two. Trends have shifted; predictions were never realized; unprecedented developments have startled the observers; and more than a few surprises have confounded the experts.

## The American Religious Scene

Americans are still a "religious" people. Ninety percent profess a belief in God; we perceive ourselves to be a believing people. But what deeper meaning is contained in that profession of faith? In what way does it have an impact on or affect the lives of individuals? In a survey published in March 1984, Gallup asked: "Is religion very important in your life?" In 1952, at the height of the great national religious revival, 75 percent responded affirmatively; in 1983, the number dropped to 58 percent—61 percent of Protestants, 56 percent of Catholics, and

25 percent of Jews. As to church and synagogue going, Gallup and others pollsters found that only 40 percent of Americans attend services in a given week—including 17 to 24 percent of Jews. A study of New York worship patterns revealed that 40 percent of the Protestants, 50 percent of Catholics, and 21 percent of Jews attend weekly services. The New York survey disclosed that 66 percent of Protestants pray daily, 58 percent of Catholics, and 30 percent of the Jews. George Gallup, Jr. concludes that while we *seem* to be a religious country, religion does not appear to be at the center of many lives. Indeed, there is widespread ignorance of the Bible, a very shallow religiosity, and a gap between the religious and the moral. Sociologist W. J. McCreedy of the University of Chicago suggests that Americans are turning away from the dictates of organized religion and are drawing upon spiritual feelings of their own to define their faith. Professor McCreedy describes the phenomenon as a decline of the influence of religious authorities and a turn to conscience and individual concepts of God and religion so that religion is important but in an *individual* way.

In a word, there is little ideological content or substance to Americans' religious faith. Consequently, both rituals and theology are anemic; Americans are more prone to *belonging* than *believing*; sociology rather than theology is their motivation; ethnicity rather than the ethical is the impetus for most of the faithful.

Yet, many perceive us to be in the midst of a religious revival, of an upsurge of faith, of a reassertion of the pious impulse. There is much evidence for this thesis in Protestant, Catholic, and, strikingly, in limited Jewish circles. The remarkable growth of Protestant Fundamentalism led by the Rev. Jerry Falwell and others and its profound impact on politics, public morality, and the media has been little short of astounding. Likewise, there seems to be a renewed interest in religion on the campuses and in other sectors of American intellectual life. Professor Harvey Cox of Harvard's Divinity School had described the tide of secularism as irreversible in his classic book of the 1960s, *The Secular City*. But in his newest volume, *Religion in the Secular City*, published in 1984, he has reversed himself and he depicts fundamentalistic and liberation theology as very vital today. "Not only are we witnessing a resurgence of traditional religion in the world, this resurgence has an undeniable —if still indeterminate—*political* significance." Cox describes both fundamentalism and liberation theology as rejections of modern society and the world: the former rejects the perversity and sin of modernity; the latter spurns the evils of capitalism. Cox is firmly convinced that we are witnessing "an era of religious revival and the return of the sacral."

Cox is not alone in detecting a turn to the transcendental and the sacred in human existence. Professor Robert N. Bellah of the University of California at Berkeley agrees that we are in the midst of a reaction against the extreme individualism and preoccupation with self that marked the 1960s as many are searching for "Roots," as he puts it. The popularity of college courses in religion (including Judaic studies) is well documented. There seems to be a ripple of religious revival among intellectuals and academicians such as writer Paul Cowan, sociologist Daniel Bell, legal expert Alan Dershowitz, and others.

It does appear, then, that the pendulum is swinging from the "do-your-thing" generation of the 1960s which was typified by boundless freedom, endless choices, and rootlessness, with politics, art, literature, music, drugs, and aberrant behavior almost a substitute for religion, to religion reborn as an acceptable intellectual option and as the source of ethical and moral commitment.

In Jewish life, this new trend is dramatically evident in the so-called *Baale Teshuvah* (repentant sinners) movement. These are young Jews, including some intellectuals and many disaffected free-spirits and rootless men and women, who have found spiritual mooring, certitude, and ethical-moral guidelines in a simple, fundamentalist brand of Judaism and in right-wing yeshivot whose party line is creedal naivete, irrationalist faith, and religious piety, all frequently orchestrated by a Rebbe or Guru-

type of leader. The rise of right-wing Orthodoxy is, doubtlessly, a reflection of the new fundamentalism sweeping Christianity and Islam.

*Church and State*

Who would have believed that the issue of church and state
would have been placed on the front burner of the 1984 Presidential election between Ronald Reagan and Walter Mondale?
Who would have conceived that prayer in the public schools
and abortion would be given top headlines in the battle for
the American presidency while nuclear disarmament and economic dilemmas were shunted aside? Yet, that is precisely what
happened in the campaign as President Reagan seemed to play
to the Fundamentalist gallery of Rev. Jerry Falwell and company. Not since the John F. Kennedy campaign when the issue
of his Roman Catholic faith was debated and finally laid to rest
has religion intruded so palpably in the election process. President Reagan set the tone in a speech in which he declared that
"politics and religion are inseparable" and from then on, the
candidates seemed to bog down in debates over theology and
religious ethics. Church groups, Catholic priests and Protestant
ministers, as well as rabbis, joined the battle as the issue of abortion, prayer in public schools, and the meaning of separation of
church and state were sharply debated and analyzed.

Actually the breaches in that wall of separation had begun to
show through before the 1984 campaign. The prohibition of
prayer in the public schools had been of concern to Fundamentalists for some time and a variety of Constitutional Amendments had been submitted to permit prayer. Then the United
States renewed diplomatic relations with the Vatican after a
hiatus of over 100 years. In a celebrated New York State case,
the Court of Appeals allowed that a *ketubah* (religious marriage
contract) is an enforceable prenuptial agreement and that the
state can be called in to compel the parties to abide by its provi-
sions. A new series of legislation has been prepared to allow

prayer meetings and Bible classes in public school buildings under the "equal access" doctrine. A host of Amendments and bills are in the works to overturn the Supreme Court's ruling allowing abortion. Most dramatically, the Supreme Court ruled in March of 1984 that a crèche showing the Nativity scene may be displayed on public property as part of the pageant of Christmas. In speaking for the Court, Mr. Justice Burger wrote:

> *The Wall of Separation between church and state is a useful figure of speech, but not a wholly accurate description of the practical aspects of the relationship that exists.*

This landmark decision has triggered a flurry of new cases and challenges, of sharply divided opinions and criticisms. The Fundamentalist Protestants, including Rev. Falwell and the Roman Catholic Church, have applauded the ruling. Even the Lubavitcher Rebbe and the National Council of Young Israel have publicly endorsed the ruling as essential to restoring religion and ethics to public life. Lutheran theologian Richard John Neuhaus, in his 1984 volume, *The Naked Public Square*, has expressed a similar viewpoint, noting that the elimination of religion from the public square leaves us susceptible to tyranny of the left or right to fill the vacuum, or to tyranny of the state itself. The liberals, naturally, have rallied on the other side of the issue and the bulk of Jewish leadership has decried the crèche decision as well as other moves to erode the wall of separation as a danger to both religion and American democracy. Clearly, the shock waves will be felt for some time to come.

What impact will this new philosophy of separation of church and state have on America's Jews? In the past, the intrusion of religion in our private lives, schooling, and business habits had a mixed effect: some Jews, out of shame and embarrassment, swam along with the tide; others opted to stand firmly, reassert their Jewishness, and exhibit a great self-pride and delight in the Jewish heritage. We shall see whether American Jews will choose the former or latter course of action.

*Demographic Changes*

In a short space of time, possibly no more than 20 years, the picture of American Jewry has changed, in some cases quite radically. The demographic scene has been fluid for some time and the trends that were adumbrated in the 1960s have taken on sharper characteristics in the decade of the 1980s. The population of American Jews never hit the expected six million and the best guesses of Professors Fred Massarik, Sidney Goldstein, U.O. Schmelz, Sergio della Pergola, Roberto Bachi, and others, are that we have possibly 5.7 million Jews in America and maybe as few as 5.3 million. This decline has been caused by several factors: a dipping birthrate; delayed marriage and single lifestyle; and a fast-rising rate of mixed marriages with only about 22 percent of the non-Jewish partners converting to Judaism. Of course, not all factors are negative and some trends do reverse themselves. For example, not all out-marriages result in losses to Judaism and the Jewish people. Professor Egon Mayer, sociologist at Brooklyn College, has demonstrated that 10 to15,000 non-Jews convert to Judaism yearly and that there are between 150,000 and 200,000 "Jews by choice" in America today. Nor may we assume that birthrates will stay constant or that Jews will continue to delay marriage. In fact, there is some evidence of an upswing in marriages and births in the Jewish community. The experts seem to concur, however, that unless the current patterns shift there will be a downward trend in Jewish population in the years ahead.

Another new fact of demography is the migration of great numbers of Jewish population primarily to the Sunbelt states of Florida, Texas, California, Arizona, and New Mexico. In their study (1984) of the population of greater New York, Professors Paul Ritterband and Steven M. Cohen discovered that the Jewish population of New York City had declined to 1.133 million in 1981 and that the population was aging, bearing few children, and moving away. Even the suburban counties were experiencing population drops. At the same time, the Jewish population in Sunbelt states was increasing substantially but not yet at a rate capable of replenishing the urban losses in the northeast and midwest. Additionally, several observers have noted that the further Jews move away from major centers, the greater the chance of out-marriages and lower fertility. Needless to say, such radical population shifts have a traumatic effect on old, established neighborhoods whose synagogues, religious schools, and community services are often depleted and shattered.

## Contrapuntal Themes

The 1971 survey of America's Jews sponsored by the Council of Jewish Federations was a careful and costly study that revealed that 82 percent of heads of Jewish households identified with Judaism as a religion but that only a little more than half of that number actually belonged to synagogues. Of those who identify with Judaism, 40.5 percent considered themselves Conservative, 30 percent Reform, 11.4 percent Orthodox, and a mere 4.1 percent described themselves as atheists or agnostics. Of those affiliated with a congregation, about 50 percent were in Conservative ones. In 1981–82, the National Survey of American Jews was taken by the American Jewish Committee. It used a low sample (1,400 respondents) in a far simpler questionnaire method. The results differed somewhat from the earlier study; they indicated that 36 percent considered themselves Conservative, 26 percent Reform, and 6 percent Orthodox, with some 32 percent listed as other (Reconstructionist, nonaffiliated, secular, etc.). Studies of New York and Boston Jews yielded results that were not too dissimilar: roughly 35 to 36 percent were listed as Conservative, 29 to 35 percent Reform, and 5 percent (Boston) to 13 percent (New York) Orthodox. In short, the American Jewish Community defines itself in religious terms but only about 40 to 50 percent are actually affiliated with synagogues.

The level of ritual is even more dismal. The national studies as well as the New York and Boston studies concur that most Jews attend a Seder for Passover and light Hanukkah candles;

more than half attend High Holiday worship and fast on Yom Kippur; but only a small minority keep strictly kosher homes (15 to 26 percent), observe the Sabbath in the classic fashion (5 to 13 percent), or kindle Sabbath candles (22 to 43 percent). As to synagogue attendance, the New York analysis indicated that about 7 percent of heads of households and spouses attend weekly. The Boston study clearly proves that second-generation Jews observe less than their parents, third-generation Jews even less, with some stabilization and even slight increases in peripheral *mitzvot* among the fourth. While the number of Orthodox has been declining steadily, the proportion of those who observe more stringent rituals has grown. The Reform group, on the other hand, has displayed greater laxity in observing rituals such as Sabbath candles and its synagogue attendance has dropped sharply from 1965 to 1975. Of course, there are untallied American Jews whose religion is UJA or Federation, Israel Bonds or a Jewish hospital, Zionism and the State of Israel. For them, ritual and religious experiences have taken a radically different route.

The Jewish education scene is one of mixed patterns, too. Estimates differ sharply as to how many Jewish children receive some Jewish education between age three and seventeen. Some say only 28 percent receive a Jewish education; others insist that 50 percent receive an education; and others maintain that the figure is 60 percent. But the facts are clear that a huge segment of Jewish children receive no Jewish education whatsoever.

Small wonder, then, that Dr. Rela Geffen Monson's study of Jewish college students revealed that 50 percent do not oppose mixed marriage and that two-thirds are seriously dating non-Jews, while over one-quarter indicated that religion is not a factor in choosing a mate. On the other hand, Professor Monson concluded that there is a high correlation between intense Jewish education, home rituals, and parental involvement and student involvement in Jewish activities and worship at college.

Paradoxically, even as ritual observance has been declining in most segments of American Jewry, the right-wing groups have intensified their commitment to rituals and obscure *mitzvot* of which few if any had heard, much less observed. And more remarkably, we are witnessing rich theological and scholarly creativity in North American Jewry. Professors Abraham J. Heschel and Mordecai M. Kaplan are gone; their legacy bears fruits still. But we are not lacking other great thinkers and theologians. Rabbi Joseph B. Soloveitchik stimulates us with his profound, brooding existentialism and unresolved dialectics. His disciples in the Orthodox group including Norman Lamm, Walter Wurzburger, Shubert Spero, and David Hartman, as well as the older scholars such as Eliezer Berkovits have augmented Orthodox thinking in many areas. Emil Fackenheim, formerly of the University of Toronto and now in Jerusalem, has produced solid philosophical works and has expounded a theology of the Holocaust in such writings as *Quest for Past and Future, God's Presence in History*, and *The Jewish Return into History*. Eugene Borowitz, Jacob Petuchowski, W. Gunther Plaut, and Levi Olan are but a few of the stellar Reform thinkers whose studies have stimulated and enlightened. Among the Conservative thinkers, the late Max Kadushin, Robert Gordis, Seymour Siegel, Jacob Agus, and England's Louis Jacobs have been remarkably prolific and creative theoreticians. Harold Schulweis has brought his rich insights to Reconstructionist views of God, human suffering, and Jewish problems.

American Jewish thinkers have even created a radical, "death-of-God" trend in theology. Richard Rubenstein, professor of philosophy at the University of Florida, has shocked more traditional thinkers with his *After Auschwitz* (1966) and other works. He writes that "Since Auschwitz I cannot believe in the God of history who chose Jews because then God must have willed six million to slaughter." Consequently, Rubenstein rejects the notion of a good, omnipotent God, and he redefines God as the "Omnipotent Nothingness." Rabbi Sherwin T. Wine, a Reform rabbi in Michigan, takes an even more radical approach. Describing himself as an "ignostic," he has founded a Society for Humanistic Judaism. His program declares that there are no "forever answers" in life and values must be drawn from a heightened sense of the individual. In his temple there are no sanctas; sacred texts are secondary to contemporary psychology and philosophy; Judaism is second to individual welfare and our American culture. For him, Judaism is a "cultural and aesthetic option" with numerous different intellectual commitments.

Such a variety of creative theologians and philosophers is surely a sign of vitality in American and Canadian Jewry as is the existence of a rich harvest of young, American-trained scholars who are producing solid works of scholarship in Bible, Talmud, Midrash, Hebrew, Jewish history and literature, and related fields.

So we are faced with a strange paradox: On the one hand, we observe the intensification of the core leading to fundamentalism; on the other hand, we are witnessing the unravelling of the periphery hurling us into assimilation. Fred Massarik has discovered that 6.4 percent of residents in Jewish homes are non-Jews (i.e., gentile spouses and children) and that 9.5 percent of people raised as Jews now indicate no preference for a specific faith. If we combine the two figures, we perceive that an appallingly high number of Jews and their families are either marginal, non-Jews, or no longer Jews! At the same time that this bleakness has enveloped Jewry, the number of yeshivah and Day School students is at an all-time high, thousands of collegians take courses in Hebrew and Judaica, thousands more visit and study in Israel, and observances such as *kashrut* or Shabbat are no longer bizarre aberrations upheld by a few diehards and "kooks."

Which of these divergent trends will prevail? Is it to be a continued, mutually enriching symbiosis between American culture and Jewish culture? Or is the dominant civilization to submerge the Jewish component? Whatever is to be the future of the Jewish religion, we may anticipate that American Jews will continue to play their contrapuntal themes with their customary passion.

# The Religious Development of American Jewry

## I

### How It All Began

When those three frail boats left the harbor of Palos, Spain, in search of the Indies under the command of Christopher Columbus, little did they imagine that they were about to discover a new world. And little did the several Marranos, or secret Jews, who were aboard dream that their tortured and harassed people, just then expelled from Spain and soon to be banished from Portugal as well, would find their greatest haven in the new continent they were to discover in 1492. The old Talmudic sages taught that even before God sends forth His punishment He has prepared the antidote. How aptly put! The calamity of the expulsion from the Iberian Peninsula was simultaneous with the discovery of America. Truly, a miracle!

Of course, only isolated Jews found their way to New Spain in the fifteenth and sixteenth centuries. And those who came were hardly able to practice Judaism, for the Church-controlled colonies enforced the Inquisition in some instances until the early nineteenth century. Judaism was an illicit faith in Spanish and Portuguese colonies, and Marranos who feigned Catholicism but secretly observed Judaism were liable to be burned at the stake. But Jews could live freely and even worship freely in British or Dutch settlements—and so they did. The earliest Jewish communities flourished in South America under Dutch rule. When, however, the Dutch lost their hold on Recife, Brazil, to the Portuguese, the grim clouds of persecution began to obscure the sun of freedom. The Jews could still smell the pungent odor of singed flesh from the *autos da fé* of Spain and Portugal, Italy and France. With the coming of the Spaniards, they knew it was time to pack and leave in quest of a new home. Some ended up in the Dutch West Indies and built notable communities in places like Curaçao; others went further north to New Amsterdam. And so it was that in 1654 the *St. Charles* brought twenty-three Jews to the shores of North America. Actually, some isolated Jews had been in the colony several months earlier, but with the arrival of the twenty-three, the American-Jewish chronicle began to unfold.[1]

From then on, little clusters of Jews began to appear on the east coast of America. They came to Newport, Rhode Island, and Savannah, Georgia; they settled in Charleston, South Carolina, and Philadelphia, Pennsylvania; they found their way to Richmond, Virginia, and Montreal, Canada. And minuscule Jewish settlements and isolated Jewish immigrants were to be seen on Long Island and in New Jersey, on the Thames River of Connecticut, in the forests of Massachusetts, and in the swamps of Florida.[2]

The Jewish community grew very slowly. After all, even in contrast to all of the problems of living as a Jew in Europe, the New World was no paradise—it was scarcely more than a howling wilderness filled with hostile Indians and enormous personal perils. And we must not overlook the tremendously dangerous ocean crossing that took several months and which many never survived. So they came slowly, in a trickle rather than a flowing stream. By the time of the Revolution, there may have been 2,000–3,000 Jews (some say there were but 1,300). The Napoleonic Wars gave a bit of a nudge to Europe's Jews to leave, so that by 1826, Isaac Harby, the American-Jewish writer, playwright, and religious reformer, estimated the Jewish population at 6,000. The era of revolution in Europe (1830–1848) sent more to the freer shore of America, and with each frustrated liberal movement in Europe, there came an increasing flow to the New World. By 1840, 15,000 Jews lived in America; there were 50,000 in 1850, and 150,000 on the eve of the Civil War. Gradually, they began to venture away from the East Coast and the secure sight of the Atlantic, and to faraway homes. After the Louisiana Purchase, Americans moved west of the Alleghenys— and Jews went too—so that by 1880, there were Jews in every state, save Oklahoma. In fact, 173 towns listed Jewish populations with a higher percentage out West (1.6 percent) than in the Northeast (.06 percent). They entered any and every kind of trade, business, and profession. The early Sephardic (Spanish-Portuguese) refugees became planters, merchants, shippers, manufacturers, writers, lawyers, doctors, and statesmen. The Ashkenazim (German, Polish, East European Jews) excelled as itinerant peddlers, petty traders, shopkeepers, bankers, and stockbrokers. Only later in the history of American Jewry was there a discernible shift into professions such as teaching, law, dentistry, medicine, accounting, and pharmacy.[3]

After 1880 the entire demographic picture changed radically. The infamous May Laws of Czar Alexander III which were adopted in 1881, squeezed the Russian Jews economically beyond their endurance. The government-supported pogroms helped destroy the last shreds of their security, and Russian Jews flocked to America and Canada in torrential streams. Of course, Russian and Polish Jews had been there before the Civil War (Hyam Salomon, for example, was from Posen), but the masses came after the 1880's. In fact, between 1881 and 1924, over two and a half million Jews found a haven in the United States, and many others settled in Canada. Their arrival truly ushered in a new era in American-Jewish history.[4]

The tragedy of the Holocaust in Europe further swelled the wave of immigrants to America. In the 1930's, as the noose of

Nazism tightened around the necks of German and Austrian Jewry, thousands of refugees flocked to America, including many of the followers of Rabbi Joseph Breuer and the neo-Orthodox Agudat Israel faction. In fact, as many as 150,000 German, Austrian, and Czech Jews made it to America before the trap swung shut. After the Holocaust, another 100,000 survivors of the calamity were admitted to the United States. Many of the new group came from Hungary, Rumania, Poland, and Russia, and many were ultra-Orthodox followers of the Satmar Rebbe, the Lubavitcher Rebbe, and various other Hasidic leaders. This latter migration further altered the character of American Jewry and, in fact, gave Orthodoxy a much-needed shot in the arm and a far more pietistic and fanatical cast than had previously obtained.[5]

Meanwhile the older immigrant groups settled down to the task of Americanization and integration. They set up their religious, charitable, communal, and social institutions. Synagogues, religious schools, old-age homes, Jewish hospitals, social agencies, fraternal groups, Zionist groups, and labor organizations dotted the land. Jews began to play increasingly prominent roles in secular activities. The Sephardim and old German settlers nestled into comfortable respectability and material success. After World War I, native-born Jews like Cyrus Adler, Louis Marshall, Julian Morgenstern, Louis Lipsky, and others, made their mark in Jewish and general affairs as leaders of great institutions and movements. Rabbis stepped out of their parochial roles and acquired national and even international prestige. The drive for Americanization and the impetus to "make it" shaped an unbridgeable gap between the immigrant generation and their offspring. The older generation looked sadly upon the young disaffected, alienated Jews who despised the Old World Orthodox ways of the parents, who ran away in droves from the fetid *shtieblach* and dank *heders,* who scoffed at the Yiddish patois of the elders, and whose great drive was to get educated, make money, and be Americans. A whole generation became a "lost generation" as a result of this conflict of life-styles and values. And the new generation promptly slipped into middle-class patterns, championing foresight, sobriety, education, and docile, law-abiding children—championing everything, in fact, except Judaism, Torah education or religious observances.[6]

Happily, World War II changed the patterns of thinking and acting of the post-World War I generation of Jews. The Holocaust shook American Jewry to its very foundations. Gone was the great thrust to be Americans. Gone was much of the old alienation. Gone was the desire to run away from Judaism. Gone, too, perhaps, was the sense of complacency that proclaimed "It can't happen here." Jews became Jews again—reluctantly perhaps, but nonetheless positively. Synagogues burgeoned; Jewish suburbs grew; Jewish education was enriched and Day Schools proliferated; Reform and Conservative Jewry expanded phenomenally; Orthodoxy streamlined its operation and became credible and even fashionable. The American Jew felt a greater Jewish identification; he needed to *belong* even if he felt no need to *believe*. And when a reborn State of Israel was a distinct possibility, he thrust himself wholeheartedly into its gestation and identified totally with its progress and perils. Ironically, the American Jew never felt more at home here while at the same time he never felt more of a kinship with the Jewish People.[7]

Was the process of integration into American society an easy one? Did the Jew find the path of acceptance a smooth one? Was he compelled to fight for acceptance? Or has America been different from other lands?

The answer is: yes—and no.

America has been different from other lands, and, at the same time in some respects, has not been different. America has generally adhered to the notion of separation of church and state and the federal constitution has proscribed an established church. Freedom for the Jew, as for other religious groups in America, has been unparalleled and unrestricted. In fact, state and local governments have often aided and abetted Jewish religious institutions. There has not been an organized political anti-Semitism here as existed, for example, in Germany, Austria,

Poland, Russia, or France. Nor has the government been party to any anti-Jewish legislation, pogroms or Inquisition. In America, anti-Semitism has been confined to the "lunatic fringe." Jews enjoy a sense of being "at home" with little feeling of living in *Galut,* exile, or even Diaspora. The pluralistic society in which Americans live has also made Jewish life a fairly simple one here. Americans tend to identify themselves along religious rather than ethnic or national lines. Consequently, Jews are just another "religious denomination," one of the more than 250 such entities in this land. In such a heterogeneous society, no one objects to theological or ethnic idiosyncrasies or peculiarities. Assimilation has never proved a major threat here; Jews did not have to be baptized in order to "make it." Jews have been able to contribute enormously to American civilization in every field of human endeavor; their judges, doctors, writers, teachers, and businessmen have shared beyond all proportion to their numbers in the flourishing of America. Moreover, Jews have lived in a state of voluntarism and free choice: no one coerces them to belong to a temple; no one synagogue rules another, and no central body or chief rabbi enforces ritual practices. In America, Jews—more than other groups—enjoy congregational independence and undogmatic pragmatism. Finally, Americans tend to revere religion in general and a vague, inchoate notion of a Deity, while eschewing dogmatism and fanaticism.[8]

All of these factors have marked American Jews as a uniquely happy and singularly blessed Jewry in the long history of Israel. But there is another side to the coin as well. American Jews have not achieved what they have without a struggle: America has not been totally unlike its predecessors, and, in fact, it suffers from some of the very maladies that ailed its antecedents in Europe.

Let us recall that the people who settled the New World carried from the Old the virus of prejudice and racism. For example, when that ragged band of Jewish immigrants debarked at New Amsterdam harbor, Governor Peter Stuyvesant wanted to ship them right back. He despised Jews "with their customary usury and deceitful trading with the Christians" and he worried lest that "deceitful race—such hateful enemies and blasphemers of the name of Christ" infect, trouble, and corrupt the community. It took two letters from the Dutch West India Company (in which Jews were substantial stockholders!) to persuade Stuyvesant to let them stay. They were to receive civil and political rights but could not exercise their religion in a synagogue or a public gathering; they were not to be employed in any public service or to open retail shops, but were to carry on their business quietly and their religion unobtrusively at home and "without doubt endeavor to build their houses, close together in a convenient place on one or on the other side of New Amsterdam —at their choice—as they do here." In other words, no public worship, no free economic enterprise, no public office, and a ghetto. Not a very auspicious beginning![9]

The situation in Maryland was even worse. The "Toleration Act" of 1649 provided that "whosoever denies our Savior Jesus Christ to bee the sonne of God, or shall deny the holy Trinity . . . shall be punished with death and confiscason or forfeiture of all of his or her lands and goods to the Lord Proprietary and his heires." In 1658 the Marrano physician Jacob Lumbrozo was actually tried on this charge and nearly lost his life. In 1723 the law was "liberalized" and no one was to be executed for a first offense. Instead, the culprit was to be fined and "his tongue bored." In case of a second offense, he would be branded on the forehead with a "B" (Blasphemer); and if he persisted in his heresy, he would be executed. While the law remained a dead letter, as recently as 1968 a man in Maryland was actually tried on that ancient charge—and was convicted.[10]

We must bear in mind that most states had established churches in the seventeenth and eighteenth centuries. Some had no established religions and gave religious toleration to dissenters, while others persecuted, harassed, and even expelled nonconformists. Obviously, Jews fared best in states where the church was disestablished and where the ideas of Locke and Rousseau, Hume and Voltaire had blown a fresh breeze of religious freedom. The English were generally benevolent towards Jews. The Act of Parliament of 1740 naturalized citizens after seven years and specifically exempted Jews from Christian

oaths. Virginia ended the established church, thanks to Thomas
Jefferson; New York, Pennsylvania, and the Northwest Territory
followed the lead. And the American Revolution and the Constitution cut the Gordian knot between church and state once and
for all. Still, the states were not bound by the doctrine, and
several persisted in maintaining a Christian character and in
debarring Jews and other dissenters from public office. It was
not until 1826 that Maryland eliminated the last anti-Jewish
disabilities and allowed Jews to take office without swearing a
Christian oath. It was only in 1833 that Massachusetts did the
same. North Carolina retained its discriminatory regulations as
late as 1868 and New Hampshire held out until 1878.[11]

Moreover, Jews have been forced to do battle for their rights
on many occasions. Asser Levy had to wage a campaign for the
right to serve guard duty in New Amsterdam. Jews were humi-
liated by General Grant's Order 11 of 1862 accusing them "as
a class" of profiteering and smuggling and expelling them from
Ohio, Kentucky, and Indiana. They had to lobby to get Congress to pass the Chaplaincy Bill of 1862 to permit a Jewish
chaplain to serve in the armed forces. They combated the notion
of America as a "Christian nation"; they attacked the Blue Laws;
they sought to remove Bible readings, prayers, and Christological celebrations from public schools; they joined forces to combat the rising tide of anti-Semitism that appeared after the Civil
War and even more noticeably after World War I.[12]

No, America is not Europe. But neither is it *entirely* different.
The Founding Fathers of America did seek to make it different, however. Influenced by the English deists and French *philosophes*, Washington, Jefferson, Adams, Franklin, Paine, and Madi-
son were determined to create a land in which church and state
would be separated forever and bigotry and prejudice would
find no haven. Washington wrote to the Touro Synagogue in
Newport after the members had saluted him on his election to
the Presidency:

> *It is now no more that toleration is spoken of as if it was by the
> indulgence of one class of people that another enjoyed the exercise of*

*their inherent natural rights. For happily the Government of the United States, which gives to bigotry no sanction, to percecution no assistance, requires only that they who live under its protection, should demean themselves as good citizens, in giving it on all occasions their effectual support.*

And Thomas Jefferson wrote to Major Mordecai M. Noah, Jewish religious leader, playwright, politician, journalist, newspaper editor, and Zionist dreamer, that

*Your sect by its suffering has furnished a remarkable proof of the universal spirit of religious intolerance, inherent in every sect, disclaimed by all while feeble, and practised by all when in power. Our laws have applied the only antidote to this vice, protecting our religions, as they do our civil rights, by putting all on an equal footing.*

Jefferson warned, however, that more remained to be done because "public opinion erects itself into an Inquisition" and is often as fanatical as the flames of the *auto da fé*, as Jews knew only too well, and he urged a reformation of public opinion on this point.

The First Amendment to the Constitution declared that "Congress shall make no law respecting an establishment of religion, or prohibiting the free exercise thereof . . ." But this clear-cut affirmation of religious freedom has been far from clear-cut in practice. The Supreme Court has allowed Congress to compel blood transfusions for Jehovah's Witnesses, prohibit polygamy among Mormons, compel the Amish to send their children to public schools, require Quakers to return runaway slaves, and jail an army doctor in 1967 for refusing to teach medicine to Green Berets in Vietnam because of his moral and religious compunctions.[13]

The separation issue has been a thorny and complex one almost from the birth of our nation. In 1833 the Supreme Court held that the First Amendment applied only to the national government, and the Fourteenth Amendment had to be adopted to extend it to the states. In 1878 the Court reaffirmed the complete separation of church and state, and in the Everson case of 1948 it reiterated the principle of a "wall of separation" between the two that must never be breached. Yet, the wall has been breached time and again. Chaplains serve in the armed forces and are paid by the government; some states maintain kosher law enforcement departments at public expense; the Court has allowed the use of public buses for parochial-school children as well as the supplying of surplus food and textbooks to such schools; prayers are heard in the Congress at all sessions; the coins of the realm proclaim "In God we trust"; the Pledge of Allegiance speaks of "One Nation under God"; and churches, synagogues, and parochial schools are exempt from taxes. The Supreme Court has outlawed Bible readings and prayers in public schools and, in recent cases, has ruled direct state payment of salaries to parochial teachers unconstitutional as an "excessive entanglement." On the other hand, it does permit *indirect* aid to the students in parochial schools. As Professor Paul Freund of Harvard puts it: "If the precise meaning of the First Amendment is not clear, the application of its safeguards to the States is even more elusive."[14]

The Jewish community has been caught up in this constant struggle to define the relationship of church and state. Its long-held position has been to keep state and church separate. Back in the 1870's, Reverend Sabato Morais contested the designation of America as a "Christian nation" while Rabbi Marcus Jastrow blocked a move to call Pennsylvania a "Christian state." Rabbis Isaac Mayer Wise and Max Lilienthal were enmeshed in a similar struggle in Ohio. Then came the campaigns against the Sunday Blue Laws: Jews argued that such laws worked undue hardship on Sabbath observers. Next was the endeavor to free the public schools of sectarianism, Christmas plays, Nativity scenes, crèches, and Christological overtones. And the issue has not yet been resolved—if, indeed, it ever will be. In the past, all Jewish groups opposed federal or state aid to parochial schools. But lately, due to the financial plight of yeshivot and Day Schools, Orthodox Jews and some Conservative and Reform Jews have joined forces with Catholics in urging such aid—constitutional prohibitions notwithstanding. Clearly, the Jewish community—certainly the religious component thereof—is perfectly willing to perform about-faces if the needs of the Jewish community so require. The wall of separation between church and state has its chinks.[15]

*Religious Institutions*

Whenever Jews came to a new community, their first priorities were to establish the religious institutions that were vital for their survival. America was no different in this regard. The earliest Jewish settlers purchased Jewish cemeteries, built *mikvaot* (ritual baths), set up charity funds for the poor, for wayfarers, for messengers from the Holy Land, and established religious schools. And they persevered in building synagogues. The first New Amsterdam settlers were not permitted public worship, so they prayed in private homes. But by 1695, an early map of New York shows a synagogue on Beaver Street. In 1729 the Spanish and Portuguese congregation built its synagogue on Mill Street. Savannah Jewry constructed their synagogue in 1733; Philadelphia followed in 1740; Charleston Jewry built theirs in 1749; and the Jews of Newport erected their splendid edifice in 1759. Six congregations greeted President George Washington on his inauguration.[16]

The Sephardic Jews controlled the liturgical services. They had been here first; they dominated the scene economically, socially, and religiously. And even though Ashkenazim were to be found here as early as 1654, they could not break the Sephardic monopoly. But eventually the old Sephardim lost their hold and Ashkenazic synagogues following either the English, Dutch, or German patterns began to crop up. Easton, Pennsylvania, had an Ashkenazic synagogue as early as 1761. Philadelphia's Rodeph Shalom was founded in 1802. And when a group of English Jews seceded from New York's historic Shearith Israel Congregation in 1825 and established B'nai Jeshurun Synagogue, the Sephardic monopoly was broken forever, and new Ashkenazic synagogues proliferated. By 1825 there were some forty synagogues in America—and not one new Sephardic congregation. Ashkenazic synagogues appeared in Cincinnati (1824), Baltimore (1830), Albany (1841), New Orleans, St. Louis, Syracuse (1841), Boston, (1842), Rochester (1846), Buffalo (1847), Los Angeles (1854), and virtually everywhere else in the land. To be sure, private home services existed long before public worship was established. Thus, Jews held home services in Albany as early as 1682, although the first synagogue was not built until 1841.

Of course, we must not overlook the appearance of Reform temples in the 1840's and 1850's. There was even a sprinkling of East European *shuls*. The first was in Buffalo in 1847; then came the Polish synagogue in Chicago in 1849 and New York's famous Beth Hamidrash Hagadol in 1852. Russian, Polish, Latvian, and Lithuanian synagogues sprung up. After the mass migration of 1881 the numbers soared. In 1860 there were 77 synagogues and 34,412 seats. In 1870 there were 189 Jewish religious organizations, 152 edifices, and 73,265 seats. The number rose to 270 congregations and 50,000 members by 1875. In 1890 there were 535 synagogues, of which 316 were Orthodox and 217 were Reform. By 1916, America boasted a stupendous 1,900 congregations, most of which were East European. In 1937 there were 3,700 congregations, of which 3,000 were Orthodox with 250,000 members, 350 Conservative with 75,000, and 300 Reform with 65,000 members. But of 4.7 million Jews, only a fraction was affiliated.[17]

Much of this changed with the religious boom that followed World War II. Synagogues and religious institutions spread to new areas and grew at a dizzying pace. As of 1972, with some six million American Jews, there were 840 Conservative synagogues with a million and a half members, seven hundred Reform temples with over a million members, and an undetermined number of Orthodox *shuls* with over a million affiliates. In short, about 55 percent of American Jews are affiliated with congregations.

The American synagogue has been strikingly different from its European forerunner in a number of ways. In Europe, the *Gemeinde*, or community organization, controlled Jewish life, including synagogues, Jewish education, philanthropy, and social services. In America there never was a *Gemeinde;* the synagogue became the basic institution and each synagogue was independent of the other. Synagogues handled kosher slaughtering, matzah baking, charity funds, Jewish education, and community affairs. But little by little, the power of the synagogue eroded. After 1812 in New York, for example, Shearith Israel no longer licensed the ritual slaughterers. Instead, the butchers controlled them—opening the door to all varieties of violations of dietary laws and unscrupulous behavior. Similarly, by the middle of the nineteenth century, matzah baking became a commercial matter run by the bakers. Even the religious schools which had normally been under the aegis of the local synagogues began to go off on their own. In 1838, Rebecca Gratz set up an independent Sunday School in Philadelphia and others followed suit in establishing Day Schools, Sunday Schools, Talmud Torahs, and *heders,* separate and apart from synagogues. Cemeteries which had always been owned by synagogues were organized as separate corporations after the middle of the nineteenth century. The old fines and sanctions levied by congregations against miscreants no longer carried much deterrent force. And after the 1820's, synagogue secessions became commonplace, with new schismatic groups, Reform temples, and later on, Conservative congregations, constantly splitting off from the parent group. Finally, secular organizations developed and drew off power from the religious groups. Already in the 1830's, New York's Jews formed secular benevolent groups. B'nai B'rith was born in 1843. Then came the Zionist groups, the labor organizations, the Bund, the Farband and Workmen's Circle, the American Jewish Committee and American Jewish Congress, the Federations and Community Councils, the *Landsmanschaften* and fraternal groups. All of them weakened the power of the synagogue and detracted from the religious controls exerted by synagogues over the people.

In the mid-twentieth century the synagogue underwent a further metamorphosis and the synagogue-center emerged as the norm for American Jewish life. The synagogue-center became the hub of Jewish communal life—religious and even secular. Jews flocked to the synagogue-center not so much for prayer as for religious education for the young, social functions, club programs, athletic facilities, and communal meetings. Most recently, new synagogal forms have been tentatively evolving. Groups of young people have set up religious communes called *Havurot* in the Boston and New York areas. Others have established unstructured synagogues that meet in private homes and allow free rein in liturgical patterns. Whether such "synagogues" will prosper remains to be seen.

There were other differences between European religious life and the American pattern. Whereas Europe boasted distinguished rabbis and scholars, America's clergy were for a long time laymen, *hazzanim,* and self-styled ministers. The *parnassim,* or lay leaders, were supreme over the clergy; even a distinguished rabbi like Morris Raphall of New York's B'nai Jeshurun had to get permission from his lay board to marry off his own daughter. And in view of the lack of competent religious authorities, it is small wonder that Shearith Israel turned to the Amsterdam rabbinate for rabbinic guidance while B'nai Jeshurun paid a half-shekel to the Chief Rabbi of England to answer a religious query. The first ordained rabbi did not reach these shores until 1840, when Rabbi Abraham Rice arrived in Baltimore. The first ordained East European *Rav,* Rabbi Abraham Ash, came to New York City in 1852. And the first scholarly rabbinic volume was not published here until Rabbi Joshua Falk produced his commentary on the "Ethics of the Fathers." Before that time, laymen masqueraded as rabbis and scholarship was unknown. America was virtually a spiritual wilderness.

Of course, the problem of finding trained rabbis was compounded by the lack of a rabbinical school in America. When Simon Tuska of Rochester wanted to prepare for the rabbinate, Rabbi Isaac Mayer Wise had to send him to Breslau, Germany. Wise mused:

> *It is a sad truth, that we suffer a perceptive want of thorough theologians, and, therefore, anybody who has brass enough in his*

*face, styles himself a reverend or a rabbi, so that many of our ministers excel the Methodist preachers in ignorance and misconceived piety.*

Tuska went to Breslau, where he studied from 1858 to 1860. He never received his ordination, but he returned to take a post in a Reform temple in Memphis where he served until his death in 1871.[18]

Perceptive leaders realized that the American rabbinate could not develop properly without a rabbinic seminary. Rabbi Isaac Mayer Wise sought to establish the Zion Collegiate Institute in 1854, but failed. Baltimore Jewry attempted to create a National Hebrew College in 1864, but it, too, collapsed quickly, and Rabbi David Einhorn's plan to export American boys to study in European seminaries seemed the only feasible one. New York's Temple Emanuel tried its hand at alleviating the problem by setting up the Emanuel Theological Seminary in 1865. When the project aborted, the money was used to send worthy students to study in Germany. Benjamin Franklin Peixotto, B'nai B'rith leader and American Consul to Rumania under President Grant, urged the establishment of an American Jewish University in 1866, but his proposal fell on deaf ears. Isaac Leeser, formulator of so many great projects, finally organized America's first rabbinical school, Maimonides College of Philadelphia, which opened its doors in 1867. Leeser served as president and chief fund-raiser; he literally gave it his life. But, as usual, Leeser was ahead of his time: the school struggled for survival—its faculty was a part-time one; funds were always lacking. In 1873 the school closed for lack of support after having ordained three men—the first home-grown rabbis. It was not until 1875 that American Jewry could boast of a viable seminary—the Hebrew Union College of Cincinnati, founded by Isaac Mayer Wise. This was followed by New York's Jewish Theological Seminary in 1886 and Rabbi Isaac Elchanan Theological Seminary in 1897. Subsequently a string of elementary and higher yeshivot and seminaries cropped up. The problem of native-trained clergy was finally resolved.

There were, naturally, striking contrasts between America's

clergy and the old European *Rav.* The American rabbi received a secular education; he preached in English; he plunged into community affairs and secular problems; he worked together with his Christian counterparts; he became a communal factotum—a mixture of pastor, preacher, priest, public relations expert, ambassador to the gentiles, teacher, psychologist, fund raiser, master of ceremonies, and organizer of numerous projects. He did not shy away from controversy or challenge. American rabbis have served in the military since 1862, when the law permitting only chaplains of Christian denominations to enlist was changed, and Reverends Arnold Fischel and Ferdinand L. Sarner served with distinction. Since then, hundreds of rabbis have served in military posts under the direction of the Jewish Welfare Board, established in 1917. Today's American rabbis write books, preach frequently, appear on radio and television, and are often national spokesmen for Jewish organizations. The present-day rabbi has achieved considerably more prestige than his nineteenth-century predecessor.[19]

American Jewry was late in creating religious and cultural institutions, but once started, the process accelerated and the achievements proved substantial. Apart from the major seminaries, the Jewish community has given birth to other schools of learning and culture. A network of Hebrew teachers colleges and colleges of Jewish studies dots the land. Gratz College of Philadelphia was the first, established in 1897. Others were begun in New York by the Jewish Theological Seminary in 1909, Mizrachi in 1917, and Herzliah in 1921. Baltimore's Hebrew College opened in 1902, died, and was resurrected in 1919. Chicago set up a college of Hebrew studies in 1924, and Boston followed suit in 1927. Dropsie College of Philadelphia was founded in 1907 for Semitic and cognate studies. Yeshiva College opened its doors in 1928 and became a full-fledged university in 1945. Brandeis University was established in Waltham, Massachusetts, in 1948. Over 185 colleges and universities currently offer courses in Judaica; 60 full-time chairs in Jewish studies are to be found on various campuses around the nation. The American Jewish Historical Society was founded in 1892; the

American Academy for Jewish Research was started in 1920; the YIVO Institute for Yiddish Research began its work in 1940. Additionally, the Hillel Organization has been serving the religious needs of Jewish collegians since 1923 under the auspices of B'nai B'rith and today there are over 250 Hillel chapters in America and Canada.

Culture and learning on American soil were also slow in coming. The first work of Jewish "scholarship" was, as we have noted, a Hebrew commentary on the "Ethics of the Fathers" by Rabbi Joshua Falk, published in 1860. The Yiddish Press made its appearance in 1870 with the publication of *Die Yiddishe Gazette,* followed by the *Tageblatt, Forward, Day, Morning Journal,* and other publications that at one time had a readership of over 400,000. The first Hebrew daily was *Ha-Tzofeh B'eretz Ha-Hadashah,* which was born in 1871, but it died after several years for lack of readers. *Ha-Doar,* a weekly Hebrew paper founded in 1921, is still published, as is the monthly *Bitzaron.* Anglo-Jewish newspapers flourished for a time, and *The Jewish Messenger, The Israelite, The American Hebrew,* and the *Occident* were read avidly in the nineteenth century, although twentieth-century readers are no longer addicted to such publications. The Jewish Publication Society finally became a viable organization in 1888 and it publishes significant works of Jewish scholarship and culture in both Hebrew and English. And a host of scholarly and popular magazines in English, Hebrew, and Yiddish are also produced.

Scholarship began to make its mark with the eighties and nineties of the last century. Rabbi Benjamin Szold authored a significant commentary on Job in 1886, and Rabbi Alexander Kohut published his great Talmudic dictionary in 1889. Moses Buttenweiser and Max Margolies wrote on Biblical themes; Louis Ginzberg, Chaim Tchernowitz, Solomon Schechter, Marcus Jastrow, Moses Mielziner, and Henry Malter dealt with the Talmud; and Alexander Marx, Israel Davidson, Solomon Zeitlin, and Jacob R. Marcus turned to history and liturgy. The great *Jewish Encyclopedia* was produced here between 1901 and 1906, and the Jewish Publication Society Bible was published in 1917. Recently, American Jewish scholarship has come into its own.

Epoch-making studies in rabbinics are being written by Professor Saul Lieberman; volumes of great history are flowing from the pen of Professor Salo W. Baron; Professor Harry A. Wolfson has enriched the study of Jewish philosophy; Professor Abraham J. Heschel opened up the world of Jewish mysticism and Hasidism; and a host of young scholars are making their mark in various areas of Jewish learning. A new translation of the Bible by the Jewish Publication Society, under the editorship of Professors Harry Orlinsky and H. L. Ginsberg, is partially completed, and a never-ending stream of scholarly books and articles floods the reader's shelves constantly. No, America is no longer the cultural wilderness it once was. It is, to be sure, not Spanish Jewry of the Golden Age; but neither is it the land of ignoramuses and charlatans that broke the spirits of Rabbi Abraham Rice and Rabbi Jacob Joseph a scant century ago and less.[20]

There have been those who maintained that the level of Jewish religious life and scholarship could be elevated if only Jews would unite. Some have urged the adoption of the European Gemeinde (a view currently argued passionately by Rabbi Mordecai M. Kaplan, although in revised form). Others have endorsed the institution of a Chief Rabbi along the lines found in England or France. And some have urged the creation of a synod or American Beth Din to legislate matters of Jewish law.

For example, in 1845 three New York German congregations banded together to create a common school system under a Chief Rabbi, and they invited Rabbi Max Lilienthal to take the post. But when one of the synagogues balked, the plan collapsed. Reverend Isaac Leeser labored ceaselessly to unify American Jewry. In 1841 and again in 1844 he issued a call for American synagogues to unite, and he published a detailed plan in his journal, the Occident, in 1845. Isaac Mayer Wise echoed his sentiments in 1848 declaring that union would help Jews "to fulfill our sacred mission." Leeser reiterated his idea in 1849, demanding unity, not Reform. But his proposal fell on deaf ears. There were those who could not reconcile their religious differences. There were others who feared the loss of independent action. And there were still others to whom the surrender of power or individual prestige was anathema. Thus Reform Congregation Beth Elohim of Charleston resolved (August 10. 1841) that "all conventions, founded or created for the establishment of any ecclesiastical authority whatever, . . . are alien to the spirit and genius of the age in which we live and are wholly inconsistent with the spirit of American liberty." Baltimore's Orthodox partisan, Rabbi Abraham Rice, opposed a synod on different grounds. Writing to Leeser on December 15, 1848, he insisted that Jews need nothing more than the *Shulhan Arukh* (Code of Jewish Law). He reminded Leeser of the German rabbinical conventions that had wrought monumental reforms, and he expressed doubts that changes would encourage more religious observances. Rice was convinced that a synod would do little more than pass further alleviations of the laws and relaxations of the rules without making better Jews or augmenting devotion to the synagogue. "Our Shulhan Arukh is our Conference," he declared. "We have no power to alter one Jod [tiny letter]."[21]

Nevertheless, there were attempts to unite religious Jewry. The Board of Delegates of American Israelites was founded in 1859 by 46 delegates from 14 cities and 25 congregations who met at New York's Cooper Union. The purpose was

> to gain statistical information, to promote education and literature, to further the cause of charity, to watch over occurrences at home and abroad relating to the Israelites, and to establish a "Court of Arbitration" for the settlement of disputes between Congregations, etc., without recourse to litigation.

The Board supported Maimonides College and endeavored to enrich the quality of Jewish religious life and education. But from the outset it was sabotaged in its program by rabbis like Isaac Mayer Wise, Max Lilienthal, and David Einhorn who were fearful of being charged with dual loyalty and who resented the fact that *they* were not in the leadership ranks. In fact, when the Board of Delegates lobbied in Washington in 1861 and 1862 for the appointment of a Jewish military chaplain, these same rabbis attempted to undermine their campaign. In 1878 the Board of Delegates was absorbed into Wise's Union of American Hebrew Congregations. American Jewry's first and only successful attempt at unity died prematurely.[22]

The synod campaign did not die, however. In the 1880's, Reverend Sabato Morais borrowed the columns of *The American Hebrew* to endorse the synod as a means of ending religious anarchy and modifying the ritual code as demanded by the times. Rabbi Kaufmann Kohler also urged a synod of American rabbis, but in order to reform Judaism. Louis Dembitz and Judge Mayer Sulzberger agreed that layman and clergy ought to join forces to update Jewish practices and strengthen the religion. But Solomon Schechter opposed the project as "useless and even harmful," and he warned that synods tend to create sacerdotalism and invade the realm of personal conscience. Henrietta Szold agreed: she did not think it possible for scattered Jews to be subject to central control. By the early 1900's, the idea virtually collapsed.[23]

Over the years there have been feeble attempts to unify American Jewry without creating a formal synod. In 1881 Rabbis Gustav Gottheil, Kaufmann Kohler, Adolph Huebsch, Henry S. Jacobs, Henry Pereira Mendes, and Frederick de Sola Mendes formed the New York Board of Ministers to unite rabbis of all persuasions in common cause. Now called the New York Board of Rabbis, it consists of one thousand Orthodox, Reform, and Conservative rabbis who work together on a variety of religious, cultural, social, political, philanthropic, and public projects. The Board supplies chaplains to hospitals and prisons, runs a busy schedule of radio and TV programs, and lobbies for Jewish interests in city and state governments. Similar bodies exist in many other major cities. The Synagogue Council of America was formed in 1926 for the purpose of "speaking and acting unitedly in furthering such religious interests as the constituent organizations in the council have in common" and in order to make the synagogue "the center of Jewish spiritual influence." The Synagogue Council consists of Orthodox, Reform, and Conservative laymen and rabbis who devote themselves to social-action problems, arrange Jewish exhibits at fairs and national functions, handle interfaith matters, and generally seek to represent Jewish religious interests to the President of the United States and members of Congress. But the organization has been hamstrung by the fact that each constituent member has the right to veto a resolution of the Council.

American Jewry still remains badly divided. True, it unites on ad hoc matters of critical nature: it joins forces on behalf of Israel or Soviet Jewry; it cooperates in philanthropic enterprises such as Israel Bonds, the United Jewish Appeal, or Federations of Jewish Philanthropies. There are several loosely federated umbrella groups such as the Presidents' Conference of Major Jewish Organizations that plan strategy and meet periodically with political leaders on vital issues. But the dream of a unified religious Jewry in America is as elusive and chimerical as it was in Isaac Leeser's times. Would the quality of American Jewry's religious life have been different had there been unity? We can only speculate.

Certainly it couldn't have been much worse. For Jewish religious life in America was far from ideal even at the outset. Way back in 1748, Peter Kalm, a Swedish traveler to the colonies, observed young Jews eating pork and breaking other Jewish rituals. New York's Shearith Israel was constrained time and again to warn backsliders and fine sinners who broke ritual laws.

> *Whosoever . . . continues to act contrary to our Holy Law by breaking any of the principles command will not be deem'd a member of our Congregation, have none of the Mitzote of the Sinagoge Conferred on him and when Dead will not be buried according to the manner of our brethren.* [24]

The Congregation passed a rule in 1758 threatening to expel any Jew from membership who did not abide by Jewish law. In 1766 Isaac Pinto introduced an English translation of the prayers, clearly indicating that Hebrew knowledge was at a low ebb. In 1783 Haym Salomon wrote to his family in Posen that Jewish life was very "weak" in the New World.

And indeed it was exceedingly "weak." By 1840, there were

virtually no descendants of the original Sephardic settlers left; intermarriage and baptism had depleted the ranks. Poor Rabbi Abraham Rice of Baltimore wrote to his teacher in Germany that "the character of religious life in this land is on the lowest level; most of the people are eating non-Kosher food, are violating the Shabbos in public . . . and there are thousands who have been assimilated among the non-Jewish population, and have married non-Jewish women." Rice battled for Sabbath observance—but in vain. Isaac Mayer Wise and Max Lilienthal tried the same tack in Cincinnati, as did Rabbi Elkan Cohn of San Francisco, but the results were limited. The new Reform movement dealt heavy blows to traditional observances. Leeser and Wise decried the growing secularization of Jewish life, and they denounced "Episcopal Jews in New York, Quaker Jews in Philadelphia, Huguenot Jews in Charleston . . . everywhere according to the prevailing sect." Samuel Isaac turned his fire on the nonobservant Orthodox who wanted others—not themselves—to pray and learn. As the synagogue lost control of *kashrut*, matzah baking, ritual slaughter, and circumcision, anarchy and chaos resulted. Scheming entrepreneurs exploited the gullibility of the religious masses; incompetent scoundrels botched their religious functions; charlatans had a field day. American Jewry has still not recuperated from those wild-and-woolly times.

Things scarcely improved at the time of the Civil War. Jeremiah Berman wrote a painstakingly complete study of religious life of those days. He lists 97 communities with ritual slaughterers from 1654 to 1880 including such diverse places as New York City; Alpena, Michigan; Columbus, Georgia; and Portland, Oregon. Many of these *shohetim* also served as teachers, rabbis, *mohelim* (ritual circumcisors), and all-around religious functionaries. But by the second half of the century, Sabbath and dietary observances slipped badly. Jewish butchers had the effrontery to open their shops on the Sabbath in New York and Philadelphia in the 1860's. In 1867, in the face of widespread flouting of Sabbath laws by merchants, a number of New York rabbis and synagogues banded together to form the Hebrew Sabbath Association to promote Sabbath observance. In 1879 Rabbi Henry

Pereira Mendes wrote open letters demanding kosher dinners at public functions run by Jewish groups, while Rabbi Aaron Bettelheim fought to end lavish funerals. And a visitor to Cleveland in 1882 noted:

> *Sabbath observance is at a low ebb, and as a result, the synagogues are poorly attended. Twenty-five years ago it was the exception to break the Sabbath and dietary laws, and it was a pleasure to see the crowded "shul," and share in the happy social influence. That time has passed. There is no difference between the Orthodox and the Reformers in this respect.* [25]

Why did religious observances decline so precipitously? For one thing, materialism and the economic drive impelled many to throw off their rituals. For another, many came here with weak religious backgrounds to start with; the more scholarly Jews chose to remain in the old country. Moreover, the population of Jews was sparse, there were no good Jewish schools, and Jewish religious leadership was woefully inadequate. Finally, Jews did not—unlike their Christian neighbors—have to affiliate with congregations. They could live, marry, beget children, and die without benefit of clergy, and, indeed, many did so.

The phenomenal flood of Jews from Eastern Europe changed the picture for the good. Now there were masses of Jews living in Jewish "ghettos," and assimilation and intermarriage declined. Now there were rabbis and teachers, *shohetim* and *mohelim*, scholars and sages. Synagogues proliferated, yeshivot appeared, and religious life enjoyed an upsurge from 1881 to 1914.

But there were also severe problems. The economic squeeze was ferocious; the sweatshop bosses forced Jews to work on the Sabbath. Some Jews had already cast their rituals overboard on the steamer, determined to begin a new life in America; others made the choice to forsake rituals here in response to the inordinate pressures of making a living. Nearly everyone wanted to become Americanized, no matter the cost to tradition or self-respect. Most worshiped the "bitch goddess of success." Thousands flocked to the labor unions; thousands joined the Bund or

Workmen's Circle. And thousands more became atheists in the ranks of the Socialist or Communist parties. The muckrakers and other observers of the time were struck by the generation gap between old and new that opened up in such a short time, and they wondered at the extremes to which the young Turks were prepared to go in rejecting the values of fathers and grandfathers. Lincoln Steffens mused:

> Responding to a reported suicide, we would pass a synagogue where a score or more of boys were sitting hatless in their old clothes, smoking cigarettes on the steps outside, and their fathers, all dressed in black, with their high hats, uncut beards, and temple curls, were going into the synagogue, tearing their hair and rending their garments. . . . It was a revolution. Their sons were rebels against the law of Moses; they were lost souls, lost to God, the family, and to Israel of old. . . . Two, three thousand years of continuous devotion, courage and suffering for a cause lost in a generation.[26]

In the thirties and forties the children of the immigrants found their way to materialistic capitalism or atheistic Communism. Both proved dead ends for Jewish living, and thousands more fell by the wayside. Baptism and conversion made few inroads in American Jewry, but apathy and assimilation certainly did.

After World War II, American Jewry enjoyed a religious boom. Synagogues appeared from nowhere; suburban communities sprang up practically overnight, and with them, new synagogues as well. Judaism became fashionable; many more young American-born boys entered the rabbinate; Jewish education was enriched and streamlined; and ritual observances began to reappear in the strangest quarters. For a time, it looked as if religious Judaism, over which Kaddish had been solemnly pronounced but a short time before, would enjoy a renaissance. Orthodoxy, which seemed moribund in the thirties and forties, enjoyed a resurrection. Reform, which had thrown away more than it had gained, returned to rituals and Zionism, and captured thousands of children of the East Europeans who had utterly ignored it. Conservatism, which never was able to get off the ground before World War II, suddenly took wing and soared, especially in suburbia where the synagogue-center became the "in" thing.

Although the phenomenally rapid religious growth of American Jewish life has slowed down and even leveled off of late, this is a truly extraordinary Jewish community. There are six million American Jews with over 4,000 synagogues and 3,000 rabbis; with three major seminaries and many hundreds of Day Schools; with over 600,000 Jewish boys and girls studying in religious schools and thousands more taking college courses in Judaica, attending Hebrew summer camps, and studying in Israel.

Moreover, American Jewry can boast of more varieties of Jewish expression than at any time since the days of the Talmud. We have more schools of thought and ideologies than ever before; we have varied patterns of ritual practices; we are blessed with a score of first-rate theologians and philosophers of Judaism. There is a wide spectrum of theological searching in Jewish life today that is incomparably enriching to Judaism in our time. We are divided as perhaps never before over religious issues. But for all of that, we are one. Ironically, paradoxically, divided we stand. . . .

World Jewry draws its life spirit from the various religious trends in today's Judaism. There are now four distinctive movements in religious life: Orthodoxy, Reform, Conservatism, and Reconstructionism. Each has made its contribution to the development of American Jewry; each has undergone change and revision; each will probably continue to give American Jewry, as well as world Jewry, its uniquely piquant flavor. To comprehend religious life in North America, we must examine these various schools of thought.

It is to an analysis of these movements, their ideologies and practices that we now turn.

# Orthodox Judaism—History

## II

Regrettably, Orthodox Judaism in the United States has not yet found its historian. Whereas the stories of Reform and Conservatism have been well told by competent researchers, the oldest of all Jewish religious groupings still awaits a systematic professional treatment. The best that we can do is to clutch at bits of information here and there, weave them into some type of pattern, and try to discern trends and traditions.[1]

Orthodoxy is, to be sure, the version of unmodified Judaism dating back to the days of the Talmud and medieval codifiers. Its pattern of observance was codified in the sixteenth-century legal code, the *Shulhan Arukh*. Virtually all Orthodox Jews abide by the legal decisions of that classic code. Until the French Revolution and Emancipation, practically all Jews in Europe, Asia, and Africa were Orthodox. But with the Era of Emancipation, thousands forsook the faith of their ancestors, thousands began to modify their religious beliefs and practices, and thousands joined the new Reform movement in Europe. Still, the majority of Jews who considered themselves religious remained

Orthodox until fairly recently. The chief rabbis of the various lands of Jewish settlement were Orthodox; the vast majority of synagogues were Orthodox; Reform made little or no headway in the areas of most dense Jewish concentrations such as Poland, Hungary, Rumania, and Russia, and religious reforms were practically unknown in Moslem lands such as Algeria, Morocco, Tunisia, Egypt, Syria, Turkey, Iraq, and Yemen where hundreds of thousands of Jews resided until the birth of the State of Israel. In Eretz Yisrael itself, the only version of Judaism practiced until the last two decades was undiluted, unmodified, uncompromising Orthodoxy.

But Orthodoxy has not been quite so monolithic as one would believe. Sephardic Orthodoxy was rather worldly; secular education was acceptable; decorum prevailed in Sephardic synagogues; sexual mores were not as prudish as among East European Jews; and integration in the fabric of the general society was a fact. Orthodox Jewry in Germany reacted in a unique fashion to the crisis of Emancipation. Rather than spurn it and encapsulate themselves in self-imposed ghettos, Samson Raphael Hirsch and his Frankfort followers accepted integration in the gentile world along with secular learning, and reinterpreted Orthodoxy, but held fast to its traditional practices. On the other hand, East European Orthodoxy remained obdurate: it rejected Emancipation; it disdained secular learning; it cloaked itself in ghettos of mind and body; it refused adamantly to reinterpret Jewish ideals or practices. Until the Holocaust, East European Orthodoxy had still not made its peace with the modern world, and the differences between Russian Hasidim, German neo-Orthodoxy, and Turkish Sephardim were marked. Yet all observed the Sabbath and Festivals in similar fashion, retained the dietary laws, and adhered to the rules of Jewish marriage, divorce, and family purity, and many joined world Orthodox organizations, such as Mizrachi or Agudat Israel.

These various trends in world Orthodoxy were imported to America and at least three distinct streams converged on the shores of the New World. There was the austere and somewhat pomp-ridden Sephardic Orthodoxy imported from Holland and

England; there was the dignified intellectualized Orthodoxy of Germany; and there was the parochial Talmud-oriented, ghetto-minded, disorganized East European brand from Poland, Galicia, Russia, and Hungary. Clearly, American Orthodoxy was not a *new* creation, for it developed from the confluence of all these trends. But it followed the lines of the German neo-Orthodox school of Hirsch which sought to live in both the secular and sacred worlds and blend Torah with worldly matters rather than the insular and more parochial orbit of, say, Rabbi Isaac Elchanan Spector of Kovno, who opposed secular learning and who refused to compromise his principle that Torah and Talmud were the sum of Jewish learning. American Orthodoxy went even further than Hirsch by making accommodations to the demands of the American society that would probably have offended the sensibilities of the German neo-Orthodox and surely would have incensed the more fundamentalistic East European sages. American Orthodoxy, although true to the ideals and practices of its European forebears, has set off in many new and unprecedented directions.

Certainly, Orthodox Judaism was the only form of American Judaism prior to the formation of the Charleston Reform Temple in 1824. Therefore, any history of American Jewish life of the seventeenth and eighteenth centuries would have to be a history of Orthodox Jewry. The Orthodoxy of the day was Sephardic Orthodoxy and the model for such religious expression was to be found in the "mother congregations" of American Jewry, namely, Bevis Marks in England and the Spanish-Portuguese synagogue of Amsterdam. All early synagogues on this continent—whether it be the Spanish and Portuguese synagogue of New York City or Yeshuat Israel in Curaçao—were patterned after the Old World models. The services were austere and decorous. The preachers recited prayers in Spanish or Portuguese. The pronunciation of the prayers followed the Sephardic mode. Times changed, circumstances were altered radically —but the Spanish-Portuguese services in Philadelphia's Mikveh Israel or New York's Shearith Israel were fundamentally the same in 1970 as in 1770. And were the Reverend Gershom

Mendes Seixas, patriot *hazzan* of New York's Shearith Israel in Revolutionary days to come back today and worship at his old synagogue, he probably would get the impression that he had never been away at all.[2]

A string of Sephardic synagogues was established early in the colonies. At first, as we have noted, services were held in private homes or stores. Gradually, as the law yielded to the demands of the times, public worship was allowed. And sooner or later, buildings were erected for public services in New York, Newport, Savannah, Philadelphia, Charleston, Richmond, and possibly in two or three other eighteenth-century communities. The services were traditional: men and women were segregated; prayers were unaltered, unabridged, and undiluted. Community pressures and sanctions were powerful and fines were levied for a variety of infractions ranging from singing too loudly at services to abusing the *parnassim* (officers) at a public meeting. The *parnassim* wielded considerable power, and in the absence of properly ordained clergy, they ruled the communities with less than a benevolent touch. Even as late as 1862, Rabbi Morris Raphall, of New York's B'nai Jeshurun, had to get permission from his *parnassim* to marry off his own daughter in his own synagogue. The laity was supreme over the clergy. But then again, the clergymen of the time were not truly ordained or professionally trained in any way; they were really *hazzanim*— cantors or "ministers," with little formal training or competence in Jewish law.

The Sephardic communities established various institutions and agencies to enhance their work. Mutual aid societies, for example, are as old as the congregations. Clearly, no one wanted to run afoul of the old rule of the Dutch West India Company that the poor Jews may never become a burden to the general community.

Nor was education neglected. True, qualified teachers were virtually nonexistent, and pedagogic methods were, to put it charitably, "primitive." Still, schools for Jewish education and general learning were set up early in the New World. Shearith Israel of New York established its Yeshivat Minhat Areb in 1731.

The all-day school taught English, Hebrew, Spanish, arithmetic, spelling, and literature from nine to five o'clock, with a two-hour lunch recess. The school met year-round and charged tuition, although scholarships were available, and poor children attended free. In 1801, the name of the school was changed to the Polonies Talmud Torah. With the beginning of the nineteenth century, state grant-in-aid to parochial schools became the norm. Rich people selected private tutors or sent their children to private schools or even abroad. Jewish private boarding schools also came on the scene and Rabbi Max Lilienthal was one of the pioneers in this area, setting up his school in 1849. But the development of the public schools and the growth of Sunday Schools and Talmud Torahs sounded the death knell of the all-day schools. All-day schools did not reappear on the American scene until 1886 and their popularity was not to blossom until the 1950's and after.[3]

It is remarkable to note that there were no ordained rabbis in America until the German-trained Abraham Rice came to Baltimore in 1840 to tilt lances with the fiery reformer Rabbi David Einhorn. Prior to Rice's arrival, laymen who had some knowledge of Hebrew prayers and melodies served as "ministers" or *hazanim*. Gershom Mendes Seixas was one such self-styled minister, as was Isaac Leeser a half century later. Seixas (1745–1816) was born in the colonies and received as good a Jewish education as was available in those days. In 1768 he was engaged by Shearith Israel as *hazzan*, preacher, teacher, and communal servant at the splendid sum of £8 yearly plus firewood and other perquisites. His tenure depended on his "Decent and Good Behavior." He taught Hebrew, Bible and Siddur translation, furnished a classroom for students, and instructed the bar mitzvah boys. Seixas was a staunch Whig, who was forced to flee New York when the British captured it. He founded the *Hebrah Hesed VeEmet* benevolent society in 1802, introduced Pinto's English translation of the Prayer Book, preached English sermons, conducted Thanksgiving services, participated in interfaith worship, and became a trustee of Columbia College. In short, Seixas became a forerunner of the modern American rabbi-factotum.

But his example was soon lost, ironically, on the Orthodox rabbinate, such as it was in the nineteenth century. The pattern set by Seixas was followed by the Reform and Conservative clergy; the Orthodox rabbinate of the nineteenth and early twentieth centuries followed the East European model. Such a rabbi rarely preached, and then, only in Yiddish; he waited to be asked ritual *shealot* (queries); he studied Talmud and Codes; he shunned interfaith programs and scorned cooperation with the non-Orthodox. Not until the third decade of the twentieth century did the American Orthodox rabbinate begin to take shape and exert an influence on Jewish life.

Sephardic Orthodoxy in this country struggled valiantly to hold fast—but it failed. In all fairness, the Sephardim were not totally to blame: theirs was a small community; they could not attract a *bona fide* rabbi; they could not import sufficient teachers, and the temper of the country encouraged—rather than discouraged—assimilation. The Sephardim tried, but fell short. The arrival of Ashkenazic Jews gave American Jewry the much-needed impetus to carry on.

Of course, there were Ashkenazim in the New World from the very beginning. Jacob Barsimson, the first Jew in New Amsterdam, was an Ashkenazic Dutch Jew. By Revolutionary times, Jews from Germany, Bavaria, Poland (mainly the city of Posen), and Galicia were to be found. By the 1840's numerous German Jews and a sprinkling of Latvian and Lithuanian Jews had reached the New World and outnumbered the old Sephardic stock even in the Sephardic synagogues. The numbers increased significantly after 1870, but with the Russian May Laws and pogroms of 1881, the floodgates of East European Jews were opened. From 1881 to 1924, about two and a half million Jews came to these shores—the bulk of them from Russia. In 1880, before the watershed, 10 percent of the population came from East Europe; by 1906, 75 percent originated in Russia or Poland.[4]

The impact of German and, especially, East European Jews on American Orthodoxy in particular, and American Jewry in general, cannot be overstressed. Suddenly synagogues began to sprout in all kinds of communities—cities and towns, urban areas and remote, rural trading posts. The face of American Jewry changed radically—and with it, the face of Orthodoxy.

The first Ashkenazic synagogue opened in Easton, Pennsylvania, in 1761. Philadelphia's Rodeph Shalom followed in 1802. When New York's B'nai Jeshurun broke away from Shearith Israel in 1825, the Sephardic "monopoly" was broken once and for all, and the unified community that had prevailed from Colonial times was shattered irreparably—for better or for worse. A succession of Ashkenazic synagogues followed: Cincinnati (1824), Baltimore (1830), Syracuse (1841), Albany (1841), Boston (1842), Rochester (1846), Buffalo (1847), Los Angeles (1851), and in dozens of other communities, east and west, north and south. The synagogues were invariably composed of English, Dutch, German, and Bavarian Jews. They were nominally Orthodox (although Los Angeles' B'nai Brith Congregation had mixed seating at the outset), and they were no longer bound to the Sephardic hierarchy that had controlled American Jewry since 1654.

East European synagogues now began to proliferate. Bethel Jacob opened in Albany in 1841. New York's famous Beth Hamidrash Hagadol was founded in 1852. It soon split into two congregations, the Beth Hamidrash and the Beth Hamidrash Hagadol, and in 1852 Rabbi Abraham Joseph Ash was brought to New York as the first East European *Rav* to serve a congregation. Polish-Russian congregations sprouted in rapid succession in Buffalo (1847), Chicago (after 1849), Newburgh (after 1858), Boston (1873), Poughkeepsie, and elsewhere. After the great wave of immigrants came in the 1880's, Polish-Russian *shuls* dotted the land.

It is instructive to note, statistically, how the Sephardim lost ground while the Ashkenazim multiplied astronomically. By 1825, of 40 American congregations, no new Sephardic congregations were established, but there were new Ashkenazic synagogues in New York, Philadelphia, Cincinnati, New Orleans, St. Louis, Albany, Easton, and elsewhere. In 1872, 29 East European congregations existed in New York City alone; by 1900, the total soared to 200. Each national group seemed to want to found a synagogue—whether Rumanian, Hungarian, Polish, Russian, Galician, etc. Some even founded synagogues named for hometowns. By 1916, there were over 1,900 synagogues in America—mostly Polish-Russian. True, many were just *shtieblach*, storefront congregations, prayer rooms barely worthy of the name "synagogue." But their worshipers were no less vital or enthusiastic than were the more staid Sephardic ancestors of two centuries previous.[5]

While synagogues proliferated, scholarship and rabbinic leadership languished. Abraham Rice, German-trained Orthodox scholar, was the first *bona fide* rabbi to serve in America. He suffered severely in his rabbinate at the Baltimore Hebrew Congregation, where he did battle with Reformer Rabbi David Einhorn as well as with his own backsliding "Orthodox" flock. Sabbath violations were particularly painful to him, as was the decline in *kashrut* observance and scholarship. He wrote, mournfully, to Rabbi Wolf Hamburger in Germany: "I dwell in complete isolation without a teacher or a companion in this land whose atmosphere is not conducive to wisdom," and he wondered "whether a Jew may live in a land such as this." In 1849 he quit his post, dabbled in business, wandered back into the rabbinate, and died in 1862—still wondering whether Orthodoxy could survive.[6]

Much the same spiritual malaise afflicted the career of Rabbi Abraham W. Edelman, Orthodox rabbi of Los Angeles' B'nai Brith Congregation. Edelman took over the pulpit in 1862, and struggled to keep a semblance of Orthodoxy in his German congregation. But the effort was doomed from the start: mixed seating—a serious breach of Orthodox practice—was introduced at the very outset. While the prayers were traditional and chanted in Hebrew, reform pressures were unrelenting. Confirmation entered the scene in 1870; the Hebrew School was replaced by a Sunday School; organ and mixed choir, plus the Jastrow semi-Reform *Siddur* were introduced in 1889—and Rabbi Edelman finally had to quit. He served the newly formed Moses Montefiore Congregation, which was of more conservative leanings, and was promptly replaced by Reform Rabbi Emanuel Schreiber in his old post.[7]

One could tell the same story over again perhaps a hundred times. In essence, Orthodoxy before the 1880's was fighting a hopeless battle. There were no good schools, no yeshivot, few rabbis (and of those who were here, virtually all were part time), no authority, no semblance of organization—only a welter of confusion and failure.

Out of this confused state, Orthodoxy sought to create a semblance of order. The chaos that followed the European immigration of the 1880's is indescribable. Apart from the appalling socio-economic problems, spiritual life was anarchic. Any scoundrel could pass himself off as a rabbi; *kashrut* was a total mess; inept ritual slaughterers and *mohalim* desecrated Israel's most sacred rites; Jewish education was a travesty. The older, "establishment" Jews treated the *Ostjuden* with condescension and discrimination ("more polish and less Polish," they beseechingly demanded). And so, Orthodoxy sought to put its house in order and acquire a semblance of respectability by creating, after the British example of Rabbi Nathan Adler, the office of Chief Rabbi.[8]

As early as 1845, Reverend Isaac Leeser had urged that a Chief Rabbi be appointed for American Jews. There was a tentative attempt to make Rabbi Ash of New York's Beth Hamidrash Hagadol Chief Rabbi. When Ash temporarily resigned his post, an effort was made to bring the eminent Bible scholar, Rabbi Meir Malbim, to these shores as Chief Rabbi. There had been groping attempts in the 1880's to form a United Hebrew Orthodox Association. Finally, when Ash died in 1887, New York's Orthodox Jewry found itself in the following lamentable state of affairs: 100–120,000 families, 130 Orthodox congregations, and only three or four part-time rabbis.

In 1887, some fifteen congregations formed the Association of American Orthodox Hebrew Congregations and offered $2,-500 as the salary for a Chief Rabbi. Soliciting letters were sent to European rabbis; several prospects were contemplated. A charter was drawn up that stated that the purposes of the group was "to encourage, foster, and promote the observance of the Orthodox Jewish religion, to spread and disseminate the doctrines and learning of the said religion, to improve and elevate the moral, social, and spiritual condition of the Jewish people, to designate, support, and maintain a Chief Rabbi and such other officers as may be deemed necessary or advisable, and to do, perform and effect all other charitable and benevolent acts and purposes, as may be specified in the Constitution and By-Laws." Ominously, imprudently, stupidly, no Orthodox rabbis were present when the laymen set up this significant body.

In 1887 the famous Vilna *Rav* Jacob Joseph was brought to New York for a six-year term. He was to set up and handle congregations, serve as Chief Orthodox Rabbi, supervise *shehitah* and *kashrut*, establish a Beth Din, and administer religious schools. His income was to be derived from *kashrut* seals (another fatal error!). The Association retained financial control over *kashrut*, licensing of *shohetim* and *gittin* (yet another blunder). When Rabbi Joseph arrived in 1888, huge throngs greeted him and the masses were captivated. As might be expected, the "establishment" sniped: Isaac Mayer Wise mocked; the *maskilim*, Reformers, anarchists, socialists, and secularists poured out their derision; and Henry Pereira Mendes, of Shearith Israel, and Sabato Morais of Philadelphia's Mikveh Israel carped (no doubt jealous of their old, established Sephardic hegemony— although Mendes later recanted).

But the *kashrut*-economic package was destined to ruin the plan (and poor Rabbi Joseph) from the start. Housewives, butchers, jealous rabbis, and malcontents rallied against Rabbi Joseph. Joseph responded with dignified restraint: he appointed his *dayanim* (ritual judges) for the Beth Din, including Rabbi Israel Kaplan (father of Rabbi Mordecai M. Kaplan) and later on, Rabbi Osher Noah Rapeport. Still, the critics grew in numbers. Rabbi Joshua Segal declared himself Chief Rabbi of twenty other congregations—and others followed suit. A new Beth Din Hagadol was set up to compete with Joseph's Beth Din. "Who made you a Chief Rabbi of America?" asked an East Side Jew of a neighboring rabbi. "The signpainter," came the reply.

Poor Jacob Joseph was ruined in body and health. He spent five years of agony and penury as an invalid till his death in 1902. The first Orthodox Chief Rabbi and the great promise held by the post died of petty jealousy and unconscionable greed.

There were, however, imprints left by the tawdry episode. In Baltimore, for example, twenty-eight Orthodox congregations merged in 1908 "for the promotion of learning and other activities helpful to Judaism and to advance every interest affecting Orthodox Jews." *Kashrut* supervision, of course, was one of the main purposes of the group. In 1910, Rabbi Abraham Schwartz was chosen Chief Russian Rabbi. But little more came of the effort. Similarly, after World War I, ten Los Angeles Orthodox *shuls* united and designated Chief Rabbi Isaac Werne to set up a Beth Din and supervise *kashrut*. Again, few practical results were to remain. Buffalo's Orthodox community elected Rabbi Nachum H. Ebin Chief Rabbi of eight congregations in 1917, but Ebin left in 1921 and the plan collapsed.[9]

The next area in which Orthodoxy endeavored to make its mark was in the field of education. Jewish education was in a state of incredible disarray from 1860 to 1940. The old Day Schools disappeared in New York, Baltimore, Philadelphia, and elsewhere with the emergence of the public schools. Sunday Schools tried to fill the gap—and failed. The wretched *heder* system, so graphically described in the novels of Abe Cahan and Henry Roth, and in the nonfiction of Jacob Riis, Hutchins Hapgood, Lincoln Steffens and others, drove more boys from Judaism than it saved. And education for the girls was totally nonexistent.[10]

In 1854 seven synagogues in New York had conducted Day Schools with 35 teachers and 857 pupils. By 1860, all were closed and the children had shifted for the most part to public schools. Uptown Jews who were more affluent hired private tutors in Hebrew. Community Talmud Torah schools opened and conducted classes after school and on Sunday mornings. In 1857 the Downtown Talmud Torah opened its doors under Rabbi Pesach Rosenthal's principalship. Then came the Machzike Talmud Torah (1883), the Uptown Talmud Torah, and others. Jews were horrified to learn that Christian mission schools were weaning Jewish children from their homes and hearths. The uptown Jews set up the Hebrew Free School Association in an attempt to serve the poor Orthodox children and immigrants. At its peak in 1898, there were 4,966 students in these schools. But the downtown Jews were not attracted to them: the uptowners wanted the schools to "refine, uplift, and Americanize" immigrants; the Hebrew content was diluted; the Reform slant was undisguised (e.g., a confirmation class was added in 1884 under the tutelage of the New York Board of Ministers). In fact, at the very end, half of the students in the Hebrew Free Schools received *no* religious education at all. In 1899 the Educational Alliance absorbed the Free Schools.

The community Talmud Torahs in New York and elsewhere flourished. For example, in 1888, the Machzike Talmud Torah numbered 690 boys, a principal, and eight teachers. These were solid institutions that taught Hebrew, Bible, Mishnah, Talmud, and other subjects never touched in the disreputable *heder* system. But the *heder* flourished; in 1890, there were 251 such one-room "schools" on New York's East Side alone! Clearly, the need for meaningful education of Orthodox youth was the great priority of the hour.

The Orthodox group of New York felt the need to establish an elementary yeshivah. In 1886 Etz Chaim Yeshivah was established for the "improvement of the spiritual, mental and social condition of Hebrew boys, to provide for their Teachers and instructions in *Hebrew*, to foster and encourage the study of the *Sacred Scriptures*, the Talmud, and the Hebrew language and literature, to hold religious services in accordance with Orthodox Judaism: also to provide teachers and instructors for said *Hebrew boys* in reading, writing, and speaking the English language." The school met in a room on New York's Lower East Side and the pupils ranged in age from nine to fifteen years. They paid a small tuition and the faculty included the young Abe Cahan. But the secular studies were downgraded, financing was fragile, student unrest great. By 1900, there were over 80 students, 4 teachers, and a building; by 1905, over 150 students attended, many of whom were ultimately to enter New York Jewry's Harvard—namely, City College of New York. But there were no rich Jewish supporters of the yeshivah and no Isaac M. Wise came along to organize the school. The Orthodox rabbinate was so weak and divided that it, too, failed to rally support for Etz Chaim.[11]

In 1897, Rabbi Isaac Elchanan Theological Seminary was organized on the East Side for advanced Talmudic studies for older lads and to "promote the study of the Talmud and to assist in educating and preparing students of the Hebrew faith for the Hebrew Orthodox Ministry." Secular subjects were also included in the afternoons and by 1902 there were over fifty students at the school. The Union of Orthodox Rabbis endorsed the Rabbi Isaac Elchanan Theological Seminary in 1903 as the only legitimate yeshivah of higher learning in this country. The guilding light of the resolution was the eminent Philadelphia rabbi Bernard Levinthal. But the school struggled, and despite the growth in enrollment by 1908 to 125, there was only a one-man faculty (Rabbi Benjamin Aronowitz), inadequate weekly stipends, a woefully insufficient facility at 156 Henry Street, and utterly neglected secular studies. A student revolt broke out in 1908 as the students demanded the addition of secular studies. The students won their battle and a secular curriculum was added, but many left for the Jewish Theological Seminary; others formed a new yeshivah; and others just dropped out forever.

With both Etz Chaim and Isaac Elchanan Yeshivot virtually bankrupt, the two schools merged in 1915. A high school program was added and Dr. Bernard Revel was appointed president. Revel had been born in Kovno in 1885 and was considered a great student of the Talmud. He came to America in 1906, received an M.A. at New York University and the first Ph.D. awarded by Dropsie College of Philadelphia in Semitics. He headed the Seminary from 1915 until his death in 1940, although in the early years, he treated the post as a part-time position and even spent part of each year oil prospecting in Oklahoma.

Revel was a man of great vision. Fearful of the secular or even anti-Semitic atmosphere of the colleges in America, he dreamed of a college under Jewish auspices. He warmly espoused the blend of "orthodox Judaism and Americanism" and favored the training of Orthodox rabbis who would preach in English. A teachers college (formed by Mizrachi in 1917) was joined to Revel's institution in 1921. But his fondest dream was realized in 1928 with the establishment of Yeshiva College, an institution that fused both Jewish and secular disciplines. Dr. Revel stated the goals of the school in 1925:

> The Yeshiva proposes to establish a College of Liberal Arts and Sciences . . . with the double purpose of educating both liberally and Jewishly a number of Jewish young men who have been already imbued with the spirit and the sanctity of Judaism and its teachings, so that these men may not be lost to us . . . Secondly, Jewish young men who consider Jewish learning an indispensable part of the moral and mental equipment that they wish to attain through a college education are to have the advantage of such a combined education.

The path was far from smooth: opposition was leveled from right and left. The uptown Jews sneered at the parochial East European greenhorns; the ultra-Orthodox Agudat Harabanim opposed the secular education. Still, Revel prevailed and a splendid campus was purchased overlooking New York's Harlem River. A graduate school was added in 1937 and the faculties were expanded. After Revel's death in 1940, Dr. Samuel Belkin was selected, after three years of debate over a successor, to succeed him.

Belkin, a Talmudic prodigy, was born in Poland in 1912, and was ordained in the Chafetz Chaim Yeshiva in Radun. He came to Philadelphia in 1930, took a Ph.D. in Greek and philosophy at Brown, and in 1935 joined the Yeshiva faculty as instructor in Greek, Talmud, and Hellenistic literature. During his presidency, the Yeshiva expanded phenomenally: the school became a university in 1945; a medical school was added in 1955; various graduate divisions, a college for girls, and a West Coast branch were created; and the school had over 7,500 students in all departments in 1970, with 750 in the college alone. Since the first three graduates received *semikhah* in 1906, over 1,000 rabbis have been ordained, about 300 of whom currently occupy Orthodox pulpits. Many Hebrew teachers, scientists, lawyers, doctors, engineers, and prominent laymen have come from the halls of the school that began so insignificantly in 1886.

Other yeshivot and Day Schools were to follow the example of New York's Etz Chaim and Rabbi Isaac Elchanan Theological Seminary. New York had four such schools by 1918. Chicago's Etz Chaim opened in 1895; Baltimore and Philadelphia started yeshivot, as did other cities. In 1938 the United Yeshivas Foundation was established; then the Central Board of Yeshivah Education and, finally, Torah Umesorah, the most important Orthodox Yeshivah Agency, were set up. Chicago's Orthodox community opened its Beth Ha-midrash La-Torah—Hebrew Theological College—in 1921. It attempted, under presidents Saul Silber, Oscar Fasman, and Simon G. Kramer, to do for Midwest Jewry what Yeshiva College was doing in the East. It added a preparatory school, a Teachers Institute, a library, and a graduate school. Lately, it has moved to a suburban campus in Skokie, Illinois, and has sought to add a junior college and create another Jewish university. As of 1970, over 335 rabbis had been ordained and over 185 serve in pulpits.

The more fundamentalistic ultra-Orthodox were never totally at ease with Yeshiva University or Hebrew Theological College. These groups denigrated secular learning; they stressed more piety and fundamentalistic beliefs; they were, at one time, anti-Zionistically inclined. Consequently, these Orthodox groups created their own higher yeshivot and hundreds of rabbis have come forth from Brooklyn's Torah Vadaat, Chaim Berlin, and Lubavitcher Yeshivah; Manhattan's Jacob Joseph and Tifereth Yerushalayim; Baltimore's Ner Israel; Cleveland's Telse Yeshivah; Lakewood's Beth Midrash Gavoha; and Spring Valley's Beth Midrash Elyon. Ironically, the Orthodox community that struggled to create *one* yeshivah a century ago boasts of several on the graduate level and hundreds on the lower level. Unlike Reform and Conservatism where one institution officially ordains the rabbis, teachers, and cantors of the movement, Orthodoxy draws its clergy from a score of institutions. It is, however, extraordinary to contemplate that in 1970 Orthodoxy maintained 65,000 children in over 300 schools.[12]

The impulse to end chaos in Orthodox Jewry certainly did not die with the Jacob Joseph fiasco. Henry Pereira Mendes of Shearith Israel and Bernard Drachman, both of whom were identified with the newly formed Jewish Theological Seminary, sought to rally Orthodox and proto-Conservative forces. Mendes and Drachman hoped that the new Seminary would train the rabbis needed to fill the rapidly developing synagogues. They joined with Cyrus Adler, Max Cohen, David Sulzberger, Louis Dembitz, Joseph Blumenthal, Solomon Solis-Cohen, Moses Dropsie, Judah D. Eisenstein, Rabbi Joseph Hertz, and others in an attempt to create an antidote to the Union of American Hebrew Congregations of the Reform movement—namely, an Orthodox Congregational Union.[13]

In 1898 a thousand delegates gathered at New York's Shearith Israel—scene of so many historical events—to form the Union of Orthodox Jewish Congregations. Pereira Mendes was elected president. The Union spelled out its program and flung the gauntlet in the face of the Reform, with pointed references to the Pittsburgh Platform. The purpose of the group was to "advance the interests of positive Biblical, Rabbinical, Traditional, and Historical Judaism." The group disclaimed any intention to become a synod, declaring itself merely a representative body. It did, however, proclaim itself in favor of the convening of a synod of certified rabbis, elders, men of wisdom and piety. Ideologically, the Union affirmed its belief in Divine revelation of the Bible and ceremonial law, and it emphasized its commitment to "the authoritative interpretation of our rabbis as contained in Talmud and Codes" and the Maimonidean thirteen principles of faith. The Union stated its desire to unite with fellow citizens of other faiths while maintaining its separate rites and ceremonies. The delegates reaffirmed belief in a personal Messiah, circumcision, and baptism for converts, protested strongly against intermarriage, and, in a clear refutation of the Reform

Pittsburgh Platform denied emphatically that Jews are merely a religious sect. "We are a nation, though temporarily without a national home." The yearning for Zion was also endorsed, as the Union affirmed its adherence to the legitimacy of the aspiration to return to the Holy Land. It emphatically rejected the charge of dual loyalty that the Reformers had conjured up.

The uneasy match between the Orthodox group and the Historical School that ultimately was to crystallize in the Conservative movement crumbled rapidly. There were, after all, profound differences of ideology, breeding, culture, and social loyalties. More divided the Yiddish-speaking Russian Jews, perhaps, from the English-speaking Germans and Sephardim than united them. The East European immigrants were looked upon with disdain as uncouth, fanatical separatists; the German-Sephardic group was suspected of ignorance and assimilationist tendencies. While Mendes lived, he was able to hold the coalition together; after his death, it disintegrated. It did not soothe the moderates to hear the Slutzker *Rav*, Rabbi Jacob David Wilowsky, chide them at the 1900 convention for coming to the sinful land of America. Others, such as Louis Dembitz, resented the title "Orthodox." Then criticism of the Seminary and its graduates mounted. As a compromise, some had urged dual support for the Seminary and the new Yeshivah Etz Chayim. In 1902 the proto-Conservative School left and never returned. It was ironic: twice the Historical School sought to work with the other factions in American Jewry—first the Reform and then the Orthodox—and twice its attempt at unity failed.[14]

The Union of Orthodox Jewish Congregations grew slowly, painfully. It endorsed the new Isaac Elchanan Theological Seminary as the fountainhead of Orthodox-trained rabbis. It added a Women's Branch in 1923. It attempted to establish Jewish university clubs to service collegians. It called for a Teachers College for girls which, however, was not to come into being until years later. It established the National Conference of Synagogue Youth, which in 1970 was divided into fourteen regions with 420 chapters, 15,600 members, and a staff of eleven. Most of the youngsters, significantly, came from non-Orthodox homes; 2,000 eventually found their way to yeshivot (755 of whom came from nonobservant families). In 1960, Yavneh, a college Orthodox organization, was established. By 1964 it numbered 40 chapters and 1,000 members—of whom 25 percent came from non-Orthodox backgrounds. Yavneh has successfully introduced kosher kitchens on several campuses.

The Union of Orthodox Jewish Congregations has made its mark in the *kashrut* field and half of its annual budget of $750,-000 is allotted for that purpose. It has ended much of the chaos in *kashrut* supervision and the U label on products has aided the consumers immeasurably. The Union also gives subventions to young Orthodox congregations (the shortage of such congregations and surplus of Orthodox rabbis necessitate this move), and it publishes a slick bimonthly magazine called *Jewish Life.* The Association of Orthodox Jewish Scientists is loosely affiliated with the UOJC, as is a new legislative and lobbying group called COLPA (National Jewish Commission on Law and Public Affairs). COLPA was formed in 1965 by Rabbi Moshe Sherer, Dr. Marvin Schick, Reuben Gross and others to represent Orthodox interests in legislative and legal matters. Although the UOJC is represented in the Synagogue Council of America and the National Community Relations Advisory Council, Orthodox interests have divided sharply since 1962 from the other groups —especially over the question of public funds for parochial schools. Consequently, the UOJC has helped form COLPA and has dissented more frequently from opinions of the various national bodies to which it belongs.

The UOJC refuses to divulge its membership. It claims 3,000 congregations and approximately 3–4.2 million members, assuming that any Jew who is neither Reform nor Conservative must be Orthodox. But a careful statistical study by sociologist Charles Liebman concluded that there are probably 205,640 men in 1,603 known Orthodox *shuls* in the United States. Many nominally Orthodox synagogues have mixed pews and are therefore not truly Orthodox; many are merely storefront *shuls* or private *shtiebels.* And, of course, many Orthodox Jews—perhaps one-third to one-half—are truly "non-observant Orthodox" whose affiliation with the movement is rather superficial. Of the various national congregational groups, the UOJC is the weakest, has made less impact on its constituent congregations, and is the least representative of the membership's views.[15]

Having discussed the history of Orthodoxy's congregational and educational bodies, it is proper to glance at its rabbinic bodies. Orthodox rabbis in America had long been pleading for a national Beth Din and a rabbinic organization that could end religious anarchy. Rabbis Judah Levin of Detroit and Asher Zarchy of Louisville sought in 1897 to rally their colleagues with (ironically!) the old Reform cry: "It is time to act for the Lord!" At the Boston convention of the Federation of American Zionists, in 1902, New York's venerable Rabbi Moses Z. Margolies, joined by Rabbi Bernard L. Levinthal, strove to organize the rabbis, and failed. A group of Western rabbis tried again and this time they succeeded. They called for "the training of ordained rabbis, teachers and preachers who have mastered the English language and who will be fit to wage combat against the forces of Reform." Thus was born in 1902 the Agudat Harabanim, the Union of Orthodox Rabbis.[16]

The Agudat Harabanim rallied the Yiddish-speaking rabbis of America. It disavowed graduates of the Jewish Theological Seminary because its alumni did not possess the traditional *semikhah.* The moving force behind the resolution was Rabbi Bernard Levinthal, whose son, as well as the sons of many other rabbis of the group, were ultimately to become graduates of that Seminary. At any rate, the Agudat Harabanim threw its full weight behind the Rabbi Isaac Elchanan Theological Seminary as the only legitimate training ground for American rabbis.

With the passage of time and the Americanization of Orthodoxy, the Agudat Harabanim declined in influence. The role of the rabbi was changing; the gap between the European Yiddish-speaking *Rav* and the American English-speaking rabbi was widening; the new Orthodox generation demanded secularly trained, modern rabbis; and the Agudat Harabanim had insisted on unrealistically high *semikhah* standards for membership in the group. Moreover, the organization has been so wracked by political dissension that in 1960 a presidium of three had to take over the leadership. Charges of *kashrut* corruption and anarchy also weakened the group. In 1964 there were over six hundred members, but the group's power, except in *kashrut* and lobbying for Fair Sabbath Laws and *shehitah* (kosher slaughter) had waned considerably.

Meanwhile, the American-trained Orthodox rabbis had formed an organization of their own, and it proved to be the most potent force for Orthodoxy in America. Out of the Alumni Association of the Rabbi Isaac Elchanan Theological Seminary (1923) developed the Rabbinical Council of America (1935). Graduates of the Hebrew Theological College of Chicago joined the group in 1942 and strengthened it greatly. By 1971 there were over nine hundred members of the RCA, of whom six hundred occupy pulpits. About half the membership are alumni of the Isaac Elchanan Seminary; 15 percent come from the Hebrew Theological College with the rest divided among various American and European yeshivot. Approximately half the members occupy pulpits with mixed seating—a serious breach of Orthodox practice. In fact, over the past decade, three of the presidents of the RCA branch on Long Island (The Long Island Commission of Orthodox Rabbis) occupied Conservative pulpits. Officially, these men have five years to convert the aberrants to true Orthodoxy or else resign; in fact, very few have ever done so. Rabbi Emanuel Rackman, past president of the RCA, has justified Orthodox men taking Conservative pulpits "in the hope that these congregations may one day revert to the traditional practice." He argues that one may temporarily flout the Torah for the sake of God and that such rabbis are not to be diminished in their commitment, for they are more "prophetic" and may reclaim many.[17]

The spiritual leader of the RCA and charismatic leader of most of modern Orthodoxy is Rabbi Joseph B. Soloveitchik. Born in Pruzhan, Poland, in 1903, he was raised in White Russia and trained privately. He went to the University of Berlin and received a Ph.D. in philosophy in 1931. In 1932 he came to Boston as a rabbi and began to teach Talmud and philosophy at Rabbi Isaac Elchanan Yeshivah in New York. Soloveitchik is without peer in Orthodox circles: he is a phenomenal Talmudist, master homiletician, superb lecturer in English or Yiddish (his public lectures never fail to pack the hall), and a profound philosopher. He is also a very lonely, remote, austere person. He often writes of his sense of loneliness. "From my youth," he once reflected in a Hebrew essay, "I learned to suppress my feelings and not to display my emotional development." He records that his father, Rabbi Moses Soloveitchik, had taught him the sanctity of human emotions and their privacy. "He never once kissed me," recalls Rabbi Soloveitchik. Although he has written only a bare handful of Hebrew, English, and Yiddish articles, Soloveitchik is *the* charismatic leader of modern Orthodoxy in America.[18]

Of late, the RCA has moved perceptibly to the right. The men are more fundamentalistic; there is greater self-confidence in Orthodoxy and more acculturation; and Orthodoxy feels more secure and less inhibited in attacking Conservatives and Reformers, especially on legal matters. The more radical-liberal views of Rackman have been losing ground, and some have even suggested that Orthodoxy follow the precedent of German Orthodoxy, secede from the national groups, and go it alone.[19]

Yet another rabbinic group, the Igud Harabanim (Rabbinical Alliance of America), was established in 1944. It consists primarily of more ultra-Orthodox graduates of yeshivot other than Isaac Elchanan Seminary and Hebrew Theological College. It numbers about 250 members, of whom 100 are in pulpits. Approximately half are simultaneously members of the RCA. There are also smaller rabbinic bodies such as the Union of Grand Rabbis, which is made up of Hasidic rabbis. But clearly, only the Rabbinical Council of America wields any influence, for it alone represents the mainstream of what has come to be known as "modern Orthodoxy."

That "mainstream" is more in keeping with the German Orthodoxy of Samson Raphael Hirsch than with the East European brand. Hirsch, the great neo-Orthodoxy leader of the nineteenth century, had sought to counter the double challenge of assimilation, on the one hand, and Reform, on the other. His slogan was, "Torah with worldly learning"; he sought to synthesize classical Jewish knowledge with modern culture. Interestingly, although East European Jews form the vast majority of American Jewry, the Orthodox have followed the German pattern set by Hirsch rather than the more parochial East European one.

Two other significant organizations of American Orthodoxy should be mentioned: the National Council of Young Israel and the Religious Zionists of America. The Young Israel Movement was founded in 1912 by Professors Israel Friedlander and Mordecai M. Kaplan—both of the Jewish Theological Seminary—Rabbi Judah Magnes, and several laymen. The ideal was to unite the Orthodox youth of New York's Lower East Side, develop decorous services with congregational singing, and introduce Friday-evening lectures and cultural programs. A model synagogue embodying these principles was established at the Educational Alliance. The services were marked by English sermons, a synopsis of the weekly portion of the Torah, and a dignity totally lacking in other Orthodox *shuls*. In 1922 the increasingly Orthodox faction disavowed the Seminary leaders (especially Dr. Kaplan) and charted a new course. The group was incorporated in 1926 "to awaken a love for Orthodox Judaism and the Jewish people within the hearts of American Jewish youth." By 1939 its membership had grown to thirty-five synagogues in the United States and Canada, and it issued its own newspaper, the Young Israel *Viewpoint*. Although originally the more liberal Orthodox element, Young Israel has moved sharply to the right of late. It insists that officers of Young Israel be Sabbath observers; it rigidly maintains the *mehitzah* (curtain separating the sexes); and it has vigorously attacked the non-Orthodox. Moreover, the decorum aspect that originally motivated its formation has been virtually overlooked in recent years, and many "Young Israel" synagogues are truly congregations of older people. The organization has taken positions on national and world issues and has been staunchly allied with religious Zionism. It has created a Council of Young Israel Rabbis, half of whom are *not*

Yeshiva University men and who, therefore, have exerted a rightist pressure on the movement. By 1971 there were slightly over 100 member synagogues with about 25,000 families and an Inter-collegiate Council of Young Israel. It is significant that virtually all the new Orthodox synagogues sprouting up around suburbs are Young Israel synagogues.

The Religious Zionists of America is the national organization of Zionists who are Orthodox-minded. It represents a merger of several old religious Zionist groups, Mizrachi and Hapoel Hamizrachi, Mizrachi Women's Organization, and their youth affiliates, B'nai Akivah and Mizrachi Hatzair. In 1957, these organizations, numbering today perhaps twenty thousand members, joined forces in order to improve their services to Israel and solidify their ties with Israel's National Religious Party.

The roots of the Religious Zionists of America go back to the late nineteenth century, when Orthodox Zionists such as Dr. Joseph Bluestone affiliated with the East European Hoveve Zion (Lovers of Zion) organization. While the ultra-Orthodox (like the Reform leaders of the day) refused to acknowledge the new secular-political Zionist movement, more enlightened Orthodox, such as Bluestone, Rabbis Philip Klein, Moses Z. Margolies, Bernard Drachman, H. Pereira Mendes, and publisher Kasriel Sarasohn, joined the ranks of Herzl and the political Zionists. In 1901 the Orthodox group seceded from the Federation of American Zionists and formed the United Zionists of America, with Rabbi Philip Klein as president. Bluestone was sent to the 1903 World Zionist Congress as the delegate of the new group. Jacob de Haas formed the Mizrachi from that group, and he organized chapters in New York, St. Louis, and Pittsburgh, with Rabbi Dov Ber Abramowitz of St. Louis as director. Rabbi Meir Berlin gave great impetus to Mizrachi as one of its new leaders in 1913. He spearheaded its first separate convention in 1914, established a Teachers Institute and Board of Orthodox Jewish Education, and in 1915 moved Mizrachi's central office to New York. By 1916 over a hundred affiliates were registered and a Mizrachi Women's Organization was organized in 1925. Today most Orthodox Zionists are found in the Religious Zionists of

America, whose primary thrust is to blend Zion and Torah, the Jewish State and Jewish law. Rabbi Joseph Soloveitchik is the spiritual leader of the RZA and his word is generally accepted in policy matters. The organization maintains educational and social facilities in Israel, publishes *Jewish Horizon* and other journals, and seeks to provide yeshivot with culture and Zionist material.[20]

No picture of Orthodoxy would be complete without a discussion of what Charles Liebman has called (perhaps incorrectly) "the sectarians." These are the fundamentalist ultra-Orthodox groups. They are generally foreign-born and in the lowest economic brackets. They cluster in self-imposed ghettos in Brooklyn or Lakewood or Spring Valley. Their spiritual leaders are *Roshe Yeshivot*—the late Rabbi Aaron Kotler (Lakewood), Rabbi Shragai Mendlowitz (Torah Vadaat), Rabbi Isaac Hutner (Chaim Berlin), Rabbi Moses Feinstein (Tifereth Yerushalayim), or the various Hasidic rabbis and rebbes. These groups maintain 31 yeshivot and 4,000 students, some of whose alumni enter pulpits (even Conservative and Reform!), while most become teachers or businessmen. Secular education is frowned upon; separatism from the evils of this world—television, movies, sexual frankness—is espoused; and refusal to cooperate even with other Orthodox Jews whose piety is suspect is endorsed. These fundamentalist yeshivot are coordinated by a yeshivah council and they publish their own educational material and journals. Their rabbis generally are found in the Union of Orthodox Rabbis, the Rabbinical Alliance, or the various Hasidic groups. Some, such as the K'hal Adath Jeshurun of Rabbi Joseph Breuer in New York's Washington Heights, are of German extraction; most, however, are of Rumanian, Hungarian, Polish, or Russian origin. Some are of Hasidic persuasion; others (such as the Torah Vadaat and Lakewood Yeshivah) are non-Hasidic. They are generally non-Zionists or religious Zionists and more inclined to membership in the world Union of Agudat Israel rather than the Religious Zionists of America. The Satmar Hasidim, a group of perhaps five thousand ultra-pious Hasidim led by Rabbi Joel Teitelbaum of Brooklyn, are bitterly anti-Zionist.

Affiliated with Israel's Neturei Karta, they refuse to acknowledge the "secular-Zionist" Jewish state, preferring to wait for the coming of the Messiah who alone will rebuild Zion. This vitriolic group takes ads in the New York *Times* attacking Israel, accuses the state of permitting criminally ghoulish autopsies, and denounces the Zionists for having collaborated with the Nazis in order to increase immigration to Israel. It has even gone to the extreme of accusing the Zionists of having trumped up charges of Soviet anti-Semitism in order to swell immigration of Russian Jews to Israel.

More representative of contemporary Hasidic thinking—and certainly far more respectable in Hasidic circles—is the dynamic Lubavitcher movement. Imported to this country from Russia in 1940 by the then Lubavitcher Rebbe, Joseph Isaac Schneerson, the movement has made extraordinary strides forward. With its central headquarters in Crown Heights, Brooklyn, the world movement has perhaps 150,000 members with 14 yeshivot, a rabbinical school, a Beth Rivka School for girls, and over 4,000 students in America alone. It has issued numerous English, Hebrew, and Yiddish publications and sends out "missionaries" to remote parts of the world to spread the word of Hasidism, to teach Torah, to win Jews back to such *mitzvot* as *tefillin*, and to capture the hearts of collegians.

The charismatic head of the Lubavitcher is Rabbi Menachem Mendel Schneerson, son-in-law of the late Rebbe. Born in 1902 in Mikolayev, Russia, he studied privately with his father, Rabbi Levi Yitzhak, and received the degree of electrical engineering at the Sorbonne. He came to New York in 1941 to assist his father-in-law and in 1951 he succeeded him as the Lubavitcher Rebbe. He has been a dynamic leader. He has established a network of schools, a college organization, a youth movement, the World Council of Lubavitcher Men and Women, vocational schools and yeshivot in Israel, Canada, Australia, and elsewhere. And while he believes in a strong emotional appeal, the Rebbe writes that "intellect is the most important element in religion; emotions or faith alone are not enough."[21]

Although they are by no means "sectarian" Jews, insofar as

Sephardic Jews tend to remain aloof from other Jews and cluster in self-imposed ghettos and synagogues, they might be legitimately considered as a separate entity in American Orthodoxy. The old Sephardim who, as we have noted, had all but died out by the 1830's, have enjoyed something of a renaissance in this country. Many Sephardim found their way here after 1900 from the Balkans; still more came in the wake of World War II. These are mostly Greek or Turkish Jews, with a sprinkling of Yugoslavian, North African, Syrian, Iraqi, Egyptian, and Persian Sephardim. The largest community is in Brooklyn, although many are now on Long Island, the Jersey shore, and even the Pacific West Coast. They tend to be isolated; they used their Ladino (Judeo-Spanish) dialect in speech and publications until fairly recently; they rarely married Ashkenazim (until this post-World War II generation); and they maintain Orthodox synagogues only, even though their personal observances have been badly diluted.

The Sephardim made several abortive attempts to unite, beginning with the Federation of Oriental Jews of America in 1912. The great and princely leader of the Sephardim who brought a semblance of unity and glory to the community was the late Rabbi David de Sola Pool of New York's historical Spanish and Portuguese Synagogue. Assisted by Dr. Nissim J. Ovadia and others, he formed the Sephardic Jewish Community of New York (1924), the World Union of Sephardic Congregations (1929), the Central Sephardic Jewish Community of America (1941), issued new editions of the Sephardic Prayer Book with English translation, and helped publish *The Sephardi* magazine. Since there is no seminary to train Sephardic rabbis in America, Yeshiva University set up a special program for the purpose in 1962 and brought Rabbi Solomon Gaon from England to head the project. The attempt has failed and Sephardic congregations either import their rabbis or utilize Ashkenazic rabbis from Orthodox or Conservative seminaries.

Today there are over 25,000 Sephardim in 63 known congregations. Most are first-generation Americans whose traditions are fading. In fact, more and more are slipping into Conservative or Reform congregations and are marrying non-Sephardic mates. Since the death of Rabbi Pool, no acknowledged Sephardic leader has come to the fore. It seems as if history is about to repeat itself: America's Sephardim will probably dissolve into the American melting pot before too long.[22]

To sum up this historical survey of American Orthodox Jewry, we can say this: Orthodox Jewry, whose demise had been predicted several times in the past, first in the nineteenth century, and again in ours, is far from giving up the ghost. If anything, it is enjoying an extraordinary renaissance. Its institutions are flourishing. Its Day Schools and camps are crowded. Its congregations have proliferated. Its national organizations have gained new stature and influence. No longer does Orthodoxy appeal only to low-income immigrant Jews. Many chic, well-educated American Jews can be found in newly built Young Israel synagogues. And most important, many children and teenagers are to be found at Orthodox *shuls* on a Sabbath morning. Although the absolute and relative numbers of American Orthodox have shrunk over the past decades, there is a small, dedicated hard core of men and women and children who are carrying on Orthodoxy's purpose. And their achievements are far from over.

Lately, Orthodoxy has begun reaching out to brethren abroad in an attempt to organize a world-wide movement. Let us remember that in most countries Orthodox Judaism is either the only official or else the dominant religious expression. In countries such as England, France, Italy, and in various South American nations, there is an Orthodox Chief Rabbi who controls the Jewish religious establishment and who is frequently the official Jewish representative to the government. In these countries the Reform and Conservative groups are either terribly weak or nonexistent. Of course, the power of Orthodoxy in these lands is more apparent than real: while officially the people are Orthodox, in practice the majority is far from religious commitment and ritual observance. In Israel the religious establishment is in the hands of two Chief Rabbis—one Ashkenazic, the other Sephardic—both of whom wield considerable influence. The overwhelming majority of *religious* Jews in Israel is Orthodox

(there are only a dozen or so Reform and Conservative synagogues in the land), although the majority of the *country* is not
truly Orthodox. American Orthodoxy has been endeavoring to
cement relations with kindred groups in order to strengthen
world Orthodoxy and to coordinate activities on a global scale.

Thus, the Rabbinical Council of America joined with the Union of Orthodox Jewish Congregations in 1970 in convening in
Jerusalem the first World Conference of National Synagogue
Organizations and Religious Councils. Both groups have sought
to place world Orthodox groups under the legal hegemony and
influence of Israel's chief rabbinate. The RCA has also arranged
to bring young French rabbis to America for in-field training.
There have also been meetings between Israel's Chief Rabbis
and several European Chief Rabbis in an effort to join spiritual
forces. It remains to be seen, however, whether—in view of
Orthodoxy's allergy to centralization—such attempts will succeed.

Nevertheless, in light of these new developments, it appears
that the historian of American Orthodoxy will have a good deal
more to write about the oldest group in American Jewry in
tomorrow's history books.

# Orthodox Judaism—Ideology

# III

Any analysis of the ideology of Orthodox Judaism's ideology is fraught with difficulties. Orthodox Judaism, until the past decade, exerted little effort in the area of ideology or theology; it concentrated its efforts on Halakhah, Jewish law. In addition, Orthodox theology has been, for the most part, warmed-over teachings of the great German neo-Orthodox leader Rabbi Samson Raphael Hirsch (1808–1888) and, to a lesser degree, his disciples Israel Hildesheimer and Isaac Breuer. Little originality appeared in Orthodox writings that were published over the past years. Most Orthodox rabbis and writers have been content to reformulate either the classic dogmatic schemas of Maimonides, Yehudah Halevi, Crescas, and Albo, or the neo-Orthodox refinements of Hirsch. Moreover, "the main body of Orthodoxy in the United States," as Charles Liebman notes, "appears at present to be doctrinally untroubled." With absolute faith in God's existence and the infallibility of His Torah and the absolute necessity to abide by that Torah as interpreted by the rabbis, Orthodoxy has remained blithely indifferent to contempo-

54

rary challenges by arguing that there have been similar dilemmas in the past, and that each time Judaism has met the challenges and survived by holding fast to its classical doctrines while refusing to bend with every blowing wind. Hence the paucity of theological literature. Finally, since Orthodoxy is so splintered and fractionalized, there is really no *one* authoritative central body, not even one official rabbinic group or synagogal body, and certainly no *one* charismatic leader whose word is universally accepted by American Orthodoxy. Thus the difficulty of untangling the skeins of Orthodox thought in the search for its main patterns and dominant trends.[1]

On the other hand, since most Orthodox leaders agree on the basic meanings of Judaism's fundamental concepts of God, Torah, revelation, etc., it is easier to summarize Orthodox thought than the multi-faceted mosaics that comprise Reform and Conservatism. In the *Commentary* symposium on Jewish theology, for example, virtually *all* Orthodox contributors agreed on basic notions. Only an occasional dissent was registered in one or two areas out of all those covered. This too, is symptomatic.[2]

Yet Orthodox thinkers are finally beginning to stir and theology is once again attracting some devotees. Rabbi Soloveitchik (whose turgid style conceals great profundity and originality), Eliezer Berkovits, and Emanuel Rackman, among the older generation, as well as Norman Lamm, Walter Wurzburger, and Irving Greenberg, among the younger, have resuscitated Orthodox theology. Some years ago, *Tradition* magazine conducted a symposium on the need for theology. Rabbi Shubert Spero urged a new turn to theology in this age when the atmosphere is saturated with science, when Judaism is no longer insular, and when skepticism abounds. "Orthodoxy," he writes, "must demonstrate its superiority over rival Jewish theologies." Rabbi Norman Lamm issued a similar call. He described doubt "as part and parcel of theology" and he urged a campaign to meet doubt and doubters head-on, especially on the campus and on the lecture platforms, rather than in synagogues and pulpits. Clearly, Orthodox theology is reviving, and out of these new searchings and yearnings—yes, even doubts!—we can discern the directions of contemporary Orthodox thought.[3]

## The Nature of Judaism

"Judaism is the religion of the Jew," writes Rabbi Leo Jung, "and as such is co-extensive with Jewish life in all its implications and the sum total of the interpretations and applications of that faith." This definition is perhaps most typical of Orthodox Judaism: Judaism is first and foremost a *religion*. Eliezer Berkovits employs more mystical terms as he describes Judaism as "the encounter between God, Israel, and man." Emanuel Rackman prefers to define Judaism as "a legal order rather than a religion or faith" based on God's covenant with His people. Orthodoxy, he writes, believes that the written and oral tradition "have all the answers." For Joseph B. Soloveitchik, Judaism signifies the life of Torah and Halakhah. Samuel Belkin describes Judaism as "a mode of living based upon the authority of God as revealed in the Torah and in the oral traditions" which were derived from authentic tradition transmitted from generation to generation.

What are the basic elements of Judaism? The late Rabbi Herbert S. Goldstein was of the opinion that constancy and immutability form the basic strands in the tapestry of Orthodoxy. In his presidential address to the 1927 convention of the Union of Orthodox Jewish Congregations he said: "Judaism in America must form a link in the unbroken chain of Jewish tradition, the first link of which was formed at Mount Sinai. It [the UOJC] is opposed to any compromise that will weaken the foundations of the faith, upholds the principles of the unalterable truths of the Torah, and declares against any substitutes in Judaism." Soloveitchik discerns three basic elements: 1) recognition that God exists as the sole, absolute end; 2) man's total, unqualified commitment to service of God coupled with subordination of his desires; 3) Torah and Halakhah are truth, and man must have faith in their essential, revealed character. Rackman defines three concepts as basic to Judaism: a personal God, the chosen people, and the Torah as the eternal bond linking God and

Israel forever. Anything that departs from these three constitutes "a new faith." Rabbi Louis Rabinowitz writes that the three
basic premises of Orthodox Jewry are these: 1) Torah was revealed from heaven; 2) the Massoretic (traditional) text of the
Bible is accurate; 3) the Oral Law is not derivative of the Written
Torah but is a portion of it and its authoritative meaning. "On
it and on it alone we base our lives, our thoughts, and our
actions."[4]

Many Orthodox leaders have begun to shy away from the term
"Orthodox." Some—like Rabbi Leo Jung—prefer the appella-
tion "Torah-true," which they borrowed from the Frankfort
neo-Orthodox school of thought. Some prefer the term "traditional Judaism." Others eschew adjectives altogether. "We are
*Jews:* Let the heterodox choose adjectives," declares one Orthodox leader.[5]

In sum, Orthodoxy sees Judaism as a religious way of life
predicated on a belief in God and in His Torah, which was
revealed at Sinai along with the Oral Law that was ultimately
unfolded by succeeding generations of sages.

### God

Orthodoxy has little to say about God except to repeat the
standard theological formulations of doxology: God exists; He
is one; He is a personal God; He is omnipotent, omniscient,
omnipresent, eternal, and compassionate; He is spirit rather
than form.

Rabbi Soloveitchik talks uniquely about God in his abstruse
essays. Soloveitchik borrows heavily from Hegel, Kierkegaard,
Scheler, Buber, and Otto, and he deftly weaves both Halakhic
and Midrashic material in constructing his theology. God, writes
Soloveitchik, is the sole, absolute end—all else is ancillary. Man
must serve God with head as well as hands and heart. Man gains
insight into God's will through the performance of *mitzvot;* his
concern must be the sanctity, not merely the dignity, of man. He
must act in awareness of his relationship to God; his total existence must be consecrated to God.

Soloveitchik detects two prototypes of man, two Adams, as he puts it. One is Adam the first, creative, striving, reaching, majestic—the would-be conqueror of the cosmos. Adam the second is the lonely man of faith, the seeker of Why? What? Who? He is a convenantal man who wonders. Admitting that the role of the man of faith is difficult these days, Soloveitchik confesses, "I am lonely." What sustains him? "I believe—therefore I am," is his response. The covenantal man of faith craves a personal and intimate relation with God so that the finite "I" meets the infinite "He" face to face. In his loneliness, the man of faith met "the Lonely One and discovered the singular convenantal confrontation of solitary man and God who abides in the recess of transcendental solitude." Adam the second is ridiculed, lonely, forsaken, and misunderstood—an outsider like Moses. He is lonely because he has no comrade, no "duplicate I." "He finds redemption in the covenantal faith community by dovetailing his accidental self with the necessary infinite existence of the Great True Real Self." In the Messianic era, the dialectic will end and the man of faith as well as majestic man will achieve full redemption in a united world.[6]

Clearly, Rabbi Soloveitchik's mystical-existential analysis of God and man is unique in Orthodox circles and has found few echoes. Orthodox thinkers, when they do speak of God, are content to reassert classical theological modes. Men like Rackman and Berkovits have also written vigorously against the naturalistic-humanistic concept of God propounded by Reconstructionism, reaffirming their belief in a personal Deity.[7]

Even the great tragedy of the Holocaust has left Orthodox thinkers untroubled. There is little theodicy among Orthodox theologians, little attempt to justify God's ways to man. Most are content to adopt the classic view: "Because of our sins have these calamities befallen us." "Six million have died: surely our sins have brought on the calamity." Or else: "We cannot fathom God's inscrutable will." Eliezer Berkovits tries to grapple with the question of evil. It exists, he writes, but it "serves a purpose which is good because it is of God." Imperfection in the world challenges man and is the source of man's freedom of will. God hides Himself for the sake of man and history to give man moral independence and responsibility.

There is little anguish, little indictment of God, little moral outrage in Orthodox circles. Orthodoxy's concept of God is fundamentally unruffled.[8]

## Torah

It is in the area of Torah and Halakhah that Orthodoxy has much to say. Since Orthodoxy is synonymous with *law* or *mitzvot*, its most creative genius has been concentrated in this realm.

The cornerstone of Orthodox thought is, naturally, revelation. Without exception, Orthodox thinkers accept the dogma that God revealed the written and oral Torah at Sinai, and that the text of the Torah as we have it today is exactly the same as that given Moses thirty-one centuries ago. Thus, Rabbi Soloveitchik writes that he is not at all troubled by Biblical criticism. The prime purpose of revelation, as he sees it, is related to the giving of the law. God is the teacher par excellence; His task was turned over to the prophet; His word is ipso facto His law and norm.[9]

All Orthodox scholars accept the view of the literal, verbal revelation of the Torah, and virtually all accept the equal value of *mitzvot*, both ethical and ritual. Rackman is singularly alone in arguing that "much of it [the Pentateuch] may have been written by people in different times" and that not all of the *mitzvot* are "of equal importance." The typically Orthodox view is that of the Lubavitcher Rebbe, namely, "Torah is indivisible. No fragment of it is 'unimportant.' " Similarly, Rabbis Norman Lamm, Aharon Lichtenstein, Walter Wurzburger, Immanuel Jacobovitz, and Professor Marvin Fox agree that the Torah is identical with the Torah revealed at Sinai, and it is eternal, authentic, and binding, with no distinction between ritual and ethical commandments and no priority of importance. Eliezer Berkovits, while interpreting revelation as an "impenetrable mystery," the details of which are allegorical ("the Torah speaks the language of man"), still agrees that one may not distinguish between one part of revelation or another, for every word is revealed. "We fulfill all *mitzvot*," he writes, "even if there is no apparent ethical motive, because we are to do God's will." For Leo Jung, revelation means: 1) that the Torah is not the fruit of the genius of Moses but came to him from a supernatural source; and 2) Torah teaching is true. "A true Jew," he adds, "believes in revelation and the divine origin of the Torah."[10]

This fundamental acceptance of revelation and the authenticity of the Biblical text has, naturally, doomed Biblical criticism. Consequently, no yeshivah teaches the Bible critically, and any such approach is treated contemptuously. Thus, the new Jewish Publication Society translation of the Bible was roundly condemned by most Orthodox scholars as untraditional and anti-Halakhic, and as the fruits of the labor of non-Orthodox ignoramuses.[11]

In view of Orthodoxy's unyielding adherence to literal revelation, we can understand why Halakhah has become the cornerstone of Orthodox theology and practice. Most of the writings of Orthodox scholars deal with Halakhah, from either a practical or a theoretical point of view. "The man of Halakhah" (to borrow the title of his most famous essay) *par excellence* is Rabbi Soloveitchik.[12]

Soloveitchik writes that Halakhah contains characteristic structures of ideas and sentiments which derive from a fundamental attitude of the human spirit. It articulates a psychic complex of ideas and values of its own and it does not stand in need of validation from any outside source. Founded on Divine revelation, Halakhah has grown in continuous awareness of the tensions and paradoxes of human nature which it sought to resolve and to integrate in its vision of the ideal personality. The life of total dedication to Halakhah leads to a "nearness to God"; the man of Halakhah is aware of tensions and crises of human personality. Religious consciousness heightens our sense of wonder at the very quality of lawfulness that holds the entire range of existence in thrall. Halakhah provides Divine answers to this human dilemma. The man of Halakhah approaches the mystery of existence with "a priori concepts" to find a satisfactory image of the universe. He comes from Sinai "armed with a body of teaching which points out to him the way to the nature of being. There is no phenomenon, event, or thing which a priori Halakhah does not approach with its ideal measurements." In a later essay he goes further:

> *There is not a single theoretical or technological discovery, from new psychological insights into the human personality to man's attempts to reach out among the planets, with which the Halakhah is not concerned. New Halakhic problems arise with every new scientific discovery. As a matter of fact, at present, in order to render precise Halakhic decisions in many fields of human endeavor, one must possess, besides excellent Halakhic training, a good working knowledge in those secular fields in which the problem occurs.*[13]

For Soloveitchik, Halakhah enables man to bend the realm of eternity into the temporal universe. There is no battle against the flesh, no Christian-like ceaseless war against the Evil Desire, for the laws of the Torah are sober and life-affirming laws and the God-given *mitzvot* enable man to build eternity here. Halakhah affords "shape and form to the amorphous, fluid, unpredictable 'feelings' of religion"; it is the "objectification of religion in the shape of fixed and lucid molds that clearly outline laws and definite principles. It converts subjectivity into objectivity and a fixed pattern of lawfulness."

In his earlier writings, Soloveitchik expressed disapproval of Hasidic feeling and enthusiasm, "for all *mitzvot* are equal before the Lord." The idea of the Halakhic man, he suggested, is to be a prophet. "Every person is called upon to renew his being in accord with the ideal pattern of the prophet and to engage in this creative process until he attains final consummation of prophetic achievement—namely, the readiness for the reception of Divine Grace." More recently, he has begun to appreciate the Hasidic value of *kavanah*—of inner, emotional experience. Cognition, he writes, leads to the experience of God's presence and some *mitzvot* involve both inner and outer moment (e.g., mourning, prayer, repentance, etc.).

Finally, Soloveitchik talks about the teleology or purpose of the Halakhah, which "manifests itself in paradoxical yet magnificent dialectic" that man gives to the covenantal community and is wanted and needed in the cosmic-majestic community. Man is fulfilled only in both communities; this is the Halakhic dialect. But since Halakhah believes in monism, man's task is to unite majesty and covenant into one with man as the creative, free agent and obedient servant of God.

No other Orthodox writer has attempted to construct such a profound and philosophical superstructure of Halakhah. While Soloveitchik's views are difficult to grasp, they have not been without partisans and interpreters. Emanuel Rackman, for example, has devoted much time and literary effort to popularizing Soloveitchik's views.

What is the purpose of Halakhah? As we have noted, Soloveitchik detects a *telos*—a purpose to the Law, namely, the unity of the creative forces in man with the Creative Force of the universe. Rackman follows this view: he sees each Halakhic rule as reflecting some Divine universal or immutable idea, a subject of revelation. He seeks the ends of the Halakhah as, for example, in Sabbath and Festivals. The purpose of the Sabbath rules is to teach us to cease the exploitation of nature. Rackman rejects the fundamentalistic view that "the Law is the Law" and no rationale or purpose need be sought. Dr. Samuel Belkin is also an advocate of this approach to Halakhah. He distinguishes between the philosophy of reason (the Greek method) and the philosophy of purpose (the Jewish approach). In Judaism the quest is Why? For what purpose? The *mitzvot*, writes Belkin, all have a higher, moral purpose—even those *mitzvot* that defy reason and seem irrational. In addition to the literal meaning of Torah, "there is a deeper purpose, a hidden meaning, obscured, imbedded in the revealed word." Eliezer Berkovits also seeks the purpose of the *mitzvot.* He stresses their educational significance and suggests that they are an *indirect* attack on the self-centeredness of the biophysical organism and they teach ethical training. The rituals engender an "awareness of the other"; they curb egocentricity and help man practice saying "No" to self-centered demands, or "Yes" in consideration of the other. By obeying

God's command we become related to God. *Mitzvot* like *kashrut,* *tefillin,* Passover, etc., bind us to Him; they fashion a "relationship with the wholly other."[14]

To be sure, there is nothing new in this approach to the Halakhah. For centuries, scholars have sought to uncover the *taame ha-mitzvot*—the reasons behind the commandments. Maimonides, in his *Guide For the Perplexed,* honed the technique to its most rational point of acuity. The Kabbalists developed the cosmic-mystical function of the Law. And Samson Raphael Hirsch brilliantly recast the technique in modern garb. The modern Orthodox school of teleology is merely continuing an age-old and respected process of seeking the recondite reasons for God's manifold laws.[15]

What of the Halakhah and change? Can the Halakhic process breathe new life into old laws? Can laws be amended, modernized, updated? Or is it frozen forever, to be obeyed by the faithful without question? This problem has occupied the best minds in Orthodoxy and the answers have been surprisingly varied.

Rabbi Soloveitchik, as we have noted, believes that the Halakhah is objective: it is an a priori system not in need of any validation and not subject to man's quixotic personality. The man of Halakhah, he suggests, is like a mathematician: he feels no conflict between the real and the ideal, between law and life. He goes his way without complaining about his lot or luck. Immanuel Jakobovitz agrees: he writes that the Halakhah is and was always decided by objective processes—rules, facts, sources; it was never governed by subjective canons of conscience. Still, he is forced to admit that a judge is human and is "subject to various influences, and his judgments are necessarily colored by objective considerations." Obviously the fundamentalist view allows for no economic, sociological, or psychological factors in Halakhah; human or societal forces play no part in the development of the Law—only God's will is decisive.[16]

Yet, there are liberals in the Orthodox camp who recognize the human factor and espouse the need for Halakhic development. Leo Jung writes that the Law is fluid and "we must not be misunderstood as saying that the Halakhah is completely rigid. It is objective . . . But we have had in Halakhah from earliest times to our own day and I pray that we shall have it also tomorrow, also the legal fiction, that means, a device by which whenever an unchanging law meets an impossible situation, the *Din Torah* within the prerogatives of the Beth Din, creates opportunity for special enactments, emergency laws." Jung delineates between valid *hiddushim* ("legitimate applications of precedent to new situations") and illegal *shinuyim* ("changes or adaption of *Din Torah* to new situations"). The former technique, when practiced by an Orthodox Beth Din through the means of *taqanah,* special enactment, is perfectly legal; the latter as used by Reform and Conservative rabbis is "an effrontery of arbitrary individual change."[17]

Rackman, although a close disciple of Soloveitchik and his "a priori system," nevertheless articulates a liberal view of the need for a growing Halakhah. To be sure, he warns that if we eliminate theocentricity we remove the heart from the appeals for the revival of Jewish Law. Yet he sees Halakhah as wavering between antinomies as it attempts to balance conflicting norms, values, and interests. He looks for the purpose of the Law and strives to preserve the ultimate goal. While endorsing the Divine objectivity of the Law, he argues that this does "not preclude diversity and heterogeneity as to methods and objectives . . . Halakhah mirrors personalities; it reflects individual *modi* existential."

> *The Halakhah is more than texts. It is life and experience. What made the Babylonian and not the Palestinian Talmud the great guide of Jewish life in the Diaspora was not a decree or a decision but vox populi . . . can a Halakhic scholar lose himself in texts exclusively when the texts themselves bid him to see what practice "has become widespread among Jews," . . . and many other social criteria?*

Orthodox rabbis must stop denigrating the role of man in Halakhic creativity, pleads Rackman, or they will fail to reach contemporaries who want to return. "Man plays a role in the development of Halakhah." Of course, when Rackman writes that *man* plays a role, he implies that only scholars and saints may play a role—never laymen. Belkin, alone among all Orthodox writers, suggests that Orthodox laymen may have a voice in the legal process.[18]

While sharply critical of Rackman's teleological approach, Rabbi Mendell Lewittes calls for frank Halakhic confrontation with problems like the *agunah* and other modern dilemmas. Orthodoxy's reticence to do so has helped give rise to "the alarming growth of the Reform and Conservative movements . . . If the qualified masters of the Halakhah were to carry on their traditional róle of being the judge of Halakhic questions . . . then the wind would be taken out of the sails of Conservative and Reform Judaism." Even more sharply critical of Orthodox timidity in the realm of Halakhah is Eliezer Berkovits, who, after adducing various examples of how Halakhah adapted itself to changing conditions for practical, economic, ethical, or spiritual reasons, proceeds to criticize as "non-authentic Halakhah" Orthodoxy's stubborn refusal to resolve pressing problems. Among the laws that Berkovits considers obsolete and ethically indefensible and archaic are those concerning autopsies, *shemitah* and the *agunah*. "The future of Judaism depends on Halakhah. The future of the Halakhah depends on our ability to restore its original function, to retrieve its spirit of authenticity." Berkovits adds: "Withdrawal from reality and continued ignoring of the challenges of the contemporary situation will not give us authentic Judaism."[19]

It is obvious that there are several Orthodox approaches to change in Halakhah. The fundamentalists deny the need for change, or else concede the need but deny that modern scholars possess the necessary competence and saintliness. The liberals urge bold action in Halakhic matters; some (notably Israeli scholars) suggest the reconstitution of a Sanhedrin for the purpose; some are bitterly critical of the Torah scholars and their refusal to face contemporary problems. All, of course, would empower only recognized *Orthodox* sages to alter or amend Halakhah.

Despite differences of approach to Halakhah, Orthodox rabbis and scholars obviously view Halakhah as the essence of Judaism. They warmly espouse the view that Halakhah can and will deal with *all* human problems. Thus, the pages of Orthodox journals, such as *Tradition, Ha-Darom, Noam, Ha-Pardes,* are replete with Halakhic items ranging from heart transplant to Sabbath observance on Mars and in interstellar space flights. The enlightened Orthodox are not at all reticent about confronting modern problems. On the contrary, they are prepared to face fearlessly the problems on their own terms. The Lubavitcher Rebbe writes:

> He who says that science contradicts religion is talking rubbish. True science is highly compatible with faith . . . The Torah is truth, and science is truth, therefore there can exist no conflict between the two. In fact, the findings of the past few years confirm what is said in the Torah—ideas which scientists a generation ago would not have believed . . . It is the duty of the Orthodox Jewish college student to dispel the myth of incompatibility.[20]

But the lack of a central authority or rabbinic body in Orthodox life makes it virtually impossible to discern a consensus on some basic issues. Responsa are written, votes are cast, opinions are pronounced, anathemas are declared—and we are as confused as ever as to where Orthodoxy stands. For example, the question of birth control has been a thorny one for Orthodox scholars. Some sages, like the Lubavitcher Rebbe, consider birth control to be a "falsification of Torah and contrary to Halakhah and the code of Jewish law." On the other hand, Rabbi Moses Feinstein (generally acknowledged as the premier legal expert or judge in Orthodox life) is much more liberal in permitting the female to use contraceptives. Orthodoxy's stand on some of the latest issues that perplex modern man, such as war and peace, transplants, abortions, etc., are not clearly defined; the water is muddy and it is difficult to discover agreement.

Of course, Orthodox scholars are in accord on certain fundamental rules of the Torah as interpreted by the Talmud and the sages, and codified in the *Shulhan Arukh*. The Sabbath is inviolate for an Orthodox Jew. He will not work, write, smoke, carry in the public domain, ride a car or public vehicle (even to get to a synagogue), use electricity or radio or television, or worship in any but an Orthodox *shul*. Similarly, he is expected to observe the Festivals faithfully—building a *sukkah* on the Sukkot holiday, fasting on Yom Kippur, scrupulously abstaining from leavened products on Passover, etc. The Orthodox male prays daily with *talit* and *tefillin*, and wears a *yarmulka* (skullcap) at all times as a sign of reverence for God. The Orthodox woman has no role in synagogue worship; but she is expected to run a Jewish home, maintain a kosher kitchen, light Sabbath candles, and go to a *mikveh* (ritual bath) after her menstrual cycle. Orthodox partisans observe the dietary laws both in and out of the home. Thus, Orthodox Jews eat only kosher meats and fish, maintain separate meat and dairy dishes, and will not even eat dairy in a non-kosher restaurant. Orthodox law requires observant Jews to marry within the faith, to receive or issue a *get* (religious divorce) before remarrying, and it generally refuses to allow its adherents to engage in converting non-Jews to Judaism. The Orthodox Jew observes a seven-day mourning period (*shivah*), tears his garment over the loss of a near relative, and recites the *Kaddish* prayer every day for eleven months after the death of a parent.

It should be obvious to the reader that Orthodoxy's focal point is Halakhah. He who would understand the ideas and ideology of Orthodoxy must survey Halakhic literature and the philosophies of Jewish law propounded by the various legal experts and Talmudists. The sum and substance of Orthodoxy today, as in the past, is to be discovered in the "four cubits of Jewish Law."

### The Jewish People

All Orthodox thinkers accept the concept that Israel is the chosen people of God. The liturgical formulation "You have chosen us from all the peoples" has remained virtually a dogma among the Orthodox. It has been a cornerstone of Orthodox theology and is considered the means that has enabled Israel to survive all tyrants and holocausts. Reconstructionism's deletion of the "chosen people" notion has precipitated a ferocious counterbarrage among the Orthodox. Eliezer Berkovits insists that Israel is chosen to be a Kingdom of Priests—a holy nation to serve not nationalism but God, a means to a higher end. In a more recent statement, Berkovits writes: "God did not choose the Jews, but the people that God chose became the Jewish people as a result of their taking upon themselves the task and responsibility for the realization of Judaism." Professor Marvin Fox accepts the concept as symbolic of Israel's mission and higher duty, while Immanuel Jacobovitz interprets it to mean that Israel, like other nations, has a national purpose. The Lubavitcher Rebbe also accepts the "chosen people" concept in terms of a national mission:

> To be sure, we recognize Golus [the Diaspora] as a punishment and rectification for failure to live up to our obligations in the past ... But we have a mission to spread the Unity of God [true monotheism] to the remotest corner of the world. Thus the ultimate purpose of the Golus is linked with our destiny to help bring humanity to a state of universal recognition of God.[21]

### The Land of Israel

In the early years of the Zionist movement, Orthodoxy was ambivalent over the question of a Jewish state. Naturally, all Orthodox Jews fervently believed in the return of the Jewish People to their ancient homeland in Zion. But many were convinced that only the intervention of a supernatural messiah could bring that about; and most Orthodox Jews maintained that "Eretz Yisrael without Torah is like a body without a soul" —that Israel's Land and Israel's Torah were one and inseparable. This explains why many Orthodox rabbis opposed the political Zionism of Theodor Herzl and denounced it as a secular attempt to force God's hand. And thus we understand Orthodoxy's ambivalence to the State of Israel with its secularistic attitude to Jewish life. Orthodox Jews still yearn for "the State of Israel in accordance with the law of Israel."

Yet, Orthodoxy in America opted early for Zionism, albeit in a religious context. The attempt of Agudat Israel, the non-Zionist world Orthodox organization, to strike roots in America failed. The anti-Zionist lunatic fringe of the Satmar Rebbe has only a few thousand followers here and in Israel. The bulk of American Orthodoxy is in the camp of the Religious Zionists of America, with a sprinkling to be found in the nonreligious Zionist Organization of America. Orthodoxy is officially represented in the Jewish Agency.

But Orthodoxy is not content with just another Levantine state in Israel; its concept of Zionism is predicated on religio-cultural values. Zion and Torah are inseparable to the Orthodox; the Land of Israel is one way of approaching the God of Israel.

Rabbi Soloveitchik sees the Jewish state as the means to a higher end—the way of fulfilling the destiny of "the community of the committed." The Lubavitcher Rebbe agrees: "But to be a Jewish state it must run according to the Messianic tradition, *i.e.*, in accordance with the laws of the Torah." Israel, says the Rebbe, is *the* Holy Land, a special place, and has never been relinquished by the Jewish People. Quoting his predecessor, the Rebbe notes that "only our bodies were sent into exile, but not our souls." Urging that the state be run in accordance with Halakhah, the Rebbe argues that the problems of observing the Sabbath in today's mechanized era are much simpler than in the days of the Temple. Is Israel the beginning of the era of redemption? No, answers the Lubavitcher Rebbe: "The redemption must always come together with Torah and *mitzvos*." In a letter to former Prime Minister David Ben-Gurion, he expressed his fears "that there exists the danger that a new generation will grow up, a new type bearing the name of Israel but completely divorced from the past of our people and its eternal and essential values."[22]

Emanuel Rackman is enthusiastic about the State of Israel for many reasons. One is that he sees in the restoration of the Jewish People to Zion a golden opportunity to restore the Law to normalcy and full application and development. The Law must "prove itself capable of meeting the challenge on every front" and yield answers "that will delight the religionist and the secularist alike." But Rackman is determined, as are virtually all Orthodox leaders, that Israel be run in accordance with the Torah. Ironically, the very same Orthodox spokesmen who warmly espouse the cause of separation of church and state in America are equally zealous in demanding that Israel be run in accordance with Halakhic canons. Thus, they favor enforced Sabbath laws, cessation of public transportation on the Sabbath, solely kosher facilities on ships and in hospitals and hotels, and they are adamantly opposed to civil marriage. Orthodox groups have firmly attacked, moreover, the implantation of Conservative or Reform Judaism in Israel or the granting of jurisdiction over marriage or divorce to non-Orthodox rabbis.[23]

A succinct statement of Orthodoxy's view of the Jewish state can be gleaned from this editorial in *Jewish Life*, the official organ of the Union of Orthodox Jewish Congregations:

> *Jewish completion is not demarked by street signs in Hebrew, by an economy built and manned by Jews, or even by a Hebrew-speaking society composed of Jews. It can be sought and found only in a community whose tenets as well as whose traditions are purely, truly Jewish.*[24]

American Orthodoxy maintains religious, cultural, and educational institutions in Israel including Bar-Ilan University and several yeshivot. Since 1970, it has launched a campaign for *aliyah* to Israel. It has a very lively presence in the State of Israel and maintains close ties with Israel's Chief Rabbis, whom many regard as the definitive Orthodox judges.

### The Jewish Community

For many years Orthodoxy has been committed to the ideal of *klal Yisrael*—the unity of the Jewish community. With the exception of the ultra-Orthodox fanatics, the modern mainstream of Orthodoxy has worked closely with Reform and Conservative as well as Zionist and secularist groups in a variety of causes concerned with Israel, anti-Semitism, education, philanthropic and welfare funds, chaplaincies, etc. Men like the eloquent Rabbi Joseph Lookstein have rallied the Orthodox groups to join with non-Orthodox confrères in a multitude of projects to benefit American Jewry as well as Israel and world Jewry.

But in recent years, there has been a tendency to sever those ties and split asunder the unity of Jewish communal efforts. Orthodoxy has felt more assured and self-confident; its ranks have swelled and solidified; its institutions are flourishing. With its new-found strength has come a new-found attitude of "Let's go it alone." There are trends reminiscent of German Orthodoxy of the nineteenth century when Samson Raphael Hirsch and the so-called *trennungs Orthodoxie* withdrew from the Jewish community and became a separate entity, shunning cooperation with the non-Orthodox.

In 1955, for example, eleven eminent yeshivah heads prohibited Orthodox rabbis from participating in umbrella groups such as the New York Board of Rabbis and the Synagogue Council of America lest a stamp of legitimacy be given to the non-Orthodox.

In 1966 Dr. Samuel Belkin was to have joined Drs. Nelson Glueck and Louis Finkelstein as the honored guests at the fortieth anniversary banquet of the Synagogue Council of America. As a result of a campaign of vilification and severe pressures from the rightists, Dr. Belkin was forced to decline the honor. At several conventions of the Rabbinical Council of America, men like past president Rabbi David Hollander introduced resolutions urging withdrawal from such cooperative groups, but the resolutions were defeated. A *shealah* (religious query) was addressed to Rabbi Joseph Soloveitchik on the matter but no reply was rendered. Several conventions of the Union of Orthodox Jewish Congregations have debated the "withdrawal" issue. Advocates of separation, such as Rabbi Ralph Pelcovitz, have warned that cooperation with non-Orthodox will dilute the message of Orthodox. Pelcovitz writes: "By submerging ourselves we lose our identity, we sacrifice our unique voice, we forfeit our opportunity to project our viewpoint in a clear, decisive, unequivocal manner."[25] Similarly, an editorial in *Jewish Life* put the question bluntly.

> *Let us not, out of misplaced courtesy, fail to state the case in plain terms. That belief which today is called Orthodox Judaism has sole claim to Jewish allegiance; it, alone, has vital Jewish force; it, alone, gives life to Jewry; it alone can unify Jewish life and the Jewish spirit, can provide the basis for Jewish life amidst epochal change.*[26]

It cannot be denied that there has been a new note of shrill and strident criticisms of the non-Orthodox. Even the more scholarly and sober pages of *Tradition* occasionally publish slurs and invectives. Contributors like Rabbis Pelcovitz and Tendler refuse to refer to non-Orthodox clergymen as "rabbis," preferring the innocuous (and debasing) title of "ministers" instead. Other journals such as Young Israel *Viewpoint* and *Orthodox Life* talk of "Heterodox" Jews and "ministers" rather than "rabbis" while the more extreme publications of the fundamentalist groups are palpably insulting. Liberals like Rackman are not beyond polemics. Rackman, for example, scorns the Reconstructionists, whom he calls "heretics." He states that it is easier to work with secular humanists than with Conservatives and Reformers, and he notes: "Even at the risk of being dubbed 'intolerant,' I too insist that there is but one authentic Judaism, while other approaches are errors, distortion, heresy, or even pretense."[27]

There is a danger to Orthodoxy itself from such a separatist, heresy-hunting approach. The liberals have been subjected to searing criticism from the fundamentalists; the progressive Orthodox like Rackman, Berkovits—yes, even Rabbi Soloveitchik! —have been the targets of right-wing attacks. Rackman has been compelled to defend his liberalism (which he concedes is a minority view) against the fanatics who would read the liberals out of the movement. Moreover, since a huge number—perhaps the majority—of Orthodox Jews constitute that strange phenomenon known as "non-observant Orthodox," it is difficult not to purge virtually everyone out of Orthodoxy's ranks. Pelcovitz tries to solve the dilemma by arguing that non-observing

Jews are Orthodox as long as they retain "spiritual allegiance to traditional Judaism."[28]

On the other hand, the Lubavitcher Rebbe has been at great pains to teach his followers that *all* Jews are members of the fold and that heresy hunting is the wrong approach. He has urged his disciples to win the stray sheep back by love—not excommunication or contempt—and indeed has had some success even among young American-born collegians.

The temper of Orthodoxy is evidently ambivalent. On the one hand, there is the mood of condescension to the non-Orthodox heretics—a mood strangely reminiscent of the Catholic Church in pre-Vatican II days. Orthodoxy is rightly fearful that if boundaries are blurred, especially between Orthodoxy and Conservatism, and differences are minimized, Orthodox Jews of the less observant type are apt to switch allegiance without too many qualms of conscience. After all, if differences of theology and practice are merely a matter of degree, of more or less *mitzvot,* why not take the easier path? Hence, Orthodoxy has been drawing up more sharply defined battle lines in an attempt to prevent the submergence of its identity and uniqueness.

Still, the liberals and progressives are not about to permit Orthodoxy to sever its ties with the non-Orthodox and separate from the community. Much good has been achieved by unified efforts in working for Israel, Soviet Jewry, civil rights, separation of church and state, protection of Jewish ritual slaughter, chaplaincy services, philanthropic and welfare agencies, and in many other areas. Certainly in matters not relating to Halakhah or theology, Orthodoxy has gained immeasurably by partnerships with non-Orthodox groups. And that is why the present Orthodox leadership has steadfastly refused to cut the ties of cooperation, if only for pragmatic reasons of self-interest. For the foreseeable future, it appears that Orthodoxy will continue to follow this curtailed program of cooperation with the Jewish community.

## The Synagogue

Generally speaking, Orthodoxy views the synagogue as the House of Prayer, with the study and social aspects as merely incidental to its true purpose. Orthodox leaders such as Dr. Samuel Belkin publicly disavowed the social-center facet of synagogues and have stressed the worship aspect. Dr. Emanuel Rackman decries the concept of a synagogue as primarily a social center and the rabbi as a public-relations man. While recognizing the social value of the synagogue in preserving the Jewish people, he argues that the synagogue should be shifted over to become a yeshivah or school.[29]

Of course, this is much more in keeping with the pattern of the European Orthodox synagogue where the *shul* was basically used for prayer and, incidentally, for adult studies in Bible, Mishnah, and Talmud. Children studied in a *heder* or a yeshivah, usually separate from the synagogue. Following this example, and sensitive to the inadequacy of the Hebrew School, the American Orthodox synagogue has all but given up on the Talmud Torah and has stressed the worth of the yeshivah or Day School as the only hope for American Jewry. Many Orthodox synagogues, therefore, maintain no synagogue school; others keep up a minuscule Talmud Torah. But the Orthodox synagogues have generally shifted their students to community-supported yeshivot.

Still, despite all disclaimers, many Orthodox synagogues are really synagogue-centers as envisioned by Orthodoxy's nemesis, Mordecai M. Kaplan. Many have gymnasiums and pools, most run club programs, and virtually all hold social functions with mixed dancing, Orthodox law notwithstanding. The modern Orthodox rabbi usually preaches in English and on a regular basis. Unlike his European predecessor who preached only several times a year and spent the rest of the time answering *shealot* (ritual questions) and studying or teaching the Talmud, the American Orthodox rabbi is virtually a carbon copy of his Reform and Conservative colleague: he preaches, teaches, administrates, serves as a pastor, acts as a counselor, and in general, fills a wide variety of roles.

In one area, however, the Orthodox synagogue has made almost no concessions, namely, in liturgy. With the exception of a few English prayers added in the worship of many *shuls,* the Orthodox synagogue has maintained the traditional liturgy with no deviations, amendments, deletions, or reforms. In fact, there seems to be virtually no theological malaise whatsoever over liturgy among the Orthodox. Whereas much of the efforts of Reform, Conservatism, and Reconstructionism has been in the area of liturgy, Orthodoxy has been untroubled and unruffled by the entire problem. Eliezer Berkovits wrote a lengthy study of the idea of prayer in Judaism in which he shows no signs of questioning the classical liturgy. He merely quotes the classic texts, reaffirms a belief in the efficacy of prayer, and reiterates the need for private and public prayer.[30]

Emanuel Rackman goes further: he denounces as arrogance any attempt to alter the liturgy. "The Orthodox Jew," he writes, "is simply too modest to tamper with the 'Siddur.' He knows that it was compiled by saints and sages whose religious fervor he wishes he could match." Decrying arrogant endeavors to reinterpret or remove prayers concerning sacrifices, the chosen people, resurrection, etc., Rackman declares that "it is not that the prayers have no appeal, but that prayer itself has no appeal." "Immodest men," he adds, "simply cannot pray. Immodest men have no sense of awe. Immodest men are rarely grateful." Officially, then, Orthodox Jews accept literally the concepts of Messiah, resurrection, Heaven and Hell, and other motifs of the liturgy.[31]

Since Orthodoxy accepts the traditional liturgy in unmodified form, it has never produced an "official" prayer book. There are perhaps six or seven popularly used editions of the traditional prayer books in Orthodox *shuls* today. In 1960 an attempt was made by the Rabbinical Council of America to issue an "authorized" *Sidur* for American congregations edited by Rabbi David de Sola Pool. The attempt was a failure and something of an economic fiasco, and the chaotic situation of varied prayer books (including different editions in *one* synagogue) has prevailed. This, too, is symptomatic of Orthodoxy's untroubled liturgical mood.

On the other hand, Orthodoxy has agonized over other dilemmas of synagogue life. Under Orthodox Halakhah, riding on the Sabbath or Festivals—even if only to synagogue—constitutes a grave breach of law. Rabbi Joseph Soloveitchik has stated that it is better to pray at home on the High Holidays than to ride to a synagogue or to pray in a non-Orthodox congregation. Yet, life is not as simple as the ideal; suburban living has forced many Jews who had hitherto not traveled on the Sabbath or holidays to do so. Orthodoxy has made an uneasy compromise with the realities of life: it closes its parking lots on sacred days so that the worshiper parks around the corner if he cannot walk to *shul*.

Yet another area of controversy in Orthodox synagogues concerns the question of mixed seating. Orthodox law requires segregation of the sexes at worship with the erection of a *mehitzah* of specified height to shield the women's gallery from view. Rabbi Joseph Soloveitchik has issued a ruling that such separation is Biblically required lest "something unseemly and immoral" be committed (Deuteronomy 23:15). His younger brother, Rabbi Aaron Soloveitchik, has taken a totally different tack in denouncing mixed seating. He argues that woman has "innate spiritual superiority" over man. Thus, she is segregated from man in the synagogue lest she embarrass him and inhibit his worship. In 1958 and 1959, Orthodox synagogues in New Orleans and Mt. Clemens, Michigan, staved off attempts to introduce mixed seating when the courts upheld the Orthodox view. *Jewish Life* exulted in its editorial columns that this marks the "end of an era of anarchy in congregational life" and it talked of "scores" of synagogues recognizing their error and restoring separate pews, for "upon this issue hinges the question whether synagogues will be Jewish sanctuaries or be made over into the likeness of the church." But Orthodoxy had won such victories in the nineteenth century only to find them pyrrhic victories as the liberal elements seceded to form new congregations, leaving a shell of the old Orthodox ones. Moreover, facts contradict fancy: scores of synagogues have *not* reinstituted the *mehitzah* and many have even dropped the segregation of the sexes. It was acutely embarrassing to several Orthodox *shuls* some years ago when the late Chief Rabbi of Israel, Isaac Herzog, chided them for not having sufficiently high curtains separating the women's gallery. While technically an Orthodox *shul* must have a *mehitzah* and one that does not is no longer Orthodox, many have de facto done away with Halakhic segregation of the sexes.[32]

Obviously, the modern Orthodox synagogue of today is noticeably different from the East European models of seventy years ago. It bears more resemblance to the decorous and dignified Conservative synagogue than to the informal and disorderly *shtiebel* of past or present. And yet, paradoxically, many people have turned their backs on the dignified Orthodox synagogues and have joined *shtiebels*. Is it because they resent bigness or confining decorum? Is it that they prefer the intimate laxity of the *shtiebel* atmosphere? In any event, numerous *shtiebels* exist side by side with dignified Orthodox *shuls*, and young and old frequent them.

*Social Action*

Until rather recently, Orthodoxy was little concerned with social action, and few rabbis or laymen were involved in communal or national problems. There were several reasons for Orthodoxy's indifference to social issues. For one, Orthodoxy was not truly acculturated to the American scene until recently. Then too, Orthodoxy was much too concerned with saving Jews for Torah to care about saving the world. With its full efforts directed to building yeshivot, strengthening *kashrut* and protecting the Sabbath, Orthodoxy could spare little time, money, or effort in the realm of social concern. The only areas in which the Orthodox movement was involved dealt with fair Sabbath legislation, battling against humane slaughter laws, and, more recently, public aid to parochial schools. These problems, of course, most intimately impinge on Orthodoxy; hence the active lobbying and fervent campaigns in those areas. If Reform was too busy tending others' vineyards to care for its own, Orthodoxy was too preoccupied with its own to tend others'.

There have been some isolated voices calling for greater involvement by Orthodox Jews in social issues. Leo Jung chided his fellow Orthodox rabbis for not teaching the social-righteousness programs of the Torah. He accused Orthodoxy of having failed to show that solutions to modern problems and world conflicts are found in *Din Torah*. By failing to teach social ethics, labor rights, and the ethical dynamism of Judaism, argues Jung, Orthodoxy has driven many into the arms of Marxism. Similarly, Emanuel Rackman has uttered a "plea for involvement" in social issues. He decried the fact that Orthodox Jews have been less involved in the social revolutions of the 1960's than other denominations. Rackman admonished his Orthodox followers that the salvation of all men should be important to all of us, and that Orthodox Jews are too "self-centered under the guise of religiosity and divine approval." Calling for the Orthodox movement to turn its attention to the economic, social, moral, and drug revolutions that assail us, he cautioned that "we cannot assure the future of Jews or Judaism simply by looking backward."[33]

These appeals have had some impact and have found increasingly evident responses in Orthodox ranks. There has been greater involvement by Orthodox rabbis and laymen in the civil rights struggle of America's black citizens. The Union of Orthodox Jewish Congregations articulated a social-actions platform at its 1970 convention calling for ratification of the genocide convention, expressing its fear over the urban crisis and deterioration of the cities, and declaring its rejection of a philosophy of "law and order" as a means of depriving blacks and other minority groups of rights and opportunities. It also demanded fair employment and housing for all citizens and the need to "improve the quality of life for all Americans," while urging the protection of the environment from pollution, and expressing concern for agricultural and mine workers and grape strikers who were battling for decent work conditions. The same convention expressed its concern for Soviet and Israeli Jewry but explicitly rejected "Jewish extremism" as preached by the Jewish Defense League as "contrary to the Torah, highly counterproductive, and a *hilul ha-Shem*" (desecration of God's name).[34]

Of late, much of Orthodoxy's social action's impetus has been focused on the question of public aid to parochial schools. Since 1962, Orthodoxy has officially espoused public aid to parochial schools because of the economic plight of yeshivot. It has broken the hitherto solid front of Jewish opposition to public aid to private education. Almost without exception, Orthodox leaders, the Rabbinical Council of America, the Union of Orthodox Jewish Congregations, and other groups have argued that without public aid, the yeshivot might be forced to close. At the 1970 convention of the Union of Orthodox Jewish Congregations, the delegates passed a resolution labeling the issue of separation of church and state as "specious." The resolution stated: "We believe opposition to such government aid to be detrimental to the Jewish interest." The convention also urged the Jewish Federations and Welfare Funds to increase their support for yeshivot and curtail their services to non-Jews. The Rabbinical Council of America, at its 1971 convention, called for a voucher system that would not violate separation of church and state. The president of the Council, Rabbi Bernard Berzon, went even further: he urged the establishment of ten liberal arts colleges in major cities under the aegis of Yeshiva University to counteract the "secular influences on Jewish youth." Berzon suggested that only in such schools can Jewish students avoid the "agnosticism, self-autonomy, sexual permissiveness, drugs" and other corrosive influences. Orthodoxy has evidently given up on both public schools and colleges.[35]

Orthodox groups have also become involved in the abortion issue. The liberalization of abortion laws in many states has touched a nerve in both Catholic and Orthodox Jewish life, since both share a general revulsion to the use of abortions. While Orthodox Halakhah does recognize the validity of abortion in certain circumstances, it does not accept the liberal views of Conservative or Reform Jews or of the Protestant-controlled state legislatures. Consequently, Orthodox voices have been raised against overly liberal abortion laws. At its 1971 convention, the Rabbinical Council of America called for a "serious evaluation" of new liberal abortion laws and decried the 100,-000 abortions in New York State as symptomatic of the general deterioration of moral caliber in our society. Likewise, *Jewish Life* editorialized against Reform and Conservative Jews for adopting a liberal stance on the issue that is not in accord with authentic Jewish belief and does not speak for the Orthodox community.[36]

On the other hand, Orthodox groups have not been generally committed to the civil rights struggle or activities on behalf of the black community. Virtually no Orthodox rabbis or laymen have been involved in the field campaign. After the passage of the 1964 Civil Rights Act, *Jewish Life* applauded the new law in its editorial column but warned of black anti-Semitism and stressed "our need to be different, to live in accordance with our own faith or tenets." While public pronouncements of the Rabbinical Council of America and the Union of Orthodox Jewish Congregations espoused the drive of blacks for equality, there has been little active participation in efforts to achieve those goals. Low-income Orthodox Jews who live in decaying urban areas and are frequently victims of black hoodlums and drug addicts are obviously not excited over Black Power or civil rights struggles. This explains, in part, Orthodoxy's diffidence concerning the Negro revolution. It also explains why the Jewish Defense League has struck a responsive chord among the masses of low-income Orthodox Jews from declining ghetto areas.[37]

Orthodoxy's attitude towards the great social issue of the 1960's and 1970's—the Vietnam war—is intriguing and perplexing. While all major Jewish religious groups—Reform, Conservative, and Reconstructionists—have officially condemned the war and urged American withdrawal from Indochina, the Orthodox movement has either supported the war or has remained neutral. Charles Liebman conducted a study of the issue: he found that the Union of Orthodox Jewish Congregations, the Agudat Israel, the Union of Orthodox Rabbis, and the

Rabbinical Alliance had publicly supported the war. In fact, he noted, no public Orthodox leader had denounced it. The editorial column of *Jewish Life*, for example, chided the new isolationist "America First" elements, propagandists, vilifiers of the Administration, and intimidators. It stated: "How depressing it is to find figures in responsible positions serving as phonographs for recorded propaganda against American military ruthlessness while detecting no relation between this propaganda and Communist terrorization and butchery of South Vietnam civilians. . . ."[38]

Still, Professor Liebman's survey of members of the Rabbinical Council of America showed that they are more dovish than the Council's spokesmen. Of the 280 who replied to his survey, 12.1 percent favor withdrawal; 53.2 percent want greater efforts to negotiate and de-escalate; 14.4 percent approve of the present policy; 1.4 percent want an increase of the war; and 16.4 percent call for any steps necessary to win the war.

Why is the Orthodox group—unlike all other religious groups—tacitly in favor of the Vietnam war? Is it because the least acculturated Jewish group seeks to prove its loyalty and Americanism? Perhaps. But it is more likely that Orthodoxy links the war in Asia to the parochial interests of Jewry. Orthodox leaders are concerned lest America retrench its forces, adopt a neo-isolationist posture, and abandon much of the world—including Soviet Jewry and Israel—to the not-so-tender mercies of the Communists. Obviously, Israel's welfare requires an American bulwark against Russian intervention in the Middle East. For this reason, perhaps, more than any other, Orthodoxy is anxious to support an American policy of intervention in wars anywhere in the world that would stem the Communist tide.

On the whole, then, Orthodoxy's involvement in social issues has been limited to those matters that impinge on the welfare of Orthodox Jewry. Issues that are of only peripheral concern to the more parochial needs of the Orthodox have been avoided or disdained.

*Interfaith Relations*

In a sense, the same attitude of "Is it good for Orthodox Jewry?" has directed Orthodoxy's involvement—or lack of it— in interfaith activities. For many years, the Orthodox community shunned or disdained interfaith activities. It has been sharply critical of Reform and Conservative leaders who have been interested in such work. Orthodox rabbis have often accused the non-Orthodox of sycophancy and boot-licking; of seeking to curry favor with gentiles in an undignified, demeaning fashion; of compromising Jewish principles, and of worrying overly about "What will the gentiles say?" instead of "What will the Jews do?" Rare, indeed, was the Orthodox rabbi or layman who involved himself in interfaith activities. Most Orthodox rabbis will not even set foot in a church. But it was inevitable that Christianity's ecumenical stirrings would evoke a reaction even among Orthodoxy.

The most definitive statement of Orthodoxy's relation to Christianity has been formulated by Rabbi Joseph Soloveitchik. Returning to his favorite theme of Adam—archetypal man— Soloveitchik declares that Jews have to cope with a double confrontation, namely Adam in nature and Adam in covenantal community. Jews, he writes, bear a double charismatic load—the dignity of man and the sanctity of the covenantal community— and it is a mistake to talk only of "single confrontation." It is absurd, says Soloveitchik, to equate the Halakhic-faith community with any other, for each faith believes that its system is best fitted for attainment of good and each is unyielding in its eschatological expectations.[39]

Soloveitchik suggests that it is a misconception in *not* realizing the compatibility of the two roles. "First, . . . we, created in the image of God, are charged with responsibility for the great confrontation of man and the cosmos. We stand with civilized society shoulder to shoulder against an order which defies us all." Second, as a charismatic faith community, we have to meet the challenge of confronting the general non-Jewish-faith community "and tell it of our otherness as a metaphysical covenantal community." Obviously, says Soloveitchik, confrontation is only possible if both parties enjoy equal rights and religious freedom and Christianity abjures self-righteous absolution of the community of the few of mythical guilt while ignoring historical responsibility for the suffering and martyrdom of the few.

There are four basic conditions for confrontation. First, each faith community is totally independent. True, there is a histori-cal-cultural Judeo-Christian heritage—but *not* a common faith. Any intimation that Jews shed their uniqueness and cease to exist because Judaism has fulfilled its mission is "undemocratic" and contrary to the very idea of religious freedom. Second, since theologies differ, confrontation is possible only at the mundane, human level in the secular—not sacred—sphere. Third, Jews must be tactful and not suggest that Christians change their ritual or emend their texts, for they must do so themselves out of conviction. Finally, we Jews may not revise our attitude to other faiths in order to trade favors and reconcile differences. We must not be servile; we must act with pride and dignity. Like Jacob vis-à-vis Esau, we draw near and then recoil; we cooperate in all fields of constructive human endeavor but simultaneously we draw back and retrace our steps into our individual faith community.

Soloveitchik's views struck an immediate response in modern Orthodoxy's officialdom. Emanuel Rackman endorsed social ac-tion with non-Jews while chiding Christendom for its silence prior to the Six-Day War and warning of dialogues with Chris-tians intent on converting Jews. The Rabbinical Council of America issued an official statement in the spirit of Soloveitch-ik's article:

> *We are pleased to note that in recent years there has evolved in our country as well as throughout the world a desire to seek better under-standing and a mutual respect among the world's major faiths.*

Warning against the dangers of materialism, secularism, and atheism, the Council agreed that dialogue is valuable provided it does not conflict with the uniqueness of the faith community, for each has a unique, intrinsic dignity and meta-physical worth.

"Only full appreciation on the part of all of the singular role, inherent worth and basic prerogative of each religious community will help promote the spirit of cooperation among faiths."[40]

But Orthodoxy has remained basically aloof from interfaith activities and has shunned interreligious dialogue primarily because many spokesmen fear that interfaith work might lead to assimilation and conversion.

*Summary*

Out of the welter of varied Orthodoxy ideas, concepts and pronouncements, we can draw some conclusions as to the basic ideology of the mainstream of American Orthodoxy.

1. Orthodoxy accepts the classical notion of God with little theological speculation. To the Orthodox Jew, God is a personal deity whose providence is a reality.

2. Orthodoxy teaches as its cornerstone the Divine origin of the Torah as interpreted by the rabbis of the Talmud and as codified in the authoritative *Shulhan Arukh*. Halakhah is Orthodoxy's guide; it is eternal, binding and irrevocable, and it can be interpreted and applied to new situations only by the *Gedole Ha-Dor*—the great sages of Israel.

3. Orthodoxy believes in the unity of the Jewish People and the need to work for the betterment of Jews everywhere. The Jewish People is God's chosen people, charged with the task of studying and teaching God's Torah. Orthodoxy is convinced that its version is the only correct interpretation of Judaism.

4. Orthodoxy is passionately devoted to the restoration of the State of Israel to be run along the lines of Torah and *mitzvot* as directed by the rabbinic sages. The Land of Israel is merely to be the means to the rejuvenation of the Torah of Israel and the dedication of the people of Israel to God.

5. Orthodoxy has worked with other Jewish groups in behalf of Jewish life, culture, and rights. It is willing to cooperate in nonreligious matters or in matters affecting Orthodoxy's vital interests. Of late, separatist trends seem to be gaining sway.

6. Orthodoxy believes that the liturgy is immutable and that

the synagogue and yeshivah are the basic institutions of Jewish life. Officially, no change in ancient synagogue practices is condoned. In practice, however, many Orthodox rabbis have accepted changes in worship and protocol.

7. Orthodoxy has been uninvolved in social action except in issues of interest to Orthodoxy and its community.

8. Orthodoxy has remained aloof from interfaith activities and has generally been critical of attempts at rapprochement between Jews and Christians.

In sum, Orthodoxy has made heroic efforts to keep its flock loyal to the traditional tenets of classical Judaism, oblivious to change and the challenges of the times, and perfectly convinced that in the fullness of time its viewpoint will be vindicated and world Jewry will return to the Orthodox interpretation of the ancestral faith.

After all, argues Orthodoxy, its version of Judaism has prevailed for over nineteen centuries; the other forms are merely contemporary fads and—in the view of the Orthodox world—passing aberrations. Orthodoxy remains confident that sooner or later these aberrant groups will disappear due to the laxity of their adherents, and the true Orthodox way will emerge triumphant.

# Reform Judaism—History

## IV

Reform Judaism was born and nurtured in Germany but had its greatest efflorescence in America. It arose originally as a response to the challenge of the Emancipation. It sought to stem the tide of disaffection, assimilation, and outright baptism that threatened to sweep away German Jewry, as well as Jews in other European lands.[1]

European Jewry had finally witnessed the end of its travail and degradation, its exclusion and segregation. By the end of the eighteenth century, French and Dutch Jews became citizens. At the beginning of the nineteenth, it was the turn of German and Austrian Jews. Then came the English Jews, the Italians, the Hungarians, the Jews of Scandinavia and Switzerland. But there was a price to pay: freedom was not to be granted gratuitiously; it was to be obtained in a quid pro quo bargain. The Jews would receive political and legal rights, but in exchange they were required to forsake their separatism and autonomous, communal structure. Clermont-Tonnère made this crystal clear when, at the time of the debates over the emancipation of French

86

Jewry, he proclaimed: "To the Jews as men—everything; as Jews
—nothing." And he added ominously: "If they accept this, well
and good. If not, let them be banished!" Napoleon went even
further. In his *opera buffa* Sanhedrin (1806–07) he insisted that
Jews forswear allegiance to any entity but the national state and
that they indicate their readiness to sacrifice their communal
integrity as the price of full citizenship.[2]

Clearly, freedom for Jews had an expensive price tag on it.
Moreover, the *Zeitgeist,* the spirit of the times, was new, dynamic,
critical. The impact of the French *philosophes* and English deists
was enormous; the notions of Voltaire, Rousseau, Locke, and
Hume were sweeping the Continent. European life was convulsed as never before since the Renaissance, and Jewish life was
similarly affected and shaken up. As the new ideas of reason,
adoration of history, criticism, logic, rationalism, deism, and
out-and-out atheism cut their swath through the churches of
Europe, so did they make their mark on the synagogue and
Jewish life.

To be sure, there were Jews who refused to traffic with these
new ideas. They closed their ghetto gates ever so tightly, en-
cased themselves in their prayer shawls, and tried valiantly to
shut out the new world. Others, despairing of any peace treaty
between Judaism and the emancipated world, flung themselves
headlong into the mainstream—abandoning in the process every vestige of their ancient faith. Like Heinrich Heine, they chose
baptism as the ticket of admission to European society. Like
Daniel Chwolson, they accepted Christianity on principle: it was
better to be a professor in Petersburg than a *melamed* (Hebrew
teacher) in Shnipishok. Thousands chose this ignominious and
lethal path.

Reform Judaism was an answer to these two unprecedentedly
difficult challenges. It sought to speak in the idiom of the *Zeitgeist;* it tried to help Jews live in two worlds simultaneously; it
labored to stem the tide of assimilation that was depleting the
ranks of Jewry.[3]

Groups of Reformers began to appear in German cities who
sought to make Judaism and its religious life congruous with

modern times. Israel Jacobson set up a Reform Temple in Seesen in 1810 that attempted to purge Judaism of "ritual offensive to reason as well as our Christian friends." His ideas were transferred to Hamburg, where, in 1817, a public Reform Temple was inaugurated with Israel Kley as preacher. The German sermons, the installation of an organ and choir, the utilization of a reformed prayer book, from which mention of a personal Messiah was removed, may have been enormously attractive to the Jews seeking acceptance as Germans; they proved anathema to the traditionalist elements who suspected a new heresy.[4]

New Reform *Vereine* spread quickly to Frankfort, Vienna, Metz, London (1842), Berlin (1844), Worms and Pesth (1848), and a dozen other communities. The most radical of these groups was in Frankfort. Its members declared their belief in the unlimited progress inherent in Mosaism, their rejection of the authority of the Talmud, their denial of a personal Messiah, and their repudiation of the return to Zion, since "Germany is our fatherland." The pages of the journals of the day trumpeted endlessly the notion that Jews are no longer a *nation*, but a *religion*—like the Catholics and Protestants. The traditionalists and Orthodox were appalled; the liberals cheered lustily.[5]

Fights were bitter. Partisans ran to the civil courts, anathemas and excommunications filled the air. When the brilliant Reformer, Abraham Geiger, was elected as associate rabbi to Solomon Tiktin of Breslau, the aged Orthodox sage reacted ferociously: he would have none of that heretic. And the sordid case dragged on for years.[6]

Then came the series of rabbinical conferences which were of far-reaching import; their decisions still reverberate today. Reform Judaism was shaped in Brunswick (1844) and Frankfort (1845), and was solidified at the Synods of Leipzig (1869) and Augsburg (1871). The heart of the message of these conferences was unmistakably clear: Judaism is a developing religion which has a mission to spread its message to the world. It must regenerate many customs and rites, adding some while deleting others. It must be studied scientifically and critically. In a word, Judaism has to be modernized and brought up to date to conform to the spirit of the age in line with the law of the inevitability of reason and progress. It must move forward with the times, not backwards to the ghetto; it must reform itself![7]

The men who propounded the program of Reform were spiritual giants in their own right. Abraham Geiger, Samuel Holdheim, David Einhorn, Max Lilienthal, Samuel Hirsch, Kaufmann Kohler, Samuel Adler—all were zealous champions of the new spirit. And they were ready to do battle with Orthodoxy, for battle was precisely Orthodoxy's tactic.

The eminent Pressburg rabbi, Moses Sofer, launched a bitter assault on the Reformers. "The new is taboo," he taught, in a pun on a rabbinic ruling. The Frankfort radicals were put in *herem* (excommunication). In 1860, a rabbinical conclave issued a ban against sermons in the vernacular, gowns for rabbis, and the placing of the *bimah* (reader's stand) at the front of the synagogue. These reforms (which are quite normal even in Orthodox synagogues today) were considered so scandalous then that they merited excommunication. In some cases, Orthodox zealots even resorted to violence against the Reformers. The battle was bitter indeed.

But Reform did not carry the day in Europe. The *Gemeinde* or *kehillah* still preserved its hold in many countries. The *Zeitgeist* shifted to more conservative religious expressions. Moreover, the Reform movement made little headway in High Church nations such as England, or Catholic lands such as France or Italy. It succeeded best in Protestant lands—Germany for example—where liberal religious views were the norm and where there was no established church.

However, the greatest advances of Reform came in the New World. Here there was a liberal, freewheeling, frontier spirit that gave wide latitude to experimentation. Here there was no stodgy High Church or established church—only a conglomeration of sects and religious groups. Here the *Zeitgeist* was liberalism, and the teachings of such progressive theologians as Theodore Parker and Henry W. Beecher were widely respected. Here there existed no Jewish community to strangle budding reforms. Here each congregation was independent to do that "which was right in its eyes." Here there was no need to placate the establishment, to engage in compromise with the moderates. Here there existed the drive to be Americanized quickly, even if it meant dropping the rituals and accepting extreme or radical reforms. It was in America, then, that Reform won its greatest victories. And it was also in America that Reform went to lengths scarcely anticipated by its European forebears.

The earliest attempt at Reform came in Charleston, S.C., in 1824 at the historic old Beth Elohim Congregation. Led by Isaac Harby and David N. Carvalho, 47 petitioners requested a shorter, more intelligible, more decorous service. Their requests were really modest: end the Spanish prayers, deliver a weekly sermon in English, introduce English prayers and a commentary on the weekly Torah portion. Evidently influenced by the Hamburg Temple, the petitioners disclaimed any attempt to abolish "such ceremonies as are considered land-marks to distinguish the Jew from the Gentile." Harby's group merely wanted to duplicate the "alterations" already introduced in Holland, Germany, and Prussia. But the *parnasim* of Beth Elohim would hear nothing of any alterations in the age-old services; the Reformers were rebuffed.[8]

Rebuffed they may have been, but not crushed. A group of twelve seceded from Beth Elohim and set about organizing the Reformed Society of Israelites. Within two years, it numbered 50 members, issued a new Prayer Book, introduced an organ and other liturgical reforms, and charted a course to adapt Judaism to the "situation of an enlightened world." Harby had proclaimed the goals of the group: "We wish not to overthrow, but to rebuild; we wish not to destroy, but to reform and revise the evils complained of; we wish not to abandon the institutions of Moses, but to understand and observe them," to worship God as "enlightened descendants of the chosen race." In obvious emulation of Maimonides' Thirteen Principles of Faith, the Charleston group formulated "The Charleston Creed," eliminating belief in a personal Messiah and bodily resurrection. But the Reformed Society was short-lived and did not survive Harby's departure for New York, where he died soon thereafter.[9]

Still, the seeds planted by the group bore fruit very quickly. In 1836 Beth Elohim became a Reform Temple, the first in America. It engaged the German-trained Pole, Reverend Gustave Poznanski as its minister. Poznanski proceeded along the path of Reform he had witnessed in Germany. He introduced the organ, deleted the *piyutim* (liturgical poems), preached in English, and abolished the second day of the Festivals. With heady optimism he trumpeted: "This synagogue is our *temple*, this city our *Jerusalem*, this happy land our *Palestine.*" That slogan was to become the theme and philosophy of Reform for an entire century.[10]

Reform began to spread throughout the length and breadth of the land. *Reform-Vereine* or *Cultus Vereine* were quickly set up in a host of cities and towns to be followed by synagogues. Baltimore established a Reform Temple in 1842; New York's Emanuel followed in 1845; Albany was next in 1850; then Cincinnati in 1854; and Philadelphia in 1856. Chicago's Sinai Temple split away from Kehilath Anshe Maarav Synagogue to found a Reform group in 1858. Some years later, Kehilath Anshe Maarav itself followed suit and went Reform. Some of Germany's leading Reform rabbis were imported to propagate the new ideas. Reverend Leo Merzbacher came to New York's Emanuel, where he prepared a new *Sidur* "free from abuses hitherto tolerated." Fiery David Einhorn went to Sinai Congregation in Baltimore where he embarked on his radically Reform career in 1855. Bernard Felsenthal landed in Chicago, where he proclaimed that Sinai Temple would set out to restore "the original spirit of simplicity, purity, and sublimity in Judaism," and where he developed services "consistent with laws of reason and truth" that would meet the demands of the times. Felsenthal announced that he would remove ceremonies that had outlived their usefulness and were erroneous, and substitute virtue and truthfulness, and "higher stages of perfection." Much the same sentiments had been expressed by New York's *Cultus Verein*— forerunner of Temple Emanuel—in 1843. The new group was convinced that by its reforms it would "will for Jews a position of greater respect among fellow citizens, enable Jews to worship

together with greater dignity, and attract the rising generation."[11]

However, the guiding genius of Reform in America was neither Merzbacher nor Poznanski, nor even Felsenthal or Einhorn.
It was an émigré rabbi from Bohemia with a bushy mustache and
muttonchop sideburns named Isaac Mayer Wise.

Wise was born in 1819, received a traditional rabbinic education and fairly good secular training, and was already attracted
to Reform in his native land. He came to America in 1846 with
his wife and child and accepted a post in Albany, N.Y. There he
introduced reforms such as family pews, an organ, and a choir.
He met considerable opposition, and in a scandalously bitter
battle on Rosh Hashanah 1850, he was physically barred from
officiating at the Ark and landed in jail. Wise and his followers
left the congregation to organize a new Reform temple. In 1854
he was called to Cincinnati, where he was to remain until his
death in 1900 and where he was to witness his greatest triumphs.[12]

Isaac Mayer Wise was not an outstanding scholar or theoretician; he was, however, a genius at organization. He edited *The
Israelite* magazine and the German-language *Deborah;* he inspired various rabbinic conclaves; he fathered the Hebrew Union College, the Union of American Hebrew Congregations,
and the Central Conference of American Rabbis; he organized
the second Jewish Publication Society; he published a Reform
*Sidur, Minhag America.* In a word, he created the American Reform movement.

Yet he was not a radical Reformer. In an article in the *Occident*
(March, 1849) he wrote:

> *I am a reformer, as much as our age requires; because I am
> convinced that none can stop the stream of time; none can check the
> swift wheels of the age; but I have always the* Halacha *for my basis;
> I never sanction a reform against the* Din. *I am a reformer, if the
> people long for it, but then I seek to direct the public mind on the path
> of the* Din; *but I never urge my principles upon another, nor do I
> commence to start a reform in a Synagogue.*[13]

And some years later, Wise mused:

> *I was never one to storm heaven; I no more wanted to change the world than I was weary of it . . . To me, Reform never was an end in itself; I considered it only a necessary means to clarify the teachings of Judaism, and to transfigure, exalt, and spread these teachings.* [14]

But with the passing years, Wise grew more radical, though never to the extent of David Einhorn. His radicalism was no more consistent than was his philosophy of Judaism, however. Thus, Wise remained a conservative in the realm of Biblical criticism and fired the newly hired Professor Louis Ginzberg (later to become professor of Talmud at the Jewish Theological Seminary) because of his adherence to it. On the other hand, he no longer abided by such basic rituals as the dietary laws.[15]

Wise had several passions in life. One was an attempt to unify American Jewry and its congregations. The Cincinnati Conference of 1871 called for the formation of a Hebrew Congregational Union "with the object to preserve and advance the Union of Israel; to take proper care of the development and promulgation of Judaism; to establish and support a scholastic institute, and the library appertaining thereto, for the education of rabbis, preachers, teachers of religion; to provide cheap editions of the English Bible and textbooks for the school of religious instructions to give support to weak congregations; and to provide such other institutions which elevate, preserve and promulgate Judaism." It was agreed that when twenty congregations with no less than two thousand members would affiliate with the Union, it would then convoke a synod.[16]

On October 10, 1872, Moritz Loth, president of Wise's Bene Jeshurun Congregation, called for a Union of congregations to set up a seminary and prepare educational textbooks. Loth stressed that the Union would never abolish circumcision, the Saturday Sabbath, ritual slaughter or the dietary laws. He also warned that any rabbi not adhering to these traditions would not be eligible for membership. In order to woo the moderates, Wise went along with these guidelines despite his personal reservations. And so, in 1873, the Union of American Hebrew

Congregations was formed consisting of twenty-eight Southern and Western congregations. Loth became president, with Isaac M. Wise as the guiding genius. The constitution stated the purposes of the Union:

> It is the primary object of the Union of American Hebrew Congregations to establish a Hebrew Theological Institute to preserve Judaism intact; to bequeath it in its purity and sublimity to posterity—to Israel united and fraternized; to establish, sustain, and govern a seat of learning for Jewish religion and literature; to provide for and advance the standards of Sabbath-schools for the instruction of the young in Israel's religion and history, and the Hebrew language; to aid and encourage young congregations by such material and spiritual support as may be at the command of the Union; and to provide, sustain, and manage such other institutions which the common welfare and progress of Judaism shall require—without, however, interfering in any manner whatsoever with the affairs and management of any congregation.[17]

The new Union was a success: Isaac M. Wise's dream of peace and unity seemed to be realized. Even the traditional Eastern congregations affiliated with the Union. By 1880, only eight of two hundred major congregations were Orthodox; the rest were Reform and the majority were affiliated with the Union.

Reform suffered a severe eclipse after the East European migration of the 1880's and 1890's. Still, the Union lengthened its cords and deepened its stakes. By 1905 it had added a Department of Synagogue and School Extension. In 1913 the Federation of Temple Sisterhoods was established; in 1923 the National Federation of Temple Brotherhoods was set up. The Union organized the Jewish Chautauqua Society to spread the message of Judaism on the campuses. The National Federation of Temple Youth was organized in 1939. The Reform movement enjoyed a phenomenally rapid growth after World War II. In 1943 there were 307 congregations in the Union. By 1971 the number had soared to 700 with a million congregants. But the organization which had initially been created by Wise as an all-encompassing congregational union that would unite all elements in Jewry had not, unfortunately, achieved its original purpose. The traditionalists could not long remain in the Union, even though its avowed intention was not originally to advance Reform Judaism. The 1946 revised constitution finally spelled out the "liberal interpretation" of the Union. Wise's dream of unity failed; but his congregational body succeeded eminently.

The second great dream of Isaac M. Wise was to create a rabbinical college in America. As early as 1854 he had called for such a school. A pioneering effort of his, Zion College, had failed before even beginning. In 1873 Henry Adler of Lawrenceburg, Indiana, gave $10,000 to found a seminary. In 1875 the Union of American Hebrew Congregations resolved to raise $60,000 for the project. Even traditionalists like Reverend Sabato Morais of Philadelphia joined Wise's great effort. Morais proposed reopening the defunct Maimonides College as the preparatory department of the projected school. Finally, on October 3, 1875, the Hebrew Union College opened at Bene Jeshurun Congregation. The president of the Board of Governors, Bernhard Bettman, declared that the school would be open to people of all faiths and women as well. Rabbi Max Lilienthal observed that "we wish to keep our students at home and raise them as genuine Americans on the virgin soil of American liberty."[18] Wise himself was too moved to speak; he called the occasion a "festival of the Lord." Several days later he noted that the event was no less important than was the development of Jamnia (Jabneh) as a center of Torah after the destruction of the Second Temple.

Wise sedulously sought to create a nonpartisan school that would serve the interests of Reform and tradition. Sabato Morais was appointed examiner and he was quite satisfied with the 1877 examinations. There were seventeen students and a faculty of four; the quarters were humble and dank. Yet Wise was filled with hope and cheer. The first graduation in 1883 saw four men ordained. Rabbi Benjamin Szold, moderate Reformer of Baltimore, was asked to deliver the commencement address. He waxed hopeful that "the outlook is no longer gloomy." All was idyllic until the banquet where, incredibly, non-kosher foods were served. Morais and the traditionalists were incensed; they walked out—never to return. Wise's attempt to build a single seminary for American Jewry failed; his Hebrew Union College, however, prospered.[19]

After Wise's death in 1900, Moses Mielziner served briefly as president. The brilliant and learned Rabbi Kaufmann Kohler followed and occupied the post until 1921, disseminating his vast erudition and his brand of "Revelation, Reform, and America—or God, Progress, and the Democratic Spirit." The College continued to expand. It opened a Teachers Institute in 1909 and built a splendid campus in 1913. Julian Morgenstern, an alumnus of the College, succeeded Kohler as president in 1921. In 1947 the eminent archaeologist, Nelson Glueck, became president, and he was followed by Rabbi Alfred Gottshalk in 1971. The faculty was excellent, the library superb, the courses vastly broadened. The school for Sacred Music was created for the training of Cantors in 1948. A West Coast Branch was opened in Los Angeles, followed by the Archaeological School in Jerusalem in 1963. Over the years, more than a thousand men have been ordained by the college.

A second school to train Reform rabbis was initiated by the fiery liberal, and phenomenal orator, Rabbi Stephen S. Wise (1874–1949). A Zionist leader, Stephen Wise was unhappy over the direction the Hebrew Union College had taken. He was displeased by its anti-Zionist stance; he felt the graduates of the college were too radically disposed and indifferent to the needs of the people; and he believed that the opportunities for graduate studies in New York were vastly superior to those found in Cincinnati. Besides, it was logical, he believed, to set up such a school in the center of the largest Jewish population in the world.[20]

In 1920 Stephen Wise approached Dr. Mordecai M. Kaplan and urged him to help found a new, nonpartisan rabbinical seminary that would be Zionistically oriented, not committed to any theological position, and totally dedicated to *Lehrfreiheit* in the spirit of Berlin's Hochschule für die Wissenschaft des Judentums. After much soul-searching, Kaplan refused, preferring to remain at the Jewish Theological Seminary. Thereupon Wise left for Europe to enlist a faculty. He sought to persuade Rabbi Emil G. Hirsch of Chicago or Professor Israel Abrahams of Cambridge to head the school—but he failed. With the backing of his own Free Synagogue, Wise urged the Hebrew Union College to sponsor the New York school, but he was rebuffed.

So, with the financial support of his own synagogue and on the strength of his own charismatic personality, Stephen S. Wise became the reluctant president of the Jewish Institute of Religion, which opened its doors in 1922 "for the training of men for the Ministry, research and community service." The school would be "liberal in spirit" and would commit neither faculty nor students "to any special interpretation of Judaism." The faculty would expound all points of view and serve as a place to disseminate Jewish knowledge "to the general public." Wise assembled a splendid faculty and, true to his promise, it propounded varied points of views and philosophies of Judaism. Most of the alumni, however, entered the Reform rabbinate, although a considerable number did ultimately wind up in the Conservative Rabbinical Assembly.

In 1947, after prolonged negotiations and much backtracking by the Hebrew Union College, Isaac M. Wise's College and Stephen S. Wise's Institute merged. Julian Morgenstern and Stephen Wise retired and turned over the reins of the unified HUC-JIR to Nelson Glueck in 1948. Stephen S. Wise's nonpartisan school was no more, for it was now officially Reform. And Isaac M. Wise's tiny Cincinnati College was now a great institution with major campuses in Cincinnati, New York, and, ultimately in Los Angeles and Jerusalem. His second noble dream had come true.

The third great dream of Isaac M. Wise was to unify the American rabbinate. He had tried valiantly all of his life to bring the widely differing elements together under one banner. In 1855, he was partly responsible for the Cleveland conference of rabbis whose motto was "peace for Israel." Along with the conservative Isaac Leeser, Wise sought to hammer out a compromise position that would satisfy Reform as well as the tradition-

alists. Four points were formulated at that meeting. The conference acknowledged "the Bible which we have received from our
fathers as the revealed word of God, given to us by divine inspiration." It added that "the Talmud contains the logical and legal
development of the Holy Scriptures, and . . . its decisions must
guide us in all matters of practice and duty." The conference
agreed that it, and all future synods, would act according to
these principles. Finally, it stated that "the illiberal assertions
contained in the Talmud are not of the kind referred to, and
have no binding force on us." Leeser left a day early and, in his
absence, Wise prevailed upon his colleagues to call for a regular
synod that would prepare a new prayer service and organize
Zion Collegiate Associations in all cities of America. He also
persuaded the delegates to condemn the all-day schools and
support the public schools with supplementary religious education. The Orthodox praised Leeser for having won over the
Reformers. Einhorn and the radicals accused Wise of a sellout.
Wise still had failed to unite the rabbis.[21]

He tried again in Philadelphia in 1869. The conference was
attended by Wise, Einhorn, Samuel Hirsch, Samuel Adler, Kaufmann Kohler, Moses Mielziner, and several others. Its tenor was
decidedly radical; Einhorn and Samuel Hirsch were in no mood
to temporize with the traditionalists. The delegates declared
that the messianic claim does not mean restoration to a Jewish
state under a son of David, but rather the union of all peoples
under one God. The conference viewed the dispersion of Israel
as a blessing that would enhance Israel's mission. It declared
that the Aaronic priesthood and sacrifices were no longer relevant but should be "consigned to the past, once and for all."
The delegates reaffirmed the selection of Israel "as the people
of religion, as the bearers of the highest idea of humanity" with
a world mission. They declared that bodily resurrection had no
religious foundation but they expressed a belief in spiritual immortality. The rabbis expressed the desirability of the cultivation of the Hebrew language, but since it is unintelligible to the
vast majority, it must give way "to intelligible language in
prayer, which, if not understood, is a soulless form." Finally,

they dropped the requirement of a *ketubah* (Jewish marriage contract), *get* (religious divorce), and sanctioned marriage between a *Kohen* and a divorcée. What a radical difference from the Cleveland conference! A disappointed Wise left Philadelphia for home wondering whether he would ever succeed in uniting American's rabbis.[22]

In 1885, at the urging of Kaufmann Kohler, another attempt to unify America's rabbis was made and a rabbinical conference was summoned in Pittsburgh. Kohler's aim, however, was very different from Wise's; he wanted to unite "all such American rabbis as advocate reform and progress and are in favor of united action in all matters pertaining to the welfare of American Judaism." Wise went along with the proposal and was elected chairman, although Kohler was the moving spirit. Little did the fifteen rabbis who attended imagine that their so-called Pittsburgh Platform would generate such far-reaching reverberations and would set the tone of American Reform Judaism for half a century.[23]

The eight points of the Platform were revolutionary and radical, much in line with the feelings expressed at the Philadelphia conference, and the philosophy of the recently deceased David Einhorn. The Platform declared that Judaism "presents the highest conception of the God-idea" and preserved and defended it amid continual struggles and trials "as the central religious truth for the human race." The delegates recognized the Bible as "the record of the consecration of the Jewish people to its mission as priest of the One God" and as the most potent instrument of instruction. But they declared that the doctrines of modern science and historical research are not antagonistic to the doctrines of Judaism, since the Bible reflects "the primitive ideas of its own age" and clothes divine providence in "miraculous narratives." The conference accepted as binding "only the moral laws" and ceremonies that "elevate and sanctify our lives" and rejected those not adapted to "the views and habits of modern civilization." It repudiated Mosaic and Biblical rules of diet, priestly purity, and dress as being of pagan and foreign origin and out of keeping with modern times, and as being more apt to "obstruct rather than further modern spiritual elevation." The fifth point was equally radical, for it detected in the modern era of culture and intellect the realization of the Messianic hope. It stated bluntly: "We consider ourselves no longer a nation but a religious community, and therefore expect neither a return to Palestine, nor a sacrificial worship under the administration of the sons of Aaron, nor the restoration of any of the laws concerning the Jewish state." Next, the Platform articulated its conviction that Judaism is a religion of reason that would work closely with Christianity and Islam in establishing truth and righteousness among men. The seventh point emphatically denied the idea of bodily resurrection and Heaven and Hell, accepting instead the notion of spiritual immortality. Finally, the conference deemed it the duty of Jewry "to participate in the great task of modern times, to solve on the basis of justice and righteousness the problems presented by the contrasts and evils of the present organization of society."

The boldly formulated document made history and changed the course of movements. David Philipson, a member of the first graduating class of the Hebrew Union College and participant in the Pittsburgh conference, described the Platform as "the utterance most expressive of the teachings of Reform Judaism." David Einhorn surely would have rejoiced, as did his son-in-law, the framer of the Platform, Kaufmann Kohler. The more moderate Reformers were shocked. Isaac M. Wise himself called it (perhaps cynically) the "Declaration of Independence of Reform." The Orthodox were outraged and the proto-Conservatives such as Morais and Jastrow realized that they would have to chart their own independent course. Although Wise never associated the Hebrew Union College or the Union of American Hebrew Congregations with the platform, and despite the fact that the Central Conference of American Rabbis never formally endorsed it, the Pittsburgh Platform marked the high-water mark of "classical" Reform, and its eight points served as the unofficial guidelines for Reform until well into the twentieth century.

Dubious that he could ever unite all factions in the rabbinate,

Wise now determined that he would at least unite the Reform rabbis. In 1889, in Detroit, Isaac M. Wise saw his third dream come true as he set up the Central Conference of American Rabbis. Ostensibly it was to be a union of *all* American rabbis; in fact, it became the rabbinic arm of the Reform movement. Its purpose, in addition to the coalescence of rabbinic forces, was to publish a yearbook and establish a pension fund for retired rabbis. The group avowed that the Reform synods of Europe "shall be taken as a basis for the work of this conference." One hundred men joined at once, electing Wise as president, a post he occupied until his death. Today, there are over nine hundred members of the conference, most of whom are graduates of the Hebrew Union College.[24]

So Isaac M. Wise, Bohemian immigrant to America, was privileged to have seen three of his most cherished ambitions realized: he established the Union of American Hebrew Congregations, he built a viable rabbinic seminary, the Hebrew Union College, and he organized the first rabbinic group, the Central Conference of American Rabbis. True, he failed in his beloved goal of unifying *all* of American Jewry. But how many humans are privileged to see all of their plans come to fruition? Wise declared in his roseate optimism that within twenty-five years all of America—yes, all of the world—would accept Reform Judaism. How incredibly naive these words now sound! But we can forgive such extravagances uttered by a man who had built an extraordinary edifice virtually from nothing.

The Reform movement prospered, then was eclipsed by the waves of Russian immigrants, then flourished again. Money was generally not lacking, as the rich German Jews gravitated to the temples. Feelings between the Orthodox and the Reform ran high; abuse was often flung at one another. The Orthodox called the Reform group "Deformed" Judaism and accused it of heterodoxy, heresy, and sectarianism. The Reformers countered by labeling the Orthodox medieval fanatics and ghetto Jews. Cooperation was difficult as the radical Reformers rode roughshod over the *mitzvot,* dessicated Jewish peoplehood, adopted the *Union Prayer Book,* introduced the organ and gentile choir, eliminated the skullcap, battled against Zionism, and turned the temples into carbon copies of the Protestant churches. Young Louis Ginzberg, who had been engaged by Wise to teach at the Hebrew Union College, came to New York from Holland at the turn of the century and was invited to the home of a famous Reform rabbi for a Sabbath evening meal. He records, with naive horror, that the only permitted food he could eat was the ice cream dessert. Clearly radicalism was in the saddle of the Reform movement.[25]

That the radical Pittsburgh spirit prevailed can be seen in the actions of the Central Conference of American Rabbis and Union of American Hebrew Congregations in the early years. In 1892, for example, the CCAR dropped circumcision as a requirement for conversion to Judaism. Many rabbis instituted services on Sunday—some to supplement the Sabbath service, others to supplant it. At the Montreal CCAR Convention in 1897, Wise won the delegates over to his view that "we cannot submit to the legalism of the Talmud, the Kabbalism of the Sohar, the literalism of the Karaites, or even the rationalism of Maimonides and Mendelssohn, because either of them was a child of his respective age and not of the Judaism of all ages." Henceforth, the Talmud, responsa, and codes were seen as merely "religious literature." The same conference expressed total disapproval "of any attempt for the establishment of a Jewish State" because such actions show a misunderstanding of the Jewish mission and harm the status of Jews by tarring them with the label of dual allegiance. The Einhorn radical spirit was triumphant; the conservatives and moderates were stilled.[26]

While Reform was propagating its radical program, it was flourishing and growing, and was reaching out for international contacts. In 1926 the World Union for Progressive Judaism was founded in London to coalesce Reform and Liberal forces throughout the Jewish world. Sparked by Rabbi Leo Baeck of Germany, Rabbi Israel Mattuck and Lady Montagu of England, Rabbi David Philipson and others of America, as well as delegates from several lands, Reform sought to transform itself into a world-wide movement. The preamble to the Union's constitution stated that Israel's mission is "to spread the knowledge of God," and thus the duty of Israel is "to work for a further recognition by Jews and by all mankind, of the religious and ethical demands of righteousness, brotherly love and universal peace." The purposes of the new Union were also to stimulate the formation of Progressive congregations throughout the world and to study Judaism and adapt it to modern life "without changing the fundamental principles of Judaism." Since 1960 the World Union has been located in New York City with affiliates in twenty-four countries—including Israel.[27]

But the *Zeitgeist* shifts and what was rational in 1885 was not necessarily rational in 1935; what was "oriental" and outmoded in 1897 was perhaps not quite so outlandish in 1937. The times were changing; the temper of religion was changing; ideologies were changing; and with those general realignments came reforms within the Reform movement, for the new philosophies that were less obsessed with rationalism altered Reform's mood. So did the teachings of Reconstructionist leader Mordecai M. Kaplan with his stress on Jewish peoplehood and his love for Zion. The influx into Reform Temples of East European Jews, who demanded "warmer" services with more rituals, affected the movement, as did the growing number of rabbis of East European rather than German origin. Nor can we overlook the impact of the European Holocaust and the rebirth of the State of Israel. The growing Conservative movement had its effect on Reform as well. Yes, Reform was reforming itself.

Actually, the process took time. For example, the CCAR and the UAHC denounced the Balfour Declaration at their meetings of 1917 and 1919. But many rabbis labored to shift that anti-Zionist stance. By 1924 the CCAR went so far as to express its agreement "to cooperate in the rehabilitation of Palestine," and by 1935 it dropped all hostility to Zionism, taking a neutral stand on political Zionism but a positive position on the upbuilding of Palestine, its economy, culture, and spiritual life.

It was the same phenomenon in the area of ritual. Gradually the old hostility to *mitzvot* diminished. Reform rabbis began to talk of Halakhah once again, and they rescued from the limbo of radical Reform the notion of "guides" to ritual practice. When Dr. Emanuel Gamoran became head of the Commission on Education of the UAHC, he proceeded to attack the anemic Sunday School system, demanding additional weekday study hours with Hebrew language, Zion, home *mitzvot* and other enrichments. There were also cries for a revised *Union Prayer Book* and a restoration of deleted Festival observances and home ritual. All of these yearnings, tensions, and strivings eventually led to the historic Columbus Conference of 1937 and its epochal Platform.[28]

The Platform began by recognizing the changes in modern life that had necessitated the restating of Reform principles. It defined Judaism as "the historical religious experience of the Jewish people," whose history shows progressive development in teaching the universal message of one God. Reiterating the old Pittsburgh Platform, the Columbus Platform endorsed the need to accept truth from all sources, whether from history or science. The heart of Judaism, says the Platform, is its "doctrine of the One, living God, who rules the world through law and love." Man is God's partner, a free creature with an immortal soul. Then the Columbus Platform departs from the Pittsburgh position: it talks of Torah (the word did not even appear in the Pittsburgh Platform!) as the progressive revelation of God. Both the written and oral Torah enshrine "Israel's ever-growing consciousness of God and of the moral law." True, certain of the laws have, due to historical processes, "lost their binding force." But "the Torah remains the dynamic source of the life of Israel" and each age must adapt the teachings of Torah to its basic needs.

Point five of the Columbus Platform marks an even more remarkably bold departure from its Pittsburgh predecessor. It states that "Judaism is the soul of which Israel is the body" and uses that long-taboo phrase "the Jewish people." While reaffirming the loyalty of Jews to their native lands, the Platform proclaims: "In the rehabilitation of Palestine, the land hallowed by memories and hopes, we behold the promise of all Jewry to aid in its upbuilding as a Jewish homeland by endeavoring to make it not only a haven of refuge for the oppressed but also a center of Jewish culture and spiritual life." It is Israel's mission to cooperate with other peoples in striving for the Messianic goal of establishing the kingdom of God, universal brotherhood, justice, truth, and peace.

The Platform stresses the role of ethics and human brotherhood, insisting on justice for all, regardless of race, sect, or class. It calls for social justice, an end to slavery and poverty, tyranny and social inequality, prejudice and strife. It denounces exploitation of children and workers, calls for charity, and insists on protection of the old and sick. It demands disarmament of mankind and an end to violence.

The final section is almost as remarkably new as the sections dealing with Palestine. It urges synagogue and home rituals, stresses the need for prayer, and reminds its partisans that Judaism as a way of life requires concrete symbols such as the Sabbath and festivals, customs and ceremonies, as well as the Hebrew language.

After a prolonged debate, the Columbus Platform was adopted 105 to 5. Doughty old David Philipson who had been present to frame the Pittsburgh Platform voted, a bit reluctantly, in favor of the new Platform. Pittsburgh was dead forever.

In the past years, Reform Jewry has greatly expanded its institutions and influence. It has opened a number of summer camps to teach Judaism to children. In 1961, after a bitter battle, it created the Kaplan Center for Religious Action in Washington, D.C. Its social-action program has been outspoken and Rabbi Maurice Eisendrath, President of the UAHC, has been a much-publicized advocate of liberal causes—sometimes to the consternation of the less liberal elements.[29] Despite sharp Orthodox opposition, the Reform group has set up a beautiful School of Archaeology in Jerusalem with a chapel in which Reform services are conducted. In addition, Reform synagogues are functioning in Jerusalem, Herzliah, Nazareth, Haifa, Netaniah, Ramat Gan, and elsewhere.

Recently, the growth of the Reform movement has slowed down— perhaps symptomatic of the peaking of America's religious boom of the 1950's and early 1960's and of the declining Jewish birth rate. But Reform's spiritual growth has not slowed down, nor has its religious dynamism and reformation abated. Who knows what directions Reform Judaism will take in the years ahead? It is doubtful if the historian can foretell the pattern. Perhaps only a prophet can do so?

# Reform Judaism—Ideology

## V

It is a far simpler task to analyze the ideology of Reform Judaism than it is to categorize Orthodox thought. For one thing, Reform has always stressed the need to engage in theological speculation and its best minds have applied themselves to the task. For another, Reform's positions over the years have been clearly and articulately stated in the official pronouncements of the Central Conference of American Rabbis and the Union of American Hebrew Congregations.

On the other hand, the student of Reform Judaism must be on guard against confusing "classical" or "radical" Reform with today's version. As we have previously noted, the Reform Judaism of the Pittsburgh Platform that held sway for fifty years was virtually overturned by the new version of the Columbus Platform. Whereas David Einhorn, Kaufmann Kohler, and Isaac M. Wise set the tone of Reform in its early stage in America, a totally new breed of Reform theologians and leaders has taken over the movement and turned it around 180 degrees. It is therefore imperative to delineate the differences between the older positions of Reform on matters like Israel, Jewish people-hood, *mitzvot*, and Jewish education, and the newer stands es-poused by the movement. Gone is the old negative attitude to Zion. Gone is the indifference to Jewish peoplehood. Gone, too, is the hostility to *mitzvot*. And gone is the former denigration of maximal Jewish education. True to itself, Reform has been evolving, reforming, growing, and modifying. Therein, perhaps, lies its greatest asset: it has stubbornly refused to harden its lines into a "new orthodoxy."

There were those in the Reform movement both in Germany and America who tried to develop creeds for Reform on the lines of the Christian catechisms. In 1903, Professor Max Mar-golis of the Hebrew Union College proposed a creed for Reform Jews, but he was sharply rebuffed by Kohler, Felsenthal, Philip-son and others who feared the growth of a schism. Leo Baeck also argued against such a move: "We know in our religion no restriction on thought, no belief which remains imprisoned in fixed ideas, in formulae, or dogmas. Every generation may, nay more, should evolve its own expression of faith." And Kauf-mann Kohler wrote that Judaism is "hallowed life, not a hollow creed."[1]

Notwithstanding its refusal to crystallize a creed, Reform has been blessed with an abundance of thinkers and theologians of the first magnitude who have enriched Jewish theology and revived the lost art of Jewish philosophical thought. Out of the corpus of their genius, we can set about analyzing the main-streams of Reform Judaism.

### The Nature of Judaism

One of the revolutionary breaks Reform made with traditional Judaism in its early stages was to deny the peoplehood of Israel. The Pittsburgh Platform stated this in unmistakable terms: "We consider ourselves no longer a nation but a religious commu-nity . . . ," and it added, "We recognize in Judaism a progressive religion, ever striving to be in accord with the postulates of reason." The hand of Kohler is evident in these passages, for he had told the conference that "Judaism is a religion of life and not a matter of the past, a system of living faith and practice which offers the guarantee of endurance and strength. . . ." Kohler wrote that "the true object of religion is the hallowing of life rather than the salvation of the soul." Kohler argued that Judaism has always been "a religion of historical growth," never static or fixed for all time by an ecclesiastical authority, but the result of the dynamic process of growth and development and "far from claiming to be the final truth, is ever regenerated anew at each turning point of history." Judaism, he wrote, is nothing less than "a message concerning the *One and holy God and one, undivided humanity* with a world-uniting Messianic goal, a message intrusted by divine revelation to the Jewish people."[2]

This definition of Judaism as an *evolving religion* formulated by Kohler struck numerous responses in the Reform movement. With practically no exceptions, Reform theologians and rabbis accepted the peoplehood-less description of Judaism. Until the Columbus Platform, Reformers considered themselves Americans or Canadians or Germans by nationality, Jews by religious persuasion.

What is the nature of Reform Judaism? The earlier spokesmen of the movement portrayed Reform as humanized religion and humanity religionized, to borrow Kohler's phrase. "And nowhere can this succeed better," he added, "than in this blessed new world." He shared with Isaac M. Wise the impassioned faith that America's soil was fertile for the growth of Reform. Kohler was harsh in his criticism of "Mosaic-Rabbinic Judaism" which he described as retrospective and lacking the courage to stand on its own feet. Traditional Judaism glorifies the merit of the forefathers and idealizes the past. "Reform Judaism, on the contrary, looks forward with hope for a far brighter future, beholding in the Messiah the ideal of mankind to be realized by the Jewish people through all the factors and agencies of civilization and progress . . ." Above all, Kohler believed that Reform reaffirmed prophetic morality over the dead letter of Rabbinism. Therefore, it is not *destructive* but *constructive;* "it desires to build up a pure and perfect manhood" by pointing to "the indestructible kernel of religion." In answer to critics who charged the Reformers with breaking with past traditions, Kohler replied that Reform is really a continuation of past progress and reforms, but now *consciously* applied in the age of historical research and reason.[3]

Isaac M. Wise listed the basic principles of Reform, as he envisioned them. He declared that unmeaning forms must be laid aside as outworn garments so as to expose the internal spirit of Judaism. Whatever makes us ridiculous before the world should be abolished; whatever tends to elevate the service and attract worshipers should be instituted. If religious observances clash with the just demands of civilized society then they must be dropped, for "our religion must make us active members of civilized society." Finally, religion is intended to make us happy, good, charitable, just, and intelligent humans. These ideas formed the nucleus of classical Reform theology, and are still normative in contemporary Reform thinking.[4]

Emil G. Hirsch, erudite radical Reformer of Chicago, son of Rabbi Samuel Hirsch and son-in-law of David Einhorn, went even further than Wise. While urging a "deepening of our Jewish consciousness," and proclaiming that the Reformers "hunger for more Judaism, not less of it," he sharply attacked traditional Judaism as a "dead Law." The Law is of non-Jewish origins, and since Judaism is *Lehre* (teaching) not *Gesetz* (law), Reform's task is to free it "from the crushing envelope." To Hirsch, "the Prophetic principles" rather than the Law constitute the essence of Judaism. This use of the term "Prophetic Judaism" has stuck, and Reform thinkers like Julian Morgenstern, Maurice Eisendrath, Sheldon Blank and others frequently invoke it in describing the gist of Reform's message.[5]

David Philipson was equally unswerving in his negativism to Jewish nationalism and Halakhah. He wrote:

> *If the Reform movement teaches anything clearly, it is the repudiation of the political and national aspects of traditional Judaism and the clear declaration that Judaism is a religion with a religious mission; Neo-Orthodoxy, Zionism, inconsistent rabbinism, with its*

*canonization of the* Shulchan Aruk *in theory and its repudiation thereof in practice, the juridical interpretation of Judaism as "law," these are the backward forces that drive the Jew of modern training and life further from his religion and leave him spiritually bankrupt.*[6]

Dynamism and universalism have always marked Reform Judaism, which stresses the organic aspect of the faith. Its more recent expositors have maintained that stance. Thus Rabbi Solomon Freehof describes Reform as "the first flaming up of direct world idealism in Judaism since the days of the Second Isaiah." Rabbi W. Gunther Plaut sees it as a "phenomenon of man's restless spirit"—a dynamic faith combining man's longing for the ways of his fathers while, at the same time, surging and struggling for new ways. To Plaut, the chief characteristics of Reform are its broad world outlook, its Prophetic universalism, its anti-mystical and non-miraculous approach to Jewish history, its confrontation with Jesus and Christianity, and its inherent dynamism. The dynamism of Reform is viewed by its expositors as perfectly in keeping with traditional Judaism. Thus, Rabbi William Silverman writes: "We believe that Reform Judaism is not only traditional Judaism but basic Judaism, deriving its inspiration from the past, applying relevance to the present and providing direction and hope for the future." Since Judaism has always meant reform and constructive, progressive growth, Reform is more historically true to Judaism than is Orthodoxy, writes Silverman, and he adds that one does not have to rely on authority or traditional observance in Reform. Therefore, it is harder to be a Reform Jew because "one has the obligation to think through for oneself the basic problems of Judaism."[7]

Reform Judaism clearly envisions Judaism as the evolving religion of the Jewish people that has always and must continue to adapt itself to the challenges of each age. Its final authority is human reason; its message is the Prophetic one of justice, love, truth, and peace; its mission is to spread its teachings to the farthest corner of the globe.

## God

Reform thinkers and theologians have had much to say about God since the very inception of the movement. Clearly, the traditional supernatural concept of a deity who speaks to man, suspends the natural order of the universe through miracles, and is described in the Bible and rabbinic literature in human, anthropomorphic terms was unacceptable to Reform theologians.

Isaac M. Wise wrote: "I believe in the revelation of God and the God of revelation" and he defined God as the "central Vital Force from which all forces in nature are materialized"—the "Genius of nature and the Logos of history fills all space and is the force of all forces, a Cosmic God who is the cause of all causes."[8]

Kohler was less Hegelian, and more Kantian, in defining God. To Kohler, God is "the still small voice of conscience" who "appears actually to step into the sphere of human life as its moral ruler." He talks about the miracle of the "whole cosmic order" and writes that "only a primitive age could think of God as altering the order of nature which He had fixed." Clearly rejecting the Orthodox view of miracles, Kohler suggests that we experience God's miracles in acts of human freedom—in "the divine power within man which aids him to accomplish all that is great and good." Kohler's Kantian views of God held sway in Reform Judaism and were codified, so to speak, in the Pittsburgh Platform, which stated: "We hold that Judaism presents the highest conceptions of the God-idea as taught in our Holy Scriptures and developed and spiritualized by the Jewish teachers, in accordance with the moral and philosophical progress of their respective ages."[9]

In the past several decades, Reform has continued its exploration of the meaning of God, although in less of the Hegelian-Kantian terms of the earlier years. The Columbus Platform still talked of God as "the heart of Judaism" who rules the world through law and love: "In Him all existence has its creative source and mankind its ideal of conduct. Through transcending time and space, He is the indwelling Presence of the world. We worship Him as the Lord of the Universe and as our merciful Father." And the late Rabbi Leo Baeck, sainted survivor of Theresienstadt concentration camp, spoke of God in Kantian terms as "the demanding God" and Author of "thou shalt" and "thou shalt not." But these Germanic notions have been replaced of late by a less rationalistic, less philosophical trend in Reform theology. Interestingly, Reform thinkers have moved back towards a personal concept of God.[10]

Professor Samuel S. Cohon, who taught theology at the Hebrew Union College, wrote that "personality is the characteristic of the Jewish idea of God. He was conceived as personal before He was recognized as cosmic. To the ancients this implied bodily form." But we moderns should think of God as "the supreme, absolute, unconditional and perfect Personality, since He alone possesses the unlimited creative power and wisdom to execute His designs," and He alone hears prayers, blesses us and reveals Himself progressively.[11]

More recently, Reform thought has reflected the diverse trends in theology that have cropped up in Protestant circles. Thus, existentialism has found its supporters in the Reform camp, as have religious naturalism and neo-Orthodoxy. Martin Buber has developed partisans in the Reform camp, as have Franz Rosenzweig and Mordecai M. Kaplan. Theology is as dynamic as ever among the Reform thinkers, and problems of the concepts of God have elicited exciting responses from the fertile minds of Reform Judaism.[12]

Jakob J. Petuchowski, who teaches rabbinic literature at the Hebrew Union College in Cincinnati, represents a neo-Orthodox trend in Reform theology. "God is not dependent for His nature or existence upon man's basic urges," he writes. "A God constructed to meet people's urges and needs is what the Bible calls an 'idol.' God has personality, though He is not a person. He is infinitely more than a person." Petuchowski insists that

God is "not a mere philosophical abstraction, but the ever-present God of Israel's historical experience" who has seen fit to reveal His Will to man."[13]

Bernard Martin, professor of philosophy at Case Western Reserve University, follows the existentialist path to God. "God —from the human side, from the point of view of man's faith— is the name we give to the object of our ultimate concern, that which we take to be worthy of our highest loyalty and deepest love." Martin believes that a God who is "not personal, or rather super-personal, is not a living, effective *reality* but a religiously valueless *idea*" and our prayers are merely philosophic meditation. Consequently, we must believe that God is super-personal, that He lives, acts, is conscious, enters into personal relationship with man, addressed him and demands man's personal response.[14]

Professor Eugene Borowitz, of the Jewish Institute of Religion, the New York school of the Hebrew Union College, is similarly attracted to the existentialist school, but his approach has traditional overtones. He talks of "covenant theology" and exhorts the modern Jew to live in relationship to God not just as an individual, but as a man "who shares in the mutual promise existing between God and Israel—that is, the Jewish people as a whole." What role must the God idea play in the life of a Jew? asks Borowitz. First, it must "make possible for him the life of Torah . . . The more completely an idea of God motivates the performance of Torah, the more acceptable to Judaism it may be said to be . . . When a Jew begins to think of God in such a way that it keeps him from fulfilling the commandments, then he may be said to have an idea which is not a permissible Jewish conception of God." For Reform Jews, writes Borowitz, an idea of God which kept Jews from social action, prayer, study, and the rest of Torah had moved to the border of Judaism or beyond. The second function of the God idea, he suggests, is that it must also give assurance of the existence of the Jewish people—it must make personal life possible for the Jew and must stand the test of intellectual coherence and Jewish history as well. While he admits that the Holocaust that annihilated six million Jews was shattering to faith, he believes that in its wake a conscious desire emerged to reclaim and reestablish Jewish existence. The Six-Day War helped us to see God even more clearly. But to say that there is no God, insists Borowitz, means that everything is permitted—including the worst brutality and cruelty.[15]

Rabbi Levi Olan takes yet another approach to the idea of God. He is an organicist: that is to say, he detects God as a living, pulsating organism in the universe. "It appears that the universe possesses three basic ingredients. It is an organism, not a machine . . . Secondly, it is a cosmos and not a chaos . . . Finally, in its development it reveals purpose moving from lower to higher forms of existence." In sum, God is "life, mind, and purpose"; God is non-absolute but "better understood as becoming even as the universe and man."[16]

Rabbi Arnold Jacob Wolf confesses that "the truth is that we do not know the truth." God is, whatever else, "a mystery," and Judaism must be, whatever else it may be, "humble before Him who spoke and theology came to be."[17]

On the other hand, Rabbi Roland Gittelsohn is a religious naturalist whose theology is heavily tinged with Mordecai M. Kaplan's Reconstructionism. God, he suggests, is the "Life force or the creative, indefinable Soul of the Universe." Gittelsohn writes:

> *I am a naturalistic, humanistic theist. Naturalistic, because I believe that God inheres within nature, rather than operating upon it from outside itself. Humanistic, because I am convinced that the loftiest human values we have been able to conceive represent the closest our finite minds can come as yet to comprehend the infinite. Theist, because I am persuaded that our spiritual propensities and capacities are reflections of something very close to the crux of Ultimate Reality.*[18]

Professor Alvin Reines of the Hebrew Union College in Cincinnati, talks of God as "the enduring possibility of being." Departing from other Reform thinkers, he posits a finite deity and rejects authoritarian supernaturalism. Only objective evidence for God can be accepted, he argues, for "as man acts, so God reacts."[19]

Clearly, Reform theological speculation on God is rich, variegated, fertile, and multi-faceted. There seems to be no *one* Reform concept of God; Reform thinkers run the gamut from the supernaturalists to the naturalists, from the believers in the Infinite Revealer of Torah to the partisans of a finite, limited deity. Perhaps Alvin Reines is correct, then, when he suggests that Reform Judaism is "polydox" in that it allows as "equally valid all opinions on the great themes of God, the nature of man, and so forth."[20]

*Torah*

It is in the area of Torah and Halakhah that Reform made its most radical break with traditional Judaism. For not since the sectarian Karaites of the eighth century had any group of Jews questioned the validity of Jewish law. And never in *all* of Jewish history since the Christian schism had any sect of Jews challenged the binding nature of Biblical ritual rules. The Reform movement not only questioned and challenged the validity of Halakhah, it swept away time-honored Biblical precepts in creating its brand of "Prophetic Judaism."

Of course, the question of revelation posed a supreme dilemma: if God revealed the Torah to Israel, then *all* the *mitzvot* are equally binding. If God did not reveal the Torah, then the underpinnings of the ethical *mitzvot* on which Reform is based crumble and fall. This dilemma still perplexes Reform Jewry today. Yet, in boldest fashion, Reform tried to resolve the dilemma, cling to revelation, and cut the Gordian knot of ritual with the same stroke. In fact, virtually all Reform thinkers have espoused the notion of revelation, though not, to be sure, in the Orthodox sense.

German Reformer Solomon L. Steinheim insisted that the Jewish religion was founded on revelation, which is "the nation-forming and preserving element of Judaism." David Einhorn agreed: "The more mere ceremonialism loses in significance and observance, the more it is necessary for us to seize upon the essential character of the Jewish faith" which stands out even without ceremonials, he wrote. And that "essential character," said Einhorn, is revelation. Isaac M. Wise believed very passionately in revelation, as did Kaufmann Kohler. True, there were some like Samuel Hirsch, Adolph Moses, and S.H. Sonneschein who viewed revelation as "mysticism" and nonrational. Emil G. Hirsch went so far as to dub it a Christian rather than a Jewish conception. There was a spirited debate at the Pittsburgh conference over whether to use the term or not. Kohler argued that he believed in revelation; that *Torah min hashamayim* (the Torah comes from Heaven) must remain one of "the foundation stones of Judaism." But he proceeded to clarify this view: "Of course, I do not believe that God stepped down in person from heaven and spoke on Mount Sinai, but when a new truth, instead of being sought for, seeks its instrument, taking hold of a single person or a people and impelling them to become its herald, this is revelation. . . ."[21]

In any event, the Pittsburgh Platform skirted the issue, contenting itself with the affirmation that "the Bible is the record of the consecration of the Jewish people to its mission as priest of the One God," and emphasized its value as "the most potent instrument of religious and moral instruction."

Two aspects of theological thinking emerged rather clearly: first, Reform accepted a progressive, non-literalistic notion of revelation; second, only the ethical commandments were accepted as divinely revealed—the ritual ones were seen as merely reflections of the passing ages of human history. Hence, only the ethical laws are to be considered as forever binding. This is boldly stated in the Columbus Platform:

> *God reveals Himself not only in the majesty, beauty and orderliness of nature, but also in the vision and moral striving of the human spirit. Revelation is a continuous process, confined to no one group and to one age. Yet the people of Israel, through its prophets and sages, achieved unique insight in the realm of religious truth. The Torah, both written and oral, enshrines Israel's ever-growing consciousness of God and of the moral law. It preserves the historical precedents, sanctions and norms of Jewish life, and seeks to mould it*

*in the patterns of goodness and of holiness. Being products of histori-*
*cal processes, certain of its laws have lost their binding force with the*
*passing of the conditions that called them forth. But as a depository*
*of permanent spiritual ideals, the Torah remains the dynamic source*
*of the life of Israel. Each age has the obligation to adapt the teachings*
*of the Torah to its basic needs in consonance with the genius of*
*Judaism.*[22]

The progressive, non-literalistic view of revelation is typical of
Reform thinkers. It was typical of Kohler's philosophy and it is,
for example, Rabbi Maurice Eisendrath's position as well. As
Eisendrath puts it, "Our God must be a *living* God who did not
reveal Himself at Sinai alone. He must come continuously to us
in every insight of our day."[23]

Today's Reform theologians are still grappling with the problem of revelation. Jakob Petuchowski, while doubting the Mosaic
authorship of the Bible, accepts "the *fact* of Revelation." What
matters is that the Torah came from God, even if in a series of
continuous revelations. Eugene Borowitz follows much the
same path. "In my opinion," he writes, "the most characteristic
theological assertion of liberal Judaism is that such knowledge
as men have of God is subjective, a human response to him,
rather than objective human reception of his formulations."
Thus, the liberal maximizes religious freedom of choice and
trusts in the responsible individual. Yet, Borowitz adds, "because I believe God still has an active role in such human experience, I still want to speak of revelation, though I do not believe
in verbal revelation."[24]

Since Reform does not accept a literal interpretation of revelation, what significance is bestowed on the Bible? And what of
rabbinic literature?

Here, too, the dilemma is a serious one. Isaac M. Wise firmly
believed in revelation and therefore refused to allow the teaching of Biblical criticism at Hebrew Union College. But most
Reformers accepted Higher Criticism while not rejecting revelation. Kohler succeeded in having the Pittsburgh Platform codify
his view that the Bible reflects the primitive ideas of its own age

and is not therefore antagonistic to modern discoveries of scientific research. Dr. Julian Morgenstern (himself an eminent Bible scholar and critic) insisted that without a critical view of Torah, reform is impossible. He believes that Biblical Science is not destructive but constructive; it has given us the Bible "re-interpreted and with a larger message and deeper and more eternal significance than ever before." Emil G. Hirsch went even further in his scientific approach, viewing the Bible as the work of men of their time who happened to have spoken Hebrew. Needless to say, if Reform was critical of Biblical literature it was even more so of rabbinic literature which was unanimously viewed as human in origin, imperfect in development, and legalistic in temper. While some defended the human genius of the Talmud and Midrash, others were particularly crude in denigrating the value of rabbinic literature.[25]

Once the Reform movement denied the literal basis of revelation of the Torah and denigrated the colossal structure of rabbinic Halakhah, the gates were opened for a full-scale attack on *mitzvot*, rituals, customs, and observances. Isaac M. Wise was curiously ambivalent. On the one hand, he said that observances are of secondary nature and "only such observances and practices which might and should become universal, because they would be beneficial to all men, are with us inherent elements of Judaism, while our opponents . . . look upon every Jewish custom as an essential element of their religion." He insisted that form must change with the times, that "legalism is not Judaism, nor is mysticism religion; the belief in fiction is superstition. Judaism is the fear of the Lord and the love of man in harmony with the dicta of reason." He sneered at the dietary laws, referring to them as "kitchen Judaism." He allowed the first commencement banquet of Hebrew Union College to be non-kosher and he permitted non-kosher food at the college.[26]

On the other hand, Wise denied that he was a frivolous Reformer seeking reform for its own sake. He insisted that he always sought a legal precedent for changes, and he argued for the preservation of some rituals that "appear ridiculous or at least superfluous to others, and stand in our way of progress, retarding our mission to the human family" to preserve the Jewish people and its mission. He warned the radicals that you cannot break the shell without harming the fruit, and he jeopardized his career in Albany by insisting that the merchants close their shops on the Sabbath. His colleague Rabbi Max Lilienthal shared this conservative tendency, demanding that Reform prove its innovations derived from classic sources and not reform out of frivolity or arrogance. The two men joined forces in urging Cincinnati merchants to observe the Sabbath. But this conservative mood was not to prevail; the radicals were to set the tone of Reform for a long time to come.[27]

Chief spokesman for the radicals was Rabbi David Einhorn, ably abetted by his two brilliant sons-in-law, Kaufmann Kohler and Emil G. Hirsch. Their view was simply this: the ethical commandments are eternally binding; but the ritual precepts reflect the *Zeitgeist*, are *not* divine, and thus are to change with the times. "Like man himself," wrote Einhorn, "the divine law has a perishable body and an imperishable spirit." He attacked the Talmud for its narrow morality and lack of universalism, and he viewed it as merely a philosophical approach that stressed the letter of the law as an end-all, rejecting progress, glorifying the past while succumbing to formalism that "makes it literally impossible to breathe." Einhorn declared in his Inaugural Sermon in Baltimore (1855):

> *Clearly we see the futility of religious usages that are dead; for the wood perished in the very flame it feeds; and the mirror serves the purpose only so long as it remains clear and bright and free from dust. But just as obvious is our need of religious forms that are still quick with religious ideas, and the sad error of those who would hold aloof from them.*[28]

Samuel Hirsch urged the removal of all *mitzvot* that "hinder us from working for the maintenance and prosperity of civil society." Any symbols that prevent the Jew from participating in the new era of prophetic redemption and messianic fulfillment must be discarded. His son, Emil G. Hirsch, was just as radical: "Judaism is not 'Law' but 'teaching'; it is not an external law, but an inward principle. It is growth, not a command." Hirsch wrote that we do not insist on observing ceremonies that have the "tendency to repel and disgust."[29]

Kaufmann Kohler was similarly negatively disposed to Halakhah. He fully accepted Biblical criticism and argued that Mosaic-Rabbinical Judaism had lost its hold irrevocably for the modern Jew. He realized that Decalogue Judaism alone would be too vague or narrow, and called for accentuation of what is essential and vital amidst the ever-changing forms and ever-fluctuating conditions. Following the lead of Samuel Hirsch, Kohler rejected the notion of Torah as Law. He insisted that ritualistic piety "fostered hair-splitting casuistry and caused the petrification of religion in the codified Halakah." Calling for a return to Biblical idealism and humanism, Kohler reminded his followers that the Prophets and Psalmists "insisted only on righteous conduct and integrity of soul, and repudiated entirely the ritualism of the priesthood and the formalism of the cult." Kohler viewed the *mitzvot* as symbols of priestly devotion and a technique for keeping the Jewish people apart from the demoralizing influences of pagan nature-worship. These external acts, he felt, became petrified and killed the spirit. True, the Law did serve as an iron wall of defense against temptations. But once the modern Jew freed himself of authority and began open inquiry into the purpose of the Law, that raison d'être was rendered invalid.[30]

Kohler appealed to Jews to end separatism and blind obedience to the Law, and to renew their world mission as a priestly people. In a ringing declaration of independence from Halakhah, Kohler stated:

> *No, I do not believe that the Mosaic statutes about the sacrifices, the incense, and the priestly apparel, or the sanitary and criminal laws, are unchangeable ordinances of God dictated from heaven. I distinguish in the Bible the kernel from the husk, the grain from the chaff, the spirit from the temporary form.*

He challenged his readers and listeners: "Is Judaism to be a sacred mummy or a fountain of life?" But even the radical, anti-Halakhic Kohler conceded that "true progress lies not in abolishing but in improving the ceremonies of religion, and in making such innovations as tend to strengthen the loyalty and reverential piety of the people."[31]

The radicalism of the men described above culminated in the Pittsburgh Platform. The two critical paragraphs dealing with ritual observance reflected the revolutionary, rather than the moderate, school of thought:

> *We recognize in the Mosaic legislation a system of training the Jewish people for its mission during its national life in Palestine, and today we accept as binding only the moral laws and maintain only such ceremonies as elevate and sanctify our lives, but reject all such as are not adapted to the views and habits of modern civilization.*
>
> *We hold that all such Mosaic and Rabbinical laws as regulate diet, priestly purity and dress originated in ages and under the influence of ideas altogether foreign to our present mental and spiritual state. They fail to impress the modern Jew with a spirit of priestly holiness; their observance in our days is apt rather to obstruct than to further modern spiritual elevation.*[32]

The Reform movement set about the task of concretizing its philosophy of Halakhah. Of course, many of the precedents were already established in Germany at the rabbinical conferences of the nineteenth century. But American Reform went markedly further in sweeping away Orthodox Halakhah and traditional *mitzvot*.

Synagogue worship was changed significantly by the Reformers; riding on the Sabbath was permitted; the second days of the Festivals were dropped; the skullcap, *talit* and *tefillin* were eliminated; and the campaign to remove all vestiges of "orientalism" went so far as to practically change the Reform temples into replicas of Protestant churches.[33]

Personal status was sharply altered by the Reformers. Circumcision was no longer required for converts, and circumcision by surgeons of Jewish babies was sanctioned. Birth control was allowed. The traditional *ketubah* (marriage contract), *get* (Jewish divorce), and other Biblical and rabbinic restrictions on marriages were dropped at the Philadelphia Conference of 1869 and affirmed at subsequent conventions. Mixed marriages were "not viewed as forbidden"—a patently ambiguous phrase that led to much confusion in Reform ranks. Abraham Geiger had ruled such marriages were valid civilly, but not religiously; but Isaac M. Wise and David Einhorn agreed with each other that mixed marriages were a "nail in the coffin of the small Jewish race." The Central Conference of American Rabbis in 1909 and 1947 declared that "mixed marriages are contrary to the tradition of the Jewish religion and should therefore be discouraged." But it is estimated that as many as one hundred Reform rabbis perform such marriages, and an astounding 40 percent of marriages in Southern California at which Reform rabbis officiate are mixed marriages.[34]

There were other fundamental changes in Halakhah that were made by the Reformers. For example, Bar Mitzvah was discontinued and replaced by Confirmation of boys and girls at age fifteen or sixteen, usually held on Shavuot. It was felt that thirteen-year-old boys are hardly "men" in any sense of the term and that an additional two or three years of study would develop better-educated Jews. Sunday Schools replaced the Day Schools and afternoon schools, and Hebrew was generally dropped from the curriculum. *Kashrut* was abolished, although some vestigial remains, such as abstention from pork, still were to be found. The traditional rules of mourning were eliminated, while nontraditional practices such as cremation, autopsies, disinterments, and congregational recitation of the *Kaddish* were permitted or introduced. Significantly, Reform equalized the role of the woman with the man and in fact the Hebrew Union College ordained the first woman rabbi in 1972.

But Reform's position on Halakhah was far from frozen and the winds of change blew early and strongly. Even the radicals were quickly disillusioned with the people's indifference to reforms. Emil G. Hirsch rebuked the people for not coming to pray even on Sunday. Kaufmann Kohler, who initiated Sunday services in 1874, dropped them in 1891, noting that "that Sabbath which is allowed to die on Friday cannot be resurrected on

Sunday," and he added that "there is something in the very air of the Sunday service that chills the heart." Criticism of the extremes of Reform began to mount, and as the old Germanic element began to decline, the new East European recruits to Reform's laity and clergy began to demand re-institution of long-discarded traditions. Rabbis Abba Hillel Silver and Felix Levy denounced the Reform movement for its Pauline attack on *mitzvot*, while Professor Jacob Z. Lauterbach, Talmudist at the Hebrew Union College, and Rabbi Solomon Freehof urged the creation of a Reform Halakhah. The impact of Conservative Judaism and Mordecai M. Kaplan's Reconstructionism also was a factor in prompting Reform to reevaluate its negativism to ritual.[35]

The culmination came at the Columbus Conference of the Central Conference of American Rabbis where the Columbus Platform was adopted that virtually repudiated most of the old Pittsburgh Platform. In the critical paragraphs on Torah, the Columbus Platform expressed its reverence for both the written and oral Torah. It urged full participation in the life of the Jewish community—in home, synagogue, school, and other agencies of Jewish life. It declared that "the home has been and must continue to be a stronghold of Jewish life, hallowed by the spirit of love and reverence, by moral discipline and religious observance and worship." But it went even further in calling for *mitzvot:*

> *Judaism as a way of life requires, in addition to its moral and spiritual demands, the preservation of the Sabbath, festivals and Holy Days, the retention and development of such customs, symbols and ceremonies as possess inspirational value, the cultivation of distinctive forms of religious art and music and the use of Hebrew, together with the vernacular, in our worship and instruction.*[36]

The response to this summons was not long in coming. The Biennial Convention of the Union of American Hebrew Congregations in 1937 called for the use of "traditional symbols, ceremonies, and customs, such as the use of only Jewish music, the use of Cantor with Choir," the employment of only Jewish singers, and the recitation of *Kiddush,* traditional hymns, etc. The gates were opened to change, or counterreformation. The newly revised *Union Prayer Book* introduced a good deal more Hebrew as well as long-discarded prayers such as the *Kiddush,* Torah reading, *Yizkor* for Festivals, etc. Temples that had abolished the post of cantor as a vestige of "orientalism" reinstated it; others allowed the optional wearing of a skullcap. Bar Mitzvah and Bat Mitzvah were introduced. Some dietary rules were revived both at temples and in homes. There was a reevaluation of Reform's ambiguity on intermarriage. The 1970 conference of the CCAR saw its president, Roland Gittelsohn, propose a motion *forbidding* Reform rabbis from officiating at mixed marriages. By a breathlessly close vote of 70 to 67 his motion was defeated and the old position *discouraging* such marriages was retained.

Similarly, Reform's evaluation of educational needs has been revised. Many Reform schools have added a second and even third day to the inadequate Sunday School. Hebrew has been introduced in practically all schools and a program of educational camping has been developed. In 1969 the CCAR had called for the creation of a network of Day Schools and urged the UAHC to support the plan. The UAHC defeated the proposal by a very narrow vote, but the trend is unmistakably in the direction of more intensive Jewish education. In fact, two all-day schools under Reform auspices were operating in 1973.

An extraordinary development in Reform ritual practices is the increasingly perceptible call in many quarters for the creation of a Reform Halakhah and a guide to ritual practices. Actually a tentative Reform *Shulhan Arukh* had been prepared by Leopold Stein in the nineteenth century, but it was shelved. In America, Rabbis Jacob Voorsanger and Joseph Krauskopf urged the adoption of a guide to Reform rituals and the creation of a synod back in 1903. Rabbi Solomon Freehof was more reserved about a guide: he urged the creation of new *minhagim,* or customs; but he resisted "early codification." Freehof argued that the Reform movement should move slowly because "Reform Jewish life is not chaotic" and is in reality "the least chaotic of all the three branches of Judaism." Jacob Z. Lauterbach ob-

served that Reform Halakhah is the youngest and latest development but is still the living stream of Jewish Halakhah. And
whereas Lauterbach believed in the need for Reform Halakhah
"to preserve Israel as the priest-teacher of the nations," he was
not an advocate of the creation of a guide.[37]

Nevertheless, in 1938 the Commission on Synagogue and
Community of the CCAR recommended the formulation of a
code of Reform Jewish ceremonial observance. In 1948 the
president of the CCAR, Leon Feuer, reiterated the need for a
guide as a means of ending the lack of observance. That same
year, the UAHC resolved to "correct a most costly error made
by the early anti-ritualistic Reformers who were earnestly intent
upon emphasizing ethical and religious principles and righteous
conduct but looking upon 'the ceremonial system to be a trivial-
izing of the noble teaching of Judaism.'" The Committee on
Reform Jewish Practice of the CCAR stated in 1950: "It has
become clearer to us also that ritual practices and ceremonial
observances give the Jew a sense of rootage in his people's past,
but they also fill him with a fortifying sense of union with all
other Jews of our time who engage in these practices." And by
1956, the former anti-Halakhist Maurice N. Eisendrath, president of the UAHC, pleaded "for an end to all this license and
libertarianism, politely dubbed liberalism," and urged frank and
full discussion of "some form of mature guide to Reform principles and practice."[38]

Two guides for Reform practice have been produced. While
neither has received official sanction from the Reform movement, they both reveal the new trends in Reform Halakhah. The
*Guide* by Rabbis Frederic Doppelt and David Polish urges that
practices of Reform be elevated to the rank of *mitzvot*. The
authors suggest that Israel Independence Day be declared an
official holiday; they call for the reinstitution of Sabbath *mitzvot;*
they disapprove of eating pork. Rabbi William Silverman in his
*Guide* follows much the same procedure. He urges that the Sabbath rituals of *Kiddush* and candles, blessing of the children,
recitation of the prayer for bread, family visits, study, and Sabbath worship be norms of life. Neither of the two *Guides* accepts

the traditional, Divine origin of Halakhah, nor do they advocate "authoritarian thought control." But, as Doppelt and Polish put it, without Halakhah we have an emasculated Judaism which cannot long abide. In their view, *Halakhot* are merely ways to go—projections of *mitzvot* into daily life. But a *Guide* is needed to bring a "greater degree of observance, self-disciplining commitment, and spirituality into our religious life" and help immortalize the historical relationship of the Jewish people and God. Whether such *Guides* will be accepted by the people remains to be seen.[39]

Present-day Reform thinking has revolutionized the Reform movement's views of Halakhah. Dr. Solomon Freehof, premier scholar of Reform Jewry, notes that the Committee on Responsa (the equivalent of a Halakhah Committee) has existed for sixty years and he has served on it for over forty. In the past, perhaps ten to twenty ritual questions were submitted annually. Today, the number has risen to over two hundred. Freehof suggests that this is because there is a greater interest in rabbinic literature, since the East European Jews who now dominate the Reform movement have ties to Orthodox roots and are seeking "to come to terms with the legal system which governs Orthodox life." Freehof is pleased with these new developments: he believes that the return to rabbinics means a return to the *mind* of Judaism, whereas Reform had merely emphasized Prophetic literature, the *heart* of our faith. Reversing his earlier views, Freehof supports the development of a guide to Reform practice— not to fix a code, but to end the new disorderliness in Reform.[40]

W. Gunther Plaut argues passionately against classic Reform bibliolatry. Unfortunately, he opines, Einhorn's spirit bested that of Wise, and Halakhah lost out. Plaut warns that if the movement does not now turn decisively away from its postclassical, radical phase, then indeed its critics will probably be right: it will have no future and degenerate into "shallow, post-Einhornian ethicism." We need no *law* or *Halakhah* in the old sense but *Halikhah*—the way to go. We must tell the Jews what to do—but with their consent and commitment, suggests Plaut.[41]

Jakob Petuchowski and Eugene Borowitz approach Halakhah from an existentialist vantage. Petuchowski views ritual as divine; *mitzvot* enable future generations to relive events of the past. First off, the modern Jew must study; then he must experiment. And while this will doubtlessly lead to a high degree of subjectivity, there are checks and balances—namely, history, the holy community, and the survival of the Jewish People.[42] Borowitz argues for "open traditionalism." He seeks some structure, yet he wants an existentialist reworking of law that traditional Judaism cannot tolerate. True, there is no guarantee that what we cherish today we will cherish tomorrow; but "that is the risk of freedom without which mature humanity is impossible." The pact between God and Israel is not fixed in immutable terms; it is meaningful only through *kiyum ha-brit*—actions, responsibility, and deeds as man feels the personal relationship with God as one of the covenanted community.[43]

Perhaps most expressive of the contemporary mood of Reform Halakhists is Freehof's statement that "the Halakhah is not our governance but our guide." When Halakhah's ethical standards do not comport with "our conscience," we turn aside from it, resolutely. The individual, in short, must decide whether or not to observe a *mitzvah;* a Reform Jew does not accept *mitzvot ex cathedra.*[44]

Clearly, Reform's views on Halakhah have undergone monumental changes. Reform is no longer disdainful of Halakhah and contemptuous of *mitzvot.* True, it is not about to accept Karo's *Shulhan Arukh;* but it is prepared to reinstitute *mitzvot* that are considered personally spiritualizing, that enhance godly living, and that ensure the survival of the Jewish People. Such decisions will not be fiats from on high or rabbinic mandates; they will be, rather, subjectively accepted commitments by Jews and Reform congregations. This is scarcely Orthodox Halakhah, but it indicates that Reform has returned to a healthy respect for ritual, and that in itself is an extraordinary phenomenon.

## The Jewish People

The Reform movement, following the lead of the so-called Sanhedrin summoned by Napoleon in 1807, stripped Judaism of its political and national elements. The Pittsburgh Platform stated the position clearly when it announced that "We consider ourselves no longer a nation but a religious community. . . ."

Yet, the Reformers did not totally denude Judaism of the aspect of peoplehood. Geiger, for example, developed a sort of religious racialism; he wrote of the "native energy" of Jews, who are "endowed with such a genius, with a religious genius" and visions of the Divine. Kohler followed Geiger's lead and wrote ecstatically of Israel's great accomplishments, primarily in one field, namely, religion.[45]

While Reform accepted the concept of the chosen people, it reinterpreted it to mean chosen by God to fulfill a *mission*. And what is the mission? Samuel Holdheim explained that "Judaism must spread the Noahide Laws to all nations" but at the same time, it must safeguard the Torah as Israel's unique possession. Holdheim added that it is the messianic task of Israel to make the pure knowledge of God and the pure law of morality the common possession and blessing of all the peoples of the earth.[46]

Kaufmann Kohler preached fervently of Israel's mission to mankind. Following Isaac M. Wise's course, he declared that "within fifty years Judaism's teachings will have become the common property of the American people." To Kohler, as well as to most Reformers, *Galut* was not viewed as a curse; on the contrary, it was seen as a blessing from God that would enable the Jew to fulfill his mission. In Kohler's words:

> *Progressive Judaism of our time has the great task of re-emphasiz-*
> *ing Israel's world-mission and of reclaiming for Judaism its place as*
> *the priesthood of humanity. It is to proclaim anew the prophetic idea*
> *of God's covenant with humanity . . . Israel, as the people of the*
> *covenant, aims to unite all nations and classes of men in the divine*
> *covenant. It must outlast all other religions in its certainty that*

*ultimately there can be but the one religion, uniting God and man by
a single bond.*[47]

Reform Judaism has taken the mission theory rather seriously.
The *Union Prayer Book,* while retaining the classic Hebrew phrase
*asher bahar banu* ("who has chosen us"), translates the phrase,
"Thou hast called us to Thy service." The Columbus Platform
reemphasized the idea in its statement that it has been "Israel's
mission to witness the Divine in the face of every form of paganism and materialism" and in its summons to fulfill the historic
task "to cooperate with all men in the establishment of the
kingdom of God, of universal brotherhood, justice, truth and
peace on earth." To varied thinkers like Jakob J. Petuchowski,
Joshua Loth Liebman, Bernard J. Bamberger, and Joseph Narot,
Israel was chosen not *per se,* but in order to do something—in
order to observe the Torah, to be covenanted to God as His
kingdom of priests, to bring spiritual insights to a world starving
for spiritual food, to teach justice, freedom, morality, and rationalism to the human race. Chosenness is thus not to be construed as superiority or ethnic chauvinism; it implies "a hard
task, a heavy responsibility, an arduous office"—to borrow the
words of Rabbi Bernard J. Bamberger.[48]

Of late, some younger Reform thinkers have been turning
away from the mission notion. For example, Rabbi Daniel
Jeremy Silver calls the mission "chutzpah" and arrogance. We
should care less about serving the world, he writes, and more
about the responsibility "to cultivate dignity and justice within
Israel."[49]

## The Land of Israel

In no other area of theology, perhaps, has there been such a
remarkable volte-face in the Reform movement as in its attitude
to Eretz Yisrael and Zionism. The Reform movement began with
total rejection of the idea of nationhood and a Jewish political
entity. All prayers for restoraton to Zion were deleted from the
Reform prayer books. Its leaders, such as Isaac M. Wise and

Kaufmann Kohler, lampooned and derided the "zionmania" of the day. The Pittsburgh Platform made it clear that we "expect neither a return to Palestine, nor a sacrificial worship under the administration of the sons of Aaron, nor the restoration of any of the laws concerning the Jewish state." The CCAR at its Montreal convention of 1897 expressed "total disapproval of the attempt to establish the Jewish State." In 1917 the CCAR denounced the Balfour Declaration and the UAHC followed suit in 1919. Reform insisted that Zionism deflected the Jew from his mission to the world; it diverted him from his loyalty to God; it was a retrogression to nationalism; it laid Jews open to the charge of dual loyalty and endangered the status of Jews in various lands of their sojourn. The 1897 pronouncement was unequivocal:

> *Resolved, that we totally disapprove of any attempt for the establishment of a Jewish State. Such attempts show a misunderstanding of Israel's mission, which from the narrow political and national field has been expanded to the promotion among the whole human race of the broad and universalistic religion first proclaimed by the Jewish prophets. Such attempts do not benefit, but infinitely harm our Jewish brethren where they are still persecuted, by confirming the assertion of their enemies that the Jews are foreigners in the countries in which they are at home, and of which they are everywhere the most loyal and patriotic citizens. We reaffirm that the object of Judaism is not political nor national, but spiritual, and addresses itself to the continuous growth of peace, justice, and love in the human race, to a messianic time when all men will recognize that they form "one great brotherhood" for the establishment of God's kingdom on earth.*[50]

Isaac M. Wise believed this statement represented the sentiment of American Judaism, "minus the idiosyncrasies of . . . late immigrants," and he called Zionism an "unpleasant episode of our history." Max Lilienthal reiterated the old slogan that "America is our Palestine; here is our Zion and Jerusalem; Washington and the signers of the glorious Declaration of Independence . . . are our deliverers." Emil G. Hirsch vulgarly compared the ancient Temple to Chicago's slaughterhouse. And

Kohler fumed over the degeneracy and demoralization of Zionism. He detected nothing of theological value in Zionism, although he conceded that religious Zionism had some validity and he admitted (with Solomon Schechter) that Zionism's response to anti-Semitism aroused among many an interest in Judaism, Hebrew literature, and Jewish history. But Kohler believed that the refuge of Israel is in its God, and not in any territorial possession. "We require a regeneration, not of the nation, but of the faith of Israel, which is its soul." Kohler called for a "spiritual Zion for all mankind" and he denounced the godless secularism of the political Zionist movement.[51]

And yet, despite this overwhelming antipathy to Zionism and Jewish nationalism, the Reform movement shifted extraordinarily. Some of the faculty members of the Hebrew Union College were Zionist sympathizers. Professors Max Margolis and Henry Malter lost their posts because of their sentiments. Professor David Neumark was undeterred: he called for a spiritual center in Zion that would also be a *religious* center. And two great and eloquent rabbis, Stephen S. Wise and Abba Hillel Silver, labored valiantly to rally Reform to the Blue and White banner of Zionism. Wise appeared at the founding of the World Union of Progressive Judaism in London in 1926 and said, "I conceive of a Jewish Mission to create a center of Jewish life, in which the loftiest spiritual and ethical ideals of the Jewish religion shall be lifted up and magnified in the sight of the Jew and of the world." And he added that if Zionists are not welcome in liberal ranks it is really the liberals who had withdrawn from "the unity and integrity of Jewish life." Although the conference took no official position on Zionism, Wise's eloquence left an indelible mark. Later, as president of the Zionist Organization of America, Wise helped marshal American Jewry behind the campaign to create the State of Israel.[52]

Silver was equally inflamed. He, too, served as president of the Zionist Organization of America; he, too, assailed the "theological abstractions" of Reform as well as its Pauline antinomianism and naive messianism. "National restoration," insisted Silver, was "the very heart of the messianic ideal from its very inception."[53]

Rabbis like Wise and Silver, along with Barnett Brickner, Felix Levy, James Heller, and others, helped change Reform's views on Zion. Historical reality did the rest. By 1935 the CCAR took a neutral view on Zionism and endorsed the upbuilding of Palestine. The Columbus Platform went further: it affirmed "the obligation of all Jewry" to aid in upbuilding Palestine "as a Jewish homeland." The UAHC followed suit in 1937 and it urged all Jews "to unite in the activities leading to the establishment of a Jewish homeland in Palestine."

The birth of the State of Israel was warmly hailed by the Reform movement. Its rabbis and laymen have labored zealously to support Israel morally, spiritually, politically, and financially. In 1967 at the Los Angeles convention of the CCAR—seventy years after the Montreal convention had repudiated Zionism—the delegates declared their "solidarity" with Israel stating: "Their triumphs are our triumphs. Their ordeal is our ordeal. Their fate is our fate." In 1969 the CCAR convention adopted a resolution declaring the fifth day of Iyar, Israel Independence Day, to be an official holiday, and the liturgy committee was charged with the creation of special liturgy for the festival. The 1970 convention of the CCAR met in Jerusalem. At the urging of Rabbi Nelson Glueck, it agreed that henceforth all rabbinical students would be required to spend one year of study in Israel.[54]

Today, with almost no exceptions, Reform is solidly behind the State of Israel. Rabbi Eugene Borowitz writes of Israel as *"atchalta d'geula* (the beginning of redemption)" and he urges that Israel be a state built on the standards of Israel's prophets, and not be just a national entity. Professor Ezra Spicehandler, director of the Hebrew Union College in Jerusalem, believes that "today the majority of Reform Jews accept Israel as the center of the Jewish people." Israel is taught in the curriculum of Reform schools, and hundreds of youngsters study and work in Israel each year. The *Union Prayer Book* is currently being revised again and will probably restore references to Zion. There is even talk of forming a Reform kibbutz in Israel.[55]

The Reform movement has not been uncritical of the State of Israel, however. It opposes a secularist concept of Zionism and

believes in the religio-moral foundations of the Jewish state. It
has bitterly condemned the Orthodox "establishment" in Israel
for refusing to allow non-Orthodox rabbis to officiate at religious ceremonies. Yet the Reform movement is a pillar of Zion
reborn. What a radical change from the position of Isaac M.
Wise and Kaufmann Kohler! Today it would be terribly difficult
to discover an anti-Zionist in the ranks of Reform Judaism.

## The Jewish Community

Despite its early repudiation of Jewish peoplehood, the Reform movement has maintained close ties with world Jewry. The
early Reformers, while renouncing the concept of *klal Yisrael*,
the Jewish community, never rejected the Talmudic adage that
"all Israelites are responsible for one another." Reformers have
worked closely with Orthodox, Conservative, secularist, and
Zionist Jews in a variety of projects. Reform rabbis have taken
the lead in such representative bodies as the Synagogue Council
of America, the Jewish Welfare Board, and the New York Board
of Rabbis, and Reform laymen have been deeply involved in
Israel Bonds, the United Jewish Appeal, and other philanthropic
and benevolent causes. The Reform movement has battled valiantly to aid beleaguered Jews the world over—whether in
Russia, Arab lands, or Israel.

While the classic Reformers stubbornly refused to acknowledge the existence of a "Jewish community" for fear of setting
the Jews apart from the mainstream of American life, that old
antipathy has all but disappeared. The modern-day Reform
movement is deeply involved in all facets of Jewish communal
endeavors. Its mission to the world has never totally obscured
its vision of fellow Jews.

## The Synagogue

The Reform movement views the synagogue as basically a
House of Prayer, and incidentally a House of Study. Most Reform congregations refer to themselves as "temples"—symbolic

of Reform's view that the movement no longer prays for the restoration of the Temple in Jerusalem, since each local synagogue is *the* temple of the Jewish people in our times. The social-center aspect of the syngagogue was long scorned by the Reform movement. But that, too, changed with the times. The Columbus Platform stated: "The Synagogue is the oldest and most democratic institution in Jewish life. It is the prime communal agency by which Judaism is fostered and preserved. It links the Jews of each community and unites them with all Israel." Today the average Reform congregation is—in common with its Conservative and even Orthodox counterparts—a synagogue-center, with the religious aspects usually incidental to the social, athletic, cultural, and communal ones.

The Reform movement intended, as we have noted, to update Jewish worship and modernize Jewish theology. Consequently, the Reform temple reflects those revolutionary changes; Reform worship services are notably different from those of the Orthodox.

The first goal of the Reform movement in this regard was to modernize and revise the liturgy. Hungarian Reformer Rabbi Aaron Chorin approved of the Hamburg Temple's worship as a needed "cleansing of the liturgy and its accretions." Rabbi Samuel Adler, who was active in the German rabbinic conferences and later served in New York's Temple Emanuel from 1857 to 1876, was even more outspoken. Rationalist by temperament, he demanded that reason rather than Talmudic legalism be the leader, and he urged the removal from the service of "lies, unintelligible items, prayers for the restoration of sacrifice, return to Palestine, personal Messiah, bodily resurrection, and all exaggeration," in order to make the service intelligible, instructive, and inspiring. Others, like Kaufmann Kohler and Emil G. Hirsch, insisted on stripping the services of all "Orientalism."[56]

New prayer books sprouted like dandelions in spring. Jakob J. Petuchowski lists over a hundred and fifty European Reform prayer books, and the number of American counterparts is little less prodigious. Starting with the early efforts of the Charleston

Reformers in 1830, each dominant Reform figure produced his version of a Reform prayer book. Merzbacher created one in 1854 at New York's Temple Emanuel; Isaac M. Wise produced his *Minhag America* in 1857; Einhorn composed his *Olath Tamid* in 1858; Szold and Jastrow followed suit, as did a host of other rabbis. The *Union Prayer Book* of 1894 crystallized all of the earlier efforts and gave Reform an official prayer book—in fact, *the* prayer book still used in virtually all American and Canadian Reform temples.[57]

Since theology was the springboard and passion of the Reformers, the *Union Prayer Book*, as well as earlier liturgical products, formalize the theology of the movement. The translation and textual emendation substituted a spiritual interpretation for the traditional notions of immortality and resurrection. They introduced a universalistic note bespeaking the belief in a Messianic *era* of justice and peace for all mankind. The *Union Prayer Book* reflects the position of the Pittsburgh Platform on Heaven and Hell:

> We reassert the doctrine of Judaism, that the soul of men is immortal, grounding this belief on the divine nature of the human spirit, which forever finds bliss in righteousness and misery in wickedness. We reject as ideas not rooted in Judaism the belief both in bodily resurrection and in Gehenna and Eden (hell and paradise), as abodes for everlasting punishment or reward.

Likewise, the *Union Prayer Book* lacks all references to the return to Zion or the restoration of the Temple and sacrificial cult, since the Reform movement had long since dropped them from its theology.[58]

The language of the prayers was also a hotly contested point among the Reformers. The historic Frankfort Conference of 1845 saw a split in the ranks over this very issue: Abraham Geiger had argued that Hebrew is a vestige of nationality and must go; Zachariah Frankel argued just as passionately that Hebrew is a vital element in Judaism and, as the language of the Bible, the external bond reminding us of God. When the conference voted that Hebrew is "not objectively required" but to be left up to the *subjective* judgment of the rabbi or congregation, Frankel walked out of the conference—never to return.[59]

The Reformers, however, could not quite decide for or against Hebrew. Radicals like Geiger and Einhorn found German more edifying; Ludwig Philippson and Isaac M. Wise countered that Hebrew is indispensable both in prayers and in Jewish education. Once again, the Geiger-Einhorn spirit prevailed and the *Union Prayer Book* contained relatively little Hebrew. However, the pendulum began to swing backwards and the Columbus Platform called for "the use of Hebrew, together with the vernacular, in our worship and instruction." The newer editions of the *Union Prayer Book* contain considerably more Hebrew than the older edition, and recent revisions have restored even more.

In a desperate attempt to attract worshipers who could not come to temple on Saturday due to economic pressures, Reform introduced the Sunday service of worship, song, and lecture-sermon. As early as 1854, the Baltimore Hebrew Reformed Association experimented with the practice. By 1874, David Einhorn made it a regular feature at Har Sinai Congregation. Kaufmann Kohler followed suit in Chicago, as did Samuel Hirsch in Philadelphia. Despite Isaac M. Wise's opposition, the Pittsburgh Conference approved the idea. Some temples used it to augment the Sabbath service; others allowed it to supplant the Sabbath service which had all but died anyway. But disillusionment with Sunday services set in rapidly. We have already noted how Kohler dropped it in despair. The CCAR affirmed the need to maintain "the historical Sabbath as a fundamental institution of Judaism and of exerting every effort to enforce its observance." And despite an effort by the CCAR to develop a supplementary Sunday service "as a means of maintaining the religious spirit of our young, getting people who work Saturdays, and attracting non-Jews," the Sunday services were gradually phased out and only a few temples still maintain them today.[60]

Isaac M. Wise had his own ideas about how to attract worshipers. In 1869 he introduced the late Friday evening service for the following reasons: first, the evening service is more impressive and solemn than the morning one; second, in the summer, the cooler evenings are preferable for worship; third, many work on Saturday mornings; fourth, gentiles can come at night and we can "remove errors and overcome misconceptions." Curiously, Kaufmann Kohler opposed the late-service innovation because it made the worshipers feel that "they have done their duty." Today the late service is the norm in most Reform temples, many of which no longer maintain Saturday morning services.[61]

Yet another innovation of Reform in synagogue worship was the introduction of instrumental music. Since the destruction of the Temple in Jerusalem, Orthodox law has banned instrumental music partly out of mourning for the Temple, partly because of prohibitions against repairing instruments on the Sabbath, and partly out of fear of aping Christian practices, notably in the use of an organ. European Reformers allowed an organ at services, and choirs—frequently with gentile choristers—were normal at worship. The service was shortened and the lengthy *piyutim* (liturgical poems) were eliminated, along with the morning Torah reading. The Reform movement was responsible for the remarkable upsurge of modern Jewish liturgical music. Distinguished composers like Lewandowski and Sulzer in the nineteenth century, and Bloch, Milhaux, Bernstein, Binder, and Freed in the twentieth, enriched the music of the synagogue immeasurably. Even jazz and rock music have entered the temples. Musical creative genius was stifled in the instrument-less Orthodox *shul*. The Reform temple opened wide new vistas for musical geniuses and creative spirits.[62]

Reform thinkers have grappled with the religious and psychological problems of prayer during the past century. Reformers do not believe in the classical notion of prayer as affecting changes in the deity: their theology could not allow such "naive" or "superstitious" notions. Kohler describes prayer as an expression of men's longing and yearning for God in times of need and of joy—an outflow of emotions of the soul and its dependence on God. He denies that prayer can affect God's unchangeable will and action. Likewise, Emil G. Hirsch writes that "prayer can exert power only over the relation of man to God, not over

God Himself." Kohler suggests that liturgy must "throb with the spirit of continuity with our great past, to make us feel one with our fathers of yore" and must "express clearly and fully our own views and needs, our convictions and our hopes."[63]

Concerning the function of prayer, the Columbus Platform states:

> *Prayer is the voice of religion, the language of faith and aspiration. It directs man's heart and mind Godward, voices the needs and hopes of the community, and reaches out after goals which invest life with supreme value. To deepen the spiritual life of our people, we must cultivate the traditional habit of communion with God through prayer in both home and synagogue.*

*The Union Prayer Book* suggests that prayer makes us aware of God's presence, teaches us humility as we contemplate God, and enables us to experience Him through His effect on the world and in social justice.[64]

Why does modern man have trouble praying? Some Reform thinkers believe the problem lies in the liturgy, which is generally stuffy, archaic, and irrelevant. Consequently, there have been several recent symposia of Reformers rethinking the liturgy, and the Committee on Liturgy of the CCAR is working on a newly revised version of the *Union Prayer Book*.[65]

But other Reform theologians view the matter as theological and existential, rather than liturgical. Jacob J. Petuchowski writes that the difficulty with prayer is that man fails to see himself as a creature of God. Eugene Borowitz decries the failure of temples in having made worshipers passive concertgoers. He endorses the view of Professor Abraham J. Heschel that the problem of prayer is *not prayer* but *God,* and that people are religiously embarrassed to pray. Borowitz urges that we "pray as one of this historic people, identifying oneself with its membership and its mission." Borowitz cautions that we cannot make the individual worshiper the final measure of the value of the synagogue in general or the Jewish service in particular. He adds that it is a kind of blasphemy to be concerned whether every prayer moves man *individually,* for that is tantamount to demanding that God serve *him* individually. "The problem is not a better prayer book," muses Borowitz, "but a better theology."[66]

Obviously, Reform is still searching for meaningful, inspiring, and intellectually and emotionally satisfying synagogue worship. But if one were to visit any Reform temple he would find certain common elements: the main service is on Friday evenings; English predominates over Hebrew; instrumental music and a choir are used; the sermon is the highlight of the service; men and women sit together; heads are normally not covered (although some rabbis wear caps and some temples allow the worshipers to cover their heads on an optional basis); the Torah is often read at Friday evening services; bar or bat mitzvah celebrations are usually marked on Friday evenings; Shavuot confirmation is widely practiced; smoking at the *Oneg Shabbat* reception is allowed, and non-kosher food may be served; and the *Union Prayer Book* is found in the temple.

*Social Action*

From its inception, the Reform movement has been involved in the campaign for social justice for all men. Its leaders have frequently been in the forefront of liberal and progressive causes, struggling for the rights of labor, civil rights, separation of church and state, liberal abortion and birth-control laws, social and international justice and others. Significantly, Reform Judaism has set the pace for other religious groups in the Jewish community, and generally the others have followed the path blazed by Reform.

The Pittsburgh Platform sounded the tone in its Eighth Principle:

> *In full accordance with the spirit of Mosaic legislation which strives to regulate the relation between rich and poor, we deem it our duty to participate in the great task of modern times, to solve on the basis of justice and righteousness the problems presented by the contrasts and evils of the present organizaton of society.*[67]

The Columbus Platform reaffirmed this commitment in even clearer terms. It stated that in Judaism religion and morality are "an indissoluble unity" and that "the love of God is incomplete without the love of one's fellowman." Judaism emphasizes the kinship of the human race, the sanctity and worth of the individual, and the right of all to justice, freedom and economic opportunity. The Platform declared that Judaism seeks the just society through the application of its teachings "to the economic order, to industry and commerce, and to national and international affairs." Continuing the theme, the Platform stated:

> *It aims at the elimination of man-made misery and suffering, of poverty and degradation, of tyranny and slavery, of social inequality and prejudice, of ill-will and strife. It advocates the promotion of harmonious relations between warring classes on the basis of equity and justice, and the creation of conditions under which human personality may flourish. It pleads for the safeguarding of childhood against exploitation. It champions the cause of all who work and of their right to an adequate standard of living, as prior to the rights of property. Judaism emphasizes the duty of charity, and strives for a social order which will protect men against the material disabilities of old age, sickness and unemployment.*

Finally, the Columbus Platform reiterated the prophetic ideal of universal peace and abhorrence of violence and war. It urged justice among nations and "organized international action for disarmament, collective security and world peace."[68]

Reform Judaism's great thinkers and leaders were deeply committed to these principles of social justice. Emil G. Hirsch wrote zealously that "religion must be a power and factor for social readjustment. This is my religion, the final arbiter." Kaufmann Kohler described Israel's mission as that of a people striving to achieve "the ideals of liberty, law, and peace" so that Israel's teachings will become "the motive-power and incentive to the re-establishment of human society upon new foundations." Professor Abraham Cronbach insisted that "social justice is Jewish," and he added, "Even if it were not Jewish, it would behoove us to espouse social justice. For social justice is

right and the right must be done whether it is Jewish or not."
Leo Baeck warned against "making Judaism a prisoner incar-
cerated in the synagogue, a captive locked in the temple who
may not be let loose to walk upon the streets of life." Stephen
S. Wise—the giant among men—went even further. Not content
with merely pious mouthings of noble sentiments, he became a
fiery activist in virtually every social cause. He turned down the
prestigious pulpit of New York's Temple Emanuel in 1905
rather than be muzzled in his sermons, and founded the Free
Synagogue, a bastion of liberal causes. He took to the picket
lines in the steel strike of 1919—an act that cost him a new
building for the Free Synagogue. He spoke out fearlessly against
corrupt politicans; he fought against child labor; he became a
force in the Democratic party. In Wise's view, there was no
alternative, for, as he wrote to Claude G. Montefiore, leader of
English Reform: "I am a liberal Jew, but have come to feel that
I have little in common with a group which perpetuates the
name of Reform Judaism, but after all is little more than a
survival of mid-nineteenth century Reform, rationalist rather
than religious . . . without a breath of the spirit of the social
passion."[69]

Both the CCAR and the UAHC have made social action integral parts of their programs; both issue detailed social-action
platforms at their annual and biennial conventions. Already in
1918 the CCAR urged more equitable distribution of profits of
industry, minimum wage laws, an eight-hour day with a compul-
sory day of rest, regulation of working conditions, abolition of
child labor, workmen's compensation and insurance, a national
system of public employment, and the right of labor to organize
and bargain collectively. It also supported mediation and con-
ciliation boards for disputes, housing for working people, pensions for widows, and constructive care of dependents, defec-
tives, and criminals. By 1928 the CCAR was demanding
right-to-work laws, unemployment insurance, old-age pensions,
and sickness and disability insurance. In 1933 the CCAR denounced, for the first of many times, anti-Negro prejudices in
economic and civil life. The UAHC followed suit in resolving

that "no government has the right to exclude any of its people from life, liberty and the pursuit of happiness by legal discriminations or by racial or religious persecutions." Over the years, the Reform movement has been in the forefront of the struggle for civil rights, with many Reform rabbis marching shoulder to shoulder with black Americans North and South. The movement has strongly supported the United Nations and world disarmament. It has championed intelligent, liberal birth-control and abortion laws since 1929. It has battled for separation of church and state; it opposes public aid to parochial schools; it is against prayer in the public schools. It has supported, since 1936, conscientious objection to military draft, and in 1969 endorsed selective conscientious objection for those opposed to a particular war on moral grounds. The CCAR has urged urban reconstruction and ecological control, and has demanded liberal immigration laws and a minimum wage for agricultural workers. It has also opposed censorship—even of prurient literature.[70]

The Vietnam war has convulsed the Reform movement. Both the CCAR and the UAHC have called for an immediate end to the war. In 1969 the CCAR was forced to drop its chaplaincy draft because the alumni simply refused to serve in Vietnam. Rabbi Maurice Eisendrath's outspoken opposition to the war has caused some stresses and strains within the movement. When the Social Actions Center was established in Washington, D.C., Temple Emanuel of New York actually withdrew from the UAHC, partly over pique at Eisendrath's outspoken liberalism, and partly out of fear that the Center would become a spokesman on social action for the entire movement.

But true to its early liberal spirit, Reform Judaism has not swerved from its declared path of translating Prophetic Judaism into day-to-day action for social justice and peace. As Professor Emil L. Fackenheim puts it, we must, on the one hand, oppose all attempts to force religion to mind its own business and stay out of secular fields, and on the other, reject making religion an other-worldly discipline that disclaims all responsibility for the social order. Rabbi Richard G. Hirsch, director of the Social

Action Center, suggests that we develop a "theology for social action" whereby we would show the relevance of tradition to contemporary social issues. He notes that ethics requires action and action involves risks; but social actions will be a stimulus for the renewal of tradition. Hirsch also espouses the notion of a Halakhah of social action to sustain the spirit of Judaism.[71]

Obviously, the Reform movement still considers the drive for social justice as the fruition of the essential teachings of Judaism.

*Interfaith Relations*

With the emergence of the Reform movement, Judaism confronted Christianity and challenged its basic premises for the first time since the forced disputations of the Middle Ages. For the first time in history, perhaps, Judaism challenged Christianity on its own terms, fearlessly assailing its teachings and questioning its ideology. Orthodoxy had shunned all contact with Christianity, refusing, in effect, to recognize its existence, disdaining dialogue with Christian clergy and theologians, even declining to enter a church. But the Reform movement changed all of this.

Some of the earlier Reformers were frankly apologists for Judaism in an attempt to curry favor with the Christian world. But soon, the apologetic tone was replaced by one of outspoken militancy and sharply arrayed polemics. Leopold Stein and Solomon Formstecher in Germany denounced Christianity as a reversion to paganism. Kaufmann Kohler followed up this line of attack in America. He analyzed the differences between the two faiths and declared Judaism's concept of God's unity and of life's holiness to be "a far superior form" than that of Christianity, for Judaism does not base its morality on love bereft of justice. And he added:

> For Christianity in its turn succeeded by again dragging the Deity into the world of sense, adopting the pagan myths of the birth and death of the gods, and sanctioning image worship. In this way it actually created a Christian plurality of gods and a "divine family" as among Greeks and Babylonians.

Emil G. Hirsch was equally outspoken. He wrote that he found nothing new in the New Testament or teachings of Jesus that had been rejected by Jews. He criticized the flaws in Jesus' character, the shortcomings of Christian theology, and the teachings of Paul, the true founder of Christianity. Hirsch assailed Christianity as an other-worldly religion as contrasted with Judaism's this-worldly "social discontent."[72]

Isaac M. Wise and Bernhard Felsenthal were battlers in a more practical way. Both sought to counter the notion of America as a "Christian country," and both sought to end Bible reading in the public schools.[73]

And yet, the Reform movement did labor passionately to improve interreligious relations. Kohler urged the study of Christianity and Islam, and introduced courses in the New Testament and Church history at the Hebrew Union College. Wise wanted Christians to come to synagogues to learn about Judaism and dispel misconceptions. The Pittsburgh Platform—elaborating on the views of Maimonides and Menahem Meiri—acknowledged that Christianity and Islam, as daughter religions of Judaism, had "a misson to aid in the spreading of monotheistic and moral truth." And the Columbus Platform urged cooperation "with all men in the establishment of the kingdom of God, of universal brotherhood, justice, truth and peace on earth."[74]

Some went even further. From time to time, a passion for Jesus has surfaced in the movement—a strange desire to capture Jesus for Judaism, so to speak. Thus, Rabbi Hyman G. Enelow declared that the "modern Jew realizes the ethical power and spiritual beauty of Jesus" because he taught a phase of Judaism that was vital and Jews should glory in what Jesus meant to the world. Stephen S. Wise delivered a sermon in 1925 urging that Jesus be accepted by Jews as a prophet which led to an explosion in the Jewish community and unequaled vilification from the Orthodox. Claude G. Montefiore echoed these sentiments in England, and Maurice N. Eisendrath picked up the theme in 1963. As recently as 1971, a member of the CCAR urged the acceptance of Jesus as our brother, teaching the Judaic ethical system, as a means of cementing bonds between Jews and Christians. His recommendation was sharply denounced by Rabbi

Balfour Brickner who said, "It is not the Christian Christ which Jews must discover but the Jewish Jesus which Christians must become more aware of."[75]

While "Jesusmania" has not captured the Reform movement, interfaith activities have. Reform rabbis have generally been involved in interreligious work, exchanging pulpits with ministers and priests, speaking before Christian groups, teaching Judaism to Christian students, working on community projects with Christian clergymen and laymen. In some cases, Reform congregations and Protestant churches have actually shared buildings.

The CCAR and UAHC have maintained a Joint Commission on Interfaith Activities, and the Reform rabbinate has consistently supported interfaith dialogue and studies. As Eugene Borowitz sees it, dialogue is vital to combat "the paganization of our civilization," to work on social issues together, and to understand differences between the faiths. A full manifesto on interfaith relations was drawn up by the CCAR in 1969. The statement welcomes interfaith conversations, with several caveats. It warns against conversion attempts and ill-informed spokesmen. It also notes that Israel is the touchstone of Judeo-Christian relations and that Christianity must relate positively to the State of Israel. It urges Jews and Christians to apply mutual respect and calls upon both groups to examine and reevaluate texts, teachings, and attitudes.[76]

*Summary*

By now it should be clear to the reader that there have been *two* Reform movements in history. One, the classical or radical Reform movement, has been theologically oriented to naturalism and social optimism, anti-Halakhic, anti-nationalistic and anti-Zionistic, and strongly inclined to ethical humanism or "Prophetic Judaism." The other, newer Reform movement retains the older theological interest, social liberalism and moral drive, while adding a new note of Zionism and nationalism as well as a healthy respect for ritual practices. The present-day

Reform movement is truly different from its older forerunner. Today's Reform Judaism contains these elements:

1. Reform sees Judaism as an evolving, ever-dynamic religious culture that adapts to every age. Flux is the only constant in Judaism.

2. Reform believes in a varied interpretation of the God concept with wide latitude for naturalists or mystics, supernaturalists or religious humanists.

3. The ethical aspects of Torah are God's revelation and forever binding. The ritual *mitzvot* are valuable means of infusing spirituality, ennobling the individual, instilling Godlike traits, and uniting the People. The Halakhah is valuable, but is not to be accepted on blind faith as coming from Heaven. It is to guide, not govern, the life of the Jew, whose conscience must be his final guide.

4. Reform believes in the unity of the Jewish People as a spiritual world entity. It urges all Jews to help one another and it seeks cooperation with Jews of all stripes.

5. Reform is deeply committed to the survival of the State of Israel, which it hopes will become a religio-spiritual center to the world and a beacon light of social justice and morality.

6. Reform is a movement in flux. It is "process" rather than a static, fixed movement. Hence, liturgy, ritual practices, and theology must constantly be revised and changed.

7. Reform is passionately committed to social activism in battling for equity, justice, and peace for all men.

8. Reform welcomes interfaith activities as a means to hasten the Messianic redemption when God's Kingship on earth will be established.

In a word, Reform believes that the strength of Judaism has been its ability to evolve and change. The survival of Judaism depends on the maintenance of that protean quality in the future. If constancy is the hallmark of Orthodoxy, then flux is the hallmark of Reform.

# Conservative Judaism—
# History

## VI

Hegel, the eminent German philosopher of history, viewed history as a process of thesis countered by antithesis, culminating in synthesis. In the case of Conservative Judaism, this analysis seems to hold true: Orthodoxy represented the thesis, Reform offered the antithesis, and Conservatism was the synthesis of the two schools of thought. Thus, if Orthodoxy is equated with tradition, while Reform's rallying cry is change, Conservatism seeks to balance the two and find a median between the poles. Whereas Orthodoxy stresses ritual and Reform emphasizes ethics, Conservatism strives to blend the two.

There are, of course, significant differences between the three ideologies. It is an erroneous simplification to define Conservative Judaism as merely "the Reform movement of East European Jews," or the middle-of-the-road compromise between the two extremes. Orthodox Jewry's rallying point, as we have noted, is Torah and Halakhah; Reform finds its axis in God. But Conservatism predicates its system on the Jewish People. Sociologically, there are differences between the groups: Reform has generally attracted the upper-class Jews; Orthodoxy's appeal has been primarily to the lower economic brackets; and Conservatism has attracted mainly the middle class. While these differentiations of socio-economic strata are rapidly disappearing, they still hold some validity.

Basically, then, Conservatism represents an attempt to check the excesses of Reform while prodding Orthodoxy into dynamic action. Conservatism seeks to conserve tradition while simultaneously recognizing the need for orderly, organic, disciplined change. It acknowledges the validity of Jewish Law as integrally related to Jewish life and survival. At the same time, however, the Conservative movement has parted with Orthodoxy over what Conservative thinkers call its intransigent refusal to adapt Halakhah to the needs of the times. In a word, Conservative Judaism emerged from the clash of German Orthodoxy with Reform; it sought to blend the best features of the two wings; and it still attempts its delicately balanced synthesis today, over a century after the Conservative approach made its unofficial debut.[1]

Conservative Judaism was born in nineteenth-century Germany. That same small community that spawned the Neo-Orthodoxy of Samson Raphael Hirsch, and the Reform of Abraham Geiger, also produced the Conservative school of Zachariah Frankel. What a superlative Jewry Germany possessed!

The German Conservative school of thought never really crystallized into a formal movement, but it was an identifiable entity nonetheless. And the man who gave it its *élan vital* was a Czech rabbi and Talmudic scholar named Zachariah Frankel (1801–75). Frankel had received a traditional yeshivah training plus a good secular education including a Ph.D. in Semitic languages. He served as rabbi in Dresden and Berlin, and finally as president of the Jewish Theological Seminary of Breslau, the first modern seminary of its kind in Germany. As we have noted previously, Frankel attended the rabbinical conferences of the 1840's, and could be described as a "moderate Reformer." But when the rabbis at the 1845 Frankfort conference ruled that the Hebrew language was no longer objectively a *sine qua non* for

Jewish life, liturgy, and learning, Frankel broke irrevocably with the Reformers. He did not found a formal movement, but he did create a new school of thought or "tendency" which he labeled with the preposterously cumbersome title of "positive-historical Judaism." His approach was "positive" because he was positively oriented towards traditional practices and laws. Yet he was also "historical" because he acknowledged the need to analyze critically and historically, scientifically and dispassionately, the institutions created by Judaism throughout its history.

Frankel incorporated this approach into his seminary in Breslau, as well as in his journal, *Zeitschrift für jüdische religiöse Interessen,* his sermons, and his scholarly writings. Aided by such giants as Yom Tov Zunz, master of liturgy and lore, and Heinrich Graetz, historian par excellence, Frankel battled both Geiger and his Reform colleagues, as well as Hirsch and the Neo-Orthodox groups. Frankel called for evolutionary rather than revolutionary changes, and he insisted that change must come from the people, for ultimately the will of the community decides the fate of law and lore. But Frankel never approved of abrogating *mitzvot* or Halakhah: he demanded religious action that would not be devoid of spirit or merely mechanistic.[2]

Frankel's positive-historical approach found some partisans in Germany, Italy, Austria, Hungary, Rumania, Poland, and England. A few synagogues in the major European cities became eventually what we would term today "Conservative" congregations. Then, too, the Jewish Theological Seminary of Vienna and the Jewish Theological Seminary of Budapest, as well as London's Jews' College, were patterned after Frankel's great Breslau school. But the Conservative movement made little headway in Europe. Like its older Reform brother, Conservatism's greatest achievements came in the New World—in America and Canada.

The unofficial "founder" of the Conservative tendency in America was Isaac Leeser (1806–68), who was born in Prussia, came to Virginia in 1828, and served as minister-*hazzan* of Philadelphia's old Spanish and Portuguese synagogue, Mikveh Israel, from 1830 to 1850, and in Beth El Emeth from 1857 until his death. Leeser was not a rabbi, nor was he even a particularly learned Jew. But he was an ardent worker for the Jewish People, a zealous battler for modern traditionalism, and a capable organizer of wide vision. He preached regularly in English; he edited the widely read magazine, *The Occident;* he advocated moderate reforms of rituals; he wrote educational texts and translated the Bible into English; he founded the first Jewish Publication Society; and he sought to unify all American Jews and rabbis in a union of peace and respect. Leeser also founded the first rabbinical seminary in America—Maimonides College —in 1867, and he served as its president until his premature death.[3]

In every way, Leeser set an example for the Conservative rabbi of the twentieth century. He introduced decorum into the service and favored "improvements" in Jewish law and liturgy, but not done "hastily, or contrary to law," so as to "bring backsliders and the lukewarm back to the pale of religion." He accepted the authority of Halakhah and wrote about the need to unite *klal Yisrael* (Catholic Israel) in synagogue federations and rabbinic bodies. He tried to work with Isaac M. Wise and the Reformers and, as we have noted, participated in the first rabbinic conference in Cleveland in 1855. The Reformers dubbed him "Orthodox," an adjective he rejected; the more traditionally inclined accused him of Reform tendencies. He ceased cooperation with Wise after the latter published his *Minhag America Prayer Book.* Leeser never forsook the dream of intergroup cooperation, however, and he remained on cordial terms with the Reformers as well as with the Orthodox rabbis like Abraham Rice and Bernard Illowy. Additionally, he was a lover of Zion and he used the pages of *The Occident* to propagate the need to colonize agricultural settlements in the Holy Land. In a word, Leeser was really the prototype of today's Conservative spiritual leader.

After Leeser's death, the void in the "Historical School" (as Professor Moshe Davis dubs the middle-of-the-road theological tendency) was filled by Reverend Sabato Morais of Philadelphia's Mikveh Israel, Rabbi Benjamin Szold of Baltimore, Rabbi

Marcus Jastrow of Philadelphia, and Rabbis Alexander Kohut, Bernard Drachman, Henry Pereira Mendes, and Frederick de Sola Mendes of New York City.[4]

Sabato Morais (1823–97) was the self-sacrificing, open-hearted leader of the Historical School. Born in Leghorn, Italy, he worked as an educator in London and came to Philadelphia in 1851, succeeding Leeser at Mikveh Israel. He endeavored to unite all dissident factions in Jewish life; he even offered to drop his beloved Sephardic ritual and accept Ashkenazic practices if that would heal the rifts in Jewish life. Morais believed in the Mosaic authorship of the Bible, under the inspiration of God. He also viewed the Oral Law as "coeval with the written statutes of the Five Holy Books." Yet, he appreciated the value of Biblical criticism and maintained that isolation from Reform Jews was an impossibility. Indeed, Morais helped Isaac M. Wise in organizing the Hebrew Union College and he served as one of its Examiners until the fateful commencement dinner of 1883.

Actually there were two distinct trends in the Historical School of the nineteenth century. Morais, Henry Pereira Mendes, and Bernard Drachman were basically traditional and rather close to the Orthodox. In fact, Mendes and Drachman helped organize the Union of Orthodox Jewish Congregations and, later on, both left the emerging Conservative group to cast in their lots with the newly reconstituted Orthodoxy. On the other hand, Szold, Jastrow, Kohut, and Frederick de Sola Mendes were moderate Reformers whose synagogues permitted mixed pews and organs, and whose personal ritual observances were far from Orthodoxy. These two camps coalesced and were united by two significant factors: Morais' inspiring leadership, and the revulsion for the radicalism of the Reform movement.

Undoubtedly, the increasing extremism of Reform had alienated the more traditional elements in American Jewry. The radical surgery of the Reform prayer books, the introduction of nontraditional practices at worship in Reform temples, the flouting of ancient *mitzvot*, such as dietary laws and marriage rules, had infuriated even the moderate Reformers. Then, too, when the Board of Delegates of American Israelites was absorbed by the Union of American Hebrew Congregations in 1878, the Historical School and the traditionalists felt—and with justification—that they had lost their voice and last vestige of influence. Nor should we forget the ever-increasing flow of East European immigrants to these shores. They were not about to worship in some austere Teutonic temple; their world was not that of Isaac M. Wise or David Einhorn.

But it was Reform's radicalism in ritual practice that really solidified the Historical School and galvanized it into action. We have already alluded to the first commencement dinner of the Hebrew Union College in 1883 at which shrimp cocktail and other *trefa* dishes were served. Morais, who was present, was incensed: he walked out forever. And as he traveled back East, he must have determined in his heart that the traditionalists would have to go it alone; the coalition with Reform was at an end. The Pittsburgh Platform was the final blow to union and cooperation. Even moderate Reformers like Szold and Jastrow were shocked, and both insisted that their congregations withdraw from the Union of American Hebrew Congregations. Morais urged like-minded rabbis and laymen to spurn the Cincinnati school and its radical leaders, and to rally to create a traditionally oriented seminary, preferably in New York City. Thus was born the Jewish Theological Seminary of America.

Morais set about studying the other modern European seminaries in Padua and Breslau for a blueprint with which to create his institution. At first, he suggested that it be called the "Orthodox Seminary." But Kohut disagreed: he wanted a more universal, consistent whole and he stated that he did not "desire it to be destined for a sect, whether reform, conservative, or orthodox." Kohut's view prevailed and the school was named the Jewish Theological Seminary of America.[5]

Morais rallied rabbis like Kohut, Szold, Jastrow, Aaron Wise, Henry Mendes, Frederick Mendes, Drachman and others to his side. In addition, he won the support of laymen of the stature of Jacob Schiff, Dr. Solomon Solis-Cohen, Joseph Blumenthal, and young Cyrus Adler. On January 31, 1886, twelve delegates gathered at New York's historic Spanish and Portuguese synagogue to establish the Jewish Theological Seminary "in conservative principles." In March of that year, sixty congregations sent delegates to Shearith Israel to help concretize the program. The term "conservative" began to be used more or less officially by partisans of the new school. It had two connotations: first, it implied a conservative rather than radical philosophy, much as the term is used in American politics today; second, it suggested thereby the desire to *conserve* or *preserve* Jewish traditions, unlike the Reform movement. Morais urged that the new school counter Reform Judaism and dedicate itself to the "knowledge and practice of historical Judaism." The preamble to the constitution stated:

> *The necessity has been made manifest for associated and organized effort on the part of Jews of America, faithful to Mosaic Law and ancestral tradition; for the purpose of keeping alive the true Jewish spirit; in particular by the establishment of a Seminary where the Bible shall be impartially taught and rabbinic literature faithfully expounded, and more especially where youth, desirous of entering the ministry, may be thoroughly grounded in Jewish knowledge and inspired by precept and the example of their instructors with the love of the Hebrew language, and a spirit of fidelity and devotion to the Jewish law.*

The by-laws indicated that the purpose of this Seminary Association was "the preservation in America of the knowledge and practice of historical Judaism as ordained in the Law of Moses *(Torat Moshe)* and expounded by the prophets *(Nebiim)* and sages *(Hakamim)* of Israel in Biblical and Talmudic writings" and the establishment of the Jewish Theological Seminary for the training of rabbis and teachers.

On January 2, 1887, the first class of eight students met at Shearith Israel. Sabato Morais became president and professor of Bible, commuting twice weekly from Philadelphia. Kohut and Jastrow, both eminent Talmudists, became professors of Talmud and rabbinics. Several other men were added to the faculty. Kohut outlined the philosophical thrust of the new school:

*This spirit shall be that of* Conservative Judaism, *the con-
serving Jewish impulse which will create in the pupils of the Seminary the tendency to recognize the dual nature of Judaism and the
Law; which unites theory and practice, identifies body and the soul,
realizes the importance of both matter and spirit, and acknowledges
the necessity of observing the Law as well as of studying it.* [6]

Joseph Blumenthal, president of the Seminary Association,
described the new institution as a place for learning "historical,
traditional Judaism based on the Bible as interpreted by our
sages." He noted that the teachers would recognize the validity
of Jewish law, would adhere strictly to the Jewish faith, but
would also propagate secular studies as well as American citizenship. The mood would be one of "wise and reverent Conservatism" and reaction against the radicalism threatening to
engulf American Jewry. In an obvious thrust at Isaac M. Wise,
Blumenthal called for "Judaism in America" rather than
"American Judaism."

The Seminary set up a Preparatory course, a Junior course,
and a Senior course. The Bible, which was to be the principal
text, would be critically and accurately taught; the Talmud
would be made applicable to the conditions of Jewish life; Jewish
history would be stressed. Moreover, every graduate was expected to receive a college degree from a recognized university
by the time of ordination. After a time, the school moved to
Cooper Union and then to a Lexington Avenue brownstone.
Later it acquired its own building on Morningside Heights, near
Columbia University. The first graduate was ordained in 1893
and became world famous in later years as Chief Rabbi of the
British Empire, Rabbi Joseph H. Hertz. There were other distinguished alumni like Rabbi Mordecai M. Kaplan. Yet the student
body remained small, funds were lacking, there was no library,
the faculty was part time, and American Jewry seemed uninter-
ested. After Morais' death in 1897, Henry Pereira Mendes and
Bernard Drachman tried valiantly to keep the school going. But
it was no good: by 1901, it seemed that the Seminary would
collapse and leave the field to the Hebrew Union College.

Leaderless, without purpose or direction, losing out to the Reform college and failing to attract the newly arrived Orthodox masses, the Seminary was financially bankrupt and spiritually barren. But a group of dedicated and zealous laymen refused to let it die. Dr. Cyrus Adler gathered with several of the supporters of the old Seminary, such as Jacob Schiff and Adolphus S. Solomons, and added a distinguished group of leaders including Felix Warburg, Louis Marshall, Daniel and Simon Guggenheim, Isidor Straus, Leonard Lewisohn, and Judge Mayer Sulzberger. Most of these men were Reform; yet Adler was able to persuade them to support the Seminary in order to service the East European masses who would surely not be attracted to the Teutonic, antiseptic Reform, and in order to maintain a rabbinical school in New York City, the center of the American Jewish community. Adler became executive administrator of the newly reorganized Seminary and he persuaded his rich friends to raise $500,000 for an endowment fund. The Seminary was saved financially; but the spiritual leader was yet to be found.[7]

That leader had been in the mind of Cyrus Adler since 1890. From that time, Adler had sought to woo a young Cambridge professor to come to the Seminary. The professor had made quite a name for himself: born in Rumania in 1849, educated first in traditional yeshivot and later in Vienna's Jewish Theological Seminary and in Berlin, he also studied at various universities and was ordained a rabbi in 1879. As tutor to Claude Montefiore in England, he found entrée to the English cultural world. The red-bearded Rumanian Hasid was appointed reader in rabbinics at Cambridge and, later on, professor of Hebrew at the University of London. He achieved world renown as discoverer of the Cairo *genizah*, the hoard of ancient Hebrew manuscripts. The man was none other than Solomon Schechter.[8]

Schechter had been rather happy in England. But several factors helped him decide upon beginning a new career in the New World. He complained to Judge Sulzberger that he was grossly underpaid. He was anxious to raise his children in a more congenial Jewish atmosphere than prevailed at Cambridge. He objected to England's role in the Boer War and he disdained English snobbery and class-consciousness. Above all, he was excited by the challenge of teaching Torah to young American Jews in a free, unfettered, unrepressed atmosphere. And so Solomon Schechter accepted the call to head the newly reorganized Seminary in 1901.

The reorganized Seminary that Schechter was to lead was established, as the preamble to its charter put it, "for the purpose of establishing and maintaining a theological seminary for the perpetuation of the tenets of the Jewish religion; the cultivation of Hebrew literature; the pursuit of Biblical and archaeological research; the advancement of Jewish scholarship, the establishment of a library; and for the education and training of Jewish rabbis and teachers." Moreover, the new institution would champion "the preservation in America of the knowledge and practice of historical Judaism, as contained in the Laws of Moses and expounded by the Prophets and Sages of Israel in Biblical and Talmudic writings. . . ."

When Dr. Schechter came to New York in 1902, he found a demoralized institution with virtually no full-time faculty, little broad support among the laity, and no rich or famous alumni on whom he could count. Yet he plunged into his task with unexcelled zeal. In his inaugural address, he expressed the hope that the Seminary would be a "theological centre which should be all things to all men, reconciling all parties, and appealing to all sections of the community." He wanted the Seminary to eschew partisanship or polemics; rather, Schechter urged that the school should solve difficulties of Torah and doubts, bring back the estranged, and give peace to the world. He insisted on absolute academic freedom:

> *I would consider my work . . . a complete failure if this institution would not in the future produce such extremes as, on the one side, a raving mystic who would denounce me as a sober Philistine; on the other side, an advanced critic who would rail at me as a narrow-minded fanatic, while a third devotee of strict orthodoxy would raise protest against any critical view I may entertain.* [9]

These words proved to be prophetic: the same Seminary that boasted of its great iconoclast, Dr. Mordecai M. Kaplan, also had on its faculty in later years the neo-Hasid, Dr. Abraham J. Heschel. In fact, the Seminary has consistently maintained academic freedom and a liberality of viewpoints and theological expressions.

Schechter set about creating a great faculty. He brought Dr. Louis Ginzberg as professor of Talmud, Dr. Alexander Marx to teach history, Dr. Israel Davidson as professor of medieval literature, Dr. Israel Friedlander to teach Bible, and Dr. Mordecai M. Kaplan, a graduate of the old Seminary, as instructor in homiletics. With the help of Judge Mayer Sulzberger, Schechter founded the library that was ultimately to become the leading library of Judaism in the world. In 1909 Schechter organized the Teachers Institute and invited Mordecai M. Kaplan to head it. The Seminary was true to the ideals of *Jüdische Wissenschaft* which Schechter had imbibed from his masters, Isaac H. Weiss and Meir Friedmann of Vienna. It taught classics in a critical light, and though Schechter disdained Higher Criticism of the Bible, the approach to Biblical and rabbinic subjects was far from Orthodox. Schechter insisted that "a school of Jewish learning which should embrace all the departments of Jewish thought, and give it that scientific thoroughness and finish which alone deserves the name of research" would also enable Judaism to compete with the hostile intellectual forces "often more dangerous to us than pogroms and direct persecutions."[10]

The newly re-organized Seminary had a great impact on the American community, and Schechter rapidly rose to eminence in Jewish life. But it failed to fill the needs of the East European masses, partly because of Schechter's negativism to Yiddish, partly because of the gap between the two worlds involved, and partly because the Orthodox disdained Seminary alumni and impugned their rabbinical qualifications. We have already noted how the Union of Orthodox Jewish Congregations disavowed Seminary graduates in 1903 and 1914, accusing them of ignorance in Talmudics and laxity in observance. Still, there were attempts to merge the Seminary and the Rabbi Isaac Elchanan

Theological Seminary. But the attempt to bridge the gap between Jacob Schiff's "rich man's uptown institution" and the humble yeshivah of the downtown East European Orthodox failed. A last approach was made by Louis Marshall in 1927 and it, too, was abortive. The Seminary has remained the training ground of Conservatism alone, despite Schechter's hope to shape it into a school for all Jewry.[11]

Schechter's impact on American life and on the emerging Conservative movement was considerable. It was Schechter, for example, who swung the Conservatives into the Zionist camp with a public espousal of that cause in 1906. That move proved painful: it provoked a nasty controversy in the public press with the Seminary's Maecenas, Jacob Schiff, who, along with the other "Our Crowd" Jews who sustained the Seminary, resented any attempt to nationalize Judaism or dilute their Americanism. Still, Schechter persevered, and although he warned against secular Zionism in a 1915 statement, the Conservative movement remained solidly in the ranks of Zionism.[12]

Solomon Schechter also preached the need to work for what he called "Catholic Israel"—*klal Yisrael,* or universal Jewry. He strove to cooperate with Jews of all stripes in order to advance the cause of Torah on these shores. Despite his sharp criticism of the Reform movement, he was on very cordial terms with Kaufmann Kohler, president of the Hebrew Union College. Schechter lectured at the Cincinnati school and Kohler was awarded an honorary degree by the New York institution. Schechter joined others in the great work of the *Jewish Encyclopedia,* the Jewish Publication Society translation of the Bible, and a host of other cooperative endeavors that transcended party lines. He set the tone of intergroup cooperation that has become part of Conservatism's philosophy down through the years.

That the Seminary became the center for Jewish critical scholarship was due in no small measure to Schechter's personal commitment to critical research. He produced a stream of works in theology and rabbinics as well as important textual studies. Louis Ginzberg proved to be a Talmudist par excellence; Israel

Davidson published basic studies in liturgy and medieval literature; and the rest of the faculty were equally seminal. The hopes
placed in Solomon Schechter by the lay backers of the reorganized Seminary were not frustrated or dashed.

After Schechter's death in 1915, there was a tremendous void
in the movement. It was not clear who was to succeed the charismatic Cambridge Hasid: some favored Professor Friedlander,
others preferred Professor Ginzberg. After several years of indecision, Dr. Cyrus Adler, who had served as acting president,
was appointed president, occupying the post until his death in
1940. However, Adler was not a rabbi; moreover, he was simultaneously president of Philadelphia's Dropsie College and active
in a score of organizations. Obviously he could give the Seminary neither the time nor the ideological thrust it needed so
desperately. Apart from the construction of its present campus
in New York City in 1929, the movement made slow and insub-
stantial progress during Adler's regime. There were very few
Conservative congregations and Seminary alumni either took
Orthodox posts or else drifted into the Reform movement.
Ideologically, the movement languished under Adler's pallid,
creedless theology that eschewed party labels and sought to
satisfy everyone. His non-Zionist stance further alienated the
masses of East European Jews, as did his condescending attitude
towards the Yiddish-speaking population. By the end of the
Great Depression, Conservative Jewry was still a weak, ineffectual, floundering school in American Jewish life.[13]

Adler was succeeded at the helm of the movement in 1940 by
an American-born alumnus of the Seminary, Rabbi Louis Finkelstein (born 1895). Finkelstein restored much of the charismatic leadership that marked Schechter's tenure. He expanded
the Seminary's activities vastly and developed Conservative Judaism into a world-wide movement. Finkelstein opened the Jewish Museum in New York City in 1947; he began the Cantor's
Institute in 1952; he added the University of Judaism in Los
Angeles in 1947 and the Jerusalem campus in 1962; he greatly
expanded the faculties and the student bodies. In an attempt to
convey Judaism's message to the general public, Dr. Finkelstein

helped sponsor the highly successful *Eternal Light* radio and TV programs which won numerous awards. Moreover, he was the moving force in the creation of the Institute for Religious and Social Studies, which, since 1940, has brought together scholars of all faiths and traditions in an attempt to foster interreligious dialogue and fraternal understanding. The more than thirty years of Finkelstein's leadership have proved to be the era of greatest growth and expansion for Conservative Judaism in the United States, as well as in Canada, South America, Israel, and other lands. In 1972 Dr. Finkelstein retired and was replaced by Professor Gerson D. Cohen as chancellor and head of the faculties. Today there are over 1,000 students and 100 faculty members in the various divisions of the Seminary.

The second organ of the Conservative movement was its rabbinical body, established in 1901 as the Alumni Association of the Jewish Theological Seminary. In 1919 the name was changed to the Rabbinical Assembly of America, and non-Seminary graduates were also admitted provided they fulfilled the requirements of the group. The Constitution of the Assembly states:

> *The object of this organization shall be to promote Conservative Judaism; to cooperate with the Jewish Theological Seminary of America and with the United Synagogue of America; to advance the cause of Jewish learning; to promote the welfare of the members; and to foster the spirit of fellowship and cooperation among the rabbis and other Jewish scholars.*

Now known as the Rabbinical Assembly, the organization comprises over 1,000 members in several countries. The Rabbinical Assembly holds an annual convention, publishes a yearly *Proceedings,* and in conjunction with the laymen of the Conservative movement, issues the quarterly *Conservative Judaism.*

The third institution of Conservative Judaism is its congregational body, the United Synagogue of America. There had been attempts as early as 1868 in New York City to form a congregational union to strengthen Sabbath observance. The delegates bemoaned the fact that despite the beautiful temples, organs,

choirs, eloquent preachers, and decorous services, the synagogues were shockingly empty. Twenty-three congregations
joined forces in an effort to remedy the situation. The group met
again in 1870 seeking to improve the liturgy without discarding
Hebrew, but there were no practical results. Reverend Sabato
Morais and Reverend Samuel Isaacs then issued a call for an
American *minhag* that would be both traditional and modern.
Morais even offered to abandon the Sephardic usage in order to
unify American Jewry. He declared that the time had arrived for
"reconstructing" another perfectly uniform and more conform-
able Judaism to meet changed conditions. "We must work to
preserve historical Judaism, though for its sake concessions for
which we are unprepared may be demanded. . . ." Still, the
Historical School was unable to muster its forces.[14]

Finally, in 1910, eleven Seminary alumni joined with faculty
members of the Jewish Theological Seminary, Dropsie College,
and Gratz College in Philadelphia to form a union of Conservative synagogues. Schechter had given the impetus a year earlier
when he called for such a union, which he envisioned as his
"greatest bequest" to American Jewry. Among the driving
forces was Dr. Mordecai M. Kaplan. Kaplan, Herman Rubenovitz, Charles I. Hoffman, and other seminary alumni, devoted
their convention at Arverne, N.Y., in 1911 to developing a Conservative Union. Dr. Schechter, Dr. Adler, and Judah Magnes,
the former Reform rabbi, added their talents to the project.
Finally, in 1913 the new group was about to be born. The name
posed a problem: some insisted on "Conservative Union"; others wanted to include the adjective "Orthodox." Schechter
sought to avoid partisan labels and prevailed upon the group to
accept the innocuous name of a British synagogal organization
—and so it became the United Synagogue of America.[15]

In New York City in 1913, twenty-two congregations from
New York, New Jersey, Philadelphia, Baltimore, Kansas City,
Boston, Denver, Detroit, Norfolk, Rochester, and Montreal
joined in what Schechter dubbed a "work of Heaven" to form
the United Synagogue of America. The Preamble to the Charter
stated that the purposes were:

*The advancement of the cause of Judaism in America and the
maintenance of Jewish tradition in its historic continuity.*

*To assert and establish loyalty to the Torah and its historical
exposition,*

*To further the observance of the Sabbath and the dietary laws,*

*To preserve in the service the reference to Israel's past and the hopes
for Israel's restoration,*

*To maintain the traditional character of the liturgy with Hebrew
as the language of prayer,*

*To foster Jewish religious life in the home, as expressed in tradi-
tional observances,*

*To encourage the establishment of Jewish religious schools, in the
curricula of which the study of the Hebrew language and literature
shall be given a prominent place, both as the key to the true understanding of Judaism, and as a bond holding together the scattered
communities of Israel throughout the world.*

The Preamble further indicated that while the United Synagogue would not endorse innovations introduced by its con-
stituents, it would embrace "all elements essentially loyal to
traditional Judaism" and in sympathy with the stated purposes.
At the outset, then, congregations that worshiped with bare
heads or prayed from the *Union Prayer Book* were excluded, while
congregations using organs or allowing mixed seating were not
—even though these departures from Orthodox norms were not
endorsed.

Schechter was chosen first president of the United Synagogue. In his inaugural address he reiterated his nonpartisan
conviction that "life is too short for feuds." He declared:

*Indeed, what we intend to accomplish is not to create a new party,
but to consolidate an old one, which has always existed in this
country, but was never conscious of its strength, nor perhaps realized
the need for organization. I refer to the large numbers of Jews who,
thoroughly American in habits of life and modes of thinking and, in
many cases, imbued with the best culture of the day, have always
maintained Conservative principles and remained aloof from the
Reform Movement which swept over the country. They are sometimes*

*stigmatized as the neo-Orthodox. This is not correct . . . It was the normal state of the Jew in Spain.* [16]

Schechter called for decorum in services as well as English sermons as the only means of stemming the flight of young Jews from the synagogues. He demanded modern religious schools, Jewish education for girls, and a role for women in the work of the United Synagogue. In his 1914 address he appealed for higher standards for religious schools and deeper Hebrew knowledge. In line with Schechter's appeal, Dr. Mordecai M. Kaplan, vice-president of the United Synagogue of America, plunged into a study of educational needs and produced a gloomy report that painted a bleak picture of the anemic religious schools that comprised the movement. Clearly, the first priority of the day was to create good textbooks, curricula, and teachers, and to upgrade school standards.

After Schechter's death, several other faculty members headed the United Synagogue, including Dr. Louis Ginzberg and Dr. Cyrus Adler. But in the last few decades the presidents of the United Synagogue of America have been laymen, although the executive directors have always been rabbis. The organization grew painfully slowly at first, for, truth to tell, there were virtually no truly Conservative synagogues in those early years. The National Women's League was formed in 1917 as a female adjunct to the United Synagogue of America. The Young People's League began its program in 1921 and the National Federation of Jewish Men's Clubs was organized in 1929. The United Synagogue of America sought to introduce its brand of Judaism into Palestine in 1926 with the erection of the famous Yeshurun Synagogue in Jerusalem. But the Orthodox "establishment" quickly squelched the attempt and Conservative Judaism was unable to make much headway in the Holy Land until rather recently. By the 1940's the movement had grown to over 300 congregations but still lagged behind its Orthodox and Reform counterparts. However, after World War II, Conservative Judaism and the United Synagogue of America enjoyed a phenomenal growth. By 1972 there were 830 congregations and about one and a half million members affiliated with the movement. So rapid was its expansion that the Seminary has not been able to supply enough rabbis to fill the Conservative congregations.

Conservative Judaism officially became a world-wide movement in 1959 with the founding of the World Council of Synagogues. The goal was to create Conservative congregations throughout the world and unite them under the aegis of the United Synagogue of America and the Seminary "to advocate the centrality and preeminence of the synagogue in the life of the Jewish people, . . . to deepen our dedication to the prophetic ideal of creating in the land of our fathers a Jewish community which shall pattern its life by the ideals and teachings of the Torah, and which shall seek to be a 'light unto the nations'; and to relate the ideals and practices of Judaism to contemporary life and thought. . . ." By 1972 the Council had created a Seminary for teachers and rabbis in Buenos Aires, Argentina; had published texts and prayer books in Spanish; and had established congregations in Central and South America, India, Israel, and Australia. While rabbis in England, Denmark, and Sweden are affiliated, there is still no *formal* Conservative movement in Europe.

As to the situation in Israel, the Conservative movement was notably tardy in building a formal structure, notwithstanding its long-standing commitment to Zionism and the State of Israel. Chancellor Louis Finkelstein had opposed exporting American brands of religion to Israel, and the Orthodox parties adamantly rejected any efforts to establish Conservative synagogues or to grant permission for Conservative clergymen to officiate at marriages, divorces, or funerals.

Nevertheless, the Conservative movement made its presence felt in 1962 with the erection of a student center, dormitory, synagogue, and classrooms at Neve Schechter near the Israel Museum in Jerusalem. The Schocken Institute for Jewish Research in Jerusalem was given to the Seminary, further expanding its holdings in Israel. By 1972, Conservative congregations were operating in Jerusalem, Tel Aviv, Rehovot, Ashkelon,

Netanya, Haifa, and Kiryat Tivon, and over sixty members of the Rabbinical Assembly were living and working in Israel. Increasingly, the Conservative movement has been pressuring the government for full recognition of its legitimacy and right to equal treatment by the State of Israel, and the 1971 Convention of the Rabbinical Assembly was held in Jerusalem specifically to establish a Conservative presence. Finally, the United Synagogue of Israel opened a building in Jerusalem in 1972 and a full-time director has begun to coordinate its activities.

The Conservative movement has also developed a vast program of youth activities. In 1951 it founded the United Synagogue Youth, which numbered over 25,000 members around the world by 1972. Its élite students have been formed into the Leaders Training Fellowship, a product of Mordecai M. Kaplan's planning genius. Long opposed to Day Schools as "parochial" and "un-American," the Conservative group has now joined wholeheartedly in such educational projects, and by 1972 there were 42 Solomon Schechter Day Schools in the United States, Canada, and Israel, with over 7,000 students. The movement has spearheaded the idea of Hebrew-speaking summer camps, and today there are ten Ramah Camps in the United States, Canada, Argentina, and Israel, with an enrollment of over 3,000 children. A college organization, *Atid*, was set up in the 1960's and now has a membership of 1,000 collegians.

One may ask why the Conservative movement has exploded so dramatically. There are several answers. After World War II, American Jewry experienced a religious revival—no doubt precipitated by both the Holocaust and the birth of the State of Israel. As a result, thousands of new synagogues proliferated throughout the land. Most of these synagogues sprang up in suburbia—in the suburbs of Long Island and Westchester; the San Fernando Valley of Los Angeles; the Elkins Park suburb of Philadelphia; Oak Park, outside of Detroit; Highland Park and Skokie near Chicago. These were basically middle-class areas; the reason that the Conservative movement held its greatest attraction for the middle class was that it seemed to epitomize middle-class values, sociologically and religiously.[17]

Additionally, the Conservative movement, being a middle-of-the-road, coalition, centrist movement, successfully captured the *Zeitgeist* of postwar America. The "vital center"—to borrow Arthur M. Schlesinger's phrase—was the dominant force in America; extremes in politics and religion were assiduously eschewed. Consequently, Conservative Judaism, as a centrist religious ideology, captured the fancy of the vital center of American Jews who were repelled by old-fashioned Orthodoxy, on the one hand, and churchlike Reform, on the other.

Finally, the vast majority of American Jews are children or grandchildren of East European Jews who were scarcely attracted to the Germanic flavor of American Reform. The cold, austere, hatless service of Reform temples did not appeal to them; they were seeking a blend of the traditional and the modern—and that blend they found in Conservative Judaism.

The observer looks in vain for great programs or pronouncements from Conservative Judaism. There are no Pittsburgh or Columbus Platforms in the movement's history; no grand pronouncements have been issued by its leading lights or rabbinic organizations. Yet its impact has been deeply felt and its organic growth has been powerful. Many have criticized Conservative Judaism for failing to issue a platform; many have attacked it as a movement of all things to all men. Conservative leaders have countered that by avoiding dogmatic stands, the movement has attracted a coalition of diverse forces. And indeed it cannot be denied that apart from its own internal growth, the Conservative movement has exerted a great influence on its sister movements: it has brought Reform back to more traditional practices, and it has forced Orthodoxy to modernize its views.

The Conservative movement has had its internal problems. We have already noted that its leaders emanated from the ranks of the rabbis and Seminary professors. The rabbis created the Jewish Theological Seminary; the Seminary professors fashioned the United Synagogue of America. Tensions between the rabbinical, lay, and congregational bodies have never been totally resolved. For years the Seminary faculty controlled the Rabbinical Assembly—much to the annoyance of the rabbis. For example, the Law Committee was totally dominated by Seminary professors. They represented a very conservative, cautious trend, and the responsa of Professors Louis Ginzberg, Boaz Cohen, and Michael Higger are virtually Orthodox in tone. A significant revamping of the Law Committee took place in 1927 with an eye to granting a voice to varied ideological views. But nothing terribly dramatic resulted from that step. In 1948 a revolution occurred and a new committee on Jewish Law and Standards was set up by the Rabbinical Assembly with representation from all shades of the movement—right, left, and center. As a result of the reorganization, far-reaching and revolutionary decisions were arrived at by the Committee that changed the direction of the Conservative movement and altered its hitherto timorous approach to Halakhah.[18]

The attitude of the Conservative movement to Zionism and Israel is another case in point. Dr. Cyrus Adler, while a believer in the *religious* validity of Zion, was never a *political* Zionist and rejected attempts to link the Seminary or the United Synagogue to political Zionism. Likewise, Dr. Louis Finkelstein rejected any secular-political Zionist movement and kept the Seminary officially aloof from Zionist activities. But faculty and student sentiments were overwhelmingly pro-Zionist and the Rabbinical Assembly had always been in the Zionist camp. After 1948 the Seminary's administration finally swung over to total support for the State of Israel and the old tensions disappeared.

The stresses and strains within the movement and resentment of Seminary domination of the various wings of Conservative Jewry have been alleviated, but have not totally evaporated.

With the passage of the years, Conservative Judaism has ceased feeding off Orthodoxy for its lay and rabbinical leadership. Already in the 1950's Rabbi Arthur Hertzberg found that the students of the Jewish Theological Seminary were predominantly from Conservative homes. Obviously, the movement is reproducing itself and no longer needs Orthodox dropouts to survive.[19]

But the movement has been drifting of late. Its phenomenal growth of the forties and fifties began to taper off by the end of the sixties. Its approach to ritual observance—even among the lay leadership—is a crazy-quilt pattern, ranging from full observance to virtual non-observance. The vast majority of Conservative Jews are almost indistinguishable from their Reform brothers. The coalition of the various groupings seems to be breaking up; in fact, the Reconstructionist wing has virtually seceded from the parent body to form its own movement. Many are calling for an ideological platform; others fear heresy-hunting dogmatism should that come to pass. Then, too, the blurring of borders between left-wing Orthodoxy and increasingly traditional Reform has made the Conservative position less secure and less definitive. Is Conservative Judaism merely a passing movement, just a more-or-less Reform variation, as David Philipson had suggested? Will the Conservative movement coalesce with the Reform group as was predicted by Maurice Eisendrath? Will the gap between the rabbinic leadership and the lay masses become unbridgeable?[20]

There are no simple answers to these problems. Whether there will be a continued growth of the movement or a gradual convergence with Reform will be determined, perhaps, by the forthcoming decade. But this is certain: Conservative Judaism helped stem the tide of rampant Reform and won thousands to Judaism who would have gone nowhere. For this alone, Conservative Judaism has earned a place in Jewish history.

# Conservative Judaism— Ideology

# VII

Conservative Judaism is a protean movement. Consequently, it has produced no definitive program of beliefs and practices, nor any one "accepted" ideology. Moreover, it is a coalition of many diverse elements ranging from the almost Orthodox to the almost Reform. This, too, explains its reluctance to congeal into a monolithic theology. Finally, it is a pragmatic movement: life and practical realities have set the pattern for Conservatism rather than platforms and ideologies.

Actually, this feature was true of classical rabbinic theology, which was protean, organismic, and undogmatic. Solomon Schechter had observed that "the best theology is that which is not consistent, and this advantage the theology of the Synagogue possesses to its utmost extent." Schechter also concluded that any attempt at an orderly and complete system of rabbinic theology "is an impossible task" because "whatever the faults of the Rabbis were, consistency was not one of them." The old rabbis seem to have thought that "the true health of a religion is to have a theology without being aware of it; and thus they hardly ever made—nor could they make—any attempt towards working their theology into a formal system." Louis Ginzberg agreed with Schechter's evaluation that rabbinic theology lacked a systematic structure. With God as reality, revelation as a fact, the Torah as a rule of life, and the hope of Redemption as a most vivid expectation, the sages felt no need for formulating their dogmas into a creed, wrote Schechter. And while the contemporary Conservative theologian Dr. Max Kadushin criticizes this view and insists that there was a rabbinic value-system—albeit an organismic rather than a logical one in the Greek mode—he is nevertheless forced to admit that the rabbinic pattern of thought is dynamic rather than static, and that it lacks neat propositions. Moreover, Kadushin shows that even the most basic value-concepts have an indeterminacy and elasticity about them. Conservative Judaism has made a virtue out of the rabbinic predilection for undogmatic thinking that allowed for a wide range of beliefs.[1]

Conservative Judaism has proved to be rich in thinkers and ideologists. Alexander Kohut gave shape to the proto-Conservative movement; Solomon Schechter's impact is still felt today; Louis Ginzberg, Louis Finkelstein, Max Kadushin, Robert Gordis, Abraham J. Heschel, and a flock of others have created an imposing superstructure. And Dr. Mordecai M. Kaplan, the *enfant terrible* of the movement, has left an indelible impression on Conservative Judaism. Whereas Orthodoxy virtually abandoned theology and Reform forsook Halakhah, Conservatism has sought to fuse the two elements of Judaism. Schechter insisted that there *are* dogmas in Judaism and he rebuked those who preached "Believe what you like but conform to this or that mode of life." He noted: "We usually urge that in Judaism religion means life; but we forget that a life without guiding principles and thoughts is a life not worth living." More recently Dr. Heschel echoed these thoughts, calling for "depth theology" and insisting that "religious behaviorism" is only one aspect of Jewish life.[2]

Periodically, there have been demands for the formulation of a creed for Conservative Jews. Rabbis Morris Adler and Robert

Gordis have repeatedly espoused the view that the formulation of a creed or set of guiding principles would help end much of the anarchy that seems to reign in the Conservative camp and would strengthen the movement. Heschel, on the other hand, sharply criticized creeds and dogmas; he described them as dangerous "vicarious faith." The essence of Judaism, he said, is a demand rather than creed, faith in God, Torah and Israel. But so far, Conservatism has shunned all such efforts at creating either a theological creed or a ritual code. Conservative Judaism has preferred to remain in flux, allowing the widest latitude to its adherents.[3]

Although the writings and thinking of Conservative theologians and leaders are bafflingly inconsistent, there are "emphatic trends" that are discernible. By careful sifting, we can pinpoint consensus and generally held opinions on some issues, although an inconsistent and variegated pattern persists in other areas.

### The Nature of Judaism

What is Judaism? Is it a religion? an ethnic entity? a culture? a civilization? Here Conservative Judaism has had a good deal to say.

Solomon Schechter described Judaism as a divine religion, not a mere complex of racial peculiarities and tribal customs. It is also a proselytizing religion; its mission is to bring God's kingdom on earth, and to include in that kingdom all mankind. Finally, when we describe Judaism as a religion we imply chiefly a *Weltanschauung* and the worship of God by means of holiness both in thought and action. While Schechter conceded that a definition of Judaism is no less perplexing than a definition of God, he sharply criticized the effort of Geiger and the Reformers to reduce Judaism to the status of merely a religious sect, stripped of all national content.[4]

Professor Israel Friedlander wrote passionately of a "Jewish culture." He agreed with Schechter that it is a fatal error to think of Judaism as merely a *creed* rather than a *culture* or the full inner life of the people. Friedlander argued that if Judaism is to withstand external pressures, "it must again break the narrow frame of a creed and resume its original function as a culture, as the expression of the Jewish spirit and the whole life of the Jews." He envisioned that the modern Jew will stress less the ceremonial and more the cultural features of our people—including literature, art, music, and the best of the modern world. Friedlander died tragically early—a victim of Russian pogromists who killed him on his mission of mercy to the Ukraine in 1920. But he left followers, notably Rabbi Mordecai M. Kaplan, who defined Judaism as "an evolving, religious civilization." Kaplan's approach (which we will treat in the next chapters) profoundly influenced the Conservative movement. He attracted numerous disciples, as well as critics.[5]

Louis Ginzberg, the eminent Talmudist, was one of the sharpest thinkers in the movement. He insisted that "Judaism is a religion of deed, expressing itself in observances which are designated to achieve the moral elevation of man and give reality to his religious spirit." Louis Finkelstein defines Judaism as "a way of life that endeavors to transform virtually every human action into a means of communion with God." Abraham J. Heschel described Judaism as an answer to man's ultimate questions, the response to the mystery of life. It is "a religion of history, a religion of time rather than things or places."[6]

But the most common definition of Judaism found in virtually all writers is Kaplan's definition: Judaism is the evolving, religious civilization of the Jewish People. Judaism is more than mere creed, more than merely a legal, Halakhic order; it is a complex of law, lore, literature, *mitzvot*, history, ethics, culture, and loyalties. It is a total civilization.

What is Conservative Judaism? Interestingly, early leaders of the movement, such as Kohut, Schechter, Adler, and Ginzberg, eschewed party labels. They preferred to speak of a "Conservative tendency" rather than a movement. Schechter nurtured a fond dream that he would unite the traditional elements in American Jewish life rather than create a new party or sect;

Adler assiduously pursued the same course. But the dream was naive and party lines were drawn willy-nilly.

Actually, the Conservative school of thought began to articulate its philosophy rather early. The new movement set out to *conserve* or *preserve* tradition. In this sense, it resembled Orthodoxy. But at the same time, it was convinced that Judaism was a living organism that had evolved historically, had grown organically, had adapted periodically to new conditions. "History reigns supreme," opined Schechter, and he insisted that Judaism is an organism with natural growth rooted in the Torah. In this regard, Conservatism resembles Reform Judaism. Schechter urged a blending of rationalism and mysticism, of critical scholarship with Hasidic piety.

> *Is it not time . . . that we revise our theology and even learn from the Zionists about the necessity of perpetuating the Jewish nation, if Judaism is at all to survive the crisis? . . . The new theology should consist in the best that all men of Israel, including Geiger, gave us, as well as Akiba Eger's and Mordecai Baneth's loyalty to the law, Zunz's and Krochmal's insights into Jewish history, Baal Shem's mysticism and love for Israel's nationality of Herzl or Ahad Ha'am.* [7]

Schechter insisted that the history of the interpretation of the Scriptures is liable to variations through "subjective notions of successive generations regarding religion and the method and scope of its application." At the same time, he was equally insistent that "we cannot create halting places at will. We must either remain faithful to history or go the way of all flesh. . . ." In an obvious jibe at Reform, he cautioned against "radical amputations" because "Judaism is absolutely incompatible with the abandonment of the Torah," for such a program is "Paulinism." Torah is the very life of Judaism, as is Hebrew, he declared. And universalistic Judaism minus ceremonies is contrary to the Bible, Talmud, and all Jewish opinion.[8]

This delicate balance between tradition and change has not been easily maintained by Conservatism. For years, the radicals and the traditionalists have been exchanging blows, with the one wing stressing the need for dynamic change, the other insisting upon tradition. The more traditional Louis Finkelstein sought to enunciate "the principles that unite us" in an address to the Rabbinical Assembly in 1927. He indicated that he was prepared to discard certain anachronistic laws, except marriage laws and Sabbath and Festival rules. He agreed that change is valid "provided always that the ultimate purpose of the change is to strengthen the attachment of Israel to the whole of the Torah, and that it does not defeat its own end by striking at the fundamentals of Judaism." What, then, unites the Conservative movement? asked Finkelstein. Our concept of God, Torah, the validity of change in the *mitzvot*, love for the Land of Israel, Hebrew, the Jewish People, and loyalty to the Jewish Theological Seminary, was his answer. But immediately Rabbi Eugene Kohn, prominently identified with the Reconstructionist wing, challenged the *entire* thesis and insisted that "only our common devotion to the Seminary unites us."[9]

An equally thorny dilemma for Conservatism has been posed by the challenge of the *Zeitgeist,* the changing spiritual and philosophical moods of the day. Schechter—obviously piqued by what he considered Reform's obsequious acceptance of the *Zeitgeist*—proclaimed that "there is something better even than 'modernity'—which is, eternity." And Heschel, in much the same vein, wrote that "it is not *utility* we seek in religion but eternity." And yet, Conservatism has absorbed and digested the best thought of the day—be it Rosenzweig's existentialism, Dewey's pragmatism, or Buber's and Heschel's neo-Hasidism.[10]

Others have labored valiantly to define the undefinable. Robert Gordis writes that Conservative Judaism is "modern, traditional Judaism, or to be more explicit, the modern interpretation of the traditional Judaism." The late Rabbi Morris Adler viewed Conservative Judaism as a median approach between Orthodoxy's reverence for tradition and Reform's adulation of change, and he called for "positive and unambiguous affirmations" of the Conservative approach. Rabbi Mordecai Waxman describes Conservative Judaism as a technique for understanding and teaching Judaism marked by several principles: 1) re-

spect for the Jewish past and discernment of its guiding principles; 2) the internal dynamism of Judaism interacting with the
external circumstances; 3) a doctrine and a tradition that
changed by *evolution* rather than *revolution*. Waxman adds that
Conservatism believes in "vertical democracy" in that the past
and the future have a voice in ongoing institutions; that it is
enriched by modern thought; and that it blends authority with
interpretation. Rabbi Simon Greenberg declared that the Conservative movement in Judaism (he avoids the use of the more
sectarian term, "Conservative Judaism") has been closest to the
spirit of traditional, historical Judaism in that *"it did not define itself
in dogmas or in publicly announced platforms."* But Greenberg delineates the several components of the movement as consisting
of: 1) the scientific knowledge of Judaism; 2) the emphasis on
Judaism as a Torah-centered civilization; 3) the acceptance of
*klal Yisrael*, the Brotherhood of Israel, as a vital need, notwithstanding the diversity of Jewish life; 4) the importance of innovation without regimentation.[11]

Obviously, Conservative Judaism has been reluctantly groping to define itself, partly by choice and partly by virtue of the
facts of life. Perhaps Rabbi Jacob Agus has put his finger on the
reason for its reluctance in his statement that Reform followed
the Maimonidean approach in establishing rationalistic guiding
principles, while Conservatism is more in the tradition of Yehudah Halevi, for whom Judaism is emotionalism, poetry, and
divine revelation. At any rate, Conservative Judaism is unquestionably a living force—notwithstanding its avoidance of self-
definition—and a vital movement that seeks to blend tradition
and change, law and ethics, history and theology, the rational
and the mystical, nationalism and culture.[12]

*God*

While Conservative thinkers have devoted some thought to
the idea of God, their interpretative motifs have not been as rich
or multi-faceted as among the Reform. Generally, Conservative
theologians have presupposed the existence of God without

much theological or philosophical speculation. Nevertheless, varied interpretations of the God concept have been developed by leaders of the Conservative movement.

Professor Schechter, for example, was more in tune with his Hasidic background than with his German training when he quipped that "monotheism is good, but God is better" because monotheism is too abstract. Schechter wrote: "God is not a mere figurehead. He not only reigns, but governs. Everywhere —in the temple, in the judge's seat, in the family, in the farm, and in the market place—His presence is felt in enforcing the laws bearing His *imprimatur* . . . With the Jew, God is the only reality. . . ." Professor Louis Ginzberg followed much the same path of a personal, experiential deity: "How baseless is the view that the Pharisees only thought of God as a distant, inaccessible, hard taskmaster." God is accessible and near—He needs no mediator. Ginzberg added that conformity to the will of God and communion with God are the two outstanding features of spiritual religion. Louis Finkelstein writes that all the world is "but an island in the sea of truth which transcends it, and which is most clearly reflected in the human mind and conscience . . . We must teach our people to feel the presence of God" and not think of Him in human or anthropomorphic terms. And he adds that our God-concept must be based on emotions and intuition but with a proper recognition of scientific fact. Rabbi Ben Zion Bokser also develops a personal notion of the Deity. He writes that "God is not a person—He is greater than a person."[13]

On the other hand, Mordecai M. Kaplan's naturalistic notion of God as the power or process that makes for human salvation or self-fulfillment has found numerous Conservative partisans. Rabbi Robert Gordis writes that there is a force for social, political, and scientific progress in the world—and that force is God. "God is the creative Power in the universe," suggests Gordis, "whose ways are manifest in laws of nature and processes of history. He reveals unity, creative power, wisdom, and righteousness." Gordis repeats the view of medieval philosophers that God's *essence* cannot be perceived—only His *effects* in the world. He is convinced that evolution and astrophysics display interrelated unity and an upward thrust in the cosmos. Moreover, God is more than Aristotle's First Cause: God is the force of history; He is concerned with men, their deeds, and their destinies. His is "the great moral principle of reward and retribution" which is more than just a fancy for the Jew; it is, in fact, "a law of the universe."[14]

Professor Abraham J. Heschel produced many significant works on theology and God. His approach was an existentialist, neo-Hasidic one; his pietism and poetic language sought to set a mood rather than a rationalistic proof-system of God's existence. He nowhere sought to prove that God exists: that idea is axiomatic in Heschel's theology, for God is suprarational, *not* irrational. "God is *He* to whom we are accountable" and "our conscience is open." Heschel perceived God in the sublime mystery of nature and history. Following Kant, he detected Him in "the starry heavens above and the moral law within." There is in man a sense of the ineffable as he confronts the mystery in life. "We apprehend but cannot comprehend," he wrote, and that sense of "radical amazement" which man experiences in meeting the sublime in nature and history leads him to an affirmation of God. Man has a feeling of terrible loneliness; hence he searches for God in the world of man. He finds God in the ineffable—namely, "that aspect of reality which by its very nature lies beyond our comprehension, and is acknowledged by the mind to be beyond the scope of the mind. . . . God is Him who is beyond the mystery."[15]

Heschel suggested that "we have no nouns by which to describe His essence; we have only *adverbs* by which to indicate the ways in which He acts towards us." When we speak of one God we do not merely deny polytheism; we declare God's incomparable *uniqueness* in that He is *not* an aspect of nature but "a reality that is over and above the universe." Moreover, we imply thereby that "He alone is truly real" and that "He is a being who is both beyond and here, both in nature and in history, both love and power, near and far, known and unknown, Father and Eternal, Creator and Redeemer." Man approaches God through the sense of the ineffable, the participation in Torah and Israel, and the "leap of action," or, to put it differently, through worship, learning, and action. Paradoxically, God needs and searches out man even as man needs God, for "Judaism is the awareness of God's interest in man."[16]

Heschel's neo-Hasidism has not had much of an impact on Conservative theologians in their conceptions of God. But he made his mark in other areas of Jewish thought and life. Still, Heschel's theology is uniquely rich in nuance and subtlety, and his position in world Jewry as theologian par excellence was uncontested.

Theologian Max Kadushin takes a different approach to the idea of God. He resembles Heschel somewhat in his existentialist slant. He writes that we experience God in "normal mysticism," in the day-to-day, personal and intimate relation with the divine "You." These occasions are manifold; the simple act of eating bread or reciting a blessing heightens the experience. Kadushin says that "holiness is a mystical experience of God, and holiness means imitation of God who is totally other." We imitate Him through ethical behavior—through love, adherence to universality, and commitment to the worth of the individual. Kadushin is scornful of the God of the philosophers (as was Heschel), for he believes that "the experience of God—not the concept of the philosophers—is what characterizes Judaism."[17]

What of the problem of evil in the Conservative theological structure?

Heschel considered evil to be a mystery that cannot be fathomed. The supreme issue is not good and evil but "God and His commandments to love good and hate evil; not the sinfulness of man but the commandment of God." Evil enters as a result of man's disobedience to God; evil is "divergence," while good is "convergence or union." Heschel was frankly pessimistic about man and the world. He stated that "there is one line that expresses the mood of the Jewish man throughout the ages: *'The earth is given into the hand of the wicked'* " (Job 9:24). Having witnessed the horrors of this generation, we are beginning to realize "how monstrous an illusion it was to substitute faith in man for faith in God." All of history, suggested Heschel, is a mixture of good and evil. Man's task is to separate the two, for redemption is contingent upon that separation. "At the end of days, evil will be conquered by the one; in historic times evils must be conquered one by one."[18]

Robert Gordis is more hopeful than Heschel. He agrees with Martin Buber that evil is the not yet hallowed. Gordis sees evil as performing indispensable functions in life: it is a moral discipline; it is a spur to creative achievement; it is an instrument for progress towards justice and freedom. But in the last analysis, as Job discovered, evil is one of the elements of mystery in the universe. Just as there is a natural order to the world—though not always penetrable by man's intellect—so, too, there is a moral order to life, an order which likewise eludes man's ken.[19]

Fundamentally, Conservative theologians seem to divide along two ideological lines: 1) the naturalists, humanists who follow Kaplan's approach; 2) the supernaturalists, who adhere to a more traditional personal God, Creator of the universe and Lord of history and human events.

*Torah*

Conservative thinkers are nonliteralistic in their understanding of revelation. With the exception of the left-wing Reconstructionists, all Conservative thinkers affirm the doctrine of revelation. But there are varied interpretations of its meaning.

Proto-Conservatives such as Isaac Leeser, Morris Raphall, and Samuel Isaacs accepted divine revelation in a literal sense. But Sabato Morais hedged: he upheld the notion of verbal inspiration rather than verbal communication. H. P. Mendes evaded the subject by turning to Maimonides; Kohut cited Albo; Szold and Jastrow were nonliteral in their understanding of doctrines like revelation, resurrection, and reward and punishment. Kohut noted that the Bible does not teach revelation or evolution or philosophical principles; it must not be read literally because it is "only concerned in the fact that the world had a beginning, produced by God, and is unbiased to report that for a time chaos existed."[20]

Solomon Schechter was equally nonliteral in his conception of revelation. But he was appalled by the excesses of Higher Criticism, which he dubbed "Higher Anti-Semitism." He set out to restore the sanctity of the Bible and to rescue it from the not-too-tender mercies of Protestant radical critics. Morais had already allowed the teaching of "lower" or textual criticism of the Bible at the Seminary, although the Pentateuch was still considered sacrosanct. Schechter continued the same policy at the Seminary, and criticism of the Pentateuch in the rabbinical school curriculum is still taboo.[21]

Fundamentally, the Conservative approach is that revelation is a fact. Heschel wrote that "Judaism is the relation between *man with Torah and God.*" The Torah is the destiny and essence of Israel; the Bible is the answer to the supreme question, What does God demand of us? Heschel described revelation as an extraordinary event rather than a process; it was a mystery that lasted a moment, whereas acceptance of Torah continues. But Heschel was not a fundamentalist and he accepted much of Bible criticism. He warned against literalism and anthropomorphisms, and he rejected the "theological exaggeration" that every iota of Torah was given at Sinai. In fact, Heschel devoted a great deal of space to proving that some of the Talmudic sages did *not* believe that the entire Bible or even the entire Pentateuch was revealed to Moses at Sinai. Additionally, Heschel saw revelation as a dialogue between God and man. The Prophets were not passive recipients or recording instruments. In fact, Sinai was both divine proclamation and human perception; the Bible is the word of God *and* man, and we need continuous understanding with a "minimum of revelation and a maximum of interpretation."[22]

Robert Gordis follows much the same premises, although he accepts revelation as a progressively unfolding process rather than an event. He, too, recognizes man's role in revelation and he insists that revelation is refracted in the human personality. "We regard the Law, both Written and Oral, as the revelation of God" but not merely dictation; rather, it is a process with "*two* active participants." The Torah "is not necessarily Mosaic; but the relationship is like that of an oak tree to an original acorn." Following Kaplan's lead, Gordis defines Torah in its broadest sense as inclusive of "everything significant that the Jewish genius has produced from the days of Moses to the present." Consequently, the Torah is binding, and neither ethical nor ritual rules may be set aside out of caprice or regard for changing fashions.[23]

Essentially, then, Conservative theologians accept revelation as both an event in history and a process in life that involves a dialogue between God and man. The original revelation of the Bible is not to be literally construed; the process of revelation is ongoing and subject to ever-changing human appreciation and interpretation in every age.

But where does this leave Halakhah? And what happens to the *mitzvot*? Here we come to one of the sticking points of the Conservative philosophy: if revelation is a fact, then all *mitzvot* are binding; if revelation is dynamic and subject to changing interpretation, then which *mitzvah* is valid? And who is to determine validity?

The proto-Conservatives were sharply divided over ritual practices. The more traditional group, consisting of Leeser, Morais, and H. P. Mendes, opposed the use of an organ and family pews, and insisted on Hebrew and unmodified adherence to Sabbath and *kashrut*, although they acknowledged the need for liturgical changes and updating of certain anachronistic laws. The liberal group, including Szold, Jastrow, Kohut, and F. D. Mendes, were willing to introduce an organ, choir, and family pews, and favored relaxation of Sabbath and *kashrut* laws. Jastrow and Szold agreed that reforms may be introduced which will give the congregants an enlightened understanding of the deeper contents which lie in Judaism. Both favored reforms designed to enhance the religious fervor of the congregation; both favored dropping or adjusting obsolete *mitzvot;* and both sought the golden mean between the mobile and the static. Hence, they produced a revised and abridged prayer book, they introduced the Reform-style late service on Friday evening, they shortened the Torah reading for Sabbath morning, and they abolished the Second Day of the Festivals, rode on the Sabbath, and modified some of the dietary laws.

But both schools of thought united in bitter opposition to some of the extremes of Reform. For example, all attacked the Sunday services. Morais wrote that in them he heard "dirges sung over the death of my father's religion." When Wise denigrated *kashrut* as "Kitchen Judaism," Jastrow and F. D. Mendes chastised him publicly and pulled their congregations out of the Union of American Hebrew Congregations. Whereas Einhorn and Kohler were negative toward Hebrew, Morais and F. D. Mendes defended it as vital to Judaism. While the Reformers denigrated the traditional Sabbath, the Historical School's partisans defended it. While the Reformers abolished marriage and divorce rules, the proto-Conservatives preserved them and took the radicals to task. And yet they felt the need for change—even a traditionalist like Morais called for an up-to-date, clear, brief code "with due respect to our changed condition."[24]

The ideologist of the Historical School of early Conservative Judaism was Alexander Kohut. Kohut affirmed the chain of tradition but argued for the need for change in every generation. We, too, can make changes in our times, he noted. True, our ancestors were giants and we may appear to be pygmies; but a pygmy on a giant's shoulder can see farther than the giant. Kohut argued that since religion has been given to man, it is man's duty to modify religion and help it grow. This process of growth must be supervised by recognized teachers who acknowledge Divine authority as well as the need for change in accordance with the exigencies of the times. Kohut assailed Reform as a deformity, a skeleton without flesh and sinew, spirit or heart. "Suicide is not reform," he declared, insisting that we must preserve "Mosaic-rabbinic Judaism, freshened with the spirit of progress, a Judaism of the healthy golden mean." Kohut's challenge to Reform did not go unanswered: Kaufmann Kohler joined the battle in a lively exchange of views of two titans of different schools. Kohut's views were rather typical of those of the nascent Conservative movement.[25]

Solomon Schechter dabbled but little in Jewish law. He was more concerned with theology and folklore. Still, he was sharply critical of Reform's amputations of Halakhah. "The frequent appeals to 'prophetic Judaism' are largely verbiage; you cannot live on oxygen alone," he wrote. He insisted that "ethics are good, but laws and commandments bidden and commanded by God are better . . ." and he described Halakhah as "the central springs both of Jewish reason and of Jewish emotion." Schechter conceived of Torah as much *more* than just law and he chided critics for casting Judaism as merely a legalistic faith. "Torah means teaching in its widest sense," he wrote, and he asked of the Reformers: "Is it really one of the deadly sins to observe the dietary laws or keep the Sabbath in the way prescribed by Orthodox Judaism? Is it really this adherence of Orthodoxy which prevents the moral regeneration of our or any other age?" Schechter spurned the Reform charge of "Orientalism," sarcastically reminding the Reformers that the Occidentals had evinced no particular genius for religious creativity. He urged that the home be the basic unit of Jewish living, and he called for home *mitzvot* including the observance of *kashrut*, Sabbath, matzah, and other rituals.[26]

But Schechter's uniquely original contribution to Halakhah was his view on how law changes. In his opinion, the authoritative interpretation of Scripture is the product of changing historical circumstances, and he believed that the center of authority had actually been removed from the Bible "and placed in some *living body* which, by reason of its being in touch with the ideal aspirations and the religious needs of the age, is best able to determine the nature of the Secondary Meaning." This living body Schechter called the "collective conscience of Catholic Israel as embodied in the Universal synagogue." Catholic Israel was composed of the Prophets and Psalmists, the rabbis throughout the ages and, above all, general custom which "forms the rule of practice." Schechter never fully developed his concept of Catholic Israel, and the tantalizingly brief allusions to the notion have given rise to some confusion. Evidently, Schechter meant to say that in the final analysis, *klal Yisrael*, the Jewish People, would put their stamp of legitimacy on various practices and would reject others.[27]

The master of Halakhah and guiding legal light of the Conservative movement was Professor Louis Ginzberg. Ginzberg agreed with Schechter that Torah is more than *law*: it is instruction or teaching of any kind—the sum total of the contents of revelation, and the eternal truths about God's love and justice. Ginzberg wrote that it is impossible to understand the past of Jewish life without a knowledge of the Halakhah because it is the "true mirror, reflecting the work of the Jew in shaping his character," it includes conduct, life in all of its manifestations, "religion, worship, law, economics, politics, ethics, and so forth." For the Jew, "law is religion—and religion is law." Like life itself, Halakhah is not free from all logical inconsistencies. Additionally, one must not judge the laws by their *origins* but by their *subsequent development*. But since Halakhah "gives us a picture of life in its totality and not of some of its fragments," it is most representative of the character of the Jewish people and it is the "specifically Jewish expression of religiousness" and must be studied with an approach that fuses classical learning and piety with modern, critical scholarship.[28]

Ginzberg was in theory a radical. He wrote that when a law code could no longer be stretched to the breaking point, legislation came to the rescue abrogating old laws and adding "new ones which conform to the demands of the age." In his pioneering rabbinic works, he showed how Halakhah had reacted to socio-economic conditions and he maintained that "Immutability must not be confounded with immobility." Yet, he never sanctioned legal changes in practice, and as head of the Law Committee of the Rabbinical Assembly he served as a restraining force in bridling the more radical members whom he often lampooned. He insisted that a Torah-less Judaism is impossible; that we must assimilate the good we find among our neighbors, adapting our surroundings to us while *not* adapting ourselves to them.[29]

Ginzberg's numerous disciples followed his radical theories while adopting cautious practical conclusions. The late Professor Boaz Cohen, for example, who taught Talmud and Codes at the Seminary for many years and was chairman of the Rabbinical Assembly's Law Committee, was a radical theoretician but an arch-conservative in practical matters. Cohen was a master of comparative law and one of the world's experts on Roman law. Yet, he declared that "we cannot and dare not be swayed, in our interpretation of Jewish law, by considerations from the study of comparative religion, or take cognizance of the data of the anthropologists. . . ." Cohen cautioned that our task is more difficult than that of our ancestors because we are conscious of what we are doing and therefore cannot pretend to be performing an unconscious act. Cohen suggested the following basic principles of Halakhah:

1) The Law is of Divine origin.

2) The Law is immutable, although liberal interpretations of the rabbis rendered the law viable and pliable. Biblical law cannot be abrogated but it can be emended by interpretation.

3) The Law has developed historically.

4) The Jewish People—*Knesset Yisrael*— is one Community in regard to basic laws.

5) The primacy of the Talmud, rather than the codes, is acknowledged.

6) Ordained sages are authorized to rule on laws.

7) The principle of interpretation is affirmed to mean that "modifications of ritual and ordinances required by new exigencies and contingencies should transpire through due process of Jewish law." But hands should be kept off family law, since that impinges on the Jewish People.

8) "The determining factor in our decisions is the question whether we are preserving genuine Jewish religious values or not."

9) The much-maligned *Shulhan Arukh* is not *authoritarian,* but *utilitarian.* We need it because it restates the Talmud, it is the code of the majority, and it is convenient.

10) In seeking canons of interpretation, we should pursue the "general aim and spirit of the Law," accepting the consensus of codifiers and following the minority if need be. We must also be attuned to the psychological consequences of our decisions.

11) We must realize that some problems are simply irremediable within the Halakhah.[30]

Louis Finkelstein has followed much the same route charted

by Louis Ginzberg and Boaz Cohen. Finkelstein has expressed very radical theories about Jewish Law. His magnum opus, *The Pharisees*, is frankly a socio-economic structuring of the Halakhah. But his scholarly radicalism has never been translated into practical terms. Finkelstein declared that Judaism is a developing religion that has undergone change, growth, self-expression, and foliation. Rabbinism is the natural outgrowth of prophetism; the Torah is "Israel's most effective protection from disintegration and assimilation." Finkelstein chides both those who accept Jewish law without reinterpretation as well as those who see law as a dead letter, and he maintains that Jewish Law must be preserved by being interpreted by those who have mastered it. We must revere these interpretations because this is authentic Judaism. Finkelstein agrees that if shifting values and the introduction of new devices will actually bring Jews back to God, Torah, and synagogue, then they will win acceptance. But he will not hear of changes that strike at "the fundamentals of Judaism." Thus, he has steadfastly sought to bridle the Rabbinical Assembly in the areas of personal status, marriage and divorce laws, and calendar changes.[31]

Speculation on the role of Halakhah and the meaning of the *mitzvot* has produced particularly rich and stimulating thought in the Conservative movement. Rabbi Robert Gordis, for example, has much to say on the matter. Gordis accepts the Divine origin of the written and oral Torahs—although not in a literal sense —but he argues for continuous revelation and the active role of man in revealing God's word. Demonstrating the capacity for growth and reinterpretation in our tradition, Gordis calls for the implementation of *takanot* (amendments) and *gezerot* (prohibitions) to make the law viable and fluid: "There are unsuspected resources within the Halachah for its continued creative unfoldment and its contribution to the ennobling of human life." Gordis believes that "growth is the law of life, and Law is the life of Judaism." We are not neutral where Jewish law is concerned, writes Gordis. Law is, however, not an end in itself but a means to an end, and it must be kept alive by utilizing social, economic, and political conditions. "If we surrender our adherence to Jewish law, we shall be courting anarchy; if we suffer it to petrify, we shall be inviting disaster." Gordis delineates the functions of ritual in several areas: 1) cosmic or religious function that binds man to the universe; 2) ethical or social function; 3) esthetic or play function; 4) group association for community preservation. The final authority on change in Jewish law must be Catholic Israel, argues Gordis in following the footsteps of Solomon Schechter. But Gordis reinterprets the notion: he notes that obviously Catholic Israel is not a valid doctrine if the majority of Jews are heretics. "Catholic Israel," writes Gordis, "is the body of men and women within the Jewish people who accept the authority of Jewish law and are concerned with Jewish observance as a genuine issue." Gordis maintains that it is a vertical and horizontal concept, for it includes past and present generations. Changes in observance become part and parcel of Jewish law *only* when they emanate from Catholic Israel; the present low status of Jewish observance is "only temporary."[32]

Professor Abraham J. Heschel offered some perceptive insights into the meaning of Halakhah. He attacked those who are "pan-Halakhists," who view Judaism as nothing more than *deeds,* and he labels such a theology "sacred physics." He wrote that

> *It is a distortion to say that Judaism consists exclusively of performing ritual or moral deeds, and to forget that the goal of all performing is in* transforming *the soul. Even before Israel was told in the Ten Commandments what* to do *it was told what* to be: a holy people. *To perform deeds of holiness is to absorb the holiness of deeds. We must learn how to be one with what we do. This is why in addition to halacha,* the science of deeds, *there is agada,* the art of being.

Heschel described the *mitzvah* as a means to a higher end: it is a prayer in action, a partnership of God and man. He urged us to develop more *kavanah*—intent, soul, inwardness—for "Judaism is *a way of thinking,* not only a way of living." We must avoid "religious behaviorism" and fuse the heart with the deed. Calling for a "leap of action" to help us perceive God's presence and develop faith, Heschel stressed that

*We do not explore first and decide afterwards whether to accept the Jewish way of living. We must accept in order to be able to explore. At the beginning is the commitment, the supreme acquiescence.*

Heschel had some critical words for Orthodoxy which, in his opinion, has made the Law into a *"lo* with an *aleph"* ("No" with a capital *n*). "We speak of it as if it were endowed with negative attributes. Even celebrations are regarded as restrictions and as if the primary object of halachah is to deny and deprive." Equally repugnant to him was the "all-or-nothing philosophy" which he considered unjustified theologically and historically. The great *mitzvot* epitomized for Heschel the great truths of Judaism. For example, he expatiated at length on the sublime values of the Sabbath. Sabbath laws teach man that he comes from royalty, that there is no distinction between master and slave, rich and poor. On the Sabbath we build a "palace in time" and become independent of civilization, achievement, and anxiety. The Sabbath fills us with *"holiness in time"*; it is a moment of eternity, majesty, joy; it teaches us "the art of surpassing civilization." Unquestionably, Heschel was the foremost exponent of the theology of Halakhah in the Conservative movement.[33]

Among the younger Conservative theologians, Professor Seymour Siegel has been the most articulate and persuasive. He does not share the "fundamentalist belief that the specific laws in their precise formulation are God's revelation." Specific laws, he suggests, are *responses* to revelation—not the *content* of revelation.

*The demands of morality are absolute. The specific laws are relative. Thus, if because of changing conditions the specific laws no longer express the ethical values which Tradition teaches . . . we have the responsibility to revise the laws, rather than allow them to fall into desuetude.*

Hence, Siegel supports the Conservative leniencies permitting a *kohen* to marry a divorcée, the nullification of a marriage to free an *agunah,* and he urges an end to the religious designation of bastardy.[34]

But all of these writings are merely theoretical. What of the practical position of the movement? How does it stand on specific *mitzvot*?

The left-wing spokesmen have been clamoring for concrete action and bold initiatives in alleviating classic Halakhic problems for many years. Rabbi Morris Adler, for example, urged that "no gradual and slow process of interpretations will suffice to evolve a Judaism compatible with our needs . . . In such spheres of Jewish law as Sabbath, dietary laws, laws relating to the problem of the *agunah*, we cannot any longer be content with revisions by the strict, slow process of law." There were those who demanded that non-Halakhic criteria be adopted by the Law Committee; others simply gave up on Halakhah as a viable system. There was much discontent with the dilatory and ultraconservative approach of the Law Committee of the Rabbinical Assembly, and impatience seethed among rabbis and laity. Finally the Law Committee was restructured in 1948. It would henceforth be representative of all trends of thought in the movement and would record both majority and minority opinions. But unanimous opinions would be binding on all members of the Rabbinical Assembly. The Seminary's faculty was deeply offended and it refused at first to join the newly formed Committee. Ultimately, the faculty agreed to serve on the Law Committee, although some faculty members remained unreconciled to its new character.

As a result of the reorganization of the Law Committee, radical and far-sweeping proposals were adopted. In 1950 a majority ruled it permissible to drive to the synagogue on Sabbaths and Festivals if the distance was too great to walk. The Committee also sanctioned the use of electricity on the Sabbath. In 1954 the Rabbinical Assembly finally adopted a new *ketubah* (marriage contract) designed to protect the woman from unscrupulous husbands who might refuse a *get* (Jewish divorce) and thus leave the wife an *agunah* (a woman unable to remarry). Ever since 1930 the Rabbinical Assembly had tried to remedy this tragic situation; each proposal had been shelved in the face of furious Orthodox opposition. This time—despite a barrage of attacks from the Orthodox—the Rabbinical Assembly acted. Many felt that the measure was inadequate and subsequently, in 1967, the Law Committee passed a resolution allowing the nullification of marriages in order to free the wife from a recalcitrant husband. In 1969 the Law Committee adopted a recommendation to make the observance of the Second Day of *Yom Tov* optional, in accordance with the practice of the Land of Israel. The Rabbinical Assembly endorsed the proposal and urged the Reform movement to restore the Second Day of Rosh Hashanah so as to unify the calendars of Reform and Conservatism with that of the Holy Land. Clearly, the Law Committee has been moving in radical directions since that historic reorganization of 1948.[35]

But the new thrust of the Law Committee has provoked considerable controversy. The Orthodox have been contemptuous; the left wing scornful; and the masses of the laity—indifferent. Many considered the Law Committee's new philosophy an attempt to straight-jacket practices and curb the power of the local rabbi; others were wary of heresy-hunting. In 1971 the entire Committee resigned and a chaotic situation ensued. Professor Robert Gordis was empowered to head a special committee to reorganize the Law Committee and he submitted a report calling for a more representative Law Committee which would be traditional in family and personal status but innovative in personal observance, liturgy, and synagogue practice. The special committee's recommendations were voted down at the 1972 Rabbinical Assembly Convention and a compromise was adopted.[36]

The picture of ritual observance in the Conservative movement resembles a crazy quilt. In some areas there is basic uniformity; in others, chaos seems to reign. The Law Committee and the Rabbinical Assembly seem to be divided into three schools of thought: left, right, and the vast center. And these divisions are reflected in the patterns of observances among the grass roots of the movement. *Kashrut* is officially maintained with the alleviation that one may eat dairy products in a non-kosher restaurant. In practice, however, very few laymen adhere to dietary laws out of the home. The Sabbath is formally observed, but riding to synagogue and the use of electricity are sanctioned. But in fact, there is only a scattering of true Sabbath observers in each congregation. Naturally, Sabbath and *kashrut* are strictly maintained in the synagogue. The variations in other practices are, however, amazingly broad. Most synagogues have family pews; some use organs, some don't; some allow mixed choirs, others don't; all require hats at prayer but only some call women to the Torah. Conservative rabbis will never perform an intermarriage without conversion; but some will marry a divorcée without requiring a *get*. Since the 1969 Law Committee rulings, some congregations have discarded observance of the Second Day of *Yom Tov*, while most have not. If one looks for consistency of observance in Conservative Judaism one is not likely to find it.

What one is apt to find is an official, de jure commitment to tradition coupled with a belief that traditions must modify, grow, and change. But de facto and in reality, there appears to be a yawning gap between theory and practice, and a chasm between the observant clergy and the nonobservant laity. Halakhah is honored more in the breach than in its observance. And therein, perhaps, lies the greatest dilemma of Conservatism.

### The Jewish People

The Conservative movement has always stressed the validity of Jewish peoplehood. Unlike Reform, it sees nothing in the notion of peoplehood that diminishes its spiritual mission or creates a conflict of loyalties. If Orthodoxy's focal point is Torah and Reform's is God, Conservatism begins with and is extraordinarily devoted to the Jewish People—*Am Yisrael*.

Solomon Schechter had underscored this approach in his emphasis on Catholic Israel and its role in shaping Jewish law and practice. His deeply felt love for the Jewish People and his concern for their welfare were known to all; his attachment to spiritual nationalism was equally renowned. Men like Israel Friedlander, Mordecai M. Kaplan, Cyrus Adler, and other spiritual heirs to Schechter's teachings preserved that spiritual nationalism. This explains the movement's heavy involvement in the affairs of world Jewry, here and abroad, in Israel or the Soviet Union. Conservative Jews have frequently been the catalysts of action to help world Jewry.

Additionally, the Conservative movement has preserved the classic attachment to the notion of the chosen people. True, early proto-Conservative rabbis like Szold and Jastrow reinterpreted the concept to conform to Reform's idea of a priestly mission to disseminate God's teachings to mankind. But the idea is very much alive in Conservatism, and the official Prayer Books of Conservatism retain the classic formula, "You have chosen us from all the nations." Nevertheless, the idea has undergone some reinterpretation. Robert Gordis takes it as a reference to Israel's religious genius. Israel is "chosen not for domination but for the service of humanity," he writes. Jews are to live up to higher ethical standards, individually and collectively, and lead all men to God by example. Max Kadushin proves that the doctrine never crystallized into a formal dogma, and he notes that the idea connotes no superiority of Jews; rather, it implies a mission to abide by God's *mitzvot.* Ben Zion Bokser interprets chosenness to mean spiritual maturity and a mark of the miraculous survival of the Jew. He also views chosenness as an indication that Jews are forever linked with Torah and have the grave responsibility of living by that Torah; that they must serve as missionaries in seeking to convert the world to love of God and man. Professor Heschel described Israel as a "holy people," whose task is to prove that "in order to be a people we have to be more than a people." Israel, he wrote, is a "spiritual order": by abandoning Israel, we desert God; but our belonging to Israel is in itself a spiritual act—a *kiddush ha-Shem.*[37]

The fervent attachment of Conservative Judaism to the Jewish People and the ideal of spiritual nationalism has never flagged over the years.

## The Land of Israel

With virtually no exceptions, the Conservative movement has labored for the reconstruction of the Jewish community in the Holy Land from its very inception. Isaac Leeser argued that no nation but the Israelites has a claim on the soil of Palestine to reconstitute it as a homeland. Leeser served as chairman of the "Agricultural Committee at Jaffa" and he established a sort of "United Jewish Appeal" to settle immigrants in Palestine. Other members of the Historical School cast in their lot with the Zionist movement either officially or unofficially. Sabato Morais, while opposing a secularist Zionism and cautioning against false messiahs, joined the Hovevei Zion (Lovers of Zion) and preached Zionism from the pulpit. Marcus Jastrow became vice president of the Federation of American Zionists; Benjamin Szold joined with Henrietta Szold and Dr. Harry Friedenwald in organizing the Zionist Association of Baltimore in 1893. H.P. Mendes viewed Zion as the "spiritual center for the world and ultimately the establishment of the Kingdom of God on earth"; Bernard Drachman and Gustave Lieberman of the Seminary faculty became active members of Hovevei Zion. In fact, Seminary students formed the first Young American Zionists chapter at New York's City College in 1897 and the first national Zionist fraternity (ZBT) in 1899. And some of the early laymen of the movement, such as Solomon Solis-Cohen, Louis Dembitz, and Harry Friedenwald, helped create the Zionist Organization of America, while Henrietta Szold founded Hadassah. The only significant non-Zionist in the group was Frederick de Sola Mendes who opposed Herzl's political Zionism because he felt that the Moslems and Christians would never countenance a reborn Jewish state, although Mendes did support colonization schemes.[38]

It was Solomon Schechter who stamped the Zionist label on the Conservative movement for all time. He had always felt that Jews needed a homeland of their own; his philosophy of Judaism included Jewish nationhood and the hope for return to Zion. He had wanted to attend the 1898 Zionist Congress in Basle but time did not permit him to do so. He was, however, somewhat leery over "extreme Herzlism," and he foresaw the need to colonize before a nation might exist. In 1899 he wrote that he was "prepared to go to the Holy Land whenever [he] would have bread to eat and raiment to wear, in spite of doctorship at Cambridge and professorship." He believed that a return to Zion was essential for Israel to achieve its sacred mission.[39]

Because of his disappointment with the irreligious conduct of the Herzl circle, he considered Zionism divorced from religious ideals a "menace." He was drawn to Ahad Ha'am's spiritual or cultural Zionism, rather than to Herzl's political version. He envisioned Zion as a spiritual center and he blistered the Territorialists who were willing to accept Uganda in lieu of Palestine as the national home. After several years of indecision, he finally announced in a public address in December 1905 that

> *To me personally after long hesitation and careful watching, it [Zionism] recommended itself as a great bulwark against assimilation, . . . loss of identity and disloyalty to Israel's history and its mission.*

He paid his dues and became an official member of the Zionist Organization of America. Schechter's public espousal of the Zionist cause provoked his leading lay supporter, Jacob Schiff, to accuse him of dual loyalty in a public letter to the New York *Times* in 1906. The struggle could have been disastrous, but Schechter prevailed and the Seminary swung into the Zionist camp. Schechter published a pamphlet that year describing himself as a religio-nationalistic Zionist, arguing that Zionism had aroused Israel's national consciousness. He mentioned his admiration for Ahad Ha'am and he described the movement as "the Declaration of Jewish Independence from all kinds of slavery, whether material or spiritual," for only when the Jewish soul will be redeemed from the Galut "can Judaism hope to resume its mission to the world."Schechter upbraided the Zionists for failing to settle in Palestine. In 1908 he attended the Zionist Convention and called for a "Jewish polity hallowed by sacred memories, equipped with Jewish institutions, taught and propagated through the medium of the Holy language." At the Vienna

Congress in 1913, he felt drawn to the Mizrachi wing. He spoke to the Congress in Hebrew and accepted the honorary presidency for Hebrew language and culture. In his final statement on the subject, Schechter reaffirmed his belief that Zionism "was, and still is, the most cherished dream I was worthy of having." But he cautioned that "Jewish nationalism is holy to the Lord, and any attempt to sever it from the historical Jewish ideals attached to Biblical terms, God's people, or Holy nation, will fail in the end."[40]

Schechter's views evoked ardent echoes in the philosophical outlooks of his colleagues. Professor Friedlander took an active role in the Zionist movement, and he, too, was drawn to the position of Ahad Ha'am. Professor Ginzberg spoke out for religious nationalism. While he refused to negate the Diaspora, he espoused the Zionist cause in a religious context urging that "Jewish nationalism without religion would be a tree without fruits; Jewish religion without nationalism would be a tree without roots." Dr. Mordecai M. Kaplan walked much the same path and has profoundly shaped the entire movement's Zionist orientation.[41]

Dr. Cyrus Adler had been an early member of the Federation of American Zionists. Later he resigned because of his annoyance over the nonreligious orientation of the Zionists. Adler followed Schechter's approach in speaking of Palestine as a spiritual-religious center for world Jewry. Later he became a member of the Jewish Agency and a vigorous supporter of colonization after a visit in 1929. His successor at the Seminary, Dr. Louis Finkelstein, continued the same pattern. In a 1927 speech to the Rabbinical Assembly he declared:

> We want to see Palestine rebuilt; we have for it, too, an intuitional, unreasoning and mystic love. We want to see Palestine rebuilt as the spiritual center of Israel . . . We want to see Eretz Yisrael established as a Jewish community; and if possible as an autonomous one. We should like to persuade its present generation of colonists and workers that the interests of their people demand their observance of the Torah, and the interests of Truth their recognition of God.[42]

Finkelstein was never wholly at ease with the secular Zionist state. Moreover, the Seminary faculty was badly split until, finally, after 1948 and the birth of Israel, the Seminary leadership shifted to the Zionist camp.

If there was some ambivalence in the halls of the Seminary, that ambivalence was totally absent among the members of the Rabbinical Assembly. As far back as 1928 and in every year since, the presidents of the Rabbinical Assembly have articulated pro-Zionist positions, and the Assembly has followed a course of support for the Jewish Agency, the United Jewish Appeal, Israel Bonds, and the State of Israel. A full statement on Zionism was articulated at the 1937 Rabbinical Assembly Convention. Its fourteen-point Pronouncement on Zionism outlined the position of the great mass of Conservative Jewry. It expressed the yearning to rebuild Zion where Jewish religion and culture might flourish; it urged free immigration to Zion while opposing any partition schemes; it expressed disappointment over the neglect of religious observance among the settlers; and it reaffirmed allegiance to the World Zionist Organization and Jewish Agency. Two of the presidents of the Zionist Organization of America—Rabbis Israel Goldstein and Solomon Goldman—came from the ranks of the Rabbinical Assembly. Goldman insisted that "Zionism is Jewish history. It is the Jewish people. The negation of Zionism is the denial of the Jewish past." Rabbi Robert Gordis wrote that Israel is a *sine qua non* for Jewish life, for only in Israel can Jewish culture, civilization, and life grow and develop freely and naturally, and only a flourishing spiritual center in Israel can enrich world Jewry. But Gordis refused to negate the survival of Diaspora Jewry, and he espoused the ideal of a creative partnership between Israel and world Jewry based on "religion, culture, and Jewish peoplehood."[43]

Some have endorsed the concept of *aliyah* to Israel as the ideal of Zionism. Professor Moshe Davis, former provost of the Seminary, has called for personal settlement in the Holy Land in order to fulfill the religious duty of *aliyah,* and, in fact, Davis now lives in Jerusalem. Davis believes that Israel must vitalize the

*Galut* and its institutions by permeating the educational, synagogal, communal, and individual aspects of Jewish life. Professor Abraham Heschel suggested that Jews maintain twin residences in America and Israel. Heschel wrote very much in the mystical-Zionistic vein of the late Rav Kook: he spoke of the mystic bonds between Israel and the Diaspora. Heschel stated that "Israel reborn is holy. The State of Israel is holy." And he believed that Israel performs the supreme act of spiritual and physical rescue of a people. Israel's rebirth has filled the world with light, said Heschel; Diaspora Jewry has the duty to give and the right to receive inspiration and faith from Zion. In a neo-Kabbalistic vein, Heschel mused:

> *Let us confess: there is no wholeness in the Diaspora. There are sparks but no flame, individuals but no community, schools, synagogues but no Jewish spiritual atmosphere. Only he who has been in the land of Israel knows what the Diaspora lacks.* [44]

The Conservative movement has been at pains to define its political relationship vis-à-vis the Zionist movement and Israel. The Orthodox had affiliated with the Mizrachi and, later, with the umbrella Religious Zionists of America. Most Reform rabbis gravitated to the Zionist Organization of America or to the Labor Zionist groups. The Conservatives felt uneasy about not identifying with a religious Zionist body. Back in 1939, Rabbi Simon Greenberg recommended affiliation with Hapoel Hamizrachi, the religious labor party. Men like Robert Gordis flirted with the same idea. In fact, a 1950 study mission of the Rabbinical Assembly recommended formal affiliation with Hapoel Hamizrachi and the creation of a Conservative Zionist organization. But nothing came of the proposal, primarily because the Mizrachi partisans rebuffed the Conservative rabbis as not sufficiently pious. Then from 1959 to 1961 the movement debated an invitation to become affiliated with the World Zionist Organization. Professor Mordecai M. Kaplan supported the plan for the sake of Jewish unity; Professors Abraham Heschel and Simon Greenberg opposed it as a detraction from the role of the synagogue. Nothing came of the proposal. [45]

The Conservatives have also been aggrieved over the Orthodox monopoly in Israel and the Chief Rabbinate's refusal to allow non-Orthodox rabbis to function in the State. In 1964 the Conservative leadership joined with Reform, as well as several secular organizations, in petitioning the then Prime Minister, Levi Eshkol, to break the Orthodox stranglehold over the religious life of the nation.

The Conservative movement has attempted to establish a viable presence in Israel. There are over sixty members of the Rabbinical Assembly living and working in Israel. There are several Conservative synagogues as well as the Seminary's Center in Jerusalem. Camp Ramah and the United Synagogue Youth both run summer seminars to Israel; rabbinical students spend a year of study in Jerusalem; an extensive tourism program has been launched by the United Synagogue. But the impact of the movement on Israeli life has, thus far, been insignificant, partly due to Orthodox hostility, partly because of the Seminary's reluctance "to export our ideas to Israel," to quote Dr. Finkelstein. However, the Rabbinical Assembly held its Convention of 1971 in Jerusalem with the expressed goal of establishing a Conservative "presence" in the Holy Land, and in 1972 the United Synagogue building was officially opened in Jerusalem.

Clearly, the Conservative movement through its Rabbinical Assembly, United Synagogue, and youth groups has been the leading and consistently devoted partisan of Zionism and the State of Israel throughout the years. Israel Independence Day is officially marked in Conservative congregations and a special liturgy has been prepared for the occasion. It would be safe to say that the Conservative movement is wholeheartedly devoted to the cause of Zion reborn.

*The Jewish Community*

In view of Conservative Judaism's stress on *klal Yisrael,* or Jewish peoplehood, it should come as no surprise that the Conservative movement has been keenly interested in the well-being of the community at large and in the needs of all Jews everywhere. It has been the most "ecumenical" of all the trends in Jewish life; it has eschewed partisanship and vituperation. Whether attacked from the left, or, as has been the more frequent occurrence, from the right, Conservative leaders have shown superlative forbearance in refusing to be drawn into internecine squabbles.

Schechter had set the pattern for intergroup cooperation by his notable efforts to work on friendly terms with his Reform colleagues. Adler continued the policy; his efforts in the American Jewish Committee and a host of other organizations bespoke his desire to build a strong Jewish community. No one, of course, surpassed Mordecai M. Kaplan's deeply felt passion for transcending party lines in building a strong and vibrant Jewish communal life. He had been a founder of the ill-fated Kehillah of New York City that strove to bring unity and cohesion to that great but cruelly divided aggregation; he has steadfastly championed the notion of an "organic community" that would build an interrelated Jewish world whose goals would be demarcated and whose techniques would be coordinated. As usual, Kaplan's teachings in this regard had a marked impact on the Conservative movement, as well as on others. Finkelstein, too, has championed the idea of intergroup cooperation on a host of projects. He had tried, unsuccessfully, to entice the Orthodox and Reform groups to form a partnership in sponsoring *The Eternal Light* radio and television project; he had also struggled to create a nonpartisan Jewish Museum. And only when he was rebuffed in those overtures did he set off on his own.[46]

Conservative lay and rabbinic leaders have been in the forefront of a variety of projects designed to strengthen the Jewish community here and abroad. Whether in the struggle for Soviet Jewry, political and economic campaigns to aid Israel, communal charity drives, coordinated campaigns to combat anti-Semitism, or projects to strengthen Jewish education, Conservative Jews have been deeply involved. And with virutally no significant exceptions, the Conservative leadership has espoused the need to create a vibrant, coordinated, integrated, organic Jewish community akin to the classic *kehillah* or *Gemeinde* that existed in days gone by. The Conservative movement warmly endorses inter-group cooperation with fellow Jews; it does not shy away in the least from being labeled "parochial" because of its stress on the needs of the Jewish community.

*The Synagogue*

The synagogue-center has been the unique contribution of the Conservative movement to American Jewry. Dr. Mordecai M. Kaplan proposed that the synagogue be more than just a house of prayer or study: it must be a center for all Jewish communal activities, including prayer, education for young and old, social activities, secular programs, communal meetings, athletic events, etc. The idea was to bring Jews, young and old, into the synagogue for whatever reason in order to win them over to a Jewish way of life. Kaplan concretized his idea in the creation of the Jewish Center in Manhattan. Rabbi Israel H. Levinthal followed suit in 1920 by establishing the Brooklyn Jewish Center, the most famous prototype of a synagogue-center in the nation. Levinthal wrote:

> *If the synagogue as a* Beth Hatefilah *has lost its hold upon the masses, some institution would have to be created that could and would attract the people so that the group consciousness of the Jew might be maintained. The name center seems to work this magic with thousands who would not be attracted to the place if we simply called it Synagogue or Temple. . . . The center is a seven-day synagogue not a one-day synagogue. From early morning to late at night its door should be open. It is true that many will come for other purposes than to meet God. But let them come.*[47]

Consequently, Conservative congregations are commonly re-ferred to as "centers"; they boast large ballrooms and social halls, gymnasiums and swimming pools, and their non-liturgical projects invariably dwarf their worship services in attendance and frequency. But the idea of the synagogue-center has not been confined to the Conservative movement alone, and as we have observed, many Orthodox and Reform groups have emulated the pattern.

What of synagogue practices among Conservative Jews? Here we find a wide variety, ranging from the almost Orthodox to the almost Reform. The early pioneers of the Conservative movement had not been able to reach a consensus on ritual patterns in the synagogues. The more traditional, such as Morais and H.P. Mendes, conducted a service virtually indistinguishable from that of a modern, decorous Orthodox *shul*. The more radical, such as Kohut, Jastrow, Szold, and F.D. Mendes, allowed the use of an organ, mixed choir, family pews, and abbreviated prayer. Under Schechter's aegis, several minimal criteria were established for all Conservative congregations: worshipers had to cover their heads, and synagogues using the *Union Prayer Book* were ineligible for membership in the United Synagogue. Later on, synagogues who failed to maintain kosher kitchens were expelled from the United Synagogue. But aside from these few basic norms, practically anything is valid in Conservative synagogue worship. Thus, New York's prestigious B'nai Jeshurun Congregation, the oldest Conservative synagogue in the land, uses an organ and mixed choir. Montreal's equally prestigious Shaar Hashomayim Congregation, on the other hand, still maintains separate pews for men and women. Some synagogues use more Hebrew than others; some allow women to take *aliyot;* some observe only one day of the Festivals; and some chant in Sephardic rather than Ashkenazic Hebrew. The latitude is wide and experimentation is popular. However, all synagogues do insist on kosher kitchens, head coverings and prayer shawls for males, and basic Sabbath observance on synagogue premises.[48]

The prayer-book issue proved to be somewhat controversial in Conservative theology. Curiously, even a relatively Orthodox man like Sabato Morais was dissatisfied with the liturgical service. He called for a simpler prayer book with the deletion of prayers for sacrifices and other abstruse passages, less repetition, and the creation of new compositions by modern philosophers, poets, and rabbis "suited to our existing wants." Morais insisted on retaining Hebrew as the unifying lingua franca of the

Jewish People, and he opposed the introduction of an organ and a choir because such practices brought "Gentile players and choristers into the shrine." Attacked from both the right and the left, he was unable to develop his liturgical reforms.[49]

But Szold and Jastrow were not deterred. Szold produced a German-Hebrew revised *Sidur* in 1864; Jastrow followed suit in 1871. Their prayer books were moderately Reform in style but essentially traditional in mood. Due to the imprecise nature of Conservative theology, no official prayer book evolved, however. Solomon Schechter was mostly concerned with installing English sermons and "strict order and decorum" in the synagogues in order to attract the youth, and his rabbinic disciples adopted his approach. A variety of prayer books was in use in Conservative synagogues—generally of Orthodox ideology.

Finally, after many years of wrestling with the problem, an official High Holiday *Mahzor* was adopted as edited by Rabbi Morris Silverman. Since this edition was, with the exception of the excision of some *piyutim* and addition of English readings entirely traditional, the dissatisfaction remained. A commission to revise the prayer book was appointed under the chairmanship of Rabbi Robert Gordis. After many years of study and drafting, the official Rabbinical Assembly United Synagogue *Sabbath Prayer Book* was issued in 1946. In his introduction, Rabbi Gordis states that the purpose of the volume is to "perpetuate traditional Judaism in the modern spirit." Three criteria were adopted in preparing the volume: 1) continuity with tradition; 2) relevance; 3) intellectual integrity. But the mountain gave birth to a mouse, and except for its new translation, supplementary readings, and minor textual changes, the *Sidur* is virtually the traditional one. The esoteric rabbinic passages have been deleted; the prayer for the restoration of sacrifices has been retained but the verb has been changed to the *past* rather than the *future* tense; the pejorative blessing, "who has not made me a woman," has been removed; and some supplementary prayers have been added. In addition, the beliefs in the chosen people, a personal Messiah, and resurrection have been retained even though the editors themselves admit that they do not take these concepts literally. Subsequently the Rabbinical Assembly produced a Daily *Sidur* and other special liturgical pamphlets, and a new *Mahzor* was issued in 1972. While the Conservative movement has finally standardized its liturgical texts, much discontent still smolders and prayer remains a problem for Conservative theologians as well as laymen.[50]

Robert Gordis, for example, seeks to answer the question whether prayer is relevant or efficacious. He cautions against equating God's knowledge with man's, because if we naively do so, we surely cannot fathom that God answers our prayers. Prayer is efficacious for several reasons: it utilizes nature's powers; it affects the worshiper psychologically; it keeps ideals alive and closer to fruition; it engenders a spirit of thanksgiving in man; and it actuates the presence of the Divine.[51]

Professor Max Kadushin has demonstrated how the rabbis utilized prayer "to transmute the commonplace into the significant." The Halakhah helps fix these concretizations by developing regularity and steadiness. Jewish worship is praise of God at the same time that there is an experience of God's love or justice, says Kadushin. "In that experience there is an awareness of the self as an object of God's love, but an awareness of the self that includes society as well."[52]

Perhaps the most acute and sensitive critic of the function of prayer had been Abraham J. Heschel. Prayer, suggested Heschel, is an "ontological necessity"; we pray because we cannot help praying. The true source of prayer is not an emotion but an insight, the "ineffable," the sense of miracles in daily life and of continual marvels. Heschel called for greater *kavanah* (devotion of the heart) in worship. He decried "prayer by proxy" and "religious solipsism or auto-suggestion." Unfortunately, although dignity is present in the modern synagogue, *life* is missing; too much "spiritual vulgarity" abounds. We need a revitalization not of prayer, he urged, but of ourselves—a revision of the soul rather than the text. We have lost the power to pray because we have lost the sense of His reality and because of our "religious bashfulness." In an obvious swipe at Reconstructionism, Heschel insisted that we cannot pray to "the sum total of values; I can't pray to an it." Heschel believed passionately that God indeed listens to prayers: "If God doesn't listen, we are insane to talk to him," wrote Heschel.[53]

While Conservative Jewry has debated the nature of liturgy with much vigor and dissension, it has been virtually unanimous in its approach to Jewish education. Schechter had urged the development of intensive Jewish education for young and old and the preparation of qualified teachers and texts. The original Sunday School pattern was dropped, and today most Conservative schools require five years of studies, six hours a week, prior to Bar or Bat Mitzvah. The old prejudices against "parochial" schools have been discarded and the movement has followed the Orthodox lead in developing a chain of Hebrew Day Schools. There were, as of 1972, 42 Solomon Schechter Schools with 7,500 pupils. Moreover, the Conservative synagogues have created a network of Hebrew High Schools as well as the Hebrew Ramah Camps for summer learning experiences. The National Academy of Adult Jewish Education has been successful in disseminating Torah among adults in hundreds of Conservative synagogues. Yet, despite the significant advances in raising educational standards in the movement, educators like Professor Moshe Davis and Dr. Morton Siegel decry the failure of Jewish education and describe the standards as still shamefully low and unenforced. Siegel suggests that this is because we make no demands of any *adult,* so we make none of children, too. Many have come to the conclusion that the only salvation lies in a day-school education with its maximum Jewish cultural milieu and total immersion in a Jewish ambiance.[54]

In sum, if one were to visit the typical Conservative synagogue in America or Canada, one would probably find the following pattern: the main service would be on Friday evening at 8:30 with a cantor, choir, and in some instances, an organ; the Bat Mitzvah girls would officiate on Friday nights, the Bar Mitzvah boys on Saturday morning; the morning service is more sparsely attended than the evening one; the evening service has a good deal of English and is less traditional than the Sabbath morning one; the men all wear a *yarmulka* and a *talit* at the morning service and sit next to the women; the rabbi preaches Friday evening and Saturday morning; the synagogue runs a daily Hebrew School and a Sunday School for children under eight, as well as a host of youth and adult activities; and there is a Hebrew High School and an adult school for Judaica either in the congregation or in conjunction with several neighboring ones. Finally, most synagogues use the Rabbinical 'Assembly/United Synagogue *Prayer Book,* and most still conduct services on the second days of Passover, Shavuot, and Sukkot.

## Social Action

The Conservative movement has not been as swept up in the social-action vortex as has been the Reform movement. But it has not remained aloof either. In 1890 in Philadelphia, Morais and Jastrow devoted their *Kol Nidre* sermons to chastise the cloak manufacturers for exploiting their workers and precipitating the costly cloakmakers' strike. In Baltimore, Szold was preaching—and practicing—help for the flocks of new immigrants who were pouring in from Eastern Europe. And in New York, H.P. Mendes was urging rabbis to live with and teach slum immigrants. Morais involved Judge Sulzberger, F.D. Mendes, Moses Dropsie, Cyrus Adler, and Solomon Solis-Cohen in aiding Jewish farmers through the Baron Hirsch Fund. Clearly, the developing Conservative movement was not merely tending its own vineyards.[55]

But a formal social-justice program was a long time in coming. It was not until 1934 that a Pronouncement on Social Justice was issued. The Pronouncement declared that

> *Judaism has always recognized certain basic principles for social organization and has endeavored to apply them to the changing social situation. The authors of this pronouncement believe that its essence is traditional. For its general principles, historic Judaism is the sanction. Only its specific applications to contemporary social problems are their own.*[56]

Over the years, this Pronouncement's general ideals have been translated into concrete action in various fields.

For example, the Conservative movement has espoused the cause of organized labor. It called for a repeal of the Taft-Hartley Law back in 1950 and defended the grape workers' strike (1965–71); but it has also urged greater democratization of unions. The movement has been involved in the civil rights struggle: rabbis marched with Martin Luther King, Jr., in Birmingham and Selma; the United Synagogue has consistently called for equal opportunities for blacks, fair housing laws, and fair employment practices. Additionally, the Rabbinical Assembly and the United Synagogue have repeatedly urged liberal immigration and abortion laws, nuclear disarmament and test bans, ratification of the Genocide Pact, support of the United Nations, and separation of church and state, including repeal of Sunday closing laws and opposition to federal aid for parochial education.[57]

The issue of federal aid to parochial education has proved to be a thorny and contentious dilemma. For years, both the Rabbinical Assembly and the United Synagogue had opposed such aid as a breach in the wall of separation between church and state. But increasingly, as the Solomon Schechter schools proliferated and the financial burden became intolerable, more members of the movement began to rethink their positions on the question. Rabbis Robert Gordis, Harry Halpern, and other past presidents of the Rabbinical Assembly continued to oppose vigorously such aid as counter to the "non-establishment clause" of the First Amendment. But Rabbi Edward T. Sandrow, who as president of the Rabbinical Assembly had taken the same position, shifted ground and came out in favor of government aid, as did Professor Seymour Siegel of the Seminary faculty and the Rabbinical Assembly's Executive Vice President. A change of attitude in the ranks of the rabbis and many laymen is discernible, although the movement still officially opposes government aid to parochial schools.[58]

Another source of agonizing soul-searching and convulsive controversy has been the Vietnam war. Since 1966 the Rabbinical Assembly has called for an end to the Vietnam war, and the United Synagogue has followed suit. This has led to a sticky dilemma over the chaplaincy. In 1968, seven young graduates, revolted by the war, refused to enter the chaplaincy as required of all alumni of the Seminary. Consequently, the Rabbinical Assembly was compelled, after an acrimonious debate, to drop the voluntary draft and substitute service assignments in the community or needy congregations instead.[59]

A number of Conservative theologians have been grappling with a theology of social action. Professor Seymour Siegel suggests that Halakhah cannot give all the answers in this area but it can be normative "paradigmatically." It can serve as guide, goad, and goals for social behavior. Professor Gordis has attempted to deal with a variety of problems, such as international affairs, church and state, and law and ethics, in the light of Jewish tradition. Dr. Finkelstein has edited a number of significant volumes representing the fruits of various seminars and institutes convened by the Seminary on a variety of legal, moral, educational, and spiritual dilemmas. Professor Heschel became an impassioned social activist in the past decade. He marched with Negroes in Alabama, protested against the Vietnam war, spoke for Soviet Jewry, and espoused the cause of the aged. He wrote sardonically:

> Little does contemporary religion ask of man. It is ready to offer comfort; it has no courage to challenge. It is ready to offer edification; it has no courage to break the idols, to shatter callousness. The trouble is that religion has become "religion"—institution, dogma, ritual . . . an impersonal affair, an institutional loyalty. It has lost sight of the person.

Heschel urged compassionate treatment of the sick, the young and the aged, the blacks and the poor. He labeled racism "an eye disease, a cancer of the soul" and described it as satanism and unmitigated evil. Warning against the "evil of indifference," Heschel described Judaism as "the theology of the common deed" and a religion that seeks to give us "a bad conscience."[60]

Unquestionably, the Conservative movement and its leading proponents have made social action a cornerstone of faith and have attempted to formulate by theory and deed a theology of involvement in the issues of the day.

*Interfaith Relations*

The Conservative movement has been far less aloof from interfaith work than the Orthodox, but it has not been nearly as deeply involved as the Reform. Early liberals like Leeser, Szold, and Jastrow did cooperate with Christian clergy and laymen in a variety of communal endeavors; but no theology of interfaith relations was evolved and, in fact, no program was articulated until very recently.

Several of the leaders of the Conservative movement have been attuned to the need for interreligious dialogues. Dr. Finkelstein, for example, was an early pioneer of "ecumenism"—long before the word became popular. In 1940 he established the Seminary's Institute for Religious and Social Studies to plumb the depths of wisdom of various faiths. Ever since then, Jewish, Christian, Moslem, Buddhist, and Hindu theologians have gathered together at periodic conferences to explore the common heritage of the various faiths and to seek joint solutions to contemporary dilemmas. A number of significant volumes have been born of those conferences.

Rabbi Robert Gordis has also been involved in interreligious conversations. While he strongly favors such activities, he insists on several prerequisites: he demands that Christians stop drawing invidious comparisons between the Old and New Testaments and between the Jewish tribal "God of Justice" versus the Christian universal "God of Love"; he insists that Old Testament quotes expropriated by the Gospels be properly credited; and he urges Christianity to reappraise its understanding of Judaism to include the rabbinic reinterpretation of Biblical faith. On the other hand, he also implores the modern Jew to rise above the heavy burden of historic memories. Professor Heschel was also swept up in the interfaith movement. He served as consultant to Cardinal Bea in formulating Vatican policies vis-à-vis the Jew; he called for a "relationship of reverence for each other" and declared it "barbaric" to oppose vital interfaith work. Professor Seymour Siegel, who has taught at Christian seminaries, states flatly, "We must have dialogue" in order to combat secularism, teach the need for standards of law and ethics, and defend "tribalism and traditionalism."[61]

Although the Rabbinical Assembly affirmed the need for Judeo-Christian dialogue at its 1965 convention, it did so with the proviso that "only scholars deeply steeped in the teachings of our tradition should engage in discussions with any other historic faith." A full-scale debate on the value of Jewish-Christian dialogue was held at the 1967 convention with Jewish and Christian participants. Rabbi Stuart Rosenberg heartily endorsed dialogue by observing that "We have been listening to Christianity for two thousand years, without having an opportunity to talk back"; now, said Rosenberg, at least they listen. Rabbi Jacob Agus declared it a positive *mitzvah* to teach non-Jews the seven basic principles of Noah, and since separation of faiths makes "very fertile soil for anti-Semitism," we must teach. Moreover, Agus describes it a *kiddush ha-Shem* (sanctification of God's name) to uproot misconceptions about religion. Rabbi Ben Zion Bokser, however, presented a critical paper assessing the pitfalls of interreligious activities. He warned that the sugar-and-spice approach often merely conceals a missionary drive. Still, Bokser agreed that Jews should not spurn offers of friendship and should welcome "any gesture that marks a diminution of prejudice." He urged Jews to help Christians "shed rigidity" and unite in battling "moral and spirtual darkness and violence." The negative goal of such a program would be to "expose the falsification of Judaism; the positive purpose would be to expound the Jewish solution to the problems of interfaith tension." As a result of this symposium, the Rabbinical Assembly unanimously adopted a resolution establishing a committee to investigate the problems and pitfalls of interreligious dialogue.[62]

*Summary* .

Obviously, the Conservative movement is every bit as protean as the Reform movement, and clear-cut ideological views are hard to come by. But the general consensus and emphatic trends that seem to emerge are these:

1. Conservative Judaism defines Judaism as an ever-changing religious civilization that has adapted in the past and must constantly adapt itself to new challenges and crises.

2. Conservative Judaism is a middle-of-the-road approach to Judaism. It seeks the golden mean; it attempts to balance the two polarities of tradition and change; it is convinced that this is, historically, the correct approach and, existentially, the sane approach to preserving a vibrant Judaism.

3. Conservative Judaism starts out from the focal point of the Jewish People. It posits the view that the basic function of Judaism is to preserve the Jewish People.

4. Its concept of God is nondogmatic and flexible. It believes that this is historically and theologically a sound position; it allows latitude for a variety of views ranging from supernaturalism and neo-Hasidism to naturalistic humanism.

5. Torah is taken to be the culture of the Jewish People. It is the word of God, although not in the literal sense. It has always developed in response to socio-economic needs; it must continue to do so. As the Talmudic rabbis gave vibrancy and dynamism to classical Judaism, so must the modern-day sages reinterpret the faith to make it viable. While the movement has a positive prejudice *in favor* of tradition, it is willing to amend or emend that tradition when specific *mitzvot* seem to be outmoded or arbitrarily unethical. Both ethical and ritual rules are, however, binding on the Jew.

6. The Jewish People is a solid, cohesive entity. Jews must feel a responsibility for one another; their fates are inextricably intertwined. Cooperation to build a flourishing Jewish community is essential.

7. The Land of Israel is holy. It is the historical, religious, and spiritual center of world Jewry; it must again assume that role. It is a positive *mitzvah* for every Jew to support Israel financially, politically, morally. But the State is merely a means to an end; for out of Zion must go forth Torah and God's word from Jerusalem.

8. The synagogue is viewed as the basic institution of Jewish life. It is a center for a host of activities—sacred and secular. Its liturgy shoud be traditional, but must be revised and updated

constantly. The core of the prayers is retained as is Hebrew; but innovation and experimentation to make the service relevant are encouraged.

9. Maximum Jewish education, complemented by Hebrew camping and Jewish club activities, is basic to the Conservative movement. Many clergy and laymen are now convinced that Day Schools hold forth the most promise for Jewish survival.

10. Social action is considered a primary Jewish obligation by the Conservative movement. The consensus is for civil rights, universal disarmament, separation of church and state, an end to the Vietnam war, and a war on poverty, crime, corruption, and exploitation.

11. The Conservative movement supports interreligious dialogue but only on a high, theological level conducted by experts, and with the proviso that conversion motives are ruled out of order.

To sum it up, Conservative Judaism seeks to combine the strong points of Orthodoxy and Reform: it adheres to the warm, tangible, traditional symbols of Orthodoxy; it espouses the Reform teaching of the need to grow, adapt, reinterpret, and develop. By fusing tradition and change, Conservative Judaism has succeeded in winning a flock of followers from among those who, on the one hand, are disenchanted with Orthodoxy's intransigence, but for whom, on the other hand, Reform represents too radical a break with tradition. Conservatism has proved to be a meaningful philosophy for this vital center of American and Canadian Jewry.

# *Reconstructionism—History*

## VIII

The only purely native-born and native-bred religious movement in American Jewry is Reconstructionism. Orthodoxy had its roots in Central or Eastern Europe; Reform and Conservatism are German imports; but Reconstructionism is uniquely American—historically, ideologically, and institutionally.

To be sure, many Reconstructionist theories are derived from European sources. For example, Simon Dubnow's conception of *Galut* nationalism plays a significant role in the Reconstructionist notion of organic Jewish communities flourishing around the world, cultivating their religion and culture in a semiautonomous state. Likewise, Ahad Ha'am's doctrines of a "spiritual center" in Zion that would serve as a focal point for Diaspora Jewry, as well as his nontheological reinterpretation of Jewish values, have become pillars of Reconstructionism. The German historical school of Zunz and Frankel implanted in Reconstructionism its recognition of the natural origin and continuity of Jewish institutions, while Durkheim's and Robertson Smith's theories of religion as an expression of social life and a means to group survival and cohesion were integrated by the move-ment. Moreover, the concepts of God of Immanuel Kant and Matthew Arnold and the social Darwinism of Herbert Spencer occupy a prominent position in Reconstructionist theology.

But American ideas have been dominant in Reconstruction-ism. John Dewey's pragmatism, William James's psychology, Felix Adler's Ethical Culture, Arnold B. Ehrlich's Biblical criti-cism, and the democratic *Zeitgeist* of the New World have formed the raw material from which Reconstructionism has risen. In addition, its leaders have all been either American-born or American-trained, and in fact the movement has *exported* its ideas to England, Israel, and other lands in a reversal of the classic pattern of *importing* religious doctrines to these shores. More than anything, Reconstructionism bears the stamp "Made in America."[1]

There is another unique quality of Reconstructionism that sets it off from the other religious movements we have studied: Reconstructionism is virtually synonymous and coextensive with the life and times of one man—Dr. Mordecai M. Kaplan. Kaplan is the charismatic leader, founder, and architect of Reconstruc-tionism: he conceived it, he formulated its program, he shaped its liturgy, he has devoted over seventy years of his rich and seminal life to expounding his ideology devoted to "the ad-vancement of Judaism as a religious civilization, to the upbuild-ing of Eretz Yisrael, and to the furtherance of universal freedom, justice and peace." The leading lights of Reconstructionism—the late Rabbi Milton Steinberg, Eugene Kohn, Ira Eisenstein, Jack Cohen—are merely satellites revolving around the central luminary that is Mordecai M. Kaplan. Nothing of value in Recon-structionism has emanated from any hand but that of Kaplan; all ideas and notions, institutions and projects reflect the influence of the most creative American Jewish religious leader of the twentieth century.[2]

Mordecai M. Kaplan was born in Lithuania in 1881, the son of the eminent Orthodox rabbi Israel Kaplan and an equally pious and intelligent mother. Kaplan grew up in the Torah-saturated suburb of Vilna and at an early age his parents decided he should become a rabbi. In 1889 Kaplan's father came to New York City to assist the newly elected Chief Orthodox Rabbi Jacob Joseph. Young Mordecai, his mother, and sister tarried in Paris for a year. There he encountered his first conflict of "living in two civilizations" as he tried to resolve the problem of attending school on the Sabbath without desecrating the day by writing his lessons. The second such childhood conflict occurred aboard the steamer that carried him to join his father in New York. It was Bastille Day one Sabbath at sea; young Mordecai wanted to witness the fireworks display. But it was also the Sabbath and Kaplan's pious mother refused to let him watch the spectacle. Ever since then, records Kaplan, he has been wrestling with the dilemma of living in two worlds—the Jewish and the secular.

At age eight Kaplan came to America. He was taught at home for several years, and at twelve he entered public school. Simultaneously, he enrolled in the preparatory department of the Jewish Theological Seminary with which he was to be associated for seventy years. A visitor to the Kaplan home in those days was the brilliant Biblical scholar Arnold B. Ehrlich. Ehrlich read his critical commentary to young Mordecai and inadvertently undermined the lad's faith in Divine revelation and the Mosaic origin of the entire Torah. Young Mordecai also began to study Maimonides' *Guide for the Perplexed* and was introduced to the world of medieval philosophy and critical theology. Kaplan was graduated from New York's City College in 1900 and was ordained by the Seminary in 1902. That same year he received a Master of Arts degree from Columbia University. By this time Kaplan no longer believed in the Mosaic authorship of the Pentateuch or miracles, but he was still—by force of habit and emotional temperament—a scrupulously observant Jew. Kaplan continued postgraduate rabbinic studies and he read widely in philosophy, psychology, history, sociology, and anthropology.

And so, the young firebrand with the goatee and the clear blue eyes set out to serve his people and teach them how to live creatively as Jews in two worlds and two civilizations simultaneously. He was called to the pulpit of a prominent Orthodox congregation in New York, Kehilath Jeshurun, where he was to be minister and English preacher, and associate to Rabbi Moses Margolies. There was some difficulty over his credentials, and the more fanatical refused to call him Rabbi. On his honeymoon trip through Europe in 1908, Kaplan received the traditional *semikhah* (ordination) from Rabbi Isaac Reines. Still, his gnawing doubts and questions persisted.

In 1909 Professor Solomon Schechter invited Kaplan to head the new Teachers Institute of the Seminary. Kaplan decided to leave his pulpit and throw himself full time into academic life. A year later he became professor of homiletics at the Seminary's rabbinical school. This appointment saved Kaplan for Jewish life, for he had been unhappy in his Orthodox *shul* and had actually contemplated becoming an insurance salesman. From then on, Kaplan never swerved from his chosen path of helping the Jewish People to find their way in an age of disbelief. His reading of Ahad Ha'am had convinced him of the need to fortify the "will to live of the Jewish People" and he set his course accordingly.

Mordecai Kaplan was not just a book scholar. He joined Judah Magnes and Samson Benderly in creating New York's Kehillah, serving as chairman of its Board of Jewish Education from 1908 to 1922. He was, with Israel Friedlander and others, one of the founders of Young Israel, and from 1912 to 1922 he walked for miles on Sabbaths to help inspire young Jews at their synagogues. Despite his heterodox views, he accepted a call to New York's Jewish Center in 1915. He sought to actualize his concept that a synagogue should be more than merely a house of prayer or study, that it should be a *center* encompassing all aspects of Jewish expression—religious and cultural, social and athletic. But Kaplan quickly found himself in trouble. He had criticized the Seminary and the Conservative movement for being too timorous; he expressed doubts about miracles and the Mosaic authorship of the Torah; he challenged some basic Orthodox theological norms. And although he received a vote of confidence from his board in 1921, he decided to resign from the Jewish Center. In 1922 Kaplan and twenty-two former members of the Jewish Center formed a new synagogue—the Society for the Advancement of Judaism. A new synagogue was born; a new movement was developing; Reconstructionism was about to emerge from the cocoon of Kaplan's fertile brain.

Actually, Kaplan had already called for the "reconstruction" of the tottering edifice of Judaism in 1920. In July of that year he founded the short-lived Society for the Jewish Renascence. He disavowed any sectarian motive or separatist purpose; he wanted, rather, to strengthen the existing structure of Jewish life. The platform of the new group delineated several goals and principles:

> *1. The continuance of the Jewish people as a nation in the land of Israel and in lands of the Diaspora with a religio-national culture of their own.*
>
> *2. The need of humanity for faith in God and the belief in the dignity and sacredness of human life, the worth of human progress, and the ultimate triumph of freedom, justice, and truth.*
>
> *3. Divine Revelation is the manifestation of God in the spiritual experiences and aspirations of mankind.*
>
> *4. Scripture is the record of those experiences of God revealing Himself to Israel and humanity.*
>
> *5. Halakhah, rooted in the Talmud, must be accepted as the norm of Jewish life, although man has the right to interpret and develop it in accordance with the needs of modern life.*

Kaplan insisted that all members of the new group must affiliate with a synagogue, attend services, read and study Jewish history and literature, strive for social and civic betterment, encourage a minimum of five hours of study for children in religious schools, engage in adult Jewish education, and work for the rebuilding of the Land of Israel. Although the group died a premature death, its ideology was incorporated into Kaplan's new synagogue, the Society for the Advancement of Judaism.[3]

The Society for the Advancement of Judaism—or SAJ, as it is popularly known—became the laboratory of Kaplan's ideas in theology, sociology, and Zionism. He borrowed the name from Dr. Judah Magnes, and in obvious emulation of the Society for

Ethical Culture, preferred to call his congregation a "society" rather than "synagogue," and referred to himself as "leader" rather than "rabbi." He issued a *Bulletin,* later called the SAJ *Review;* in 1935 he began to publish the *Reconstructionist* magazine. In his pulpit, in his magazine articles, and in his classes at the Seminary, Kaplan expounded his philosophy of Judaism. At the Seminary, he became the *enfant terrible* and his views were anathema to Dr. Cyrus Adler and several faculty members. In 1927 he reached another crisis in his life and he resigned from his beloved Alma Mater. He felt stifled in its conservative atmosphere; he wrote to a disciple, Rabbi Solomon Goldman of Chicago, that he had resigned in order to devote himself "wholeheartedly to the furtherance of Conservative Judaism." In his letter of resignation, he stressed that "both the national and the religious element in traditional Judaism must be conserved and developed. By omitting either of these elements, we are bound to break completely with the Judaism of the past." He added that in the "reconstruction of Judaism new principles of observances will be evolved to sanction and enlarge ceremonials in Judaism."[4]

But Dr. Alder and several colleagues at the Seminary and in the Rabbinical Assembly prevailed upon him to stay on. A number of Kaplan's disciples—Rabbis Solomon Goldman, Herman Rubenovitz, and others—proposed forming a liberal bloc within the Rabbinical Assembly and the United Synagogue. Goldman wrote in 1927 that he was "prepared to bore from within for at least a year or two. If at the end of that period, we find ourselves helpless, we should attempt an independent organization." Rabbi Eugene Kohn was opposed to secession but he suggested extending the work of the SAJ. Rabbi Max Kadushin favored quiet, individual efforts on their own while remaining part of the Conservative movement. Rubenovitz was anxious that the little group translate into concrete action the term "historical Judaism" and he urged his colleagues to help Jewish liberalism reassert itself in revision of prayers and ritual and in public programs. But Kaplan was reticent: he was reluctant to fragmentize Jewish life any further. Until 1968, Kaplan steadfastly refused to break away from his beloved Alma Mater or the Conservative movement; he did not want Reconstructionism to add another set of competing institutions to the already splintered condition of Jewish life in this country. Instead, he preferred that Reconstructionism cut across partisan boundaries and unify all groups. This reluctance to strike out on his own crippled the growth of Reconstructionism—and may have doomed it to ineffectualness forever.[5]

The year 1927 was critical in another sense for Kaplan and Reconstructionism. Dr. Stephen S. Wise, who, several years earlier, had founded the Jewish Institute of Religion, had been searching in vain for a president for the school. In 1920 he had approached Kaplan and invited him to become a co-founder of the Institute, but he refused. In 1927, knowing of Kaplan's disenchantment with the Jewish Theological Seminary, and believing that Mordecai M. Kaplan was the most remarkable Jewish thinker on these shores, Stephen Wise again invited him to head JIR. After much soul-searching, Kaplan declined: he felt it would be an act of disloyalty to an institution with which he had been associated for thirty years. Wise tried once again in the 1930's; Kaplan was sorely tempted, as he felt frustrated in his quest to shift the direction of the Seminary. But his sense of loyalty to his Alma Mater deterred him. In retrospect, Kaplan wonders whether he hadn't committed a colossal blunder, for as head of the Jewish Institute of Religion he could have shaped it in his own image; he would have trained a generation of Reconstructionist rabbis; he would have had a ready-made institution from which to disseminate his ideas; he might have captured American Jewry. Who knows? But this is purely speculation. The fact is, he stayed with the Seminary until his retirement in 1963.[6]

Kaplan continued to write, teach, and preach. In 1934 he produced his magnum opus, *Judaism as a Civilization.* It made an immediate impression and has remained one of the landmarks of American-Jewish thought and the "Bible" of the Reconstructionist movement. In it, Kaplan offers a critique of the various movements of Jewish life, and he analyzes their strong and weak points. Then he proceeds to argue that none of these ideologies can shore up the rotted house of Judaism; nothing short of reconstructing the edifice can save it. He then presents his program. He describes Judaism as an evolving, religious civilization; he insists on retaining Jewish spiritual peoplehood; he views Zion as an indispensable cultural-religious center; he rejects literal revelation of God's Torah; he describes *mitzvot* as *sancta* and folkways that must be reinterpreted, emended, and amended; he denies belief in other-worldly salvation. In short, he argues for a Copernican revolution in Jewish life if we are to save the intellectuals and if we are to preserve Judaism. The book has become a classic; essentially it states everything that Reconstructionism has to say, and with certain exceptions, it has remained the normative position of Kaplan and his followers till the present.

From that point on, Kaplan continued to pour out articles and books in profusion. He taught at the Graduate School for Jewish Social Work from 1925 to 1937. He was also a professor at Columbia's Teachers College and the University of Chicago. In 1935–37 he was professor of education at the Hebrew University in Jerusalem. After considerable soul-searching and with great personal ambivalence, he decided to return to America. He has visited Israel many times since, however, to lecture at the Hebrew University and at various *kibbutzim.*

Always the man of action, Kaplan was elected president of the Rabbinical Assembly in 1932 after an acrimonious battle. He sought desperately to reshape both the Rabbinical Assembly and the United Synagogue. He was a leading theoretician in the Zionist Organization of America. He was a builder of the Board of Jewish Education in New York; he helped develop the Menorah Society; he had a great impact on social workers as well as rabbis and educators. His fertile mind conceived the synagogue-center, the University of Judaism (the California school of the Jewish Theological Seminary), the Bat Mitzvah ceremony for girls, the Leaders Training Fellowship to cultivate teenage boys and girls for Jewish leadership, equal religious rights for women in synagogue life, as well as a flock of other institutions and seminal ideas that have affected all branches of American Judaism.

Kaplan also sought to concretize his theology in liturgical efforts. In 1941 he produced a new *Haggadah* for the Passover *Seder*. It was hailed by the liberals and damned by the conservatives. But the furor that greeted the *New Haggadah* in 1941 was insignificant compared to the tempest that engulfed Kaplan upon the issuance of his new *Sabbath Prayer Book* in 1945. A group of ultra-Orthodox rabbis of the Agudat Harabanim, gathered at a New York hotel, excommunicated Kaplan, and burned a copy of the new *Sidur*. Even some of Kaplan's colleagues at the Seminary turned on him. In an article in the Hebrew weekly *Ha-Doar*, Professors Louis Ginzberg, Alexander Marx, and Saul Lieberman described him as "unlearned in the Law" and suggested that he ought to stop dabbling in Halakhah and return to homiletics. Kaplan was deeply hurt; he felt forsaken and alone. At a ninetieth-birthday tribute in his honor tendered by the New York Board of Rabbis, he described those days as the most painful and anguished in his career. But many rallied to his side. The Rabbinical Assembly unanimously condemned the action of the Agudat Harabanim members as well as the Seminary opponents. They labeled such action a desecration of God's name, an act of "irresponsible hysteria," and a violation of freedom of conscience. Kaplan rallied his strength, the storm abated, and when he issued his *Festival Mahzor* and *High Holiday Mahzor* several years later, scarcely a ripple troubled the waters.[7]

In 1946 Kaplan became dean emeritus of the Teachers Institute. He continued as professor of philosophies of religion at the Rabbinical School of the Seminary from 1947 until his retirement in 1963. He had trained three generations of rabbis, teachers, and social workers in an unprecedentedly long and fruitful career of teaching and lecturing. After his "retirement," he produced articles and books, novel ideas and conceptions, and he indefatigably devoted himself to the development of the Reconstructionist movement. In his ninetieth year of life, he was still running like a stripling, his mind as fertile and creative as ever.

Most of Kaplan's success has been due to his charismatic and magnetic personality. As a teacher, he was often pedantic and talked over the heads of his students. But he could also be inspiring and exalting and on more than one occasion his students were moved to applaud a lecture. He had a monumental temper, and was impatient with dolts and intolerant of ignoramuses. On the other hand, he has always owned a rich sense of humor, he cared about his students, and he loved his classes. Preeminently, he was respected because he asked the right questions, and whether one agreed with the answers or not, all concurred that he forced his students to clear away their mental cobwebs, rethink their positions, and utilize merciless logic and cold clarity in analyzing the problems of Jewish life. Studying in Kaplan's class was like an exhilarating plunge into an icy stream: one may not have always been happy or comfortable, but one was certainly awakened with a jolt.

Kaplan is a man of many parts. He is an amateur sculptor, he loves music, he has kept a remarkable journal for over half a century. He has both a Copernican and a Maimonidean complex. He wants to reorient Jewish priorities just as Copernicus reoriented the concept of the universe; he seeks to reconstruct Judaism in the light of present-day knowledge, even as Maimonides (whose books were also burned) did in his time. In short, Mordecai M. Kaplan has been perhaps *the* American-Jewish thinker of the twentieth century and perhaps one of the great Jewish ideologists of all times.

But Kaplan failed miserably in one key area: he could never make up his mind whether Reconstructionism was to be an interdenominational school of thought, or "quality of life," or a full-blown institutionalized movement. Kaplan wanted to avoid further factionalism; but he did not realize that a movement cannot grow on oxygen alone—it needs a structure, a body, institutions to flesh out its spirit. His vacillation in this area hurt the movement and stunted its development.

Some of Kaplan's colleagues felt more strongly about the need for structure. In 1928, for example, a national organizational conference of Reconstructionists was summoned. The Midwest Council of Reconstructionism was established in Chicago with Rabbis Max Kadushin, Felix Levy, and Dr. Alexander Dushkin at its head. Later, there was an abortive attempt to do the same on the East Coast. Educators like Dushkin, Israel

Chipkin, Jacob Golub, Samuel Dinin, Abraham Duker, Judith Epstein, and Albert Schoolman flocked to his banner as did Reform and Conservative rabbis who begged Kaplan to set his own course. The *Reconstructionist* magazine, published as a fortnightly, then a monthly, made an impact despite its modest format and limited readership. In 1935, Reconstructionist clubs were organized for the first time. In 1938 the leaders set up a summer institute and a press, and 2,100 subscribers signed up as Friends of Reconstructionism. Kaplan needed help; he invited Rabbis Max Kadushin and Milton Steinberg to become his assistants, but they both refused. Finally, Ira Eisenstein, who was still a Seminary student, joined the staff at the SAJ, becoming its leader in 1945 and reintroducing the title "rabbi" in 1950. Rabbis Eugene Kohn, Milton Steinberg, and Ira Eisenstein became Kaplan's closest collaborators; others like Israel Goldstein, Ben Zion Bokser, Solomon Goldman, Mortimer Cohen, Morris Adler, as well as Reform rabbis like Felix Levy, Joshua Trachtenberg, Charles Shulman, among many, became nominal affiliates of the group and editors of the *Reconstructionist*.

The Reconstructionist Foundation was set up in 1940 in an attempt to shape a movement and capture formal support from Reform and Conservative rabbis as well as laymen, secularists, and Zionists. Many members of the Rabbinical Assembly were attracted to the Foundation as were those of the Central Conference of American Rabbis. But some of the earlier followers either broke with Kaplan's increasingly radical views or just drifted away. Thus, Max Kadushin, Ben Zion Bokser, Morris Adler, and Solomon Goldman left the ranks, and even Milton Steinberg—notwithstanding his loyalty to Kaplan and sympathy with Reconstructionism—uttered sharply critical views of Kaplan's concept of God and rejection of the chosen people in the last days of his tragically short life.

Reconstructionism issued its *New Haggadah* in 1941, its *Sabbath Prayer Book* in 1945, a *High Holiday Mahzor* in 1947, and a *Festival Mahzor* in 1958, as well as a *Daily Prayer Book* and lesser liturgical compositions and numerous books, pamphlets, and brochures. In 1943 the struggling Reconstructionist fellowships tried unsuccessfully to convene a national convention. Groups in Brooklyn, Westchester, Baltimore, Philadelphia, Los Angeles, Oakland, Kansas City, Milwaukee, Arlington, Va., and Alexandria, Va., tried to coalesce under the directorship of Rabbi Jack Cohen in 1944. Cohen (who was later to succeed Eisenstein as rabbi of the SAJ) urged the creation of an "activist religious movement," but the plan aborted. An effort to establish the Reconstructionist Youth Fellowship in 1946 also died aborning.

The groping towards a formalized movement proceeded painfully. In 1950, forty Conservative and Reform Rabbis organized the Reconstructionist Rabbinical Fellowship. By 1951, 86 had enrolled and eventually 285 rabbis and 250 educators, social workers, and laymen were paper members. In 1950 the Reconstructionist School of Jewish Studies was opened—and promptly collapsed. When Rabbi Ira Eisenstein was elected president of the Rabbinical Assembly in 1952, Reconstructionist hopes waxed again. But nothing came of it and it was evident that the Conservative movement would not follow the Reconstructionist path. The Reconstructionist Press was revamped in 1953 and issued some notable works, chiefly by Kaplan, Kohn, Eisenstein, and Cohen. In 1955 the leaders tried once more to form a fellowship of congregations. Several synagogues, including the SAJ and others from Skokie (Illinois), Buffalo, Indianapolis, and Cedarhurst, N.Y., joined. In 1957 three more affiliated. But the association was little more than a loose union rendering financial support to the Reconstructionist projects. In 1953, Ira Eisenstein went to Chicago to succeed the late Rabbi Solomon Goldman in an attempt to propagate Reconstructionism in the Midwest. But Eisenstein failed and returned to New York in 1959 to become president of the Reconstructionist Foundation. A Reconstructionist Women's Organization was set up in 1957 and the *T'hiyah* Youth Organization in 1959. Neither, however, has enjoyed much success.

Finally, in 1959 a formal Fellowship of Reconstructionist Congregations was established. Ira Eisenstein pressed for an end to Reconstructionism as a "school of thought" and the beginning of an active program with agencies and institutions. In 1961 the organization, now known as the Federation of Reconstructionist Congregations and Fellowships, tried to open its own summer camp—and failed. Meanwhile, the Rabbinic Fellowship had gone out of existence, and the *Reconstructionist* magazine, for all its prestige, still had fewer than five thousand paid subscribers. In 1961, Rabbi Jack Cohen left the pulpit of the SAJ and went to Israel as Director of Hillel at the Hebrew University. Although he did not succeed in developing a Reconstructionist service, a new synagogue called Mevakshay Derekh was established in Jerusalem by Reconstructionist sympathizers. It has become a sort of unofficial Reconstructionist congregation and Rabbi Kaplan was fond of worshipping there. Meanwhile, Rabbi Allan Miller was brought over from London to succeed Cohen at the SAJ—striking evidence of the paucity of competent American Reconstructionist rabbis. By 1969 there were only ten members of the Federation of Reconstructionist Synagogues and nine small *havurot* (fellowships) scattered throughout America, Canada, and the West Indies. Of the ten synagogues, two were occupied by alumni of the Jewish Theological Seminary. Rabbi Arthur Gilbert, a Reform rabbi, became assistant to Eisenstein in running the Reconstructionist Foundation. By 1970 there were 82 Conservative and 50 Reform rabbis affiliated with the movement and 2,300 families, 1,300 of whom came from two congregations.

The problem of a school for training Reconstructionist clergy proved to be most thorny. In the 1950's Kaplan had tried to have Jack Cohen appointed to the Seminary faculty. While Cohen was allowed to teach and assist Kaplan, he never received a faculty appointment. It was obvious that after Kaplan's retirement the Seminary would not permit Reconstructionism to make its case at the Seminary again.

The leadership of Reconstructionism finally convinced Dr. Kaplan that unless the group began to train its own rabbis, it would atrophy and die. In 1968 the Reconstructionist College was established in Philadelphia for the training of rabbis. The move was long overdue, and when a survey of 1,500 rabbis trained in various seminaries indicated that a bare sixty said they would accept a Reconstructionist synagogue, the case for a seminary was clinched. The College was established to train men and women to lead the movement. It was innovative in ideology and techniques; it affiliated with Temple University and expected its students to work for a Ph.D. degree simultaneously. The course of studies is a minimum of five years, and the cirriculum is unique in that each year of study is devoted to a different period in Jewish history with all subjects revolving around that core. The freshman class enrolled thirteen students, including women, and the first ordination is slated for 1973. But the College has suffered from both financial and personnel problems, and most of the faculty teach on a part-time basis. The first dean of the College, Rabbi Arthur Gilbert, resided in New York, as does Rabbi Ira Eisenstein, its president. Whether the College will survive or not is still a moot point; but the students are enthusiastically committed to the school and there have been more applicants than the College can handle.

For whom has Reconstructionism had its greatest appeal? Sociologist Charles Liebman shows that it had its greatest impact on second-generation Americans, especially in the twenties and thirties. These children of East European immigrants found Reconstructionism to be closest to the American *Zeitgeist* and pragmatic mood. They were attracted to Kaplan's definition of Judaism as a religious civilization; they concurred in his non-supernatural concept of the Deity; they accepted his views on social progress, social justice, ethics and social Darwinism. Moreover, Kaplan's partisans were charmed by his positive—if basically nostalgic—commitment to *mitzvot.* For Kaplan has remained personally an observant Jew, and many of his earlier partisans shared his loyalty despite their rationalistic reinterpretation of revelation, although latter disciples have not been too meticulous in observing the ritual rules. Additionally, Reformers, Conservatives, Zionist leaders, and secular Jewish culturalists have been inspired by Kaplan's notion of Jewish peoplehood. The classical Reformers who had stripped Judaism of the notion of the Jewish People fought his ideas bitterly. But gradually he won them over to his point of view. Intellectuals and some academicians have also become devotés of Reconstructionist views on God and society.[8]

However, Reconstructionism has lost its impetus in recent years. After World War II the mood of the country changed sharply. Gone was the naive optimism and artless faith in human progress. Gone was the simple trust in man and nations. Gone was the unquestioning belief in science and technology. Existentialism made great inroads; crisis theology and pessimism left their marks. Dewey was out, Kierkegaard was in, and Kaplan's influence waned considerably. From 1920 to 1945, 25 percent of the students at the Jewish Theological Seminary were sympathetic to Reconstructionism. But by 1967 only 17 percent of the seniors and 10 percent of the freshmen listed themselves as Reconstructionists. As to the ordained rabbis, 15 percent of the Conservative rabbis *under* forty and 24 percent of the Reform men consider themselves Kaplan partisans.[9]

And yet, ironically, Charles Liebman shows that the bulk of American Jews subscribe to Kaplan's views—if only unconsciously! They *do* view Judaism as a religious civilization. They *do* prefer his rationalistic approach to Torah, revelation, and *mitzvot*. They *do* subscribe to his non-supernatural God idea. They *do* accept his conception of Jewish peoplehood. They agree with his spiritual Zionism. And they accept his reinterpretations of Jewish values. Why, then, are there not several million Reconstructionists? Partly because Kaplan himself refused to allow his philosophy to be institutionalized until so recently. And partly, too, because his views are not as well known as they should be. Numerous American Jews are like Molière's *bourgeois gentilhomme* who spoke prose all his life and didn't know it—they have been Reconstructionists all of their lives, unwittingly![10]

The impact of Reconstructionism and Mordecai M. Kaplan on American Judaism has been significant. All branches of religious Jewry—including Orthodoxy—have assimilated, knowingly and unknowingly, many of the salient features of Reconstructionism. Kaplan's synagogue-center is a widely accepted institution; the validity of his concept of peoplehood is generally acknowledged, as is his "New Zionism"; his emancipation of the Jewish woman has become the norm for many congregations; his reinterpretations of Jewish laws and values have been applauded and followed.

What of the days ahead? Will Reconstructionism, with its new institutions and College become a viable, dynamic *movement* rather than merely a school of thought? And what will happen when Kaplan is no longer on the scene? Has he built a cult of the personality that will leave an unfillable vacuum? Only time will tell. In the meantime, Reconstructionism seeks to consolidate its gains, plot its future course, and deepen its stakes. It is determined to be more than a passing ideology created in the image of one giant of a man—Mordecai M. Kaplan.

# *Reconstructionism—Ideology*

# IX

Reconstructionism is the most philosophical, intellectual, and cerebral of all the movements in Jewish religious life. It began as a revolt against prevailing ideologies; it has continued to function as a gadfly seeking to reformulate Jewish ideals and values.

It is far easier to evaluate and analyze Reconstructionism than the other religious schools of American Jewry. For one thing, most of the ideas, insights, and innovations are Mordecai M. Kaplan's; all of the other proponents, such as Milton Steinberg, Eugene Kohn, Ira Eisenstein, and Jack Cohen, merely play variations on Kaplanian themes. Because Reconstructionism is virtually synonymous with Mordecai M. Kaplan, its founding father, he who would write a study of its ideology must master Kaplan's writings; all else is merely commentary on the basic tenets of his approach. Moreover, Reconstructionism has held a handful of formal rabbinical or congregational conventions and has issued few officially formulated pronunciamentos. Consequently, if one reads Kaplan's numerous writings or leafs through the pages of the *Reconstructionist* magazine, one receives a fairly complete picture of Reconstructionist thinking. Unlike the other movements in Jewish life, its tenets are clear, concise, and rationally structured, and the ideological axioms are lucidly presented. Reading Kaplan is not easy, but at least the philosophy is consistent. And one emerges from reading his works with little of the confusion and perplexities that cloud the ideologies of the other schools of Jewish thought.[1]

## The Nature of Judaism

Perhaps the most widely accepted definition of Judaism is Kaplan's formulation that Judaism is an *evolving religious civilization*. As we have previously noted, virtually all Conservative rabbis and many Reform ones accept this notion.

Why does Kaplan reject the conception of Judaism as a *religion*? The answer is that he finds that to be too narrow and confining a definition. Judaism is much more than just a religion: it is culture, language, art, music, folkways, customs, *sancta*, etc. Kaplan has some peculiarly new notions as to the role of religion in the life of the Jew. He writes that "a specific religion . . . is the acceptance of life as having meaning by virtue of what certain persons, objects, events, and other concrete elements in the career of a specific people—in brief, certain *sancta*—have contributed toward the self-realization of that people." Religion is a "natural social process which arises from man's intrinsic need of salvation or self-fulfillment"; it is both a social phenomenon and an individual experience, and whatever helps to produce creative social interaction among Jews rightly belongs to the category of Jewish religion, because it contributes to the salvation of the Jew. Paradoxically, writes Kaplan, "the spiritual regeneration of the Jewish people demands that religion cease to be its sole preoccupation." For the sake of religion, it is necessary to foster other interests besides religion, for Judaism is a way of life—not life itself—and it must include such elements as poetry, drama, art, esthetics, music, etc.[2]

But why the adjective "religious" in Kaplan's definition? Why

not merely describe Judaism as a "civilization?" Kaplan replies
that religion is a necessary ingredient in civilization:

> *The role of religion in human life is to humanize men by enabling*
> *them to transcend the limits of present nature. It emphasizes that*
> *which differentiates man from the beast; it identifies the divine element*
> *in that which man can make out of himself. . . . To the extent that*
> *any civilization contributes to this end of achieving the good and full*
> *life and realization of the holiness of human life it is religious. Hence*
> *Judaism is a religious civilization.* [3]

Obviously, since religion helps man achieve his fullest potential
as a human being and enables him to rise above the beast, it is
an indispensable facet of Jewish civilization. The main problem
of the Jewish religion today, suggests Kaplan, is not the God
idea but what common purpose which makes for enhancement
of human life will gain commitment and passionate devotion of
Jews and enable them to see therein the manifestation of God.
Milton Steinberg argues that the retreat of religion has been a
contribution to the tragedy of our time and has been of supreme
importance and influence in changing the norms of today's
world. [4]

Why does Kaplan insist on describing Judaism as an "evolving" religious civilization? The point is that, historically speaking, Judaism never stood still. It changed, it adapted itself to new
conditions, it consciously or unconsciously absorbed and assimilated unto itself the cultural and religious influences that
surrounded it. Kaplan delineates several stages in the development of the Jewish civilization. First came the *national* stage
when Jews were an *am*, a people. Then we became an *ecclesia*,
*Knesset Yisrael*. Afterwards we entered the *rabbinic* stage when the
*hakhamim* (sages) held sway. And now we have reached the democratic stage in our development. In the past the various challenges to Judaism confirmed us in our loyalty. Moreover, we
derived solace and inner strength from our belief in salvation in
*olam ha-ba*, the world to come, as well as in observing the *mitzvot*
and studying Torah. In the Middle Ages, we sought to harmo-
nize faith and reason, miracles and science. Giants like Mai-

monides succeeded in reconciling reason and faith by rationalism; others turned to Kabbalah and mysticism. But the modern era destroyed the medieval corporations and shattered the tightly woven, self-contained Jewish community. Jews lost control over their civil laws, and the state encroached upon the realm of marriage, divorce, and education. Jewish intellectuals rushed to be integrated as quickly as possible in the New World, discarding Judaism in the process. Jews no longer accepted a belief in other-worldly salvation. The combination of naturalism and this-worldliness, plus emancipation and freedom, proved lethal to traditional Judaism, and Jews were simply not prepared to resist the shock.[5]

There were, of course, attempts to meet these modern challenges. Kaplan analyzes and criticizes each one in turn. Reform was wise in accepting the need to adapt Judaism but it denationalized our civilization. Neo-Orthodoxy did elicit greater self-sacrifice than other groups and insisted on maximum education and living. But it desiccated nationhood by treating it as a theological concept and it was obsessed with supernaturalism. Conservative Judaism stressed the primacy of the Jewish People and its historical quest to live. But it was overly afflicted with romantic nostalgia, and lacks the courage to revise or update Jewish law. Zionism is based on the ineradicable nature of anti-Semitism and rightly appeals to the will of the Jewish People to live and create in its own land. But it has failed to reckon with the Jewish People as a whole in *Galut.* Obviously, each movement, despite its advantages, is crippled by its inherent shortcomings and cannot adapt Judaism to the changing times. In fact, nothing short of a reconstruction of Judaism can achieve that.[6]

Jews must be taught how to live creatively in two civilizations, writes Kaplan. They must draw the best from both the Jewish civilization as well as the dominant secular one in which they live. But Judaism must undergo—as it has so many times in the past—transvaluation of its concepts and reevaluation of its ideals. Religion can no longer operate with a tradition which speaks in terms that are alien to the *personal* experience of the average intelligent man or woman. It must aim at the intellectuals—at the people who are "scientifically oriented." In an oblique refutation of Schechter, Kaplan states: "Not timelessness but timeliness is the desideratum. Religion is necessarily rooted in the soil of tradition, but its life depends on its ability to send forth new shoots into the light of our own day." Judaism must assimilate in a "deliberate and planned fashion" the best in contemporary civilization "and it must be brought into harmony with the best ethical and social thought of the modern world."[7]

What is Reconstructionism, then? Kaplan had steadfastly refused to call it a new movement, and until very recently he insisted that "Reconstructionism should become a *quality* of existing Jewish institutions and movements rather than another addition to their quantity." Kaplan had cherished the notion that his interdenominational approach to Jewish life would cut across partisan boundaries and unite the splintered elements in Judaism. He selected as the symbol of his school of thought a wheel, and he interpreted its significance as follows:

> *The form is that of a wheel. The hub of the wheel is Palestine, the center of Jewish civilization from which all the dynamic forces of Judaism radiate. Religion, culture, and ethics are the spokes by which the vital influence of Palestine affects and stimulates Jewish life everywhere and enables it to make its contribution to the civilization of mankind. The wheel has an inner and an outer rim. The inner rim represents the Jewish community that even in the dispersion, maintains its contact with the Jewish civilization rooted in Palestine, by the spiritual bonds of religion, ethics and culture. The outer rim is the general community, for us the community of America, with which the Jewish civilization as lived by the Jewish community maintains contact at every point. The seal thus symbolizes the whole philosophy of the Reconstructionist movement.*[8]

Despite Kaplan's dream to the contrary, and despite the fact that Reconstructionism studiously avoided institutionalization for over forty years, it was inevitable that Reconstructionism would either have to become a movement or else wither away.

Consequently, Reconstructionism has become a small movement of Reform and Conservative rabbis and laymen that is pragmatic in philosophy, liberal in theology, and nationalistic in emphasis. Its impact should not, however, be measured in terms of the number of its adherents. For it has exerted great influence on the other religious philosophies in Jewish life as well as on the secular and Zionist schools of thought. Reconstructionism has not belied its founder's early hopes and aspirations.

*God*

Kaplan's conception of God has struck traditionalists as being even more audacious than his definition of Judaism, for Kaplan is avowedly a naturalist-humanist who rejects supernaturalism, miracles, and any anthropomorphic or human representation of the Deity. He describes God as the power or process that makes for human salvation or self-fulfillment. Kaplan defends the legitimacy of his naturalistic approach, pointing out that Maimonides did much the same for Jewish theology in the twelfth century when he defined God in Aristotelian terms as the "Active Intellect" and equated God with His attributes, thereby, in effect, describing God as a process.[9]

Kaplan follows John Dewey in defining an idea, a concept, an institution by its function—its affect and effect. Thus, the function of the God idea has been salvational. It has enabled man to find self-fulfillment and realize his greatest potential as a human being; it has implanted in him ideals such as goodness, truth, beauty, justice, love, and peace. The idea of God for modern man must accordingly enhance the striving of the human being for salvation and for worthwhileness and the realization of his fullest potential. Taking a cue from Ahad Ha'am, Kaplan suggests that even if God did not exist, the idea of God is a real and efficient cause in Jewish life serving as a symbol of justice in the people's psyche and acting as an urge to righteousness. God may not actually exist as found in Jewish writings, but the conception has been an efficient factor in the life of the Jewish People. Kaplan shows how the God idea has been dynamic rather than static, and that it is scientifically incorrect to maintain that there is a specifically Jewish *conception* of God. There is, rather, a specifically Jewish *application of the God idea to the sancta* of Jewish living.[10]

Kaplan defines God in various writings and at considerable length. Utilizing Matthew Arnold's definition, Kaplan describes God as the power that makes for salvation. God is the expression of belief that affirms what ought to be or can be, "the Power that endorses what we believe ought to be, and that guarantees that it will be." God reveals himself in the human spirit as the urge that impels man to become fully human and to realize himself, to attain his destiny—in short, to achieve salvation. God reveals himself in the cosmos in the organicity, polarity, creativity, and authenticity that reside therein. God is the "highest ideal for which men strive and at the same time, points to the objective fact that the world is so constituted as to make for the realization of those ideals." Whenever man has a sense of moral responsibility he experiences the revelation of God. "To believe in God is to reckon with life's creative forces, tendencies and potentialities as forming an organic unity, and as giving meaning to life by virtue of unity."[11]

Kaplan devoted an entire book, *The Meaning of God in Modern Jewish Religion,* to reconstructing traditional theological notions. In it he calls for a "revaluation," not just a transvaluation, of the traditional concepts, and he urges us to disengage those elements in tradition which answer permanent postulates of human nature and integrate them into our own ideology. He insists that Judaism divest itself of supernaturalism, sensate notions of the Deity, mysticism, and miracles. Salvation must no longer be taken as other-worldly, for modern man seeks his self-fulfillment in *this* life rather than in paradise. Only by dissociating the Jewish religion from the supernatural can the universal significance of our ideas and values take effect in the world, he writes. Since religion and belief in the existence of God are rooted in human nature, man will have to ascribe attributes to Him that derive from and refer to the experience of the average man and woman. And that experience leads us to a *faith* (yes, Kaplan uses the term *faith!*) that the universe is so constructed and man so created as to evince a power which orients us to life and elicits from us the best of which we are capable or renders us immune to the worst that may befall us. To fail to reconstruct Jewish religion in harmony with this modern, scientific approach, states Kaplan, is to sin against the light.[12]

In a brilliantly original analysis of the Jewish Festivals, Kaplan demonstrates how each one articulates an aspect of man's striving for salvation, and how each is so constituted as to highlight that ideal. The Sabbath, for example, exemplifies the threefold yearning for creation, holiness, and covenantship. In underscoring the notion of creation, the Sabbath reaffirms our belief in God as "the sum of the animating, organizing forces and relationships which are forever making a cosmos out of chaos." Rosh Hashanah features the idea of social regeneration; Yom Kippur teaches us the power for the regeneration of human nature. The Pilgrim Festivals—Sukkot, Shavuot, Passover—emphasize God as the power in nature and history, making for cooperation, joy, freedom, and righteousness. Hanukkah and Purim highlight the notion of God as the means to national survival.[13]

Is Kaplan a pantheist, as many charge? Not at all: he does believe emphatically in God as a process in man and the world. He writes that our civilization must be religious lest we yield to cynicism or despair. Moreover, he does not equate God and nature, as do the pantheists. He detects God as a process in nature forever making cosmos out of chaos; an abstract force that we concretize by using the term "God." But He is just as real as the force of gravity which we personify in a similar fashion. Kaplan has been challenged for depersonalizing God. He responds by saying, "A God who makes a difference in one's personal life should be designated as a personal God." He has, moreover, a deeply abiding faith in God and human potential, and he insists that "if we cannot believe in the potentialities of human nature, we have nothing on which to base our faith in the goodness of God."[14]

The only Reconstructionist thinker to have challenged Kaplan's God concept was the late Milton Steinberg. Rabbi Steinberg felt that Kaplan had overintellectualized his God idea, and had made it too rationalistic and cold-blooded. He wrote that in adapting Judaism to a world setting, one must not make it "a religion of reason" based only on demonstrable propositions in which mystery has been muted, for all reality is *not* reason. Steinberg, moreover, criticized Kaplan's non-absolute God because He is "more than just the sum total of forces making for salvation." Steinberg conceived of God as "the essential Being of all beings, though all beings in their totality do not exhaust Him. His reason is rationality of nature, cosmos rather than chaos; His power is dynamism of physical reality; His will is impulse behind upsurge. He is the soul of man—thought, morality, creativity, and ethics." God is the only tenable explanation for the universe, for it is one, dynamic, creative, rational, purposive, and contains consciousness as evidenced by the creation of man. Moreover, man cannot live joyously or creatively or hopefully without God. To lead the moral life, man needs God and man learns to believe in God from his historical experience.[15]

How does Kaplan handle the problem of evil? He proposes a finite notion of the Deity. Evil, he says, is that aspect of reality not yet permeated by divinity. "God's omnipotence is not an actualized fact at any point of time, but a potential fact." Evil, he suggests, is chaos still uninvaded by the creative energy, sheer chance unconquered by will and intelligence. Natural evils such as floods and earthquakes are not part of God's plan or purpose; they are simply that phase of the universe which has not yet been completely penetrated by Godhood. This notion of a limited God is somewhat unusual, but it is not unique, and an occasional medieval philosopher posited a similar view.[16]

How should we deal with evil? Kaplan urges man not to keep faith in miracles but to persevere courageously and persist faithfully, apply human intelligence to life's problems, and release the creativity to solve them. Man must focus his attention on the reality of goodness and "will the abolition of evil." Moreover, we must shift the problem from thought to ethical action by summoning all the latent power residual in human nature. Religion should indicate to man some way whereby he can act to transform the world into a better place if evil is within our control; if it is not, then religion must show us how to transcend it.

> *Evil is not the last word. When we put our wills to the task of improving the world, we find them mysteriously reenforced by natural powers that seem to have been waiting for our action to make such use of them.*

In the final analysis, Kaplan admits that we must "be satisfied with a modest fare of faith" in confronting the challenge of human suffering.[17]

Milton Steinberg shares much the same view, describing evil as "the still unremoved scaffolding of the edifice of God's creativity." Suffering men, he writes eloquently, "are participants, even if in the smallest degree, in God's travail as He gives birth to a new order, not only of things, but of being."[18]

The Reconstructionist idea of God is, clearly, a non-supernatural one that derives from human experience and that posits its faith that there is in man and the universe a process or power or force that drives for salvation, for goodness, for morality, for ethics, for life, for peace, for harmony, for order. And this power or process is what we call—for lack of a better term, perhaps—God.

## Torah

The Reconstructionists have scandalized the traditionalists in their analysis of Torah more than in any other facet of their program. They alone of the religious movements in Jewry *deny the validity of revelation*. God did not reveal the Torah to Israel, insists Kaplan, the Torah reveals God to Israel. Kaplan accepts Biblical criticism and views the Bible as a collection of documents reflecting different ages and authors with much moral immaturity. "Torah means a complete Jewish civilization," writes Kaplan, and is not merely law. The Torah is the record of man's striving for salvation; therefore, Torah does not consist alone in what the text teaches, but anything that impels us to find a means of salvation—even if it is the antithesis of Torah —is, paradoxically, Torah. While the Torah is unique compared to other ancient religious doctrines, it is far from the last word on philosophical truth. When we use the phrase *Torah min ha-shamayim*—the Torah originates in heaven—we must not naively infer that God dictated the Torah to Moses and the Prophets. Rather, we should take the phrase to mean that the original prophetic discovery of the moral law is the principal self-revelation of God. Man's discovery of religious truth is God's revelation of it, since the very process of that discovery implies the activity of God. Although Kaplan denies Divine revelation he does not invalidate the grandeur of Torah:

> *We can discover value in the Torah by utilizing it as a living tradition, a sort of collective memory of valuable experience . . . Whatever is right should be incorporated in our Torah, and whatever is wrong should be eliminated from our Torah.*[19]

The denial of the Divine origin of Torah has outraged the Orthodox, who view Reconstructionists as heretics, and it has shocked many Conservative and Reform thinkers for whom Divine revelation is a basic tenet of the Jewish faith.

But if Kaplan denies revelation, what of the *mitzvot*? Are they superfluous? What validates our adherence to them? Is the term *mitzvah,* "commandment," totally unwarranted and outdated?

For a long time, Kaplan shied away from using the word *mitzvah.* Moreover, he popularized the term *sancta,* which played an important role in his philosophy. Each civilization creates its *sancta*—"those institutions, places, historic events, heroes and all other objects of popular reverence to which superlative importance or sanctity is ascribed. These *sancta,* the attitude toward life that they imply and the conduct that they imply and the conduct that they inspire, are the religion of that people." Since Jews no longer apply sanctions to lawbreakers and the Halakhic process has broken down, Kaplan eschews the words "Halakhah" and *mitzvah* and prefers to use the phrase "folkways and customs."

Rabbi Jack Cohen has gone so far as to write of "the end of the Halakhah" and the birth of "voluntarism" as the way of Jewish living.[20]

Still, argue the Reconstructionists, rituals have great social and cosmic values and are really integral parts of human nature and indispensable aspects of civilization. True, the meticulous observance of ritual is always a temptation to self-righteousness, writes Kaplan. Nevertheless, human culture cannot dispense with symbolic forms for conveying spiritual values. Ritual helps us identify with our people and gives us the spiritual essence of its experiences. We need observances as we need language to convey ideas and feelings.

> *Our position is that those* mitzvot *which, in tradition, are described as applying "between man and God" should be observed, insofar as they help to maintain the historic continuity of the Jewish People and to express, or symbolize, spiritual values or ideals which can enhance the inner life of Jews.* Their observance, however, *should* be reckoned with, not in the spirit of juridical law, *which is coercive, but in the spirit of a voluntary* consensus based on a general recognition of their value. *We shall, therefore, refer to our approach to Jewish ritual observance as the* voluntaristic approach.[21]

Kaplan, accordingly, finds no value in perpetuating legal terminology when discussing rituals, and he considers phrases such as "law," "sin," or "pardon" unjustified. He prefers the terms "customs" and "folkways" rather than "laws," and he describes folkways as the social practices by which a people externalizes the reality of its collective being. Ritual, says Kaplan (in the language of Durkheim) is essential to preserve the collective identity of the group. Kaplan does display a bias for tradition, and is even willing to consult tradition before invoking change. But, he insists, the past should have a *vote*, not a *veto*. Personally observant because of nostalgia and pious upbringing, Kaplan believes passionately in the value of such practices as wearing *tzitzit* under his shirt. He endorses *kashrut* both as a means of enhancing the Jewish atmosphere at home and as a sound technique making for Jewish distinctiveness and identification. He also believes it elevates an animal act and teaches us that we eat to live and not that we live to eat. Still, he admits that if *kashrut* away from home fosters unwarranted aloofness or creates undue hardships, it may be set aside or emended. Kaplan also insists that "a Sabbathless people cannot possibly cultivate the life of the spirit." But he is prepared to depart from traditional *mitzvot* and create new ones. If a *mitzvah* is obsolete, clashes with our highest standards, and cannot be invested with new meaning, social or personal value, or credibility by reinterpretation, it should be discarded. Moreover, Reconstructionists urge us to create new *mitzvot*, and Kaplan has done just this in the Bat Mitzvah ceremony for girls, in granting *aliyot* to women, and in many ritual changes in services at the Society for the Advancement of Judaism. Interestingly, Kaplan espoused "Women's Lib" long before the phrase was even heard of![22]

But how do Reconstructionists go about changing folkways and customs? Who has the right to do so? And by what process?

The answer is the democratic, voluntaristic approach. In the absence of an organized Jewish community that can apply controls and sanctions and coerce observance, the *individual* Jew must decide *voluntarily* whether or not he will abide by Jewish practices. Kaplan and colleagues like Steinberg, Eisenstein, and Cohen do not consider this as anarchy or license; rather, they conceive this to be liberty to pick or choose those observances that are meaningful to the individual Jew and also serve to bind him to his people. Kaplan spurns the *Shulhan Arukh* as the authoritative code of Jewish life. He prefers, instead, to consult "guides" to ritual observance and, in fact, the Reconstructionists created such a *Guide* in 1941. The *Guide* describes ritual as a *means* to group survival and the spiritual growth of the Jew, and it outlines norms and guidelines that might help the Jew practice various rituals. Thus, it suggests that on the Sabbath it is permissible to do things one could not do all week which help a person to "a way of enjoying life." What helps one to experience Sabbath should be indulged in, and "our will to live most happily and effectively must supersede the observance of the Sabbath."

The final arbiter of choice is the people, say the Reconstructionists in an obviously exaggerated interpretation of Schechter's
"Catholic Israel." This approach has, understandably, led to a
variegated pattern of Reconstructionist observances: Kaplan
keeps kosher and prays daily with genuine piety; some of his
nearest disciples do neither. But Kaplan's democratic urge and
commitment to "unity in diversity" compel him to defend the
democratic process in selecting rituals.[23]

In the past, most ritual norms have been set by Kaplan and
his inner circle, with occasional votes by members of his congregation or the Reconstructionist Fellowship. Ira Eisenstein has
felt that this procedure has not gone far enough. He wants
American-style democracy in the Reconstructionist camp, and
he rejects "Catholic Israel" as a chauvinistic and nostalgic notion that implies that everything past is good and innovations
are inherently degenerate. He urges that Jews be given a stake
in law-making, thereby increasing their sense of responsibility
that will lead to more knowledge.[24]

Clearly, Reconstructionism is the most "democratic" and
nonstructured of all the approaches to Jewish law. It shares,
along with the Orthodox and Conservatives, affection and nostalgic love for tradition; but it rejects their basic reluctance to
change and grow and their resorting to legal fictions to circum-
vent the laws. The Reconstructionist concur with the Reformers
in their stress on ethical rules and their disavowal of Halakhah
as coercive law. But they reject Reform's negativism to ritual and
criticize it as a pallid, bloodless Judaism. Reconstructionism
really wants both worlds: rich commitment to ritual—but demo-
cratically arrived at and selected.

### The Jewish People

Reconstructionism, like the Conservative movement, lays its
greatest emphasis on the notion of *Am Yisrael*, the People of
Israel. But it goes one step further: it begins its philosophy of
Judaism *not* with God who found the Jewish people, but with the
Jewish People who found God. Nor does it endorse the usually

accepted view that the Jewish People is here on earth to teach and practice Torah. It reverses the equation, maintaining that the Torah exists *for the sake* of the Jewish People. In this sense, Reconstructionism represents a Copernican Revolution in Jewish thought. For just as Copernicus proved that the sun, rather than the earth, is the center of our solar system, so Kaplan places Israel, rather than God, at the center of the Jewish civilization.

Kaplan considers peoplehood one of the basic dimensions of Jewish civilization, the others being divinity and salvation. He notes that we are an international, spiritual people with the inalienable right of any group to exist, provided we harm no one else. We must not be concerned merely with survival; rather, we must seek to achieve the highest intellectual, esthetic, and social good that validates our existence. We can meet all challenges by fostering a religious orientation to life that affirms holiness and the supreme worth of life. Politically, we are loyal to our host nation; spiritually we must nurture the Jewish civilization and relate to Eretz Yisrael. We must live in two civilizations: the American and the Jewish, enriching ourselves by feeding on both. Milton Steinberg describes the process as "cross-fertilization of civilizations."[25]

The most revolutionary aspect of Kaplan's thinking in the area of the Jewish People is his rejection of the notion of the chosen people. In his earlier writings, Kaplan equivocated; he was uneasy with the doctrine and suggested that it be reinterpreted to mean that Jews must harken to a spiritual call and fulfill a mission to teach the world. But due to the pernicious doctrine of racism propagated by the Nazis and Fascists, Kaplan abandoned the idea entirely—much to the annoyance of other Jewish religious groups. In fact, Reconstructionism is the only Jewish ideology to totally disavow the chosen-people doctrine. Kaplan calls it an anachronism, chauvinism, racism, self-infatuation, and a pernicious and undemocratic theory that implies superior racial heredity and biological traits. In more vituperative moments he has labeled it "Nazism," claiming that it justifies racial inequality and the master-race ideal. Such arrogance leads to invidious comparisons and all too often has generated missionizing, religious imperialism, and ill-will. We can no longer retain or reinterpret it so that it is compatible with our own highest ethical standards, writes Kaplan. As to those who argue that if we discard the notion we will lose the will to live as Jews, Kaplan replies: "Judaism can certainly not afford to harbor any doctrine which is in conflict with the ethical basis of democracy."[26]

Other Reconstructionists, with the exception of Milton Steinberg, agree with this view. Ira Eisenstein writes that we Jews are unique—but we should not talk about it, but should be more humble and not resort to invidious comparisons. Eugene Kohn states that "election involves rejection," and since we are committed to America's democratic ideal, "we are constrained to deny that any religious society or communion is 'chosen' for all are created equal—none is chosen and none rejected." Yet, Kaplan cannot quite be rid of chosenness; he talks of the "inherent genius of Jewish peoplehood to elicit from the individual Jew the best of which he is capable."[27]

What then do we do with the chosen people? Kaplan suggests that we substitute the concept of Jewish mission or vocation in its stead. Here Kaplan indicates that he is indebted to the Reform movement, which said virtually the same thing a century earlier. We Jews, he writes, have heard a "divine calling in which all peoples can have a share." Our vocation is to foster human salvation by getting each nation to consider national individuality as God's gift and to reinterpret the *mitzvot* so as to make them viable—the product of collective Jewish life and an indication of a Divine drive. We must show that the true nature of religion is to make people or nations a medium for nurturing the ideal human type that embodies Divinity. We must teach the moral and spiritual uses of power over nature and impel man to create a social order based on freedom, justice, peace, love, and moral responsibility. Borrowing a phrase from A. D. Gordon, Kaplan summons Jews to become "a People in the image of God." Kaplan waxes most eloquent in arguing that the Jewish nation has to be animated by Divine traits of moral responsibility, authenticity, loyalty or love, and creativity in relation to individuals and nations. "*The purpose* of Jewish existence is to be a People in the image of God. *The meaning* of Jewish existence is to foster in ourselves as Jews, and to awaken in the rest of the world, a sense of moral responsibility in action." Kaplan adds: "When that comes about, the Messianic Age will have arrived."[28]

*The Land of Israel*

Mordecai Kaplan has been an ardent Zionist since his youth. Consequently, the Reconstructionist movement has been wholeheartedly behind the effort to reconstitute the Jewish Commonwealth for over half a century. Kaplan writes: "The primary *mitzvah* of Jewish peoplehood is the rehabilitation of Eretz Yisrael as the spiritual homeland of the Jewish People." Once that comes about, Kaplan urges the establishment of a permanent advisory body—a parliament of sorts—to speak for the entire Jewish People, to help reorganize it into organic communities, to spread Hebrew knowledge, to revitalize Sabbath, Festival, *kashrut* observances, and to deepen the commitment of Jews to Judaism.[29]

Obviously, Kaplan's Zionism is much more than merely a political concept. Kaplan had been deeply affected by the writings of Ahad Ha'am, and his Zionism is of a cultural-spiritual brand. Kaplan states that a Commonwealth in Eretz Yisrael is "indispensable to the life of Judaism in the diaspora." He concedes that the fullest Jewish life is only possible in Eretz Yisrael and he detects a moral imperative to build the land. For a long time he flirted with the idea of settling in Israel. In fact, two of his closest disciples—Dr. Alexander Dushkin and Rabbi Jack Cohen—have done so. But Kaplan is pragmatic enough to realize that a total ingathering into Israel is impossible and that there will always be the twin foci of world Jewry in Israel and *Galut.* The reader will recall that the seal of the Reconstructionist movement gives expression to this notion of Israel as the spiritual center of a world Jewish community. Kaplan had long supported Labor Zionism, the Histadrut, and the Kibbutz movement as embodying the highest social ideals of Zionism. Of late, however, this aspect of Reconstructionist Zionism has diminished and the movement has concentrated more on breaking the monopoly of Orthodoxy in the State and in separating religion from politics.[30]

Kaplan has called for a New Zionism. He urges that the State of Israel provide a setting in which the Jewish People could be fit instruments of this-worldly salvation for every Jew. He suggests a public declaration similar to the Baṣle Platform and a Jewish World Assembly of men of all shades of opinion consisting of those who seek the maintenance of the Jewish People. "Without a Jewish People regenerated in spirit," he writes, "no matter how successful the state that it would establish, and how large a population that state could muster, Zion will continue to be unredeemed." Zionism is, therefore, a means to a greater goal, namely, the resuscitation of the Jewish People and its spirit. He chides the political Zionists who proclaim the State an end in itself and who negate the *Galut;* he calls for a strong sense of mutuality and interaction between Israel and world Jewry, a creative partnership between Zion and the *Golah.* Zionism must be a religious movement in that it fosters the capacity of the Jew for living a more abundant life. Jewry of Israel must be nuclear and interactive with the Diaspora "as a permanent condition." For even though Eretz Yisrael is the "only place where Jewish civilization can be perfectly at home," other lands must be rendered capable of harboring the Jewish civilization. If it fails in Eretz Yisrael, it will disappear elsewhere; if it disappears elsewhere, Israel will become a new Levantine civilization. "World Jewry without Eretz Yirael is like a soul without a body; Eretz Yisrael without World Jewry is like a body without a soul." In his most exalted sentiments, Kaplan describes Zionism as "the remaking of the Jewish People through the remaking of its land," and he admonishes his readers that "before the Torah can go forth from Zion, it will have to enter into Zionism."[31]

Kaplan is obviously a maverick in Zionism even as he is in other areas of Jewish life. His brand of Ahad Ha'am Zionism has never sat well with the political Zionists; nor has his criticism of the theocratic nature of Israel appeased the Orthodox. But he has shaped much of Zionist ideology and compelled a rethinking of the aims of the movement. Moreover, the Reconstructionist group has been a staunch partisan of the Jewish state, and the editorials of the *Reconstructionist* magazine are militantly behind Israel. Many leaders of American Zionism—notably in the Hadassah organization—are protégés of Kaplan's at the Society for the Advancement of Judaism. Reconstructionist partisans have been firm backers of Zionism and the State of Israel as the means to the creative survival of world Jewry and the flowering of its culture, spirit, and civilization.

## The Jewish Community

As we have noted, Reconstructionism has placed its heaviest emphasis on the concept of the Jewish People. Kaplan had hoped that Reconstructionism would transcend party labels and serve as a unifying force in Jewish life. He has sought to cooperate with all elements in the Jewish community for the common good with the possible exception of the Orthodox, whose vituperative attacks on Reconstructionism have provoked equally blistering counterattacks from Kaplan and his disciples. Since his early days with the Kehillah of New York City, Kaplan's ardor for a unified and integrated Jewish community has not cooled. How does Kaplan propose to achieve this goal?

Kaplan has advocated the creation of "organic communities," by which he means the unification of Jewish communities and integration of their activities, institutions, and services along the lines of the classical *kehillah*, except that the new communities are to be based on voluntarism rather than coercion. The organic communities would

1) *maintain a register of vital statistics,*
2) *induce Jews to affiliate with local or national organizations,*
3) *budget the needs of Jewish life,*
4) *activate high ethical standards and formulate codes and sanctions,*

5) *foster and coordinate Jewish education, cultural, and religious activities,*
6) *foster and coordinate health and social welfare, antipoverty work, etc.,*
7) *foster creativity in culture and the arts,*
8) *help Jews meet economic discrimination and defend Jewish rights,*
9) *collaborate with non-Jewish groups for the common welfare.*[32]

Such organic communities would integrate all congregations, social service agencies, educational institutions, and Zionist, defense, and fraternal bodies, and would thereby eliminate waste, competition, and duplication. In the 1940's, Kaplan went even further by urging that "World Jewry should unite as a people, and apply to the United Nations for recognition of its claim to peoplehood." In the 1950's he changed his tune and called upon world Jewry to join in a conference in Jerusalem and renew the *brit* (covenant) between God and Israel. In fact, as a result of his prodding, an Ideological Conference was convened in Jerusalem in 1957, but it failed to have the dramatic impact for which he had hoped. Kaplan's call for organic communities was enthusiastically endorsed by rabbis and communal workers of various stripes. Milton Steinberg wrote sympathetically:

> *What is involved is whether Jewish public affairs shall be efficiently or inefficiently run, democratically or by usurpation, co-operatively or disjointedly. It is all as simple as this, whether the House of Israel in America is to be orderly or disorderly. Between two such alternatives, can anyone hesitate?*[33]

Thus far, however, the Reconstructionist program for organic communities has not been implemented.

### The Synagogue

Mordecai M. Kaplan conceived the idea of the synagogue as a center of a variety of activities, including prayer, study for children and adults, communal gatherings, and cultural, social, and esthetic experiences. No other idea of Reconstructionism has caught on as universally as this one, for practically all Reform, Conservative, and Orthodox congregations have embodied this role.

Reconstructionist synagogues have been notably creative and innovative in dealing with liturgy. Much of Reconstructionist thinking has been devoted to the realm of prayer, and Reconstructionists have not recoiled from the modern-day problems of liturgy. Eugene Kohn, for example, writes that today's problem is that we lack a belief in the efficacy of prayer. Prayer fulfills certain valid needs of man; it helps him to have "grateful, hopeful, and serene adjustments to reality." But current prayer ritual fails and is not congruent with our conception of God, which is no longer an anthropomorphic one. Kohn suggests that the fundamental need is for a "meaningful" service. To create such a service, we must remove theurgic or magical elements, meaningless passages (such as sacrifices, vengeful statements, chauvinistic notions, etc.), and we must add new prayers that arise out of our experiences and are expressed in the idiom of modern thought. Prayer must be in harmony with the character of God as the source that endows life with value or holiness. Since religion is what men do with their interrelatedness, mutual dependency, and mutual responsibility, Kohn regards prayer as communion with God, as the effort to bring our personal lives into harmony with the "universal life." We articulate religious ideals in prayer language, although that does not mean that we have to believe in the magical power of words. We address God as an I-Thou, "as if He were a person," and we need congregational worship to identify with our group.[34]

Kaplan describes prayer as a way of articulating our aspirations and ideals and heightening Jewish consciousness. The purpose of worship, he suggests, is to influence the worshiper to bring life into harmony with God as the Power that determines the conditions by which man achieves the harmonious and abundant life. Kaplan insists that prayer be relevant, modern, intelligible, and in conformity with the highest ethical and theological ideals of modern man.[35]

Reconstructionism has attempted to translate these principles

into concrete liturgical reforms. The four major liturgical productions—the *Sabbath Prayer Book*, the *High Holiday Prayer Book*,
the *Festival Prayer Book*, and the *Daily Prayer Book*—exemplify
these ideals. In the introduction to the *Sabbath Prayer Book* the
editors suggest that modern Jews have lost their sense of need
for worship and prayer because we now accept a new concept
of God that conforms to a mechanistic universe. Consequently,
we no longer pray to God to suspend the natural order of the
universe and perform miracles. Prayer is necessary to engender
in us a sense of communion with God, the source of the will to
salvation, and to foster a mood of oneness with Israel, the Hebrew language, Zion, and Jewish culture. Prayer must be revised
so as to be relevant and up-to-date and conform with our highest
ethical ideals. Hence, the popular prayer "God, who has chosen
us from all the peoples" is emended to "God, who has brought
us near to His service" in line with Reconstructionism's rejection of the chosen-people doctrine. Prayers for animal sacrifices
are deleted, as are references to a personal Messiah, retribution,
and reward and punishment. In lieu of the prayer for the resurrection of the dead, the Reconstructionist text reads: "God
remembers his creatures for life in mercy." The text of the
Sabbath service runs 232 pages; the supplement in Hebrew and
English—including modern material—is over 330 pages! At the
end we find a modern paraphrase, "We Want," in place of the
medieval Maimonidean "I Believe." Likewise, the *High Holiday
Prayer Book* reinterprets classical prayers, changes some, deletes
others, adds new ones.[36]

The Society for the Advancement of Judaism has served as the
laboratory of Reconstructionist synagogue worship. Thus, the
distinction between the Kohen, Levi, and Israelites in receiving
honors has been abolished as a throwback to the caste system.
Women receive *aliyot* to the Torah. There is instrumental music
and a choir at services; congregational singing rather than can-
torial recitatives is encouraged. The service is basically in Hebrew because Kaplan believes that "a language is the most tangible means of conveying the reality of the soul of a people . . .
Hence, the study and use of the Hebrew language should be
urged as no less a religious duty than the use of it in the prayer

book is now regarded by the Orthodox." Kaplan insists that Reconstructionism Hebraize Jewish education and foster the study of the Hebrew language and literature.[37]

Reconstructionist synagogues have endeavored to deepen the content and raise the quality of Jewish education. Kaplan has recommended a minimum of six to seven hours weekly of religious studies, including such subjects as Hebrew, religion, history, and ethical culture. He has also championed adult Jewish education. On the other hand, Reconstructionists have strongly opposed Jewish Day Schools as undemocratic and parochial in outlook. Kaplan wrote in *Judaism as a Civilization* that they are a "futile gesture of protest against the necessity of giving to Jewish civilization a position ancillary to the civilization of the majority." More recently, he has endorsed Day Schools for the lower grades. As yet, however, Reconstructionism has not created any Day Schools.[38]

In sum, the average Reconstructionist synagogue uses the Reconstructionist prayer books, holds its main services on Sabbath mornings and in some places on Friday evenings as well, observes one day of *Yom Tov* rather than the traditional two, permits men and women to sit together, insists on men covering their heads, calls women to the Torah, uses instrumental music, emphasizes Hebrew and congregational singing, is innovative and willing to experiment, and is a synagogue-center serving as host to a multiplicity of functions and activities.

## Social Action

Social action occupies a prominent place in Reconstructionist ideology. Kaplan had long ago defined the primary function of religion as the improvement of ethics, and in his analysis of the Jewish Festivals he had suggested that their aim is the amelioration of social rather than individual evil. Kaplan states that the Torah must serve as an ethical code of behavior, engendering truth, modesty, compassion, sanctification of God's name, goodness, and equity. He believes that social ethics must conform to "certain laws that are as intrinsic to human nature as the law of gravity is to matter." He urges that we demonstrate the existence of Divinity through the practice of social justice and moral responsibility. His definition of salvation is oriented in the direction of social justice; he describes it as faith in the "progressive perfection of the human personality and the establishment of a free, just, and cooperative social order." Milton Steinberg has suggested a sifting of Jewish ethical values and the converting of ideals into habit, law, and communal practice. Moreover, he summons Jews to "evoke new Jewish ethical expression."[39]

These ideals have been translated into ethical action by Reconstructionists. Invariably, they have been involved in liberal causes, championing the needs of the underdog and espousing the rights of the individual. In the 1930's, for example, Reconstructionists were frequently socialists, anti-capitalists, and anti-Communists. Ira Eisenstein maintained that Jews ought to be socialists because competition is brutal, it leads to scapegoating and anti-Semitism, fosters class distinction, and creates an insecurity that is inimical to Jewish expression. Mordecai Kaplan was also a staunch anti-Communist, anti-capitalist, democratic socialist. And while he is still opposed to both the class struggle of free enterprise and the totalitarianism of Marxism, he is no longer as committed to socialism as formerly.[40]

Reconstructionists have taken liberal views on a variety of issues. They favor liberal birth-control and abortion laws; they oppose the death penalty; they are warmly pro-labor; they are internationally minded and support the United Nations, as they did the League of Nations in the past; they espouse the goal of racial justice and urge rabbis to involve themselves in social action; and they favor public ownership of natural resources and a curb on unbridled competition. The editorials of the *Reconstructionist* have been consistently opposed to the Vietnam war and to American involvement. Moreover, the *Reconstructionist* is not averse to endorsing political candidates, and in 1964 it opposed Senator Barry Goldwater's candidacy for the Presidency.[41]

Reconstructionists have adopted a uniquely formulated stance on the issue of religion in the public schools. While firmly in favor of separation of church and state, Kaplan believes that a nondenominational religion of democracy can and should be taught in schools. Kaplan suggests that democracy must be raised to the level of religious faith if it is to combat totalitarianism. He notes that America has its *sancta:* its flag, holidays, great personalities, etc. It even has its creed that endorses the sacredness of the human soul and the dignity of the individual. He believes that the problem of religion in the public schools could be resolved by teaching a nonsectarian brand of religion of democracy that would stress unity in diversity, American democratic values, and the ideals of freedom and justice. In 1951 Kaplan edited with J. Paul Williams and Eugene Kohn what could be described as an American prayer book, consisting of readings, songs, and prayers for the celebration of American holidays, entitled *The Faith of America.* But neither the book nor the strikingly original concept of a religion of democracy caught on in either Jewish or general circles.[42]

*Interfaith Relations*

Reconstructionism has not been overly involved in interfaith work. Kaplan has been wary of religions claiming to be truer than any other. He has also been shaken by the Holocaust and has concluded that anti-Semitism is an irrational phenomenon caused by xenophobia or religiously rooted Jew-hatred that really cannot be eradicated by brotherhood programs. He has little use for "gestures" of good will, and he notes that when we frankly state our positions vis-à-vis one another, antagonism results. The best we can do, suggests Kaplan in a position curiously close to that of Orthodoxy, is to work on common ethical ideals and strive for civic rectitude and relief of poverty, fight disease, defend oppressed and persecuted peoples, and unite for "common spiritual purposes which transcend doctrinal and creedal differences and which make for mutual respect, esteem, and affection." Ira Eisenstein espouses the same view, and notes that as long as each faith believes that *it* is the sole possessor of truth, brotherhood will remain an illusion. There can be no hope for true interreligious amity until the religions reorient

their theologies so that they see the other religions as equally
legitimate cultural expressions of different civilizations. We Jews
must drop the notion of the chosen people and also learn to
"live and let live," suggests Eisenstein.[43]

The *Reconstructionist* magazine has been similarly suspicious of
interfaith activities, as can be surmised from its editorials. For
example, several editorials applauded the decision of Vatican II
to exonerate Jews of the charge of Deicide. But at the same time,
they were bitterly critical of the arrogance of the Church in
"forgiving" the Jews, and they denounced the vitiated language
of the final draft of the Schema on the Jews. Moreover, the
editorials insisted that the Catholic Church recognize the State
of Israel and the Jewish People as the first step towards reconciliation.[44]

Obviously, Reconstructionism is not intoxicated by the ideal
of "good will" and interreligious dialogue.

*Summary*

Reconstructionism is the most liberal, free-wheeling, maverick movement in American Jewish religious life. It is uniquely
American, the product of the extraordinarily creative brain of
Dr. Mordecai M. Kaplan. Only recently shaped into a full-blown
movement, Reconstructionism's naturalistic-humanistic philosophy has made a greater mark on American Jewry than many
realize or acknowledge. Its main tenets are these:

1. Judaism is an evolving, religious civilization that has always
undergone change and reconstructed itself to meet the challenges of each era. Judaism must continue to evolve as it confronts the latest onslaughts of naturalism and science in an age
of democracy.

2. Reconstructionism is a movement that seeks to reinterpret
Jewish values and institutions and unite diverse Jewish groups
of all shades of opinion who are committed to the creative survival of the Jewish People and its civilization. Such a union
cannot be coerced or forcibly achieved; it must come about
through voluntarism and democratic choice.

3. Reconstructionism starts with the premise that the Jewish

People must survive creatively. The Jewish religion exists for the People; the Torah is one of the basic techniques of its perpetuation. All values in Judaism must be so oriented as to safeguard Jewish survival.

4. Reconstructionism defines God as the power or process that makes for human salvation or self-fulfillment. It believes that man and the universe are so constructed as to endorse the highest human values of salvation. Its idea of God is naturalistic rather than supernaturalistic, process rather than person, experiential rather than mystical. Reconstructionists generally insist that Judaism must be stripped of supernaturalism and irrationalism if it is to appeal to modern man.

5. Reconstructionists deny the divine revelation of Torah. They consider the Torah to be man's attempt to discover God as the power of self-fulfillment or salvation. Torah is taken to encompass the entire corpus of Jewish law, lore, life, culture, civilization, and creativity. The movement no longer accepts the notion of Halakhah or *mitzvot*. It prefers to use the terms "folkways," "customs," or *"sancta."* It no longer believes it possible or proper to coerce observance. Hence, it maintains that Jews should voluntarily choose to observe those customs that are personally meaningful and socially valuable for group survival. Old practices should be reinterpreted, emended or amended; new ones should be added constantly to enrich Jewish civilization.

6. The Jewish People are the cornerstone of the Jewish civilization and must be preserved and maintained. All legitimate means that abet that survival should be utilized. The Jewish People are a trans-national, spiritual nation that must live creatively in two civilizations: their own and that of their host nation. Jews, however, must no longer consider themselves as "chosen," for that is arrogant chauvinism. Jews must, rather, fulfill a spiritual "vocation" and teach moral and spiritual values to mankind.

7. Reconstructionism strongly believes that the land of Israel should be the hub or spiritual center of world Jewry. It acknowledges that only in Israel can the Jewish civilization flourish to the fullest. But at the same time, it views the Diaspora as a necessary

and valuable condition. Israel and the Diaspora must mutually enrich one another. Zionism must be a means to a higher end, namely, the spiritual and cultural renaissance of world Jewry.

8. Reconstructionists urge the organization of organic communities based on the old *Gemeinde* or *kehillah.* Jews should voluntarily join such communities, which would then integrate and coordinate their organizations, activities, and institutions. Such organic communities would eliminate waste and duplication and would go far in strengthening Jewish life.

9. The synagogue in Reconstructionism is more than a prayer house. It is a center of numerous activities, sacred and secular. Its liturgy should be creative and relevant, in keeping with the moral and intellectual tastes of the times. The use of creative music, Hebrew, and congregational participation should be encouraged. Prayer must be seen as a means of evoking man's highest potential and of uniting him with a group. The religious school should be heavily weighted in ethical culture and Hebraic content.

10. Religion is essentially a social phenomenon, says Reconstructionism. Hence, Jews must cultivate ethical action and be involved in social dynamics. Reconstructionism is, normally, politically and economically liberal, and is committed to a world government of justice and peace as well as a domestic policy of the welfare state, whose basic function is to serve the individual and protect his freedom and dignity.

11. Reconstructionism is frankly leery of interfaith activities. Since religious tenets tend to divide rather than unite men, Reconstructionism prefers to avoid religious dialogue and concentrate, instead, on common action against the social ills of society and the world.

In a word, Reconstructionism is an attempt to blend Orthodoxy's plenitude of Jewish living with Conservatism's love for Jewish peoplehood and Reform's dynamism and critical outlook. Unquestionably, Reconstructionism has been a necessary leavening agent in American Jewish life. No matter what becomes of the movement, its ideas will bear fruit for a long time to come.

# Critique and Prognosis

## X

Thus far our study of today's Jew and his religion has been totally descriptive and, hopefully, reasonably objective. We have analyzed, at some length, the history and ideology of the Orthodox, Reform, Conservative, and Reconstructionist movements without probing their strong points and weaknesses or attempting to criticize and evaluate each school of thought. Before closing this volume, it may be appropriate to present some critique and prognosis.

### Orthodoxy

Orthodox Judaism has been criticized since the inception of the Reform movement over a hundred and fifty years ago. The critics charge it with being supernaturalistic and irrational, unscientific, out of step with modern times and thought, and woefully irrelevant. Its detractors say that Orthodox Jews compartmentalize their thinking; that they refuse to meet current challenges and insist that religious principles are immune to the onslaughts of new knowledge. Moreover, Orthodoxy's views of Halakhah are assailed as unresponsive to the needs of the day and unyielding in severity. The uncompromising legal stands of Orthodoxy both here and in Israel have made it impossible to live by Halakhah in the twentieth century or create a viable, modern state run by Jewish legal norms. As a result, thousands have been driven away by Orthodoxy and repelled by its medievalism. Finally, the critics aver that Orthodoxy has become increasingly self-righteous and pietistic, stridently proclaiming that it is all-wise and possesses the true Torah while demeaning other Jews, denigrating other viewpoints, and separating itself from the community and cooperative endeavors.

Interestingly, in recent years these external criticisms of Orthodoxy have generated internal echoes from the ranks of Orthodoxy. Young Turks like Professor Irving Greenberg, of Yeshiva University, and Professor Charles Liebman, formerly of that school and currently teaching at Israel's Bar-Ilan University, as well as some of the older spokesmen of the movement, have engaged in searching self-criticism—often to the annoyance of "establishment" leaders.

Charles Liebman, for example, decries Orthodoxy's inability to produce leaders from its own ranks. He notes that laymen play no role in Orthodoxy in America, that only rabbinic leadership counts, and that the fault lies in the restrictive yeshivah education that fails to encourage bright, inquisitive minds.[1]

Many Orthodox leaders have chided Orthodoxy for failing to meet the challenges of the day by utilizing the best in both sacred and secular wisdom. Liebman suggests that Orthodoxy's critical sense has been dulled. Professor Eliezer Berkovits has been unsparing in his strictures, and describes Orthodoxy as ineffectual because "we of its orthodox branch are unwilling to accept and, therefore, refuse to understand the radical change that has taken place in the world at large, as well as in the situation of the Jew the world over. In the main we insist that Judaism must be carried on as if nothing happened." Borrowing a phrase from Kaufmann Kohler, Berkovits accuses Orthodoxy of having created a "sacred mummy" and of having read the masses out of Judaism with prohibitions galore. Professor Irving Greenberg agrees: he decries the withdrawal from the intellectual and cultural implications of American society and he insists that Orthodoxy cannot and must not be hermetically sealed because that leads to ignorance, parochialism, and a lack of concern for social justice. He calls for relevant education that employs less coercion, less repression, and is more directed to contemporary and human values and freedom of response. Orthodoxy has neglected the Jewish cultural explosion, and nostalgic shoddiness reigns supreme in its ranks. Rabbi Norman Lamm writes in a similar vein. He indicts Orthodoxy for timidity and a "failure to interpret itself to itself," and he calls on Orthodoxy to formulate a world-view, "engage the world and speak persuasively and intelligibly to the man of today about transcendent purpose, about the meaning of the Covenant, about the significance of Halachic living both for personal meaningfulness and for the fulfillment of our covenantal obligations."[2]

Similarly, Orthodox mavericks have berated the movement for its refusal to confront Halakhic dilemmas with sensitivity or sincerity. Berkovits suggests that Halakhah has not been effective because "we have not succeeded in developing the application of *Halakhah* to the complexities of a scientific-technological age." He notes no serious searches for Halakhic remedies in Israel, no attempt at new methods of application of principles, and a lack of sensitivity to ethical and moral problems. He urges an end to coercion to *mitzvot* and political entanglement for religious ends, but he affirms his faith that Halakhah has *not* broken down; rather, it is our techniques of applying it that have collapsed. Norman Lamm agrees that we have too often made a virtue, even a dogma, of irrelevance, and our finest thinkers have not yet come to grips with the great issues of the time, such as war, population control, ecology, and so forth. Even Israel's eminent Ashkenazic Chief Rabbi Shlomo Goren has called for more elasticity in the Halakhah and greater concern for human problems.[3]

The growing din of discord and dissonance and the increas-

ingly frequent calls for Orthodox separatism in certain quarters
have provoked sharp counter reactions from Orthodox leaders
who have decried such parochialism. Rabbis Joseph Lookstein
and Emanuel Rackman have been hard-pressed to counter
separatists like Rabbi David Hollander who refuse to cooperate
with the New York Board of Rabbis and who demand Orthodox
withdrawal from umbrella groups such as the Synagogue Council of America. Rabbi Oscar Fasman, president emeritus of
Chicago's Hebrew Theological College, wrote a stinging denun-
ciation of Orthodoxy's fanaticism, sectarianism, and anticultural
feelings, and he blames the heads of the newer yeshivot for
fostering such divisiveness and parochialism. It is undoubtedly
true that the level of vituperation against Orthodoxy's opponents has increased both in America and Israel during the past
years and that the more liberal Orthodox have endeavored to
check this tendency.[4]

Finally, even a staunch Orthodox partisan like Rabbi Leo Jung
admits that while Orthodox Judaism has made great institutional strides, it has made "very little progress" in raising the
level of personal observance. There are simply too many nonobservant Orthodox Jews around to allow complacency or encourage rosy optimism.[5]

And yet, as Charles Liebman writes, "the only remaining bastion of Jewish passion in America resides in the Orthodox community." Perhaps Liebman exaggerates—surely there are others. But it is a fact that Orthodoxy has enjoyed a resurgence; that
its yeshivot are jammed with children; that young Orthodox
men and women—many of them yeshivah alumni—crowd Orthodox shuls on Sabbath mornings; and that virtually the only
people in the community who close their businesses on the
Sabbath and scrupulously observe such mitzvot as the dietary
laws and mikveh are Orthodox Jews. This small hard core of
zealots is willing to go to any lengths to remain Halakhic Jews,
even to the point of building Orthodox enclaves in newly developing suburbs or urban neighborhoods.

Why the resurgence of Orthodoxy? Charles Liebman believes
its revival is due to the new religious mood of irrationalism and

supernaturalism, as well as the desire for smaller, more intimate *shuls* and fellowship with like-minded Jews who share a bond of *mitzvot*.[6] Perhaps the failure of other movements to capture the hearts of young people is also a factor.

Will Orthodoxy disappear in time? That is doubtful. As Liebman writes:

> *Earlier predictions of the demise of Orthodox Judaism in the United States have been premature, and to say the least, Orthodoxy is on the upsurge. Its inner core is growing in numbers and financial strength. It is experiencing a greater sense of confidence and purpose, but its ultimate direction and form are still undetermined.*[7]

Orthodoxy will always appeal to those who find comfort and security in the belief that the Torah is the immutable word of God. The problem is: What óf the less edifying aspects of Torah? And how do we amend the word of God to solve inequities and remove excrescences? We are told that the great sages are empowered to reinterpret the Law. But in fact, they have moved with glacier-like speed and have resolved practically nothing.

Will tomorrow's Orthodoxy differ from today's? Very likely yes, just as today's Orthodoxy differs from that of yesterday. In the past, secular education was frowned upon and beards were *de rigueur*. Today, all but the ultra-Orthodox accept the need for secular learning, and few wear beards out of religious convictions. Orthodoxy is, and has been, accommodating itself despite its denials. Tomorrow's Orthodoxy may be different from the current version—but it will be around.

### Reform

Much of the criticism of Reform has been blunted by virtue of Reform's changes during the past thirty years. This highlights one of Reform's strong points; it indicates a responsiveness to the needs of the day and a willingness to shed old doctrines and accept new realities. Critics of Reform have accused it of heresy, sectarianism, heterodoxy. Some have compared it to the Karaites, the medieval sect who denied the binding authority of Talmudic law and reverted to a literal adherence to the Bible. Others chided Reform for stripping Judaism of nationalism and peoplehood and for opposing Zionism. Many denounced its naive liberalism and slavish loyalty to the *Zeitgeist*. Since the *Zeitgeist* changes periodically, Reform must then change accordingly. Consequently, what degree of constancy can there be if the movement changes every decade and sways with every blowing wind? Reform has also been attacked for overly stressing the needs of humanity while neglecting Jewish interests; of tending others' vineyards while neglecting its own. Then, too, critics have called Reform cold, antiseptic, and devoid of passion and fervor. Reform's attack on rituals as "Orientalism" has been rightly lampooned as naive. For who says that the Occidentals have a monopoly on religious truth and that the Orientals are devoid of spiritual riches? Others charge Reform with fostering anarchy by its rejection of Halakhah and of turning Judaism into little more than an idea or an abstraction. They call Reform a religion of convenience, a path of little resistance, demanding no sacrifices of its adherents. Moreover, its approach to revelation is illogical and untenable: if the moral laws are binding forever as God's word, why not ritual laws as well? Conversely, if rituals are only valid for a specific time and place and are to be subjectively accepted or rejected, why not the moral laws, too? This denigration of rituals has also denuded Judaism of its emotions and heart and left Reform a soulless body, a shell without a spirit, a mind without a heart. Additionally, many accuse Reform of being merely a way station to assimilation. It has not, we are told, retained the loyalties of its children or served as a bulwark against religious erosion.

Finally, Reform is supposed to make Jews better human beings because of its great stress on social justice and Prophetic morality. But are Reform Jews really more moral and more honest than, say, Orthodox partisans? And if Judaism is basically social ethics, why be Jews at all? Why not be Ethical Culturalists or humanists? The Reformers counter that we must preserve the Jewish People. But how can we preserve the Jewish People with-

out the plenitude of Jewish living? of *mitzvot?* of maximal education? After all, a civilization does not live on the rarefied oxygen
of theological principles and ethical norms alone!

While some of these strictures are no longer valid, several are
still significant, and Reform's own critics are the first to concede
the point. Rabbi Louis Mann, for example, chided Reform for
having lost the old zeal of Holdheim, Geiger, and Isaac M. Wise.
He detected too much of a laissez-faire attitude nurtured by the
social prominence and financial prestige of the movement. Samuel Cohon wrote that Reform Judaism had reshaped the exter-
nals but has yet to deepen Jewish spirit or bring the modern-day
Jew to worship. Even Kaufmann Kohler had to admit that Reform Judaism had disappointed its leaders as the novelty wore
off. He asked: "Have Sunday services changed the lives of Jews
for the better? Have hearts been touched by a holier, purer life?
We need more than abstract ideas and a few sacred days." Solomon Freehof has added his eminent voice noting that Reform
had reformed services and modernized worship but "We have
failed to achieve the revival of Judaism, the new life for which
we had hoped." We need less logic and more sentiment and we
need to get away from the "High Church mood," declared Freehof.[8]

Reform thinkers have become more and more uneasy about
the movement's stand on Halakhah. Rabbi Abba Hillel Silver
assailed the Pauline attitude of Reform with its antinomianism,
its attacks on the Talmud and *Shulkhan Arukh,* its denigration of
Sabbath, *kashrut,* and *mitzvot,* and its naive messianism and Pauline sense of the apocalypse. Such a Judaism, he said, was little
more than a faith erected on "the slender, sagging stilts of a few
theological abstractions." Even an ultra-liberal like Maurice
Eisendrath decries the fact that many gems were discarded and
that there is a danger of a new Orthodoxy of Reform marked by
too much license in the synagogue and too little religious discipline. Rabbi Philip Bernstein pondered, "How far does this
liberalism go before it becomes meaningless and absurd?" He
called for some "guide posts" in Jewish ritual—a cry, as we have
seen, reiterated by others in the Reform group. W. Gunther

Plaut is another leader who demands a new Halakhah for Reform. Rightly sensing the dilemma of freedom versus authority, Rabbi Plaut asks, "If Halakhah is purely human, what is its basis? If not, what right have we to change it?" And Rabbi Daniel Jeremy Silver wonders whether a few prophetic verses represent the sum of tradition and he muses: "If the halacha and the casuistic method are abrogated, how does anyone get down to specifics?"[9]

Many have charged that Reform lays stress on the head and neglects the heart of the congregant. Plaut has suggested that Reform too long eschewed the folk element of Jewish existence and emphasized the negative aspects of religious formalism, thereby failing to capture the masses. Louis Mann declared that Reform had "overemphasized the intellectual aspect of the movement to the neglect of its mystical elements." Rabbi Joshua Loth Liebman sought to correct this failing by wedding religion to psychiatry. In his famous volume, *Peace of Mind,* he, too, decried neglect of emotion and excessive rationalism, and he called for a synthesis of feeling and intellect: "I am convinced that religion, which already has made its peace with Copernicus and with Darwin, will have to make peace with Freud."[10]

Yet, Reform is undergoing constant revisions. As Samuel Cohon has written: "The tasks of Reform have not and never can be finished. Reform is a perennial process of self-renewal, of ever regenerating the creative spirit of Judaism." Professor Ezra Spicehandler, Director of the Hebrew Union College in Jerusalem, agrees that Reform is entering a new era and is updating its theology. "Formerly the Reform movement regarded Judaism merely as a religious denomination, and the national aspect was ignored. Now the majority accept Israel as the centre of the Jewish People." Of course, Spicehandler notes that unlike the Orthodox, Reform cannot accept observances on the blind faith of a soldier who accepts orders unquestioningly. Reform Jews will pick and select only those laws "which have meaning for us today. But observances there must be."[11]

Reform has saved many Jews who would have either gone nowhere or would have assimilated or even converted. It infused in Jews the zeal to reevaluate the old, to revise and update the obsolescent and outmoded, to change the moribund. It reintroduced into Judaism the dynamic quality long lost in ages of stagnation. It restored the old Prophetic passion for social justice and reminded Jews, dulled and insensitized to social ethics by centuries of Halakhic hair-splitting and minutiae, that the essence of Torah is morality, justice, truth, and peace. It helped show the way to reconciliation between the Jew and the outside world; it harmonized Torah with science, the sacred and the secular, the classical with the modern. It taught the Jew that he need not withdraw from the world or recoil into his ghetto in the face of onslaughts from society.

How far will Reform continue to change? Will it follow the trend back to tradition? Can it fire up the zeal of young people wandering on the seas of doubt and boredom without rituals and demands? Will tomorrow's Reform differ from the classical version? It will presumably be remarkably different. How much will it vary? We shall have to be patient and see.

*Conservatism*

The Conservative movement, unlike Orthodoxy and Reform, has been vulnerable to criticism from both right and left. The Orthodox have condemned it as merely a less radical version of Reform, while the Reform have labeled Conservatives as timid Orthodox. Conservatism is by its nature a middle-of-the-road movement. Consequently, it has been assailed for its fence-straddling stance. Its critics accuse it of seeking to be all things to all men, of lacking ideology and program, of deliberately remaining inchoate, hazy, and murky in order to satisfy all extremes. Elasticity is fine in a rubber band, but not in a movement; besides, one can only stretch a rubber band so far before it snaps. Additionally, Conservatism's critics accuse it of seeking to have its cake and eat it too. If Conservatives accept revelation, then they must accept all of the *mitzvot;* if they reject revelation, then why accept any of the *mitzvot?* If Torah is man's response to revelation, what portion of it is divine? Which of its laws and teachings are binding and eternal? And which are merely human? If Conservatives affirm Halakhah to be their *governance*, how can they change it or countenance flouting it? If it is merely their *guidance*, then how can they pretend to be Halakhic Jews? If Conservatives acknowledge the binding authority of the Talmud and Codes, as well as Israel's sages, how can they authorize blatant violations of Sabbath, dietary laws, and personal status rules. And if they spurn that authority, in what way do they differ from Reform? These are, indeed, thorny dilemmas.

No other group in American Jewish life has been as self-critical as Conservatism. The movement has been unsparing in its self-analysis and in assailing its leaders, institutions, and ideology.

For example, Rabbi Morris Adler criticized the "vast vagueness" and amorphousness which Conservatives persist in seeing as an asset. "We are on the way to a strange paradox of an Orthodox school, a Conservative rabbinate, and a Reform laity." Milton Steinberg detected in the movement a confusion of character due to its adherence to slogans rather than philosophy and the "neglect of even that slight ideology." Mordecai M. Kaplan has also taken Conservatism to task for its vagueness, its failure to define its terms, and its pusillanimous avoidance of Halakhic problems. Robert Gordis has called time and again for the formulation of basic principles and an ongoing conference on the philosophy and theology of Conservatism. He has urged the issuance of guides to Jewish law, ethical standards, Jewish education, study and worship, and a program of Conservative Judaism in Israel.[12]

The Conservative movement has been wracked by inner tensions. The Seminary has dominated the Rabbinical Assembly and the United Synagogue—much to the annoyance of both. Since the Seminary faculty tends to be virtually Orthodox, the gap between the intellectual leadership, the clergy, and the laity is enormous. Many critics believe that there is, in reality, no Conservative movement. Only the rabbis and their families are truly Conservative Jews; the masses of the laity are nondescript Reform Jews whose pattern of personal observance is barely distinguishable from that of their Reform neighbors.

The movement has built its structure on the fickle foundation of "Catholic Israel"—that is, the will of the people decides which Jewish practices will be preserved, which will be deleted. But as Israel Zangwill wittily observed, Catholic Israel is eternally Protestant: the majority of American Jews have closed the book on Sabbath and dietary rules—just to mention two basic rituals that have fallen into neglect. Does that mean that such *mitzvot* are now obsolete? If the Catholic Israel doctrine is retained, the answer would have to be "Yes!"

Over the years, the Rabbinical Assembly has been champing at the bit to break loose from the Seminary faculty and set off in new directions. In the past decade, this has begun to take place, and much to the outrage of some faculty members, the Rabbinical Assembly's Law Committee has pushed through far-reaching legal changes in Sabbath and Festival rules, personal status, marriage and divorce laws, and *kashrut* principles. The question some observers raise, however, is this: Is it not already *too late* to capture the soul of the people? Why bother allowing people to ride to synagogue on the Sabbath when they no longer *care* if it is the Sabbath?[13]

Whither the Conservative movement? Will there be—as David Philipson and Maurice Eisendrath have predicted—a rapprochement of Conservatism to the Reform position? It is doubtful. For as long as Reform is not governed by Halakhah, Conservatism will never join forces with it. Will Conservatism coalesce with Orthodoxy, since both share reverence for Jewish law? Very unlikely, since Orthodoxy hates and fears Conservatism as a much-too-similar brand of Judaism and a dangerous competitor. It also rejects Conservatism's Halakhic innovations as either illegal or unwarranted. Besides, institutional loyalties are too deep.

Conservatism will probably plod along on its own, trying hard to avoid dogmatic programs, which, in all likelihood, it will be forced to adopt eventually by exasperated partisans. At all events, the Conservative movement has served Jewry well, by reemphasizing Jewish peoplehood, spiritual nationhood, and Zionism. Moreover, it has tended to balance the scales of the two extremes of Orthodoxy and Reform. It has reiterated loyalty to tradition while affirming the need for change. It has synthesized the two basic elements of Judaism—law and ethics—and redressed the imbalance fashioned by Orthodoxy (through its stress on law) and Reform (with its emphasis on ethics). It has saved numerous Jews unable to live in the fires of Orthodoxy and unwilling to plunge into the icy waters of Reform. In short, it has been a typically American, pragmatic, undogmatic, centrist movement that has won the hearts of many. Can it continue to win Jews over? Can its triumphs be deeper than mere institutional loyalties and external allegiances? Can it also persuade Jews to change their lives and observe the *mitzvot* officially espoused by the movement? Can it rediscover its lost raison d'être and convey it to its laity? These are some of the problems that vex Conservative leaders.

### Reconstructionism

Reconstructionism has been criticized, and occasionally vilified, from various quarters. Some call it a *philosophy* of life, rather than a *way* of life. Some accuse Mordecai M. Kaplan of being a thinker among men of action, and a man of action among thinkers. Secularists say he is too religious; religionists accuse him of being too secularistic. Sociologists call him a theologian; theologians dub him a sociologist. Others say he asked the right *questions* but came up with the wrong *answers.* Some critics see nothing new in Reconstructionism since the 1940's, while others believe that the *Zeitgeist* that spawned Reconstructionism is dead; the new philosophical and sociological moods are inhospitable to Kaplan's ideas which are, by now, passé.

Kaplan's concept of God has been described as too abstract, too philosophical. "How do you pray to a process?" is a frequently posed question. Milton Steinberg, the only Reconstructionist to have really subjected the movement to criticism, pondered: "Does God really exist or is he only man's notion? Is there anything objective which corresponds to the subjective conception? And who adds up the 'sum' in the 'sum total of forces that make for salvation'? Is the sum added up 'out there,' or in the human imagination?" Steinberg found Kaplan's notion of God "inadequate" because "the riddle of the universe is not so readily to be dismissed, and faith is not only a psychological and ethical venture but a cognitive one also, an affirmation concerning the ultimate nature of things." Others view Kaplan's stress on "salvation" as a Christian concept that has no place in Jewish theology. Eugene Borowitz fears that with the loss of absolutes and substitution of relativism and functions, there is the danger of Judaism breaking down into a plurality of deities, with a god for each civilization. Moreover, Kaplan's insistence that one is either a supernaturalist or a religious humanist is dogmatic and unwarranted, for there are other options. Borowitz asks, "Can an impersonal God have a personal affect on man? Can man take personally an impersonal God?" Professor Eliezer Berkovits criticizes Kaplan for reintroducing supernaturalism despite his disclaimers. Kaplan, he feels, is guilty of no less of a leap of faith than is Karl Barth. He accuses Reconstructionism of a new polytheism and pantheism or pan-anthropoism, and he derides Kaplan for preserving social and scientific theories that are either outmoded or just one among others.[14]

Reconstructionism has been sharply attacked for its position on Halakhah. Many accuse it of fostering anarchy by its espousal of voluntary choice of folkways. Great laxity and latitude exist among Reconstructionists—even among their rabbis. Moreover, if *sacred* means *any* element of human experience that helps enhance human life and achieve salvation, that would include too much. For example, the sex experience could be taken as one of the *sancta* as could the thrill of hunting or the pleasure of golf, for that matter. Borowitz queries, Which drive to self-fulfillment is legitimate? Might not some of today's vulgar folk rites receive sanction? And why should customs or folkways retain their form any longer than *mitzvot*? If we allow elasticity in *mitzvot*, will not most seek the lowest level of observance? Finally, since Reconstructionists disavow Halakhah primarily because it is inoperable and can no longer be enforced by coercive methods, would they be prepared to accept it, say, in the State of Israel, where Halakhah is enforced?[15]

Yet another vulnerable facet of Reconstructionism is its rejection of the notion of the chosen people. Without the ideal of the chosen people, why be Jews? Is it enough to survive merely because the biological law of life says that it is moral for all groups to live, as Kaplan suggests? In fact, the biological law of life determines that some organisms should *die,* and history decides that some people should become extinct! Why should Israel not go the way of all flesh? Isn't Kaplan's vocation theory merely a hair-splitting, semantic substitute for the chosen people?

Critics within Reconstructionist ranks are few, probably because the movement is so young. While Milton Steinberg believed that "the bulk of Reconstructionist theory, program, implementation, seems to me to stand up under the test of the years and indeed have been validated by it," he found it debilitated by its pallid God concept, its indecision as to whether it was a school of thought or a movement, and its lack of an "incendiary style." One of these criticisms has been obviated by the creation of the Reconstructionist College and the formalization of the Reconstructionist movement. It is ironic: Reconstructionists have for forty years disavowed any intention to become a formal movement or another party in Israel, and here they are—a full-blooded faction in Jewry. It was clearly unavoidable—a spirit cannot live disembodied for very long.[16]

Reconstructionism is, perhaps, too intellectualized, too rarefied, too philosophical for many. But for others it has been the only means of remaining a Jew in this scientific age of rationalism and naturalism. By positing a naturalistic concept of God, it has appealed to those for whom a supernatural deity is juvenile, nonsensical, even absurd. By stressing the value of peoplehood and love for Zion as the spiritual center, it has helped unify diverse elements in Jewish life. Its notion of the organic community, if adopted, could only benefit Jewish life. Its stress on voluntarism is in the mainstream of American civilization and in keeping with modern man's abhorrence of coercion and witch hunts. Its new Zionism has added a vibrant dimension to the old and has acted as a corrective to the unbridled secular nationalism of the Zionist movements. Its reevaluation of old rituals and liturgy and reinterpretation of classical norms have enabled the modern Jew to live in the past, present, and future. Its notion of living creatively in two civilizations and of the need to enhance and enrich all aspects of Jewish life, culture, and civilization is terribly important for the American Jew.

Can Reconstructionism survive beyond the life of Mordecai M. Kaplan or has the cult of the personality built around him foredoomed the movement? Will the Reconstructionist Seminary be able to flourish and attract new students? And can Reconstructionism remain a movement in view of the wide latitude in religious practices that exists? After all, the line between freedom and anarchy is not readily distinguishable.

For all of its shortcomings, Reconstructionism has been a leavening in the yeast of Jewish life. It has affected the other religious groups as well as the secular ones. In retrospect, Reconstructionism has enriched the quality of Jewish life, prodded Jews to rethink old views, and has pointed Jewry in new directions for tomorrow.

*A Final Word*

American Jewry is an impressive entity. Nearly six million strong, with over three million Jews affiliated with synagogues, flourishing seminaries, rabbis, scholars, professors of Jewish studies, and great religious institutions, it can stare down its critics with a touch of pride and even condescension. For American Jewry has belied the Cassandras who prophesied its demise. But that is the way it is with Jews: we are constantly confounding our critics and detractors.

As we have noted, American Jewry was slow in developing its religious and cultural institutions. It took a full two hundred years before we produced a work of scholarship or trained a native-born son for the rabbinate. We tend to think of two centuries as a long time. But in Jewish history, two centuries are as a breath. As Professor Salo W. Baron has written, about nine centuries elapsed before Spanish Jewry emerged from Roman ignorance and Visigoth barbarism and entered upon its Golden Age. Whether American Jewry is entering its Golden Age is hard to say. But we are no longer living in the Dark Ages, either.

Baron has also suggested that if American Jewry had one hundred good rabbis, one hundred Jewish scholars, one hundred Jewish communal workers, one hundred top writers, and one hundred talented lay leaders, we could be sanguine about the future of the community. Well, we have the requisite numbers of rabbis, scholars, lay leaders, writers, and workers, and in addition, we have the schools and seminaries and Hebrew camps to do the job. But there is another essential ingredient: *the will of the people.* That elusive will-o'-the-wisp holds the key to Jewish survival. If the people are willing, empires can be won; if they are not, then all is lost.

At present it appears that the Jewish will to survive creatively is far from ideal. The population is stable—virtually at zero growth; the Jewish community is an aging one; the number of students in religious schools is shrinking markedly; Jewish neighborhoods in the inner city are decaying alarmingly; and Jewish learning, literacy, and living are on a low level while rituals are generally ignored. Religious convictions are about as deep as the Jordan River, and people join synagogues for the most outlandish—and untheological—reasons. Some prefer Conservative congregations to Reform because they insist on wearing caps. Others go to Reform temples because they require only two hours of religious studies a week. Many join an Orthodox synagogue because it is nearer than the Reform temple. And still others belong to one synagogue in preference to another because the rabbi is more handsome, the gym and pool are attractive, the décor of the building is chic, the membership more prestigious, or the social life more bustling. The variety of "religious" motivations in American life never ceases to amaze the trained observer.

Moreover, American Jews have created a new complex of secular rituals. Cards are played religiously on Friday night; golf contests are waged on Saturday; and bagels and lox are *de rigueur* on Sunday morning. But what of *mitzvot?* They are ignored. And what of the classic love of Jewish learning? It has been channeled into secular areas. Today's Ph.D.'s would have been yesteryear's Talmudic scholars; the Jewish doctors of our times probably would have been writing Bible commentaries a century or two ago.

Furthermore, the religious boom of the fifties and sixties seems to have peaked and the upward trend had leveled off by the late sixties and early seventies. New synagogues are no longer being built with the frenetic frequency of the fifties. Only 16 percent of America's Jews attend services weekly, the lowest of any major religious group. Most Jews have been aptly dubbed "Seventh-Day Absentists." At least 45 percent are still unaffiliated with a synagogue. A poll of rabbis revealed that 63 percent believe that religion is losing its influence in American life (the Protestant percentage was 59 percent; the Catholic 61 percent). The campuses have been described as vast wastelands and cemeteries for Jewish values, and only a fraction of the 400,000 Jewish collegians (or Jewish professors, for that matter) attend religious services or participate in Hillel activities. Intermarriage—once an extraordinarily low 7 percent among American Jews—is rising sharply and probably is about 17 percent today. Basic rituals, such as *kashrut* and Sabbath, are sadly neglected while minor observances, such as Hanukkah festivities, have been magnified into major proportions. And Jewish learning and knowledge are at an abysmally low level. The gap between the clergy and the masses in Reform and Conservatism is enormous, while the nonobservant Orthodox predominate in much of Orthodox life. Rabbi Eugene Borowitz writes of the paradox of Jewish belonging without believing and the weak, peripheral factors making for affiliation. "Ironically," he muses, "it may well be that secular Judaism, which could not dominate American Judaism under its own name, now may do so under the auspices of the synagogue." Borowitz adds pointedly:

*What other religious group in America can boast of men who are zealously committed to interfaith activities, but who have no faith of their own, who worship in no church with any degree of regularity, and who observe no commandments but those that their organizational participation requires or common American decency decrees? What does it say of Jewish life in America when Reform Judaism appeals because it demands so little but confers so much status? when people blandly proclaim that they are non-observant Orthodox Jews? when Conservative Judaism makes a virtue of not defining the center so that it may avoid alienating those disaffected on either side?[17]*

And yet, all is not totally bleak and American Jewry is certainly not about to disappear. There are hopeful signs even as there are disquieting ones. It is unquestionably true that Jewish observances have declined precipitously. For example, a study of kosher-food consumption in New York in 1917 revealed that a million Jews—two-thirds of the community—bought kosher meat. Today the figure is doubtlessly the reverse. On the other hand, the Jewish community can boast of a vastly improved Jewish education system. In a survey conducted for New York's Kehillah in 1910 by Dr. Mordecai M. Kaplan, it was found that three-quarters of New York's Jewish children received *no* Jewish education whatsoever. Today at least 80 percent of America's Jewish youth receive some religious instruction, more than 600,-000 attend Jewish schools between ages five and seventeen, and approximately 70,000 pupils are in over 300 Jewish Day Schools. Thousands attend Hebrew summer camps, youth groups, and Hebrew High Schools, while scores study in Israel. Courses in Judaica, Hebrew, Jewish history and philosophy are offered at 185 colleges. Scholarly Jewish studies are produced yearly. There are over 3,000 rabbis here and perhaps 4,000 synagogues. Three major seminaries and a score of lesser ones are turning out rabbis, cantors, and teachers. And Judaism—whose demise was predicted barely a century or less ago—is very much alive, dynamic, and flourishing.

We are not living in the ignorant wilderness of which Rabbi Abraham Rice complained in the middle of the nineteenth century. American Jews are no longer the disorganized, petty, jealous, struggling masses who so cruelly broke the heart of Rabbi Jacob Joseph at the turn of the century. America is not the *trefa* land condemned by ultra-Orthodox pietists in the past. Nor is American Jewish life the sick, tottering edifice which challenged the talents and ingenuity of Mordecai M. Kaplan in the twenties and thirties. No, we have made great strides since then. And for all of its flaws and failings, its superficialities and shoddiness, American Jewry is an imposing edifice, rich in promise and ripe for achievements.

What of the future? Will we continue to have four religious movements? Will several of them coalesce? Or will they, perhaps, multiply? The sages tell us that with the destruction of the Temple, prophecy was taken from the prophets and given over to fools. Not wanting to be labeled a fool, one should forgo the role of prophet and remain a cautious observer of the passing scene. The future is far from certain and one cannot predict whether we will enjoy an upsurge of religion or be afflicted with a religious decline. Nor can we foresee the forms which tomorrow's Judaism will take. But of this we can be certain: tomorrow's Judaism will be one that is interesting, challenging, dynamic, and exciting. The Jewish People may be frustrating, infuriating, exasperating, stiff-necked, stubborn, rebellious, factious, querulous, and contentious. But they are never dull. They have not been dull these past three thousand years—and we have reason to believe that they will not be so in the next three thousand either.

The challenge is: how to revive the spirit of our people so that they will *want* to live creatively as Jews. Abraham Joshua Heschel suggested that only by touching people's *neshamot*, their *souls*, can we win them over to Judaism. Obviously, the various religious movements we have examined have tried to touch those souls—succeeding in some cases, failing with most. But how do we capture souls? What will touch *neshamot?* Unfortunately, there are no simple answers. We search, we seek, we pursue faith. For as long as we search, seek, and pursue we indicate that there is life in the Jewish People and a spark in the Jewish soul.

In Ezekiel's great vision of the dry bones, God challenged the Prophet: "Can these bones live?" Ezekiel was uncertain: "You know, Lord." And when God infused the bones with Divine Spirit, they revived and took on sinew and flesh, muscle and blood. The bones came to life again; the fossilized House of Israel was born anew. Somehow the modern Jew must recapture that resuscitating spirit.

Which of the various religious philosophies is the *right* one? Which approach to God is the *valid* one? Or are all equally legitimate? Only God knows. And in His good time, He will reveal that knowledge to man.

In the meantime, we Jews continue in our pursuit of faith.

# *Notes*

## Chapter I

1. For the general background see *Pilgrim People* by Anita Lebeson; *The Jews in America: A History* by Rufus Learsi; *Early American Jewry* by Jacob Rader Marcus.

2. See Marcus, *op. cit.*

3. Jewish population statistics pose a problem. The Federal Census forbids questions on religion. Nor has there been a survey of religious bodies in over thirty years. Consequently, we have to rely on what Salo W. Baron calls "guesstimates" in calculating Jewish population. See the studies of A. Goldberg in *The Jewish People Past and Present*, Vol. 3, p. 25; J. Lestschinsky in Vol. 4 of the same work, pp. 56–68; M. Davis, "Jewish Religious Life and Institutions," in *The Jews*, edited by L. Finkelstein, Vol. I, pp. 381 ff.; Sidney Goldstein's "American Jewry, 1970: A Demographic Profile," in the *American Jewish Year-book*, Vol. 72 (1971), pp. 3–88. The forthcoming study headed by Dr. Fred Massarik for the Council of Jewish Federations and Welfare Funds will contain a wealth of up-to-date material on American Jewry and its demographic structure.

4. See Mark Wischnitzer's *To Dwell in Safety* (Philadelphia, 1949) and J. Lestschinsky's "Jewish Migrations, 1840–1946," in *The Jews, op. cit.*, Vol. II, pp. 1198–1238.

5. See M. Davis, *op. cit.*, pp. 426 ff.; Charles Liebman, "Orthodoxy in American Life," *American Jewish Yearbook*, Vol. 66 (1965), pp. 21–97.

6. See Nathan Glazer's *American Judaism*.

7. Glazer, *ibid.* Cf. Will Herberg's *Protestant-Catholic-Jew*.

8. See the following essays in the *American Jewish Yearbook*, Vol. 56 (1955): Joseph Blau, "The Spiritual Life of American Jewry, 1654–1954," pp. 99–170; Oscar and Mary F. Handlin, "The Acquisition of Political and Social Rights by the Jews in the United States," pp. 43–98; N. Glazer, "Social Chracteristics of American Jews, 1654–1954," pp. 3–41. See also O. Handlin's *Adventure in Freedom;* Glazer's *American Judaism;* and Herberg's *Protestant-Catholic-Jew*.

9. See Hyman Grinstein's *The Rise of the Jewish Community of New York*, pp. 142 ff.; Learsi, *op. cit.*, pp. 26–28.

10. See Isaac Fein's *The Making of an American Jewish Community*, pp. 4–8.

11. See Learsi, *op. cit.*, 48–52; O. Handlin, *op. cit.*

12. See Bertram W. Korn's *American Jewry and the Civil War* (Philadelphia, 1951), pp. 121–155 and 156–188.

13. Milton Mayer, *Man v. the State* (Santa Barbara, 1969), pp. 103 ff.

14. *Ibid.* See the appropriate Supreme Court Cases discussed in Mayer's volume and in the articles of Blau and Oscar and Mary Handlin cited above in note 8.

15. Moshe Davis, *The Emergence of Conservative Judaism*, pp. 89–96.

16. See Grinstein, Lebeson, Learsi, *op. cit.*, and Davis, "Jewish Religious Life and Institutions," *op. cit.* in note 3.

17. Davis, *ibid*, p. 381, and his *The Emergence of Conservative Judaism*, p. 150.

18. Abraham Karp, "Simon Tuska Becomes a Rabbi," *Publications of the American Jewish Historical Society*, Vol. L, No. 2 (December, 1960), pp. 79–97.

19. On the chaplaincy battle see Korn, *op. cit.*, pp. 56–97. On the changing role of the American rabbi, see "The American Rabbi: A Religious Specialist Responds to Loss of Authority" by Jerome E. Carlin and Saul H. Mendlovitz in *The Jews*, edited by Marshall Sklare, pp. 377–414. Nevertheless, the American rabbi is far from content in his calling and the rate of attrition is high. A recent Gallup Poll found that more rabbis contemplate leaving the pulpit than do ministers or priests. It is also a disconcerting fact that the students in the various rabbinical schools are fundamentally unhappy with their rabbinic training. See Charles Liebman's study, "The Training of American Rabbis" in the *American Jewish Yearbook*, 69 (1968), pp. 3–112.

20. See Joshua Trachtenberg's "American Jewish Scholarship" in *The Jewish People Past and Present*, Vol. 4, pp. 411–455, and Solomon Zeitlin's "Jewish Learning in America" in *The Jewish Quarterly Review*, XLV, 4 (April, 1955), pp. 582–616. Also compare the studies of Jewish scholarship and Hebrew learning by Solomon Freehof, Jacob Kabakoff, Charles Angoff, and Harold U. Ribalow in *Judaism*, 3, 4 (Fall 1954), pp. 381–426. All of these studies need to be updated.

21. Rice's letter was published in *Tradition*, 7, 4; 8,1 (Winter 1965–Spring 1966), pp. 122 f.
22. On the Board of Delegates, see Davis, *The Emergence of Conservative Judaism*, pp. 101 ff., and Korn, *American Jewry and the Civil War, passim*, and especially pp. 72–74.
23. On the synod question see David Philipson, *The Reform Movement in Judaism*, pp. 301–2 and 328; W. Gunther Plaut, *The Growth of Reform Judaism*, pp. 21, 26, 238 f., and *passim;* Davis, *The Emergence of Conservative Judaism*, pp. 114–146, 200 ff., 275–282, and *passim.*
24. Quoted by Davis in his "Jewish Religious Life and Institutions in America," *op. cit.*, pp. 358 f.
25. See Jeremiah J. Berman, "The Trend in Jewish Religious Observance in Mid-Nineteenth Century America," *Publications of the American Jewish Historical Society*, XXXVII, (1947), pp. 31–53. Cf. Davis, *The Emergence of Conservative Judaism*, pp. 208 ff.
26. See Rudolf Glanz, "Jewish Social Conditions as Seen by the Muckrakers," *YIVO Annual of Jewish Social Science*, IX (1954), pp. 308–331; *A Bintel Brief*, edited by Isaac Metzger, *passim; The Autobiography of Lincoln Steffens*, quoted in Milton Hindus' *The Old East Side*, pp. 89 f.

## Chapter II

1. See *The Rise of The Jewish Community of New York* by Hyman B. Grinstein; *Early American Jewry* by Jacob Rader Marcus; "Orthodoxy in American Jewish Life" by Charles Liebman in *American Jewish Yearbook*, 66 (1965), pp. 21–97; Gilbert Klaperman, *The Story of Yeshiva University*, as well as the various communal studies. Also see the article by Emanuel Rackman, "American Orthodoxy—Retrospect and Prospect," in *Judaism*, 3, 4 (Fall 1954), pp. 302–309, and the article by Joseph Lookstein, "Traditional Judaism in America: Problems and Achievements," in *The Jewish Quarterly Review*, XLV, 4 (April, 1955), pp. 318–333. Cf. Liebman's study, "Orthodoxy in Nineteenth Century America," in *Tradition*, 6, 2 (Spring–Summer 1964), pp. 132–140.
2. See Grinstein, *op. cit.*, especially chapters III, IV, and V; Morris A. Gutstein, *The Story of the Jews of Newport;* Edwin Wolf 2nd and Maxwell Whiteman, *The History of the Jews of Philadelphia;* Charles Reznikoff and U.Z. Engelman, *The Jews of Charleston.*
3. Grinstein, *op. cit.*, chapter XII; Jeremiah Berman, "Jewish Education in New York City, 1860–1900," *YIVO Annual of Jewish Social Science*, IX (1954), pp. 247–275. Alvin Schiff, *The Jewish Day School in America.*
4. See Moshe Davis, "Jewish Religious Life and Institutions in America," in *The Jews*, edited by Louis Finkelstein, Volume I, pp. 361 ff.; *To Dwell in Safety* by Mark Wischnitzer; "Jewish Migrations, 1840–1946" by Jacob Lestschinsky in *The Jews, op. cit.*, II, 1198–1238; "Economic and Social Development of

American Jewry" by Lestschinsky in *The Jewish People Past and Present* 4, 56–64.
5. Davis, *op. cit.*, p. 381.
6. On Rice see *The Making of an American Jewish Community* by Isaac M. Fein, pp. 54–58.
7. See *History of the Jews of Los Angeles* by Max Vorspan and Lloyd P. Gartner, pp. 85–90 and *passim*.
8. Jeremiah Berman, "The Trend in Jewish Religious Observance In Mid-Nineteenth Century America," *Publications of the American Jewish Historical Society*, 37 (1947), pp. 31–53; H. Grinstein, "The Efforts of East European Jewry to Organize Its Own Community in the United States," *Publications of the American Jewish Historical Society*, XLIX, 2 (December, 1959), pp. 73–89; Abraham J. Karp, "New York Chooses a Chief Rabbi," *Publications of the American Jewish Historical Society*, XLIV, 3 (March, 1955), pp. 129–198.
9. See *History of the Jews of Los Angeles*, pp. 164 f; *The Making of an American Jewish Community*, pp. 178, 192; *From Ararat to Suburbia*, pp. 318 f. Other communities, such as Chicago, made similar abortive attempts. Although several Orthodox rabbis have referred to themselves as "chief rabbis" of a particular city, American Jewry has never followed the European pattern in this regard and there have never really been any "chief rabbis" in the European sense.
10. See Berman's study, "Jewish Education in New York City, 1860–1900," cited in note 3. Cf. also the selections in *The Old East Side* edited by Milton Hindus.
11. Berman's study, *op. cit.*; cf. also Klaperman, *The Story of Yeshiva University*, *passim*.
12. Cf. Charles Liebman, "Orthodoxy in American Jewish Life," cited in note 1; Alvin I. Schiff, *The Jewish Day School in America;* Moshe Davis, "Jewish Religious Life and Institutions," cited in note 4; "Jewish Educational Institutions" by Simon Greenberg in *The Jews*, edited by Finkelstein, II, 916–949.
13. See *The Emergence of Conservative Judaism by* Moshe Davis, pp. 315, 317, 318, 320–322, 334, 351.
14. Cf. Davis, *op. cit.*, pp. 318 f.
15. Cf. Liebman, "Orthodoxy in American Jewish Life," *op. cit.*, pp. 54–56.
16. Liebman, *op. cit.*, pp. 32–34.
17. E. Rackman, *One Man's Judaism*, p. 272. The Orthodox view against mixed seating has been liberalized, as evidenced by the fact that in 1933 Dr. Revel revoked the ordination of an alumnus who accepted a post with mixed pews. See Rothkoff, *Bernard Revel*, pp. 165 f.
18. On Soloveitchik see A. Lichtenstein's essay in *Great Jewish Thinkers of the Twentieth Century*, edited by Simon Noveck, pp. 281–297. Cf. Soloveitchik's Hebrew essay, *"Kedushah Geluyah Ukedushah Nisteret"* in *Shanah Beshanah*, edited by A. H. Pitchenik (Jerusalem, 5731), pp. 179–201.
19. Separatists like Rabbi David Hollander, past president of the RCA, and Rabbi Ralph Pelcovitz have espoused the go-it-alone tack. The UOJC has rejected secessionist resolutions at several conventions over the past few years.
20. See H. Grinstein, "Orthodox Judaism and Early Zionism in America" in

*Early History of Zionism in America,* edited by Isidore S. Meyer (New York, 1958), pp. 219–227. Cf. Liebman, *op. cit.,* pp. 61 f.

21. Liebman, *op. cit.,* pp. 79–85.

22. While statistics are hard to come by, there are probably over 100,000 Sephardim in America. Many are simply not affiliated with synagogues, but others are in Reform and Conservative congregations and have passed into the Ashkenazic mainstream. See now Marc Angel, "The Sephardim of the United States: An Exploratory Study," *American Jewish Yearbook,* 74 (1973), pp. 77–138.

## Chapter III

1. See Charles Liebman, "Orthodoxy in American Jewish Life," *American Jewish Yearbook,* 66, 1965, p. 47.

2. See *The Condition of Jewish Belief,* edited by Milton Himmelfarb.

3. Shubert Spiro, "Is There an Indigenous Jewish Theology?" in *Tradition,* 9, 1–2 (Spring–Summer 1967), pp. 52–69. Cf. Norman Lamm's "Faith and Doubt" in the same issue, pp. 14–51.

4. Leo Jung, *Harvest,* p. 219; E. Berkovits, *God, Man and History,* pp. 14 f.; E. Rackman, *One Man's Judaism,* pp. 4–6; J.B. Soloveitchik, *"Ish Ha-Halakhah"* in *Talpiot,* I, 1, pp. 651–734; Samuel Belkin in *Essays in Traditional Jewish Thought,* p. 38; L. Rabinowitz, *"Torah min ha-Shamayim"* in *Tradition,* 7,1 (Winter 1964–65) pp. 34–45.

5. See Leo Jung, *Harvest,* p. 289. Cf. R. Pelcovitz, "Wanted: An American Orthodox Image" in *Jewish Life,* XXIX, 1 (October 1961), p. 16.

6. J.B. Soloveitchik, "The Lonely Man of Faith" in *Tradition,* 7, 2 (Summer 1965), pp. 5–67.

7. Rackman in *One Man's Judaism,* pp. 262–283; E. Berkovits, "Reconstructionist Theology" in *Tradition,* 2, 1 (Fall 1959), pp. 20–67.

8. E. Berkovits in *God, Man and History,* pp. 78 and 148. See his more recent views in his volume *Faith After the Holocaust,* New York, 1973.

9. J.B. Soloveitchik, "The Lonely Man of Faith," *op. cit.,* pp. 6, 50.

10. Rackman in *The Condition of Jewish Belief,* p. 180; Norman Lamm in the same volume, pp. 124 f.; A. Lichtenstein, pp. 132 ff.; I. Jacobovitz, p. 110; Marvin Fox, pp. 60 f.; E. Berkovits, pp. 25 f.; cf. Leo Jung in *Harvest,* pp. 248, 286, 288.

11. See the articles by Rabbis Isaac Swift and Gilbert Klaperman, and Mr. Reuben Gross in *Jewish Life,* XXX, 4 (May–June 1963), pp. 22–41.

12. See his article *"Ish Ha-Halakhah,"* cited in note 4, and his "The Lonely Man Of Faith," pp. 50 f.

13. See his "The Lonely Man of Faith," pages 52 f. and footnotes.

14. Rackman, "Sabbath and Festivals in the Modern Age" in *Studies in Torah Judaism,* edited by L. Stitskin, pp. 38–80; *One Man's Judaism,* p. 177; "The Dialectics of the Halakhah" in *Tradition,* 3,2 (Spring 1961), pp. 131–150.

Samuel Belkin, "The Philosophy of Purpose" in *Studies in Torah Judaism*, pp. 1–29; E. Berkovits, "Authentic Judaism and Halakhah" in *Judaism*, 19,1 (Winter 1970), pp. 66–76, and his *God, Man and History*, pp. 113 f., 120, 130.

15. See Maimonides' *Guide*, III, 26–50 (selected and translated in my *Maimonides: His Wisdom for Our Time* [New York, 1969], pp. 61–63). Cf. also Y. Heineman, *Taame Ha-Mitzvot Be-Safrut Yisrael*, 2 volumes, Jerusalem, 5714.

16. Soloveitchik in *"Ish Ha-Halakhah,"* p. 688; I. Jacobovitz in *Tradition*, 7,1 (Winter 1964–65), pp. 86–88.

17. Leo Jung, "What is Orthodox Judaism?" in *The Jewish Library*, edited by Jung, second series (New York, 1930), pp. 114 ff. and reprinted in varied forms in other volumes.

18. See his review of Judge Moshe Silberg's *Principia Talmudica* in *Tradition*, 6, 2(Summer 1964), p. 129; *Studies in Torah Judaism*, p. 48; "The Dialectics of the Halakhah" quoted in note 14, p. 148; "Sabbath and Festivals in the Modern Age," p. 8; *One Man's Judaism*, p. 177. Cf. Belkin, *Essays in Traditional Jewish Thought*, pp. 140 f.

19. M. Lewittes, "The Nature and History of Jewish Law," in *Studies in Torah Judaism*, p. 303. Cf. E. Berkovits, "Authentic Judaism and Halakhah" cited in note 14.

20. See especially the various issues of *Tradition*. Cf. I. Jacobovitz, "Jewish Law Faces Modern Problems" in *Studies in Torah Judaism*, pp. 317–464. Cf. also the Lubavitcher Rebbe, "A Thought for the Week," IV, 31 (May 16–22, 1971).

21. E. Berkovits in *God, Man and History*, pp. 139 ff. and in *The Condition of Jewish Belief*, p. 26; M. Fox in *The Condition of Jewish Belief*, pp. 63 f.

22. The Lubavitcher Rebbe issued a public statement in December, 1970.

23. E. Rackman in *One Man's Judaism*, p. 312.

24. *Jewish Life*, XXXVI, 5 (May-June 1969), p. 4.

25. R. Pelcovitz, "Wanted: An American Orthodox Image," *Jewish Life*, XXIX, 1 (October 1961), p. 16.

26. *Jewish Life*, XXXIV, 1 (September-October 1966), p. 5.

27. Rackman, *One Man's Judaism*, p. 3.

28. Rackman in *One Man's Judaism*, pp. 262–283; Pelcovitz, "Who is the Orthodox Jew?" in *Jewish Life*, XXXII, 2 (November-December 1968), p. 16.

29. Belkin in *Essays in Traditional Jewish Thought, passim*, and Rackman in *One Man's Judaism*, pp. 313–324.

30. E. Berkovits, "Prayer," in *Studies in Torah Judaism*, pp. 81–189.

31. E. Rackman, "Arrogance or Humility in Prayer," *Tradition*, I, 1 (Fall 1958), pp. 13–26.

32. J.B. Soloveitchik in a letter to Rabbi Benjamin Lapidus published in *Conservative Judaism*, XI, 1 (Fall 1956), pp. 50–51. Rabbi Aaron Soloveitchik's view was expressed in a speech to the National Leadership Conference of the UOJC, Chicago, November 27–30, 1969, and is available in a pamphlet. Cf. editorial in *Jewish Life*, XXVI, 5 (June 1959), pp. 3–5.

33. Jung in *Harvest*, pp. 210 ff.; Rackman, *One Man's Judaism*, p. 386.

34. See the Resolutions of the 1970 Convention of the UOJC.

35. B. Berzon quoted in the *New York Times* of May 9, 1971. Cf. editorial in *Jewish Life*, XXVIII, 1 (October 1960), pp. 6–9.

36. RCA resolution quoted in the *New York Times* of May 9, 1971. Cf. editorial in *Jewish Life*, XXXVI, 4 (March-April 1967), pp. 4–6.

37. Editorial in *Jewish Life*, XXXI, 6 (July-August 1964), pp. 4–5. The vast majority of JDL members have been recruited from the ranks of the poorer Orthodox youth of urban ghettos.

38. Liebman in *Tradition*, 9, 4 (Spring 1968), pp. 28–32. Cf. editorial in *Jewish Life*, XXXIV, 3 (January-February 1967), pp. 3–6.

39. J.B. Soloveitchik, "Confrontation" in *Tradition* 6, 2 (Spring–Summer 1964), pp. 5–28.

40. Rackman in *One Man's Judaism*, pp. 354–360. See the statement of the RCA in *Tradition*, 6, 4 (Spring–Summer 1964), pp. 28–29. Belkin is also opposed to interfaith projects. Cf. his *Essays in Traditional Jewish Thought*, *passim*.

## Chapter IV

1. For the historical background see Graetz's *History of the Jews*, Volume V; Baron's *A Social and Religious History of the Jews* (1937 edition), Vol. II; Baron's essay, "The Modern Age" in *Great Ages and Ideas of the Jewish People*, edited by Leo W. Schwarz, pp. 315–483; Elbogen's *A Century of Jewish Life*; and H. Sachar's *The Course of Modern Jewish History*.

2. Graetz, *op. cit.*, pp. 474–499; D. Tama, *Transactions of the Parisian Sanhedrin* (London, 1807), translated from the French by F.D. Kirwan; Robert Anchel, *Napoleon et les Juifs* (Paris, 1928); Sachar, *op. cit.*, pp. 58–65.

3. See D. Philipson, *The Reform Movement in Judaism* and W. Gunther Plaut's *The Rise of Reform Judaism* and *The Growth of Reform Judaism*.

4. See Philipson and Plaut, *op. cit.*, and Graetz, *op. cit.*

5. Plaut, *The Rise of Reform Judaism*, pp. 20–62.

6. *Ibid.*, pp. 62–70.

7. *Ibid.*, pp. 74–94. Cf. Philipson, *op. cit.*, 140–226.

8. Philipson, *op. cit.*, pp. 329–334; Plaut, *The Growth of Reform Judaism*, pp. 4–7; Lee M. Friedman, "America's First Reform Congregation," in *Pilgrims in a New Land*, pp. 151–162.

9. Plaut, *op. cit.* pp. 6–7.

10. Plaut, Philipson, and Friedman, *op. cit.*

11. See Philipson, *op. cit.*, pp. 337 f.; Plaut, *op. cit.*, pp. 4–11.

12. See Israel Knox's biography, *Rabbi in America: The Story of Isaac M. Wise.*

13. Cited in Moshe Davis' *The Emergence of Conservative Judaism*, p. 153.

14. *Ibid.*

15. *Ibid.* Cf. Plaut, *The Growth of Reform Judaism*, pp. 29 f.

16. Plaut, *op. cit.*, pp. 26–28; Philipson, *op. cit.*, pp. 377–379.

17. Plaut, *ibid.*, p. 28.

18. Against Einhorn's view, which was to send the students to Germany.

19. Philipson, *op. cit.*, pp. 377–379; Plaut, *op. cit.*, pp. 50–55; Davis, *op. cit.*, pp. 175–182.

20. Carl Voss, *Stephen S. Wise: Servant of the People*, pp. 105, 137, and *passim;* Hyman J. Fliegel, "The Creation of the Jewish Institute of Religion," *American Jewish Historical Quarterly*, LVIII, 2 (December, 1968), pp. 260–270.

21. Davis, *op. cit.*, pp. 130–134; Plaut, *op. cit.*, pp. 19–24.

22. Plaut, pp. 30 f. The guiding spirit was obviously Kohler's and Einhorn's.

23. Philipson, *op. cit.*, pp. 355–357; Plaut, pp. 31–41.

24. See the *Yearbook* of the CCAR, Vols. I, II, III, 1890–1893.

25. See *Keeper of the Law* by Eli Ginzberg (Philadelphia, 1966), p. 69.

26. The appropriate volumes of the *Yearbook* of the CCAR document these decisions. The early decisions are collected in Vols. I, II, and III.

27. Plaut, *op. cit.*, pp. 89–96; *Basic Reform Judaism* by William B. Silverman, pp. 232–243. The World Union for Progressive Judaism has announced that it will shortly move its headquarters to Jerusalem.

28. Plaut, pp. 96–101; CCAR *Yearbook* 47 (1937), *passim.*

29. New York's prestigious Temple Emanuel quit the UAHC in a widely publicized action and bitterly criticized Eisendrath.

Chapter V

1. Plaut, *The Growth of Reform Judaism*, pp. 199 ff.; Philipson, *The Reform Movement in Judaism*, pp. 147–150, 458, note 28.

2. For Kohler's views see his *Jewish Theology*, pp. viii f., 4, 8, 20, and 321.

3. Kohler, *Studies, Addresses, And Personal Papers*, pp. 203, 212 f., 221 f., 223, 233, 327–329.

4. Quoted in Philipson, *op. cit.*, pp. 342–344.

5. Emil G. Hirsch, *My Religion*, pp. 294 f.

6. Philipson, *op. cit.*, p. 395.

7. Freehof in the Preface to *The Rise of Reform Judaism*, p. viii; Plaut, *The Rise of Reform Judaism*, p. xiii; Silverman, *Basic Reform Judaism*, p. xiii, and pp. 4 and 10.

8. See *Rabbi in America* by Israel Knox, *passim.*

9. Kohler, *Jewish Theology*, p. 36.

10. Plaut, *The Growth of Reform Judaism*, pp. 33 f., 96 ff., 210 f.

11. *Ibid.*, p. 211.

12. A fascinating symposium on the God idea was held at the 48th General Assembly of the UAHC and is succinctly summarized in Silverman's *Basic Reform Judaism*, pp. 92–104.

13. Silverman, *op. cit.*, p. 95; Petuchowski, *Ever Since Sinai*, p. 47.

14. Silverman, pp. 96 f.
15. Borowitz, *A New Jewish Theology in the Making*, p. 63; *How Can a Jew Speak of Faith Today?*, pp. 21 ff., 52, 56.
16. Silverman, *op. cit.*, pp. 98–100.
17. See Wolf's "On God and Jewish Theology" in *Contemporary Reform Thought*, edited by Bernard Martin, pp. 43 f.
18. Gittelsohn's view is cited in Plaut's *The Growth of Reform Judaism*, p. 355.
19. Quoted in Silverman, *op. cit.*, p. 100.
20. Silverman, p. 92.
21. Plaut, *The Rise of Reform Judaism*, pp. 127–133; *The Growth of Reform Judaism*, pp. 33–36, 206–210.
22. Plaut, *The Growth of Reform Judaism*, p. 97.
23. Philipson, *op. cit.*, p. 433. See Eisendrath's *Can Faith Survive?*, *passim*.
24. Petuchowski, *op. cit.*, pp. 82 ff., 110, 113 f.; Borowitz, *How Can a Jew Speak of Faith Today?*, p. 62.
25. Julian Morgenstern, *As a Mighty Stream* (Philadelphia, 1949), pp. 87 ff.; Plaut, *op. cit.*, pp. 23 f., 224 ff.
26. Davis, *The Emergence of Conservative Judaism*, p. 154; Knox, *Rabbi in America*, p. 129.
27. Plaut, *op. cit.*, pp. 236, 276 f.
28. Plaut, pp. 96–98.
29. Samuel Hirsch's view is in Plaut, p. 36. For his son's position, see *My Religion*, pp. 20, 61, etc., and Plaut, pp. 228 f.
30. Kohler in *Jewish Theology*, pp. 46 ff., 241, 342–353; *Studies, Addresses, And Personal Papers*, pp. 203–207.
31. *Studies, Addresses, And Personal Papers*, pp. 206 ff.
32. Cited in Plaut, p. 34. See Philipson's comments in his *The Reform Movement in Judaism*, pp. 355–357.
33. CCAR *Yearbook*, Vol. XIII (1903), pp. 168 ff.; Davis, *The Emergence of Conservative Judaism*, p. 221; Kohler, *Jewish Theology*, p. 352; Morgenstern, *As a Mighty Stream*, p. 127; and the appropriate sections in Plaut's two volumes and in Philipson's work.
34. On the mixed-marriage controversy, see Plaut's *The Rise*, etc., pp. 220 ff., and *The Growth*, etc., pp. 257 f. Cf. "The Cost of Mixed Marriages," by A. S. Maller and M. L. Raphall in the CCAR *Journal*, XVIII, 2, (April, 1971), pp. 83–85.
35. Kohler, *A Living Faith*, pp. 31–41; Freehof, *Recent Reform Responsa*, pp. 7–9, and his Introduction to Philipson's volume, *op. cit.*, p. xx; Silver and Levy cited in Plaut, *The Growth*, etc., pp. 96 ff. and 152 f.; Lauterbach, *Rabbinic Essays* (Cincinnati, 1951), pp. 262 ff.
36. The text of the Columbus Platform is in Plaut's *The Growth*, etc., pp. 96–98.
37. Plaut, *op. cit.*, pp. 236–241; Freehof in CCAR *Yearbook*, LVI (1946), pp. 288 ff.

38. Silverman, *op. cit.*, pp. 185–195; Eisendrath in *Aspects of Progressive Jewish Thought*, edited by I. Mattuck, pp. 76 f.

39. See *A Guide for Reform Jews* by Frederick A. Doppelt, and David Polish and Silverman's *Basic Reform Judaism*, pp. 196–217.

40. Freehof, *Recent Reform Responsa*, pp. 7–12.

41. Plaut, "The Halacha of Reform" in *Contemporary Reform Thought*, pp. 90–98.

42. Petuchowski, *Ever Since Sinai*, pp. 74–77.

43. Borowitz in *A New Jewish Theology in the Making*, pp. 207–209; *How Can a Jew Speak of Faith Today?*, p. 67.

44. Freehof in his Introduction to Philipson's *The Reform Movement in Judaism*, p. xx.

45. For Geiger's view see *Abraham Geiger and Liberal Judaism*, edited by Max Wiener (Philadelphia, 1962), pp. 262–264. See Kohler's *Jewish Theology*, pp. 323–330, 339–341, 365.

46. Holdheim quoted in Plaut, *The Rise*, etc., pp. 138 f.

47. *Jewish Theology*, p. 51; cf. 340 f.

48. Petuchowski in *Ever Since Sinai*, pp. 57–64; Liebman in Plaut's *The Growth*, etc., pp. 171 f; Bamberger in *Contemporary Reform Jewish Thought*, pp. 129 f.; Narot in the same volume, pp. 142 f.

49. D. J. Silver in *Contemporary Reform Jewish Thought*, p. 156.

50. Cited in Plaut, *The Growth*, etc., pp. 153 ff.; Philipson, *op. cit.*, pp. 360 f.

51. Philipson, *op. cit.*, p. 360; Kohler, *Jewish Theology*, pp. 390 f., and *Studies, Addresses, And Personal Papers*, pp. 334, 442, 453–466; Plaut, *op. cit.*, pp. 144–150.

52. Wise quoted in Plaut, pp. 150 f.

53. Silver quoted in Plaut, pp. 152 f.

54. See the appropriate volumes of the *Yearbook* of the CCAR. Cf. David Polish's "The Challenge of Israel" in the CCAR *Journal*, XVIII, 2 (April, 1971), pp. 4–11.

55. See Spicehandler's statement in *Petahim* No. 1 (15), December, 1970, p. 24 (English summary). Cf. Borowitz, *How Can a Jew Speak of Faith Today?*, p. 96.

56. See Plaut, *The Rise*, etc., pp. 152–158.

57. See Petuchowski's *Prayerbook Reform in Europe*, passim.

58. Plaut, *The Rise*, etc., pp. 152–205; *The Growth*, etc., pp. 297–316; Abraham Millgram, *Jewish Worship* (Philadelphia, 1971), pp. 569–599.

59. Plaut, *The Rise*, etc., pp. 162–164.

60. Plaut, *The Growth*, etc., pp. 269–283; CCAR, *Yearbook* XIII (1902), p. 77, and XVII (1906), pp. 87–113.

61. Plaut, *op. cit.*, pp. 277 f.; Kohler in CCAR *Yearbook*, XVI (1905), p. 62.

62. Abraham Z. Idelsohn, *Jewish Music* (New York, 1929), *passim; Jewish Liturgy and Its Development* (New York, 1932), pp. 269–300.

63. Kohler, *Jewish Theology*, pp. 271–274.
64. *Union Prayer Book*, pp. 10, 39, etc.
65. See the CCAR *Yearbook*, LXXVII (1967), *passim*.
66. Borowitz, *How Can a Jew Speak of Faith Today?*, pp. 114, 123–127.
67. Plaut, *The Growth*, etc., p. 34.
68. *Ibid.*, p. 98.
69. Hirsch, *My Religion*, pp. 131 ff.; Kohler, *Jewish Theology*, p. 475; Cronbach and Baeck cited in Plaut, *op. cit.*, pp. 118 ff.; Stephen S. Wise quoted in Voss, *Stephen S. Wise: Servant of the People*, p. 145.
70. Plaut, *op. cit.*, pp. 118–127; Silverman, *op. cit.*, 166–178. See the appropriate volumes of the CCAR *Yearbook* which contain an annual social actions statement.
71. Fackenheim in *Judaism and Ethics*, edited by D. J. Silver, p. 244. See Richard G. Hirsch's essay in the same volume, pp. 251–261, and the contrary opinions of Professor Julius Kravitz of HUC-JIR, pp. 271–284.
72. Stein and Formstecher quoted in Plaut, *The Rise*, etc., pp. 146–151. For Kohler's view see *Jewish Theology*, pp. 17, 54. Hirsch's opinion is found in his *My Religion*, pp. 29–64 and pp. 75 ff.
73. See Plaut, *The Growth*, etc., pp. 179 f.
74. *Ibid.*, pp. 34, 97 f., 284 ff.
75. *Ibid.*, pp. 181 ff. Voss, *Stephen S. Wise: Servant of The People*, pp. 132–134, 145, 231; the *New York Times*, June 24, 1971.
76. Borowitz, *How Can a Jew Speak of Faith Today?*, pp. 205–221. See the full statement of the CCAR on the question of interreligious dialogue in the CCAR *Yearbook*, LXXIX (1969), pp. 82–85.

## Chapter VI

1. See Moshe Davis, *The Emergence of Conservative Judaism*, and Mordecai Waxman (ed.), *Tradition and Change*.
2. See *Tradition and Change*, pp. 43–50.
3. On Leeser see Davis, *op. cit.*, pp. 347–349 and *passim;* Waxman, *op. cit.*, pp. 51–57; Herbert Parzen, *Architects of Conservative Judaism*, pp. 5–11.
4. See Davis for a thorough analysis of the men and their ideas.
5. Davis, pp. 15–20. Cf. Herbert Parzen, *Architects of Conservative Judaism*, pp. 17–25.
6. Kohut cited in Davis, *op. cit.*, p. 239.
7. Davis, pp. 320–326; Cyrus Adler, *I Have Considered the Days* (Philadelphia, 1943), pp. 178, 242–244; Parzen, *op. cit.*, pp. 12–25.
8. See Bentwich's biography, *Solomon Schechter, passim;* Abraham J. Karp, "Solomon Schechter Comes to America," *American Jewish Historical Quarterly*, LIII, 1 (Sept., 1963), pp. 42–62.
9. *Seminary Addresses*, p. 24.

10. *Ibid.*, pp. 11 f., 232.
11. See Gilbert Klaperman, *The Story of Yeshiva University, passim; Louis Marshall: Champion of Liberty,* edited by Charles Reznikoff (Philadelphia, 1957), pp. 888–894.
12. See Schechter's *Seminary Addresses,* pp. 91–104 and the preface, p. xxiv. Cf. Norman Bentwich's *Solomon Schechter,* pp. 314, 320 ff., 329, etc.
13. See Parzen, *op. cit.,* pp. 79–127.
14. Davis, *op. cit.,* pp. 208–210; cf. 160 ff.
15. Parzen, pp. 176 ff.; H. and M. Rubenovitz, *The Waking Heart,* pp. 35–57.
16. Schechter quoted in *Tradition and Change, op. cit.,* pp. 163 ff.
17. Marshall Sklare, *Conservative Judaism, passim.*
18. The appropriate volumes of the Rabbinical Assembly *Proceedings* tell the story. Cf. Parzen, pp. 212 ff.
19. Arthur Hertzberg, "The Conservative Rabbinate: A Sociological Study," *Essays on Jewish Thought and Life* edited by J. Blau, P. Friedman, I. Mendelsohn, and A. Hertzberg (New York, 1959), pp. 309–332.
20. David Philipson, *The Reform Movement in Judaism,* p. 381; Plaut, *The Growth of Reform Judaism,* pp. 350 f.

## Chapter VII

1. Schechter, *Studies in Judaism,* I, 231; *Some Aspects of Rabbinic Theology,* pp. 12, 16, 42, 46; Ginzberg, *Students, Scholars and Saints,* p. 92 (quoted verbatim from Schechter's *Some Aspects,* etc., without citing the source!); Kadushin, *The Rabbinic Mind,* pp. 11, 14 ff.
2. Schechter, *Studies,* etc., I, 145–181; Kadushin, *op. cit.,* pp. 340–367; Heschel, *The Insecurity of Freedom,* pp. 116 f.
3. Morris Adler at the 1948 United Synagogue Convention, quoted in Mordecai Waxman's *Tradition and Change,* pp. 277–288; Gordis in the United Synagogue *Proceedings,* 1963, pp. 178–181 and the *Proceedings* of Rabbinical Assembly, XXIX (1965), pp. 96 ff.; Heschel, *God in Search of Man,* pp. 6 f., 330 f.
4. *Studies,* I, 180, also 151; III, 78.
5. Friedlander, quoted in *Tradition and Change,* p. 82.
6. Ginzberg, *Students,* etc., pp. 206 f.; Finkelstein in *The Jews,* II, 1327; Heschel, *God in Search of Man,* p. 167.
7. *Studies,* I, 183; III, 82 ff.
8. *Studies,* I, 183; *Seminary Addresses,* pp. 22, 25; cf. *Studies,* III, 74.
9. Finkelstein, quoted in *Tradition and Change,* pp. 313–324.
10. Heschel, *Man Is Not Alone,* pp. 233 f.
11. Gordis, *Conservative Judaism,* p. 36; Morris Adler cited in *Tradition and Change,* pp. 277 ff.; Waxman in *Tradition and Change,* pp. 16–20; Simon Greenberg quoted in *Tradition and Change,* pp. 263–275, and his speech to the 1963 United Synagogue Convention, *Proceedings,* pp. 113–123.

12. Jacob Agus, "Current Movements in the Religious Life of American Jewry," *The Jewish People Past and Present*, 4, 131.

13. Schechter, *Seminary Addresses*, pp. 133 f.; Ginzberg, *Students*, etc., pp. 100 f. and 106; Finkelstein quoted in *Tradition and Change*, p. 315; Bokser, *Judaism: Profile of a Faith*, p. 53.

14. Kaplan, *The Meaning of God in Modern Jewish Religion* and his other works; Gordis, *A Faith for Moderns*, pp. 113, 133.

15. Heschel, *Man Is Not Alone*, pp. 3 f.; *God in Search of Man*, pp. 11 ff., 31, 51, 58, 101, 104, 112, 114, 118, 158, etc.

16. *God in Search of Man*, p. 161; cf. 136 and 240 f.; *Man Is Not Alone*, pp. 114–119.

17. Kadushin, *The Rabbinic Mind*, pp. 202 f., 287, 304 f.; *Worship and Ethics*, pp. 6 ff.

18. Heschel, *God in Search of Man*, pp. 70 f., 375; *Man Is Not Alone*, pp. 120 f.; *The Insecurity of Freedom*, pp. 130 ff., 135, 146.

19. Gordis, *A Faith for Moderns*, p. 186.

20. See Moshe Davis, *The Emergence of Conservative Judaism*, pp. 285–292.

21. Schechter, *Seminary Addresses*, pp. 35–39.

22. Heschel, *God in Search of Man*, pp. 167, 178, 259, 260, 274, 302 f.; *Theology of Ancient Judaism*, 2 volumes, in Hebrew (London, 1962), deals extensively with revelation.

23. Gordis, *A Faith for Moderns*, p. 150; *Judaism for the Modern Age*, pp. 153–185; *Conservative Judaism*, p. 55.

24. Davis, *op. cit.*, pp. 139 ff., 292 ff.

25. *Ibid.*, pp. 222–226.

26. Schechter, *Some Aspects*, etc., pp. 117, 125; *Studies*, I, 13, III, 74; *Seminary Addresses*, pp. 6, 59, 84 f., 134.

27. Introduction to *Studies in Judaism*, I, xviii f. and III, 89–119; Preface to *Some Aspects of Rabbinic Theology*, pp. xvii f., 117.

28. *Students, Scholars and Saints*, pp. 104, 110, 112, 114, 118; *On Jewish Law and Lore*, p. 78.

29. See Ginzberg's Introduction to his *Commentary on The Palestinian Talmud* (New York, 1941, English section), p. xiv, and his *On Jewish Law and Lore*, pp. 4, 77–124; *Students*, etc., pp. 205 ff.

30. Rabbinical Assembly *Proceedings*, XI (1947), pp. 60–61; Boaz Cohen, *Law and Tradition in Judaism*, pp. 11, 23 ff., 34, 36 f., 53–62, 96, 110, and *passim*.

31. Finkelstein, *The Pharisees*, 2 volumes (Philadelphia, 1938), pp. 2, 101, and *passim*; cf. his two addresses printed in *Tradition and Change*, pp. 187–197, 313–324, especially pp. 319–320.

32. Gordis, *Judaism for the Modern Age*, pp. 127–152, 186–194; cf. pp. 176 ff.; *Conservative Judaism*, pp. 62–77; *A Faith for Moderns*, pp. 281–283.

33. *God in Search of Man*, pp. 310, 320–332, 417 ff. (cf. pp. 197, 282); *The Insecurity of Freedom*, p. 205; *The Sabbath*, pp. 48 and *passim*. Note Heschel's

affinity with Franz Rosenzweig who taught: "Judaism is not Law. It creates Law, but is not it. It is to be a Jew."

34. Siegel, "Ethics and the Halakhah," *Conservative Judaism*, XXV, 3 (Spring 1971), pp. 33–40.

35. Morris Adler in an address to the 1948 United Synagogue Convention, quoted in *Tradition and Change*, p. 284; RA *Proceedings*, XIV(1950), pp. 112–188; XVIII (1954), pp. 55–83; XXXII(1968), pp. 229–241; *Conservative Judaism*, XXIV, 2(Winter 1970), pp. 21–59.

36. *Conservative Judaism* XXV, 3 (Spring 1971), pp. 49–55.

37. Gordis, *Conservative Judaism*, pp. 54 f.; Kadushin, *Worship and Ethics*, pp. 90 f.;Bokser, *Judaism*, pp. 258 ff.; Heschel, *God in Search of Man*, pp. 380, 422–425 f.

38. Davis, *The Emergence of Conservative Judaism*, pp. 268–274.

39. *Seminary Addresses*, pp. 91–104.

40. Norman Bentwich, *Solomon Schechter*, pp. 316–320,322 ff.; Schechter, Preface to *Seminary Addresses*, p. XXIV.

41. Friedlander, *Past and Present*, pp. 1–112, and Parzen's careful analysis in *Architects of Conservative Judaism*, pp. 155–188; Ginzberg, *Students*, etc., p. 124, and Parzen, p. 144; Kaplan, *A New Zionism*, among other works.

42. Finkelstein, quoted in *Tradition and Change*, p. 322.

43. RA *Proceedings*, V (1938), pp. 388 ff.; Solomon Goldman, *Undefeated* (Washington, 1943), p. 36; Gordis, *Conservative Judaism*, p. 34;*Judaism For the Modern Age*, pp. 118, 124; cf. pp. 41 f., 58–61.

44. Davis in a speech to the 1955 United Synagogue Convention, quoted in *Tradition and Change*, pp. 467–469; cf. his speech to the Rabbinical Assembly, RA *Proceedings*, XXXIV (1970), pp. 34–40; Heschel, *The Insecurity of Freedom*, pp. 209 f., and more fully in his *Israel: An Echo of Eternity* (New York, 1971), *passim.*

45. See the text of the debate in *Torch*, XIX, 1 (Winter 1960), pp. 7–40.

46. For Kaplan's views on the "Organic Community" see *The Future of the American Jew*, pp. 114–122.

47. Levinthal in the United Synagogue *Recorder*, IV, 4 (October, 1936), p. 19. Cf. Solomon Goldman, *A Rabbi Takes Stock* (New York, 1931), p. 20.

48. Interestingly, a hot controversy over standards developed around the Bingo issue. In 1959 the United Synagogue ruled that it would expel any congregation playing Bingo or similar games of chance and, in fact, several were dropped from membership. But in 1971 the United Synagogue attenuated that rule by a breathlessly close vote. Henceforth, synagogues playing Bingo will not be expelled: but they may not vote in the United Synagogue elections, nor may their members be eligible for offices in the organization. Neither the Reform nor the Orthodox groups has adopted anti-gambling stands. The United Synagogue also attempted to adopt standards for synagogue leaders requiring them to attend Sabbath services regularly and to study

Hebrew. But this, too, has been a failure and the resolution calling for its implementation has become a dead letter.

49. Davis, *The Emergence*, etc., pp. 163 ff.

50. See Gordis' Introduction to the *Sabbath Prayer Book*, pp. iv-xiii, and more extensively, "A Jewish Prayer Book for the Modern Age," *Conservative Judaism* II, 1 (October, 1945), pp. 1–20.

51. *A Faith for Moderns*, pp. 243–269.

52. *Worship and Ethics*, p. 69; *The Rabbinic Mind*, p. 169.

53. *God in Search of Man*, pp. 49 f.; *Man's Quest for God*, pp. 49–84.

54. Davis in RA *Proceedings*, XXXIV (1970), pp. 36 ff.; Morton Siegel in the same volume, pp. 71–76, 85; cf. Simon Greenberg in *Tradition and Change*, p. 417.

55. Davis, *The Emergence*, etc., pp. 261–268.

56. RA *Proceedings*, V (1933–38), pp. 156–164.

57. The annual *Proceedings* of the Rabbinical Assembly as well as the biennial *Proceedings* of the United Synagogue contain social actions programs. Cf. especially the 1963 Golden Jubilee *Proceedings* of the United Synagogue for a detailed social actions statement (pp. 190–195).

58. Gordis, *The Root and the Branch*, pp. 107, 112 f.; Resolutions of the 1961 and 1963 United Synagogue conventions opposing public aid to parochial schools. An attempt to pass a resolution favoring public aid to parochial schools failed to pass at the 1972 RA Convention.

59. RA *Proceedings*, XXXII (1968), pp. 201–205. The bitter debate has not been published.

60. Siegel, "Religion and Social Action," RA *Proceedings*, XXV (1961), pp. 143–163; Gordis, *The Root and the Branch*, *passim;* Heschel, *The Insecurity of Freedom*, pp. 3 ff., 12, 86 f., 90, 102; G.S. Rosenthal, *Generations in Crisis, passim.* Cf. the many volumes issued by the Conference on Science, Philosophy and Religion and the Institute for Religious and Social Studies, both sponsored by the Jewish Theological Seminary.

61. Gordis, *The Root and the Branch*, pp. 54–65; Heschel, *The Insecurity of Freedom*, pp. 179–183; Siegel in the United Synagogue *Proceedings* for 1965, pp. 113–116 and in the RA *Proceedings*, XXXI (1967), pp. 84–86.

62. See the stimulating debate in the RA *Proceedings*, XXXI (1967), pp. 70–92 and 103–148.

## Chapter VIII

1. On the sources of Reconstructionism see "Mordecai M. Kaplan and His Teachers" by Ira Eisenstein in *Mordecai M. Kaplan: An Evaluation*, edited by Eugene Kohn and Ira Eisenstein, pp. 15–25.

2. There is no biography as yet of Dr. Kaplan. For interesting autobiographical material, see Kaplan's "The Way I Have Come," in *Mordecai M. Kaplan:*

*An Evaluation*, pp. 283–321, and his "How to Live Creatively as a Jew," in *Moments of Personal Discovery*, edited by R. M. MacIver (New York, 1952), pp. 93–104.

3. H. Parzen, *Architects of Conservative Judaism*, pp. 202–204.

4. See generally, "Reconstructionism in American Jewish Life" by Charles S. Liebman, *American Jewish Yearbook*, 71 (1970), pp. 3–99. Cf. the illuminating documents in H. and M. Rubenovitz' *The Waking Heart*, pp. 77–84.

5. *The Waking Heart*, pp. 79 f.; Liebman, *op. cit.*, pp. 32 ff.

6. Carl H. Voss, *Stephen S. Wise: Servant of the People*, pp. 154–55, 308; Parzen, *op. cit.*, p. 198.

7. Parzen, pp. 198–200, 234.

8. See Liebman, *op. cit.*, pp. 46 ff.

9. *Ibid.*, pp. 49–62.

10. *Ibid.*, pp. 68–99. Cf. Milton Steinberg, *A Partisan Guide to the Jewish Problem*, p. 185.

## Chapter IX

1. Kaplan's basic writings include: *Judaism as a Civilization; The Meaning of God in Modern Jewish Religion; The Future of the American Jew;* and *The Greater Judaism in the Making.* The other volumes are merely refinements of specific problems or variations on basic themes.

2. *The Jewish Reconstructionist Papers*, pp. 9 and 11; *The Meaning of God*, etc., p. 39.

3. *The Future of the American Jew*, p. 221; *Judaism as a Civilization*, p. 47; *The Meaning of God*, etc., p. 96.

4. *Judaism as a Civilization*, p. 328; *Judasim Without Supernaturalism*, p. 216; Milton Steinberg, *A Believing Jew*, pp. 53 ff.

5. *The Greater Judaism in the Making*, p. 220.

6. *Judaism as a Civilization*, 91–169; *The Greater Judaism in the Making*, pp. 221–449; *Questions Jews Ask*, pp. 438 ff. For an analysis of the crisis of the modern Jew, see *Judaism as a Civilization*, pp. 3–15, and *The Greater Judaism in the Making*, pp. vii–xii, 171–220.

7. *Judaism as a Civilization*, p. 306; *The Meaning of God*, etc., pp. 39, 356; *The Purpose and Meaning of Jewish Existence*, p. 306.

8. *The Jewish Reconstructionist Papers*, p. xvi; The *Reconstructionist*, XI, 1 (February 23, 1945), p. 15. For a more up-to-date summary of principles, see *The Greater Judaism in the Making*, pp. 450–511, and *Questions Jews Ask*, pp. xi–xiii, 511–521.

9. *Judaism as a Civilization*, pp. 38, 394. For a full statement of Kaplan's God concept, see *The Meaning of God*, etc., *passim*.

10. *The Jewish Reconstructionist Papers*, pp. 88 ff.; *The Meaning of God*, etc., pp. vii, 321; *Judaism as a Civilization*, p. 317.

11. *Judaism as a Civilization*, pp. 306, 317; *The Meaning of God*, etc., pp. 306, 323 ff., 26, etc.

12. *The Greater Judaism*, etc., pp. 467–474; *The Meaning of God*, etc., pp. 356 f.
13. *The Meaning of God*, etc., *passim;* cf. the brief summation in *The Greater Judaism*, etc., pp. 467–484.
14. *The Meaning of God*, etc., pp. 60, 76, 194; *Questions Jews Ask*, pp. 104, 124.
15. Steinberg, *A Believing Jew*, pp. 19 f.; *A Partisan Guide to the Jewish Problem*, p. 186; *Anatomy of Faith*, pp. 81–108.
16. *The Meaning of God*, etc., pp. 63, 72–76.
17. *Ibid.*, pp. 73, 80; *The Future of the American Jew*, pp. 236–242.
18. *A Believing Jew*, pp. 28–30.
19. *Judaism as a Civilization*, pp. 414, 510; *The Greater Judaism*, etc., pp. 506–511; *The Meaning of God*, etc., p. 303. *The Future of the American Jew*, pp. 346, 382; *Questions Jews Ask*, p. 153.
20. *Judaism as a Civilization*, p. 432; *The Future of the American Jew*, p. 419; *The Greater Judaism*, etc., pp. 504 ff; *The Meaning of God*, etc., pp. 303, 318; Steinberg, *A Partisan Guide*, etc., pp. 152 f.
21. *Questions Jews Ask*, pp. 227, 265.
22. *Judaism as a Civilization*. pp. 441, 463; *The Jewish Reconstructionist Papers*, pp. 129–141; *The Meaning of God*, etc., p. 170; *The Greater Judaism*, etc., p. 487; *Questions Jews Ask*, 215–276.
23. *Questions Jews Ask*, pp. 263–275.
24. Ira Eisenstein quoted in *Tradition and Change*, edited by M. Waxman, pp. 447–454.
25. *The Future of the American Jew*, pp. 94–105; Steinberg, *A Believing Jew*, pp. 94–101.
26. *Judaism as a Civilization*, pp. 253–263; *The Future of the American Jew*, pp. 211–230.
27. Eugene Kohn, *Religion and Humanity*, p. 87; Kaplan, *The Purpose*, etc., p. 303. Cf. Steinberg, *Basic Judaism* (New York, 1947), p. 96.
28. *The Future of the American Jew*, pp. 215 ff.; *The Purpose*, etc., pp. 290, 296, 312 f., 318.
29. *The Greater Judaism*, etc., pp. 484 ff.; *A New Zionism*, pp. 12, 26, 41, 42, 119, 128.
30. *A New Zionism*, p. 149; *Questions Jews Ask*, pp. 393–421.
31. *A New Zionism*, pp. 144, 149, 172.
32. *The Future of The American Jew*, pp. 80 f., 114 f.; *A New Zionism*, p. 126.
33. *The Greater Judaism in the Making*, p. 455; Steinberg, *A Partisan Guide*, etc., p. 218.
34. Kohn in *The Jewish Reconstructionist Papers*, pp. 101–111; "Prayer and The Modern Jew," Rabbinical Assembly *Proceedings*, XVII (1953), pp. 179–191, and reprinted in his *Religion and Humanity*.
35. *Questions Jews Ask*, pp. 102–104, 241–244.
36. See the Introduction to the *Sabbath Prayer Book*, pp. xvii–xxx, and the several volumes of liturgy produced by the Reconstructionists.

37. See Kaplan's view in the *Reconstructionist*, XXXVI, 10 (October 23, 1970), pp. 15 f., and *Questions Jews Ask*, pp. 241 f., 357, 375–377.

38. *Judaism as a Civilization*, p. 489; *Questions Jews Ask*, p. 355.

39. *The Meaning of God*, etc., p. 358; *Questions Jews Ask*, pp. 520 f.; *The Greater Judaism in the Making*, pp. 482–486; *Judaism Without Supernaturalism*, pp. 101 f.; Steinberg, *A Partisan Guide*, etc., p. 187.

40. Ira Eisenstein, "Should Jews Be Socialists?" in *The Jewish Reconstructionist Papers*, p. 155. Kaplan, *The Purpose*, etc., pp. 314–318.

41. For a typical anti-Vietnam war view, see the editorial in the *Reconstructionist*, XXXVII, 3 (May 7, 1971), pp. 3 f.

42. See *The Faith of America*, edited by Kaplan, J. Paul Williams, and Eugene Kohn, *passim*. Cf. Kaplan's *The Future of the American Jew*, p. 151.

43. *Questions Jews Ask*, pp. 72–73; Eisenstein, *Judaism Under Freedom*, p. 235.

44. See the editorial in the *Reconstructionist*, XXX, 13 (October 30, 1964), pp. 3 f., in which the editors call for the Church to recognize Israel and the Jewish People as the first steps toward reconciliation and a "more positive attitude through its treatment of the Jewish community as a people equal with others in the sight of God." Cf. the editorial of October 29, 1965, in Volume XXXI, 13, pp. 3–4, which is bitterly critical of the final, diluted language of Vatican II and the arrogant tone of the Schema.

### Chapter X

1. Charles Liebman, "Orthodoxy in American Jewish Life," *American Jewish Yearbook*, 66, 1965, pp. 91 ff.

2. Liebman, *op. cit.*, and his article in *Tradition*, 9, 4 (Winter 1966), pp. 78–87. Cf. E. Berkovits, "Orthodox Judaism in a World of Revolutionary Transformation," *Tradition*, 7, 2 (Summer 1965), pp. 68–88. Incidentally, the editorial board of *Tradition* disavowed Berkovits' thesis. See, too, Irving Greenberg, "Jewish Values and the Changing American Ethic," *Tradition*, 10, 1 (Summer 1968), pp. 42–74, and Norman Lamm, "Modern Orthodoxy's Identity Crisis," *Jewish Life*, XXXVI, 5, (May-June 1969), pp. 5–8.

3. Berkovits, *op. cit.*, and his article, "Authentic Judaism and Halakhah," *Judaism*, 19, 1 (Winter 1970), pp. 66–76; Lamm, *op. cit.* Rabbi Goren's views have been expressed in several newspaper interviews.

4. Oscar Fasman, "Trends in the American Yeshiva Today," *Tradition*, 9, 3, (Fall 1967), pp. 48–64.

5. Jung in *Harvest*, p. 213. Cf. Howard Polsky's "A Study of Orthodoxy in Milwaukee: Social Characteristics, Beliefs, and Observances" in *The Jews*, edited by Marshall Sklare, pp. 325–346.

6. Liebman, *op. cit.*, p. 92. Cf. his article, "A Sociological Analysis of Contemporary Orthodoxy," in *Judaism*, 13, 3 (Spring 1964), pp. 285–304.

7. Liebman, *op. cit.*, p. 22.

8. Louis Man in a speech to the 1941 UAHC Convention; Kohler in *A Living Faith*, pp. 13 f.; Freehof in *Aspects of Progressive Jewish Thought*, pp. 42 f.

9. A. H. Silver quoted in Plaut's *The Growth of Reform Judaism*, pp. 152 f.; Eisendrath in *Aspects of Progressive Jewish Thought*, pp. 76 f.; P. Bernstein, "The CCAR: Seventy Fruitful Years," in the CCAR *Yearbook*, LXX (1966), pp. 160 f.; Plaut, *The Growth of Reform Judaism*, p. 350; D. J. Silver in *Judaism and Ethics*, p. 6.

10. Plaut, *op. cit.;* Mann, *op. cit.;* J. L. Liebman, *Peace of Mind* (New York, 1946), pp. 20 ff.

11. Samuel Cohon in *Judaism*, 3, 4 (Fall 1954), p. 353; E. Spicehandler in *Petahim*, 1 (15), December, 1970, p. 24 (English summary).

12. Morris Adler in an address to the Golden Jubilee Convention of the United Synagogue of America, published in the *Proceedings* of The Golden Jubilee Convention, 1963, pp. 110 ff. R. Gordis, *ibid.*, pp. 174–183; Milton Steinberg, *A Partisan Guide to the Jewish Problem*, p. 166; M. M. Kaplan in his presidential address of 1932 to the Rabbinical Assembly; H. Parzen, *Architects of Conservative Judaism*, p. 76.

13. See Max Routtenberg in Rabbinical Assembly *Proceedings*, XXIV (1960), pp. 190–230. Cf. the reevaluation symposium in the *Proceedings*, XXXIV (1970), pp. 86–126. Cf., too, Marshall Sklare's balanced critique, "Recent Developments in Conservative Judaism," *Midstream*, XVIII, 1 (January, 1972), pp. 3–19. Sklare notes the failure of the Conservative movement to develop ritual observances among its partisans as well as its inability to attract the young people to synagogue life and commitment. For reactions to Sklare's study, see the symposium, "Morale and Commitment," in *Conservative Judaism*, XXVII, 1 (Fall 1972), pp. 12–26.

14. Steinberg, *Anatomy of Faith*, p. 183; Borowitz, *A New Jewish Theology in the Making*, pp. 110 ff.; E. Berkovits, "Reconstructionist Theology," *Tradition*, 2, 1 (Fall 1959), pp. 20–66.

15. Borowitz, *op. cit.*, pp. 39, 120.

16. Steinberg, *A Believing Jew*, pp. 166–178. In view of the fact that Steinberg made this evaluation of Reconstructionism when the movement was barely twenty years old, it is difficult to fathom how he could have concluded that the bulk of Reconstructionist theory and program had stood up "under the test of the years." Is a scant generation enough time to evaluate the validity or efficacy of a religious movement?

17. Borowitz, *op. cit.*, pp. 33, 46.

# Glossary

**AGUNAH**

A woman who may not remarry because her husband has not given her a Jewish divorce due to either his refusal or inability.

**ALIYAH**

1. Immigration to the Land of Israel.
2. The act of going up for an honor at the Torah in the synagogue.

**BETH DIN**

A Jewish ecclesiastical court, usually consisting of three judges.

**BIMAH**

The reader's platform in the synagogue from which the cantor chants the liturgy and the Biblical portion is read.

**BRIT MILAH**

The covenant of Circumcision performed on the eighth day of a male child's life.

**DAYAN**

A judge of religious law.

**DIN**

A point of law or a ruling of a Beth Din. The final rule.

**ERETZ YISRAEL**

The Land of Israel.

**GALUT** (or *Golah*)

The Diaspora. The dispersion of Jews throughout the world. The settlement of Jews in lands other than Israel.

**GET**

A Jewish writ of divorce.

**HALAKHAH** (or *Halacha*)

Jewish law. The legal process employing Jewish legal norms, interpretations, opinions, and code books.

**HAZZAN**

The cantor who chants the liturgy at the synagogue services.

**HEDER**

The one-room Hebrew school in which youngsters used to receive their rudimentary Jewish education in America. The *melamed* (teacher) was often an incompetent who used archaic and cruel methods.

**HEREM**

Excommunication of sinners from the Jewish community.

**KADDISH**

The doxology recited by the cantor or reader. A special *Kaddish* is recited by the mourner.

**KASHRUT**

Jewish dietary laws. Foods that are prepared according to the rules of *kashrut* are called *kosher* and may be eaten by observant Jews.

**KEHILLAH** (or *Kahal*)

The Jewish community in ancient and medieval times that was basically self-contained and autonomous and ruled itself. With the Era of Emancipation, the organized *Kehillah* lost its coercive powers and was based on voluntarism.

**KETUBAH**

The Jewish marriage contract.

**KIDDUSH**

A prayer sanctifying Sabbaths and Festivals recited with a cup of wine and said both in synagogue and at home.

**KOHEN**

A descendant of the priestly clan of Aaron.

**LEVI**

A descendant of the Levitical clan that served as assistants to the temple priests.

**MAHZOR**

The High Holiday and Festival Prayer Book.

MASKILIM

The "enlightened," emancipated intellectuals of the eighteenth and nineteenth centuries in Central and Eastern Europe who sought to bring Judaism into the modern world and update its ideas and practices.

MEHITZAH

The curtain or partition separating men from women in the Orthodox synagogue.

MELAMED

A religious school teacher.

MIKVEH

A ritual pool used by Orthodox women for purification after the menstrual cycle. The *mikveh* is also used for the baptism of converts to Judaism. Some ultra-pious males use the *mikveh* for ritual purification for Sabbaths and Festivals.

MITZVAH

A religious commandment; a divine fiat; an order of the sages. Orthodox Jews believe there are 613 *mitzvot*—many of which are no longer observed since the destruction of the Temple in Jerusalem.

MOHEL

A ritual circumcisor who performs the *Brit Milah* on Jewish male babies.

ONEG SHABBAT

Literally, "the joy of Sabbath." The *Oneg Shabbat* is the festive celebration of the Sabbath with song, dance, and refreshments held after services in Conservative or Reform congregations on Friday evenings or occasionally on Sabbath afternoons. Many Orthodox synagogues have introduced the practice.

### PARNAS

The lay leader of a congregation. The term is usually applied to Sephardic lay leaders.

### SEMIKHAH

Ritual ordination of a rabbi enabling him to answer ritual questions and serve as a spiritual leader and teacher.

### SHEHITAH

Jewish ritual slaughter of animals and fowl.

### SHEMITAH

The Sabbatical Year observed every seventh year in which debts were canceled, slaves freed, and the land permitted to lie fallow. Orthodox settlers in Israel have tried to revive some of the agricultural aspects of this ancient institution.

### SHIVAH

The seven-day mourning period after the death of a near relative.

### SHOHET

A ritual slaughterer who kills animals and fowl in accordance with the Jewish laws of *shehitah*.

### SHTIEBEL

The Yiddish word for a little prayer room or informal synagogue.

### SHUL

The Yiddish word for synagogue.

### SHULHAN ARUKH

The Code of Jewish Law edited by Rabbi Joseph Caro of Safed, Israel, in 1564. The *Shulhan Arukh*, along with the glosses of Rabbi Moses Isserles of Cracow, has become the standard law code of Orthodox Jews.

SIDUR

The Jewish prayer book.

TALIT

A prayer shawl used by male Jews at morning worship.

TALMUD TORAH

1. A school for the study of Judaism, Hebrew, Bible, etc.
2. The act of studying Torah.

TEFILLIN

Phylacteries worn by Jewish males at morning worship consisting of two black boxes containing scriptural passages and wrapped around the head and arm by leather straps.

TORAH

1. The Five Books of Moses.
2. The Bible.
3. The entire corpus of Jewish law, lore, and wisdom.

TREFA

Non-kosher meat or food.

TZITZIT

1. The fringes of the *talit.*
2. A small *talit* worn by male Jews under their shirts as a reminder of God's presence.

YARMULKA

A skullcap worn by Orthodox, Conservative, and some Reform Jewish males at worship. The Hebrew equivalent of this Yiddish word is *kipah.*

YIZKOR

The prayer for the dead recited four times a year.

YOM TOV

A Jewish festival including Rosh Hashanah, Yom Kippur, Passover, Sukkot, and Shavuot.

# Bibliography

*General Background*

Adler, Selig, and Thomas E. Connolly, *From Ararat to Suburbia*, Philadelphia, 1960.
Blau, Joseph L., *Modern Varieties of Judaism*, New York, 1966.
Elbogen, Ismar, *A Century of Jewish Life*. Philadelphia, 1953.
Fein, Isaac M., *The Making of an American Jewish Community*. Philadelphia, 1971.
Finkelstein, Louis, *The Jews*. 2 vols. Philadelphia, 1955.
Glazer, Nathan, *American Judaism*. Chicago, 1972.
Goren, Arthur, *New York Jews and the Quest for Community*. New York, 1971.
Graetz, Heinrich, *The History of the Jews*. 6 vols. Philadelphia, 1940.
Grinstein, Hyman B., *The Rise of the Jewish Community of New York*. Philadelphia, 1945.
Handlin, Oscar, *Adventure in Freedom*. New York, 1954.
Herberg, Will, *Protestant-Catholic-Jew*. Garden City, N.Y., 1956.

Himmelfarb, Milton, *The Condition of Jewish Belief.* New York, 1966.

Hindus, Milton, *The Old East Side.* Philadelphia, 1969.

Janowsky, Oscar, *The American Jew.* Philadelphia, 1964.

Korn, Bertram W., *American Jewry and the Civil War.* Philadelphia, 1951.

Learsi, Rufus, *A History of the Jews in America.* Cleveland, 1954.

Lebeson, Anita, *Pilgrim People.* New York, 1950.

Leventhal, Israel H., *Point of View.* New York, 1958.

Marcus, Jacob R., *Early American Jewry.* 2 vols. Philadelphia, 1951.

Metzger, Isaac, *A Bintel Brief.* Garden City, N.Y., 1971.

Noveck, Simon, *Contemporary Jewish Thought.* New York, 1963.

_____, *Great Jewish Thinkers of the 20th Century.* New York, 1963.

Rischin, Moses, *The Promised City.* Cambridge, Mass., 1967.

Rosenthal, Gilbert S., *The Jewish Family in a Changing World.* Cranbury, N.J., 1970.

_____, *New Directions in the Jewish Family and Community.* New York, 1974.

Sachar, Howard M., *The Course of Modern Jewish History.* Cleveland, 1958.

Schwarz, Leo W., *Great Ages and Ideas of the Jewish People.* New York, 1956.

Sklare, Marshall, *The Jews.* Glencoe, Ill., 1958.

_____, *America's Jews.* New York, 1971.

Vorspan, Max, and Lloyd P. Gartner, *History of the Jews of Los Angeles.* Philadelphia, 1970.

In addition, the reader will profit from *The Jewish People Past and Present* (4 vols., New York, 1946–1955), especially Vol. 4 which deals entirely with American Jewry. *American Jewish Archives, American Jewish Historical Quarterly* (formerly the *Publications of the American Jewish Historical Society*), the *American Jewish Yearbook,* and the *YIVO Annual* (particularly the Tercentenary Issue, Vol. IX, 1954) contain valuable monographs and other material. See, too, the *Jewish Quarterly Review,* Tercentenary Issue, XLV, 4, April, 1955, and *Judaism,* Tercentenary Issue, 3, 4, Fall, 1954.

*Orthodoxy*

Belkin, Samuel, *Essays in Traditional Jewish Thought*. New York, 1956.

———, *In His Image*. New York, 1960.

Berkovits, Eliezer, *God, Man and History*. New York, 1959.

———, *Man and God*. Detroit, 1969.

Donin, Hayim H., *To Be a Jew*. New York, 1972.

Jung, Leo, *Harvest*. N.Y., 1956.

———, *The Jewish Library*. 23 vols. New York, 1928 to present.

Karp, Abraham J., "New York Chooses a Chief Rabbi," *Publications of the American Jewish Historical Society*, XLIV, 3 (March, 1955), pp. 129–198.

Klaperman, Gilbert, *The Story of Yeshiva University*. New York, 1969.

Lamm, Norman, *Faith and Doubt*. New York, 1971.

Lamm, Norman, and Walter S. Wurzburger (eds.), *A Treasury of Tradition*. New York, 1969.

Liebman, Charles, "Orthodoxy in American Jewish Life," *American Jewish Yearbook* 66 (1965), pp. 21–97.

Rackman, Emanuel, *One Man's Judaism*. New York, 1970.

Rothkoff, Aaron, *Bernard Revel: Builder of American Jewish Orthodoxy*. Philadelphia, 1972.

Stitskin, Leon D., *Studies in Torah Judaism*. New York, 1969.

Wouk, Herman, *This Is My God*. Garden City, N.Y., 1959.

The reader should also consult *Jewish Life* (formerly called *Orthodox Jewish Life*), the bi-monthly magazine of the Union of Orthodox Jewish Congregations, and *Tradition*, the semi-annual journal of the Rabbinical Council of America.

*Reform*

Borowitz, Eugene, *A New Jewish Theology in the Making*. Philadelphia, 1968.

———, *How Can a Jew Speak of Faith Today?* Philadelphia, 1968.

Doppelt, Frederic A., and David Polish, *A Guide for Reform Jews.* Evanston, Ill., 1957.

Eisendrath, Maurice, *Can Faith Survive?* New York, 1964.

Freehof, Solomon, *Reform Jewish Practice and Its Rabbinic Background.* Cincinnati, 1952.

————, *Recent Reform Responsa.* Cincinnati, 1963.

Hirsch, Emil G., *My Religion.* New York, 1925.

Knox, Israel, *Rabbi in America: The Story of Isaac M. Wise.* Boston, 1957.

Kohler, Kaufman, *Studies, Addresses, and Personal Papers.* New York, 1931.

————, *Jewish Theology.* Cincinnati, 1943.

————, *A Living Faith.* Cincinnati, 1948.

Martin, Bernard, *Contemporary Reform Jewish Thought.* Chicago, 1968.

Mattuck, Israel I., *Aspects of Progressive Jewish Thought.* New York, 1955.

Petuchowski, Jakob J., *Ever Since Sinai.* New York, 1961.

————, *Prayerbook Reform in Europe.* New York, 1968.

Philipson, David, *The Reform Movement in Judaism.* New York, 1967.

Plaut, W. Gunther, *The Rise of Reform Judaism.* New York, 1963.

————, *The Growth of Reform Judaism.* New York, 1965.

Silver, Daniel Jeremy, *Judaism and Ethics.* New York, 1970.

Silverman, William B., *Basic Reform Judaism.* New York, 1970.

Voss, Carl H., *Stephen S. Wise: Servant of the People.* Philadelphia, 1969.

The reader should also consult the *Yearbook* of the Central Conference of American Rabbis and the quarterly CCAR *Journal.* The magazine of the Union of American Hebrew Congregations, *American Judaism,* contains some valuable material.

*Conservatism*

Agus, Jacob, *Guideposts in Modern Judaism.* New York, 1954.

Bokser, Ben Zion, *Judaism: Profile of A Faith.* New York, 1963.

Cohen, Boaz, *Law and Tradition in Judaism*. New York, 1959.
Davis, Moshe, *The Emergence of Conservative Judaism*. Philadelphia, 1968.
Ginzberg, Louis, *On Jewish Law and Lore*. Philadelphia, 1955.
———, *Students, Scholars and Saints*. Philadelphia, 1945.
Gordis, Robert, *A Faith for Moderns*. New York, 1971.
———, *Conservative Judaism*. New York, 1945.
———, *Judaism for the Modern Age*. New York, 1955.
———, *The Root and the Branch*. Chicago, 1962.
Greenberg, Simon, *Foundations of Faith*. New York, 1967.
Heschel, Abraham Joshua, *God in Search of Man*. Philadelphia, 1956.
———, *The Insecurity of Freedom*. Philadelphia, 1966.
———, *Man Is Not Alone*. New York, 1951.
———, *Man's Quest for God*. New York, 1954.
———, *The Sabbath*. New York, 1951.
Kadushin, Max, *The Rabbinic Mind*. New York, 1972.
———, *Worship and Ethics*. Evanston, Ill., 1964.
Parzen, Herbert, *Architects of Conservative Judaism*. New York, 1964.
Rosenthal, Gilbert S., *Generations in Crisis*. New York, 1969.
Rubenovitz, Herman and Mignon, *The Waking Heart*. Cambridge, Mass., 1967.
Schechter, Solomon, *Seminary Addresses and Other Papers*. New York, 1959.
———, *Some Aspects of Rabbinic Theology*. New York, 1936.
———, *Studies in Judaism*. 3 vols. Philadelphia, 1945.
Sklare, Marshall, *Conservative Judaism*. Glencoe, Ill., 1972.
Waxman, Mordecai, *Tradition and Change*. New York, 1958.

In addition, the reader should consult the annual *Proceedings* of the Rabbinical Assembly, the *Proceedings* of the Biennial Convention of the United Synagogue of America, and the quarterly journal *Conservative Judaism*.

*Reconstructionism*

Eisenstein, Ira, *Judaism Under Freedom*. New York, 1956.

Eisenstein, Ira, and Eugene Kohn, *Mordecai M. Kaplan: An Evaluation*. New York, 1952.

Kaplan, Mordecai M., *Judaism as a Civilization*. New York, 1934.

———, *The Jewish Reconstructionist Papers*. New York, 1936.

———, *The Meaning of God in Modern Jewish Religion*. New York, 1937.

———, *The Future of the American Jew*. New York, 1948.

———, *A New Zionism*. New York, 1955.

———, *Questions Jews Ask*. New York, 1956.

———, *Judaism Without Supernaturalism*. New York, 1958.

———, *The Greater Judaism in the Making*. New York, 1960.

———, *The Purpose and Meaning of Jewish Existence*. Philadelphia, 1964.

———, *The Religion of Ethical Nationhood*. New York, 1970.

Kohn, Eugene, *Religion and Humanity*. New York, 1953.

Liebman, Charles S., "Reconstructionism in American Jewish Life," *American Jewish Yearbook* 71 (1970), pp. 3–99.

Rubenovitz, Herman and Mignon, *The Waking Heart*. Cambridge, Mass., 1967.

Steinberg, Milton, *A Partisan Guide to the Jewish Problem*. New York, 1945.

———, *A Believing Jew*. New York, 1951.

———, *Anatomy of Faith*. New York, 1960.

The reader should also consult the *Reconstructionist* magazine, now issued ten times yearly.

# Supplement to
# the Second Edition

# XI

# Orthodox Judaism

Orthodox Judaism has taken some surprisingly interesting turns on the road these past 10 years. For one thing Orthodoxy has matured in America. After having appeared to be on the brink of dissolution, Orthodoxy has rebounded with new vigor and creativity. Virtually counted out 25 years ago, American Orthodoxy is flourishing and growing in areas hitherto lacking an Orthodox presence. And while the Orthodox community numbers but 11 percent of American Jewry according to the National Population Study, and perhaps only 7 percent according to newer surveys, it is an increasingly vocal, organized, visible, and self-confident group. In fact, an aura of triumphalism has injected itself into Orthodox circles. As Orthodoxy has become Americanized, it has produced numerous yeshivah graduates, many of whom are successful doctors, dentists, lawyers, college professors, business executives, and even government officials. Orthodoxy has become more comfortable on the American scene and more at home with its tenets in the modern world. The old inferiority complexes have been dispelled; the feelings of being an outsider or a greenhorn have all but disappeared. The Orthodox Jew feels perfectly at home in American life and having achieved unprecedented acceptance, he has staked out positions with a new sense of self-confidence and assertiveness. In a word, Orthodox Judaism has come of age.[1]

*Swing to the Right*

Curiously, at the very moment of Orthodoxy's acceptance in American life and at the time when the liberal Orthodox version of Judaism as propagated by Yeshiva University and its rabbinic and lay alumni seems to be taking hold and developing, the right-wing, fundamentalist groups have asserted themselves in a fashion previously unknown in American Jewish life. Whether or not the new fundamentalism in Orthodoxy is a reflection of the upsurge of fundamentalism in Christianity and Islam that is currently sweeping the world is a moot point; what is beyond debate is that Orthodoxy has veered sharply to the right these past 10 years or so and the more liberal partisans have been hard-pressed to defend their position.

The newly assertive right wing, spearheaded by the Eastern European, Yiddish-speaking Agudat Israel faction, has been pressuring the liberal elements of Orthodoxy as never before. Following the lead of nineteenth-century separatist Rabbis Samson Raphael Hirsch and Esriel Hildesheimer, they have demanded that Orthodox groups end all cooperation with the non-Orthodox and secede from umbrella organizations, such as the Synagogue Council of America and the community Boards of Rabbis. The right-wing yeshivot and their rabbis have injected a more intolerant note into American Jewish life and the Conservative and Reform branches of Jewry are treated with scorn and contempt as befits "heretics." Even the progressive elements in Orthodox life are feeling the lash.[2]

Rabbi Gilbert Klaperman in his farewell speech as president of the Rabbinical Council of America in June 1984, was constrained to note that his group had *not* been cowed into withdrawal from the Synagogue Council of America, although he conceded that the recent Reform decision to follow either patrilineal or matrilineal descent to determine Jewishness has forced his group to cease cooperation with Reform rabbis in projects outside the Synagogue Council. Additionally, he decried pressures from the right wing in areas of intergroup cooperation, *kashrut*, fundraising, and projects for Torah Umesorah which controls yeshivah education. At the same convention, the newly chosen president Rabbi Louis Bernstein called on "the center of the Orthodox religious movement to assert itself and fulfill its role of guiding a delicate course between the extreme of both left and right in religious Judaism." The pressures from the right have evidently been painful as indicated by the fact that in the important symposium on "The State of Orthodoxy" run by *Tradition* magazine in its Spring 1982 issue, most of the 22 participants acknowledged the seriousness of the problem. Increasingly, the modern Orthodox have been forced to validate and justify themselves and, ironically, some, such as Rabbi Shubert Spero, have argued (in terms reminiscent of those used by Conservative and Reform Jews seeking parity in Israeli religious life) for "pluralism within Orthodoxy."[3]

Rabbi Emanuel Rackman, long a partisan of the progressive wing in Orthodoxy, has derogated right-wing separation and fanaticism. "The achievements of modern Orthodoxy dwarf the achievements of the Lakewood Yeshivah and others similarly minded," writes Rackman. Additionally, he notes that one major challenge is, "How does one put an end to the identification of Orthodoxy with intolerance, the total rejection of modernity, and the readiness to isolate from non-observant Jews?" He is also concerned that Orthodox Jews who seek to cope with modernity do so apologetically and with a sense of guilt vis-à-vis the ultra-Orthodox whom they regard as the "true representatives of the faith." He denounces their approach as "inauthentic" and he decries their neglect of Biblical studies and insularity. He describes the right-wing resurgence as due to: 1) rising fundamentalism; 2) lack of modern intellectual secondary teachers; 3) insecurity in the world that leads to blind faith; and 4) the irrational *Baal Teshuvah* (repentant sinners) movement that is little different from "foxhole religion" in its day. In a word, Rackman notes that many modern Orthodox are sickened by a type of "McCarthyism" that has infested Orthodox life these days.[4]

These liberal views have not gone unchallenged. Rabbi Yitzchak Alster, for example, rejects Rackman's label of "inauthentic" and he insists that the renaissance of Orthodoxy is due to the contributions of the heads of those very yeshivot whom Rackman denigrates. He writes that sages such as Rabbi Isaac Hutner, Aaron Kotler, Moshe Feinstein, etc., came here from East Europe, opened yeshivot and taught Torah in opposition to Reform and Conservatism. It was this yeshivah world that introduced *glatt* kosher meat (i.e., meat that has lesion-free lungs and that satisfies even the most rigorous standards of kosher laws), that made the wearing of yarmulkes in public acceptable and popular, that reintroduced traditional rather than mixed-sex dancing, etc. Adds Alster: "Had the compromising and style-conscious spirit of modern Orthodoxy been permitted to run its natural course, what would Orthodoxy look like today?"[5]

Right-wing extremism has evinced itself in several specific areas. First, the Agudat Israel has been very active in political lobbying for its own objectives. It has urged a modification of the separation of church and state and has swung virtually the entire Orthodox movement into a position demanding government support of parochial schools, the construction of *eruvin* (fictional fences that permit carrying and other activities on Sabbath), and, in the light of recent court cases, it has marshaled government sanctions to obtain a *get* (Jewish divorce) for women whose husbands have refused to grant such a writ. Second, it has injected a sharper note of intolerance towards the liberal branches of Jewry, refusing to call non-Orthodox rabbis by their titles, spurning cooperation in fund-raising campaigns of UJA-Federation, Soviet Jewry appeals, aid to Israel, and other communal drives. Third, the right wing has introduced a plethora of halakhic stringencies not hitherto demanded by Orthodox sages in America. Fourth, it has bred contempt for secular studies and college education and has stressed that only Torah study counts. Finally, the creeping fanaticism of the right has exploded into violence on more than one occasion. Satmar Hasidim, for example, have beaten and shorn the beards of Lubavitcher Hasidim and attacked Belzer Hasidim both in New York and in Israel, necessitating police intervention. Apparently, the Satmar view other Hasidic sects as less than Orthodox in ideology and practice and they are incensed by their support of the State of Israel. Similarly, Knesset member Rabbi Menachem Porush of the Agudat Israel Party landed in the hospital after being beaten by Gerer Hasidim who were resentful of his criticism of their leader, the Rebbe of Gur.

## Halakhah

The rightist mood has naturally intruded upon the area of Halakhah and Jewish observance. Thus, practices that had fallen into neglect have been revived and popularized while old stringencies that had been preserved by fringe groups have suddenly been propelled into the limelight. *Mikveh* (ritual bath) had all but disappeared in American Jewry; today *Mikvaot* are being built in posh, suburban areas. Yarmulkes are seen on college campuses, in hospitals, medical schools, public life, in streets, and even in the military. And more than one Orthodox *shul* has been constrained to raise the height of its *mehitzah* (partition between the men's and women's section) to satisfy the demands of the more pious. Few heard of an *eruv* 20 years ago; today, young Orthodox Jews battle vigorously to build *eruvin* in new neighborhoods so that they may carry or wheel baby carriages on the Sabbath. Even the *sheitel* (wig) or *tiechol* (kerchief) which married women are required by Orthodox rules to wear at all times (at least in public) and which was virtually extinct outside of Hasidic circles has made a comeback. It is not unusual to see a chic young Orthodox wife sporting a magnificently coiffed wig (often more alluring than her natural hair!) or a fashionable hat in conformity with traditional laws of modesty and chaste dress.

Additionally, the right wing has introduced new *humrot* (stringencies) and new ones are cropping up constantly. It was the Satmar Hasidim who introduced *glatt* kosher meat to America after the second world war. That stringency, not accepted

by the peerless Rabbi Moshe Feinstein, has caught on in Orthodox circles so that today, most airlines, catered affairs, kosher
restaurants, etc., serve *glatt* kosher meat. More recently, *Halav
Yisrael* has been popularized and an increasing number of
Orthodox Jews demand milk that is certified as kosher and under rabbinic supervision. Despite the fact that Rabbi Feinstein,
who is generally acknowledged as Orthodoxy's premier *posek*
(rabbinic judge and decisor) does not require the use of such
milk, it seems that this latest stringency is catching on. In sum,
the halakhic mood seems to be towards greater stringency and
less leniency.

Ideologically, this seems to be true as well. The old liberal
halakhists such as Professors Emanuel Rackman and Eliezer
Berkovits appear to be losing favor; the young, stringent decisors, notably Professor J. David Bleich, are the ones who are
riding high even among the modern Orthodox, not to mention
the right-wing fundamentalist groups. Berkovits, who moved
to Jerusalem from Chicago, has continued to articulate the liberal view of Halakhah that is not radically different from the
position of Conservative halakhists. In his latest writings he reiterates his opinion that subjective factors cannot be eliminated
from acceptance of Torah. He maintains that if there is a reason for it and it is "right and proper" we may deviate from biblical regulations, for by doing so we do not obliterate regulations
but expand them. He is incensed at the idea that the State of Israel is dependent on non-Jews to perform Sabbath labors and
he describes today's masters of Halakhah as the "New Karaites"
in their adulation of oral law and refusal to establish a Sanhedrin. He urges revisions in laws; he refuses to disqualify as
witnesses non-observant Jews; he favors the annulment of
marriages in *agunah* cases so as to free wives whose husbands
cannot or will not issue a *get*; he refuses to nullify (unlike
Rabbi Moshe Feinstein) marriages performed by Conservative
and Reform rabbis; he does not demand full ritual observance
of converts; he believes in persuasion, not compulsion, for "the
method of authority defeats the eternal validity of the Torah."
Most significantly, he calls for mutual understanding between

the groups because "there is reverence for God even among Conservative and Reform Jews."[6]

Berkovits' views, however, are increasingly shunned by the new right of Orthodoxy; he and Rackman and men of their stripe are viewed as mavericks in Halakhah. Actually, Rabbi Joseph B. Solveitchik had set the tone of a philosophy of Halakhah in his famous essay, *Ish Ha-Halakhah*, first published in 1944. At the time he insisted that Halakhah is *not* influenced by subjective canons or feelings and that halakhic man is like a mathematician, devoid of personal feelings in making decisions, and armed with a set of *a priori* principles and norms unaffected by human situations.

This objective, mathematical, computerlike approach to Jewish law is best typified by Rabbi J. David Bleich who teaches both philosophy and Talmud at Yeshiva University. Bleich (himself the product of a right-wing yeshivah), has written extensively on Halakhah, biomedical problems, responsa literature, and contemporary legal and ethical matters in light of Halakhah. He is prodigiously erudite and his writings display vast knowledge of Jewish and secular sources, especially in biomedical ethics. But his approach to Halakhah is quite different from that of Berkovits or Rackman; he insists that no subjective considerations or inclinations consciously influence scholarly opinions and it is a travesty to begin with preconceived conclusions and attempt to justify them by dialectics for the rule has always been, "Let the law pierce the mountain." Objective canons, personal piety, religious probity plus great learning and consensus rather than isolated or individual opinions must decide the law. For Bleich, "ethics and Halakhah are one and the same" and Halakhah reveals to the legalist the "transcendental worldview of the Divine Lawgiver." In all of his rulings and decisions, Bleich takes the strict view. Leniency and permissiveness are all but absent from his decisions; he is a severe hard-liner who rejects liberal opinions even when expressed by Orthodox colleagues. This seems to be the new mood among even the young American-trained halakhic scholars.[7]

*The Role of Women*

The reaction of Orthodoxy to the Women's Liberation Movement is noteworthy. Naturally, the right-wing groups are unalterably opposed to any role for women in synagogue leadership or worship; women are to follow their traditional role as homemakers and mothers whose Jewish education should be limited to basics and whose secular education must not exceed the state requirements. The question of women rabbis is not even discussed in such circles.[8]

But in the liberal Orthodox circles, despite many disclaimers, the question is very much alive. *Tradition* magazine has published a spate of articles on the subject of women in ritual, women in the rabbinate or lay leadership, women as students of Torah, etc. Orthodox girls of the more progressive types generally receive the same education as the boys, with the exception of the study of Talmud which is still viewed as in the male domain. Many liberal Orthodox synagogues have a type of Bat Mitzvah or Bat Torah ceremony for the girls. Increasingly, women are allowed to become trustees of Orthodox synagogues and some congregations have separate *minyanim* for women and allow them to dance with the Torah on Simhat Torah. In frustration over refusal to solve the *agunah* problem, an organization called GET (Get Equal Treatment) has been established in Brooklyn by Orthodox women to highlight the plight of wives whose husbands have refused them a Jewish divorce. A similar group called MITZVAH has been set up in Jerusalem with much the same purpose. Obviously, Orthodox women are not willing to accept second-rate citizenship any longer.[9]

No one argues more persuasively for a greater role for women than Blu Greenberg. Mrs. Greenberg, wife of an Orthodox rabbi and a scholar in her own right, has noted (1981): "Throughout the centuries, Judaism generated revolutionary ethical teachings. Why will it not now incorporate the lessons of feminism?" She notes the inequality of synagogue, communal and halakhic affairs with which women must contend and she urges that we train women as judges and religious decisors (*poskot*). Blu Greenberg accepts women's *minyan* as an interim solution at best. She criticizes Orthodoxy's slowness at alleviating the *agunah* tragedy: "The law should not discriminate against one sex. And if there is one woman in each generation who suffers unnecessarily as a result of the law, then the law is biased against all women." She views the women's revolution as essentially a good one and she urges a distinctive-but-equal model for Judaism and greater access of females to Torah, prayer, rabbinic, and lay leadership, etc.[10]

Of course, Mrs. Greenberg is a maverick and many reject her pleas. Professor Moshe Meiselman wrote a book on *Jewish Woman in Jewish Law* in which he opposed all such liberalization of the role of women. He rejected arguments for *aliyot* for women; he decried women who don *talit* and *tefillin* as guilty of the sin of pride; he noted that it is forbidden to teach Torah to women but in these days of college-educated females he grudgingly allowed the study of Torah as essential; he stated that all scholars deny females the right to be a witness although they may serve as judges in limited areas. Meiselman insisted that *all* contemporary rabbinic authorities, including Rabbi Joseph B. Soloveitchik, oppose a woman's *minyan* and he cited Rabbi Soloveitchik as disapproving of women dancing with Torah scrolls as a violation of age-old synagogue etiquette. In sum, Meiselman opposed women's liberation and careerism since women's primary role is the religious welfare of the family.[11]

But things are not quite so simple even in Orthodox circles. Professor Saul J. Berman studied the matter and concluded that we must avoid apologetics and be more sensitive to the needs of females. Rabbi Reuven P. Bulka urged that we recognize changing needs of females and the impact of the women's movement while at the same time honoring women in their full uniqueness and authenticity even as we reject feminism. Outgoing RCA President Gilbert Klaperman devoted part of his speech at the Convention of June 1984 to a call for a commission to "deal with the needs of women to find some form of rewarding participation in the Orthodox synagogue and issue guidelines on areas in which women may legitimately take part in women's prayer groups, as well as in the administration of synagogues within halakhic parameters." Rabbi Klaperman specifically mentioned membership on synagogue boards, carrying a Torah on Simhat Torah, study groups, Bat Mitzvah, and the like. "We must tap," he argued, "talented and dedicated women, many of whom are day school graduates." To be sure, none of this sits well with Rabbi J. David Bleich who, in the same issue of *Tradition* in which Professor Saul J. Berman's liberal position on women was presented, rejected all attempts at giving women a greater role in ritual: "Normative Judaism teaches that the Halakhah is not derived from any 'temporal world view' or 'social situation' but expresses the transcendental worldview of the Divine Lawgiver."[12]

As to the burning issue of women rabbis, Orthodoxy seems unalterably opposed to and contemptuous of the idea. Only Professor Emanuel Rackman and Blu Greenberg appear sympathetic to the idea. Rackman writes that this is less a matter of Jewish law than of psychology of Jews and sociology of the Jewish community. He doubts whether yeshivot will ever admit women in the present climate but he urges women to study and become experts in Halakhah. Mrs. Greenberg goes further: she favors ordination of women and is optimistic that it will "unfold in gradual steps" in her lifetime. Dr. Judith Bleich, wife of Rabbi J. David Bleich and herself a rare female scholar in the Orthodox community, is contemptuous of the idea. She writes: "The issue is not the ordination of women by the Jewish Theological Seminary; the issue is the ordination of men." In a word, none of the alumni of the Seminary are valid rabbis so what difference whether they are male or female graduates?[13]

### The State of Israel

The tensions and splits within the ranks of Orthodoxy evince themselves in its attitude toward the State of Israel. In truth, there is no single attitude towards Zion or the Jewish State; rather, there are many ranging from outright hostility to warm sympathy to ultra-nationalism blended with religious fundamentalism. The sources of these differences date back to the early days of modern Zionism. The ultra-Orthodox Neturai Karta and Satmar Hasidim who literally refuse to recognize the State of Israel have taken their cue from leaders such as Rabbis Elhanan Bunim Wasserman, Moshe Blau, and Joel Teitelbaum who dubbed Zionism "idolatry." While spurning political and religious or ideological Zionism, this extreme right-wing group does affirm practical Zionism and believes in settling in Israel to study Torah, live in close proximity to the Holy Land, and await the coming of the Messiah.[14]

The Agudat Israel Party has never been in favor of Herzl's brand of secular Zionism or of the Mizrahi's religious Zionism. Rabbi Samson Raphael Hirsch had opposed human actions to regain Israel and Agudah has been loathe to cooperate with non-observant Jews in building the State or in working within the structure of the World Zionist Organization. To this day, the yeshivah heads in America and Israel (the so-called *Moetzes Gedolay Hatorah*) remain hostile to a secular Israeli state and view Zionism as an aberration. For example, Rabbi Isaac Hutner, Dean of Hayim Berlin Yeshivah and member of the Council of Torah Greats, wrote that the Grand Mufti of Jerusalem became an enemy of the Jews only after "great public pressure for the establishment of a Jewish State." Despite historical proof to the contrary, his disciples Rabbis Bernard Weinberger and Yaakov Feitman insisted we must accept Hutner's views of *Daas Torah* (Torah Opinion) because he wrote in a form of *Ruah Hakodesh* (Holy Spirit). And how can one ever argue with "Holy Spirit" even if historical facts have been distorted?[15]

The Lubavitcher Rebbe has also been a powerful opponent of "the Zionist State" at the same time that he has encouraged his disciples to settle and build the Holy Land. Yet, the Rebbe has ruled that the return of any occupied lands by Israeli to the Arabs is a violation of Halakhah—a position that is, as Rabbi Immanuel Jakobovits has tartly observed, anomalous to say the least. But practical matters being such as they are, when Prime Minister Menachem Begin needed to put together a coalition for his Likud Party, he invited the Agudat Israel to join and it did so, extracting important religious considerations in the process. Nevertheless, the liberal, pro-Zionist Mizrahi Party still controls the hearts of American Orthodox Jews, despite the party's eclipse in Israel. The irony is that the anti-Zionist Agudah Party served for seven years in Israel's government while the pro-Zionist Mizrahi group was excluded.[16]

However, the Mizrahi wing has been wracked by dissension and controversy. The right-wing extremists have followed Rabbi Meir Kahane who has left America after founding the Jewish Defense League and now leads his tiny Kach Party which openly calls for the expulsion of Arabs from Israel by force if need be. His support in America is limited mostly to ultranationalist religious circles centered in Borough Park, Brooklyn.

In the more moderate wing, splits have occurred over the role of the Gush Emunim (Group of Faithful) who have settled in Judea and Samaria (the so-called "West Bank") and who, in their blend of religion and nationalism, insist that Jews have the right to settle anywhere in Israel. *Tradition* magazine has published numerous articles on this debate with views ranging from staunch support for that position to sharp criticism. Rabbi Jakobovits, for example, has openly decried the militancy of the Gush Emunim and has urged the separation of religion and party politics in Israel and the independence of rabbis from state control. Needless to say, his position has been roundly denounced by the nationalist elements and he himself was reviled at public lectures in America several years ago. Rabbi Joseph B. Soloveitchik has been silent on the matter of return of captured territories and the issue of settlements in Arab areas. He has remained a loyal supporter of the Mizrahi and publicly endorsed the National Religious Party in the 1984 elections. But in a remarkable and infrequently quoted passage in one of his essays, he urged religious leaders to get out of the Knesset and into schools and yeshivot, for salvation will not come through political leaders but by "giving meaning to the life of individual and community; by opening the gates of joyful religion to those who are lost and wandering."[17]

The more militant nationalists, including many students of Rabbi Soloveitchik, have taken a hard line towards peace with the Arabs and have supported Gush Emunim and the more extreme nationalistic aberrations. For example, Rabbi Avraham Hecht, president of the Rabbinical Alliance of America and rabbi of the Syrian Sephardic Synagogue in Brooklyn, has been outspoken on this matter: "We support the Likud, not Agudat Israel and love Arik Sharon who is the kind of tough-guy hero Americans identify with." After the arrest of over twenty Israeli citizens accused of terrorist actions against Arabs in Israel and the occupied territories, 25 American rabbis (including members of the Rabbinical Council of America, Young Israel Rabbis, and disciples of Rabbi Soloveitchik) purchased ads, in the *Jerusalem Post* and elsewhere, defending their vigilantism: "Focused action against those responsible for the maiming or death of Jews" is understandable, they declared.

> We appeal to the government of Israel to recognize that, if those recently imprisoned were retaliating against those responsible for maiming or murdering Jews and the continued instigation of further terror against Jews then the accused are guilty of no crime.

Their position has been endorsed by Rabbi Moshe Tendler who has participated in a campaign to raise money for a legal defense fund.[18]

This provoked a counterreaction from thirteen leaders of the RCA, including the current president, several past presidents, the vice president of Yeshiva University, and other eminent rabbis who denounced their view as a violation of the sacredness of life and a diminution of the sovereignty of the State of Israel by the creation of private armies of vigilantes.[19]

Clearly, the many-faceted Orthodox approach to Zion and Israel is as divisive and clamorous these days as it was in the past. In truth, there is no one homogeneous Orthodox position on the nature of the Jewish State. The Orthodox seem united only on these points: 1) the need to support a strong, free Israel based on Torah and *mitzvot*; and 2) no recognition of the Reform and Conservative movements in Israel's religious life. To the credit of Orthodoxy, however, the bulk of immigrants to Israel are Orthodox and thousands of Orthodox boys and girls are sent to study in Israeli institutions, yeshivot, and universities.

## Critique and Prognosis

Orthodoxy is currently riding a crest of optimism bordering on triumphalism. It has made a remarkable comeback from near extinction, its yeshivot and synagogues are flourishing, its young couples, many of whom are yeshivah alumni, are spearheading the growth of new Orthodox communities. But all is not quite so well as it would seem and triumphalism is not appropriate.

For one thing, American Orthodoxy is still a small minority of the Jewish Community. About 90 percent list themselves as non-Orthodox. Moreover, Orthodoxy is mostly a New York phenomenon; its great strength is in Brooklyn and several nearby suburbs; it is weak and almost nonexistent in other cities and communities in America. The Orthodox community is still poorly organized and there are several competing rabbinic and lay organizations with no hope of unity on the horizon. The proliferation of *shtieblach* (private synagogues) has complicated matters for the organized or establishment Orthodox community. And there is still no clear, articulate philosophy of modern Orthodoxy. At the same time, the unmistakable swing to the right has severely pressured progressive, secularly educated Orthodox Jews to justify their position while relations vis-à-vis non-Orthodox have worsened sharply.[20]

In a revealing symposium on the state of Orthodoxy published in *Tradition*, 22 distinguished liberal Orthodox rabbis and scholars (no right-winger agreed to participate) expressed their frank views of their own movement.[21] There was little mood of triumphalism and while almost all would like to see the return of Conservative and Reform Jews, none expect them to turn Orthodox and most do not foresee such developments before the coming of the Messiah. All indicated concern over the challenge from the right-wing fundamentalists; all were dismayed by the in-fighting, gutter-tactics and sniping. While all contributors are proud of the yeshivot produced by Orthodoxy, most resent the fact that too many graduates of those schools are smug and self-righteous. Most participants are not buoyed by the *Baal Teshuvah* (repentant sinner) phenomenon because they find such people to be smug, arrogant, even obnoxious. Several, such as Professors Emanuel Rackman and Hillel Goldberg, decry Orthodoxy's lack of philosophy or ideology and the internal intolerance. Rabbi Immanuel Jacobovits, Chief Rabbi of the British Empire, is equally concerned about the introverted, indifferent isolationism and complacency of his colleagues. A number of rabbis, including Rabbi Aharon Lichtenstein who heads the yeshivah in Gush Etzion, Israel and is Rabbi Soloveitchik's son-in-law, indict fellow Orthodox Jews for their holier-than-thou attitude. Lichtenstein (1982) also decries their corruption in civil matters and their stress on *mitzvot* between man and God rather than man and man. We place too much stress on *eruv* and kosher tuna fish, he writes, and not enough on secular culture's impact on us and the need to produce *gedolim* (Torah greats).[22]

Professor Michael Wyshograd, professor of philosophy at New York City's University and a close disciple of Rabbi Soloveitchik, was most unsparing in his criticism. While expressing his pride that "Orthodoxy is the only movement whose rabbinic and lay components have remained faithful to the interpretation of the covenant that has been classically identified as Judaism," he finds much that is wrong with it. It has produced no "holy people"; rather, it has produced "hard-hearted, rigid, self-righteous Jews" closed to human suffering. It has spawned cynics and vituperative people who feel religiously superior, who have no inner, spiritual personal relationship to God and who follow a party line. Orthodoxy has given us scientists but few poets, painters, musicians, or philosophers. Even the American Hasid is more sullen, defensive, and hard than his European forerunner. "The essential need of contemporary Orthodoxy," he writes, "is to recapture the category of the religious" and not withdraw into "Orthodox cities of refuge but reach out to the non-Orthodox."[23]

In sum, Orthodoxy seems to be hardening its boundaries. The right-wing resurgence has made the young Orthodox rabbi more intransigent, more self-righteous, less likely to co-operate with non-Orthodox colleagues, and the young Orthodox layman is more self-righteous and less community-oriented than in the past. Fewer Orthodox rabbis, for example, are willing to officiate at weddings with non-Orthodox colleagues and Rabbi Moshe Feinstein has even invalidated weddings performed by non-Orthodox clergy and has questioned their competency as witnesses. Old community projects and cooperative enterprises supported by all religious groups are breaking up and a spirit of fundamentalism and even fanaticism is abroad. The liberal Orthodox rabbi and layman are under increasing pressure from the right-wingers who are in the ascendancy. The question is: Will the swing to the right continue? Is this new mood good for Orthodoxy in the long run? Or will it have a deleterious effect? Time will tell.

# Reform Judaism

The past decade has been one of growth and expansion for the Reform movement after some years of stabilization and equilibrium. The number of rabbis in the Central Conference of American Rabbis increased to over 1,360 by 1984 while the number of congregations affiliated with the Union of American Hebrew Congregations rose from 700 to 770 as a result of a concerted and dynamic development program to create new congregations.

At the same time, Reform has had its ideological conflicts and internal turmoil and while they have not been marked by the acrimony that has been too prevalent among the Orthodox, they have injected divisiveness and polarization into Reform Judaism. Reform's controversies have centered on the issues of authority versus individualism, the role of Halakhah in Reform Judaism, and the nature of Reform Judaism in the post-Holocaust world. A sweeping attempt at a new formulation of Reform's ideology was undertaken in 1976 on the centennials of the founding of the Union of American Hebrew Congregations and the Hebrew Union College. After a period of careful study and debates, the Centenary Perspective was presented to and voted on by the Central Conference of American Rabbis. It is the latest and most accepted formulation of Reform's ideology.[1]

## A Centenary Perspective

The Centenary Perspective is a much longer and more complete summation of Reform's ideology than either the Pittsburgh Platform or the Columbus Platform. It goes beyond the Columbus Platform in projecting the newest views of Reform. It affirms that "most modern Jews within their various religious movements, are embracing Reform Jewish perspectives." The Centenary Perspective agrees that the Holocaust has "shattered our easy optimism about humanity and its inevitable progress." It reaffirms its acceptance of the universalist mission of the Jewish people in working towards messianic fulfillment at the same time that it gives the survival of the Jewish people "highest priority." The Perspective urges the restoration of Torah study as "a religious imperative and whose practice is our chief means to holiness." Whereas Judaism emphasizes action rather than creed as the primary expression of a religious life, the religious life encompasses both the ethical and the ritual, including family devotions, private and public worship, daily religious observance, keeping the Sabbath and the holy days, celebrating the major events of life, and so on. To be sure, when approaching observance, Reform Jews are called upon to "exercise their individual autonomy choosing and creating on the basis of commitment and knowledge."

The statement on Israel is extraordinarily positive:

> We are bound to that land and the newly reborn State of Israel by innumerable religious and ethnic ties . . . We have both a stake and a responsibility in building the State of Israel, assuring its security, and defining its Jewish character. We encourage <u>aliyah</u> for those who wish to find maximum fulfillment in the cause of Zion. We demand that Reform Judaism be unconditionally legitimized in the State of Israel.

At the same time, the Perspective reaffirms the mandate to create strong Jewish communities wherever we live, centered around the synagogue. It also reminds Reform Jews of their duty to be concerned with both universalistic and particular causes; to develop a passion for our people as well as mankind. Finally, it reiterates its basic optimistic faith that "the existence of the Jew is an argument against despair; Jewish survival is warrant for human hopes," for "we remain God's witness that history is not meaningless" and people "are not powerless to affect their destiny."[2]

### Freedom Versus Authority

"Individualism has been fundamental to Reform Judaism," declared Professor Eugene Borowitz. In the opinion of Rabbi W. Gunther Plaut, "Our people lack a Jewish lifestyle. They live like *goyim* . . . We need *mitzvah* or *hovah*, demand." In these sharply contrasting views we glimpse in a nutshell the major controversy within Reform's ranks.

Many Reform thinkers believe that the genius of Reform has been its emphasis on the individual and his right to select Jewish practices as he sees fit. Eugene Borowitz writes that "Jewish obligation begins with the informed will of every individual." Since it is left to the individual to choose, he suggests that Reform is *more* demanding than Orthodoxy which spells out the individual's obligations. Rabbi Eugene Lipman argues that our congregations are not prepared to accept discipline from the Union of American Hebrew Congregations or the Central Conference of American Rabbis. We are "radically individualistic" and only if we find the "Covenental intent of an act as a *mitzvah* does the individual perform it." Each Reform Jew must ask: "Shall I perform it in the traditional way? Is there a better way?" Professor Norman Mirsky agrees: "What is most sacred in Reform Judaism is the *individual* and the individual's right to find religious expression within Reform Jewish institutions." Professor Dan Cohn-Sherbok goes further, urging that "we must free ourselves from the legal system," and he warns that we must not return to a central code and rules.[3]

On the other side of the debate we find an array of some distinguished Reform scholars and rabbis who insist that without authority, Reform is doomed to assimilate. W. Gunther Plaut, surely one of the leading Reform rabbis and scholars and a champion of greater involvement in Halakhah and *mitzvah*, is particularly sharp in his critique of Reform's rampant individualism which he identifies as anarchical. He believes Reform has become too smug and it needs the prophetic spirit of dissatisfaction:

> *Above all, our people lack a Jewish lifestyle. They live like goyim; they have adapted themselves so completely that they have forgotten what it is they left behind. To defend the emptiness of their lives they shout, "Freedom!" but they mean hefkerut, license to carry on with as little as possible, or at best, with what is convenient.*[4]

Plaut insists Reform Jews need a sense of *mitzvah*, commandment, or *hovah*, demand. Rabbi Mordecai Podet (1983) concurs and wonders: "But can the constituency of Reform Judaism generate sufficient Jewish self-discipline, communal morale and commitment to be the bearer of such a lofty faith? Not under the banner of absolute autonomy." He urges a close relationship to both the content and the spirit of Halakhah. Rabbis Walter Jacob and Mark N. Staitman (1983) insist Reform Jews need guides to observance. "Freeing ourselves from the legal system can only lead to the abandonment of tradition" and "complete anarchy and bankruptcy." Other eminent voices ranging from the sage of Reform, Solomon B. Freehof, to Daniel Jeremy Silver and William Braude agree that total autonomy leads to anarchy and playing footloose with tradition is fraught with incalculable dangers.[5]

It appears that the issue of authority versus individual freedom is the number one problem dividing Reform these days. It is a profound point that goes to the heart of Reform's ideology; its resolution will surely affect the direction of Reform Judaism for the foreseeable future.

### Mixed Marriage and Conversion

Undoubtedly the most explosive conflict that has rocked the Reform movement in the decade from 1973 to 1984 has been the issue of mixed marriage and conversion. The Reform movement has been hardest hit by the problem of mixed marriages partly because more Reform Jews marry non-Jews than do Orthodox, Conservative, or Reconstructionist Jews, partly because more mixed-married couples find a more congenial home in Reform than in the other branches of Judaism. Rabbi Alexander Schindler, President of the Union of American Hebrew Congregations, announced the startling statistic that 50 percent of the children in Reform religious schools came from mixed marriages. Consequently, the question of how to relate to and absorb such families has assumed a paramount importance in Reform.

Actually, the Reform movement has been struggling with this problem for a long time. In 1909 the CCAR had voted to discourage rabbis from officiating at mixed marriages. In 1973 the CCAR went further and expressed its opposition to participation of its members in mixed marriage ceremonies. This resolution provoked the more "liberal" Reformers who insisted on autonomy and the right to follow individual conscience. Subsequently, about 100 members of the CCAR, under the leadership of Professors Eugene Mihaly and Sheldon Blank of the Hebrew Union College, formed the Association for a Progressive Reform Judaism. The group expressed its opposition to the "increasing preoccupation" by Reform organizations "with appeasing the Orthodox and Conservative establishments." The Association defended the right of rabbis to perform mixed marriages in the name of freedom of conscience; it decried the "increasing authoritarian character of our movement;" it denounced the move to accept traditional norms of Halakhah for conversion; it assailed the view of the centrality of Eretz Yisrael to Diaspora Jewry; it called for a greater role of laymen in the decision-making process of Reform; and it announced that it would publish its own journal. In a word, it seemed as if Reform was about to have a full-blown schism on its hands and the mixed-marriage issue was the catalyst.

But the schism did not come about and the new group never really got off the ground. One reason for its failure was the

move by CCAR President Robert Kahn to set the stage for the
Centenary Perspective that would submerge the old classical
Reformers' position once and for all. Another factor were the
bold actions of Rabbi Alexander Schindler to reach out to the
mixed-married couples in an effort to save what was salvage-
able.

Schindler, who had emerged as the leading spokesman of
Reform Judaism in the 1970s and 1980s, first proposed an outreach program both to the mixed-married couples as well as to
the "unchurched" of America. His plan was, quite simply, proselytizing and in 1978 the UAHC endorsed his proposal to meet
the needs of non-Jewish partners and welcome them to synagogues and encourage them to raise Jewish children, to service
the children and enroll them in religious schools, to propagate
information among prospective converts and to integrate converts into the Jewish community. And while few voices were
raised in opposition to this proposal, his next one struck like a
bolt of lightning: he urged that the traditional view that matrilineal descent determines the Jewishiness of a child be replaced
by either matrilineal or patrilineal antecedent. Thus, a child
would be Jewish if either mother or father were Jewish, providing the child was raised as a Jew. Actually, the Reform movement had *de facto* followed this norm; but Schindler wanted to
make it *de jure* and public for all to see and know.

A vigorous debate erupted over the proposal. The Israel Reform Rabbis (MARAM) were solidly against the patrilineal proposal as were the more tradition-minded American and Canadian rabbis. But in 1983, the CCAR voted to accept the
Schindler plan:

> *The realities of contemporary Jewish life as well as the highest
> ideals of Judaism require that any and all discriminatory refer-
> ences to either matrilineal or patrilineal descent be stricken from
> Reform Jewish practice and that in cases of doubt, the doubt should
> be resolved in favor of broadening the definition of who is deemed
> to be a Jew. This is all the more important in light of the decima-
> tion of our ranks brought about by the horror of the Holocaust.*

The CCAR added that the presumption of Jewishness would be established through timely public and formal identification with the Jewish faith and people and the performance of such *mitzvot* as Jewish education, Bar or Bat Mitzvah, Confirmation, or other public acts.[6]

At the same time, however, the CCAR (41 percent of whose membership acknowledged that they perform mixed marriages without conversion) passed a resolution in opposition to rabbis co-officiating with Christian clergy at mixed marriages. The patrilineal decision, however, crowded out the later decision and was widely reported on front pages of papers throughout the land. The Orthodox were incensed and spared no invectives; the Conservatives were in a dilemma and were unsure whether the close cooperation between the two movements might proceed. And the more traditional Reform rabbis feared that the move would encourage intermarriage, discourage conversion, split world Jewry even more, and jeopardize Israel's fledgling Reform movement.[7]

## Halakhah and Ritual

There has been an unmistakable swing to greater traditional observance in the Reform movement of late. More and more Reform rabbis observe the kosher food laws; more and more congregations insist on head covering for males at worship and have reintroduced Hebrew and many discarded rituals (e.g., the observance of Purim and Grace After Meals); more and more Reform families have restored home rituals such as Sabbath candles and *kiddush* for the Sabbath eve. Many applaud the trend; others are equally vehement in denouncing the new mood of traditionalism.

Among partisans of greater traditionalism we find the eminent legal scholar Rabbi Solomon B. Freehof, who has described Halakhah as the mind of Judaism and who rejoices that the Committee on Responsa has been flooded with more legal questions than ever in Reform's history. Rabbi Walter Jacobs insists that Reform must talk in terms of Halakhah or it will lose all shreds of tradition. Rabbi Robert N. Levine and Professor David Ellenson agree and suggest that Halakhah makes up the lifeblood of Judaism. Rabbi W. Gunther Plaut has called for the notion of *mitzvah* or *hovah*, of religious duty and obligation, as vital to a vibrant Reform. Professor Peter J. Haas urges Reform to write more responsa while Rabbis Bernard H. Mehlman and Rifat Sonsino have suggested a Reform text to be used as a *get* (religious divorce). Rabbis have supported the return of the long-discarded Bar Mitzvah ceremony; others have advocated traditional norms for conversion including circumcision and ritual bath; and the CCAR's Commission on Worship voted for the restoration to primacy of the Sabbath morning service since the Late Friday eve service is no longer needed and is really an artificial creation.[8]

Those who are more in the mold of "classical" Reform have resisted bitterly these moves to greater traditionalism and Halakhah. Professor Eugene Mihaly of HUC derided Rabbi Plaut's call for *mitzvot* as "mockery of ourselves, of our history, of everything we claim to represent as Reform rabbis." Mihaly argued that every individual rabbi must determine what is the "law of Moses and Israel" for that is our freedom. Rabbi Leon Feuer, past president of the CCAR, agreed that the new stress on Halakhah and ritual is a betrayal of the Reform program and in several articles he attacked the use of the skullcap, the restoration of the Bar Mitzvah ceremony, and the verbosity of the new *Sidur*. In his view, these new trends represent a loss of individual freedom and a departure from the ideals of classic Reform.[9]

Eugene Borowitz has sought to mediate the two extremes. He admits that there is some truth to the charge that Reform Jews seem free to do whatever they find comfortable for them and that theirs is "too often a religion of convenience." But if understood properly, Reform stresses the primacy of demand and that life-pervading quality remains the same for Reform as for Orthodox Jews. He agrees that while there may be a return to traditional observances, it is hardly a return to Orthodoxy, as some complain. The autonomy of the individual and the primacy of the ethical remain paramount for Reform Jews. Borowitz believes that "Torah arises from the relationship between God and the Jewish people, the Covenant, and that I and other Jews are the living bearers of that relationship." He admits that if Torah is merely "human" creation it will *not* impel Reform Jews to study or practice it. Still, he insists on autonomy and the right of every individual Jew to choose his pattern of observance. For a Reform Jew such autonomy implies he must: 1) confront obligations; 2) choose from tradition; 3) create new forms of Jewish life, even if he is but a layperson; 4) abide by limits within each area of Jewish "observance."[10]

Greater traditionalism is strikingly evident in the area of liturgy. The Reform movement has sown a rich harvest of new liturgical creations including *Shaarei Tefillah, Gates of Prayer* (for the Sabbath), and *Shaarei Teshuvah, Gates of Repentance* (for the High Holidays), as well as two companion volumes for study of the liturgy, *Gates of Understanding*. The 1975 *Shaarei Tefillah* is over 800 pages long and is replete with Hebrew. More significantly, it has restored many discarded prayers and rituals including references to Zion, prayers for Jerusalem, the blessings over the *tallit* and *tefillin*, services for Purim and Tish'a Be-Av—just to mention a few. *The Gates of the House* is a volume for home worship running 296 pages that includes Grace after Meals, Sabbath songs, *Havdallah*, Sukkot prayers, *Kiddush*, etc. We must recall that virtually none of those prayers were found in the older liturgical productions such as the *Union Prayer Book*. But under the creative leadership of Rabbi Chaim Stern, editor of the volumes, and Professor Lawrence Hoffman (who criticized the old *Union Prayer Book* as too universalistic and unconcerned with Jewish needs), Reform's new prayer volumes have been warmly received by many. Equally well received has been the new Reform Bible Commentary, edited by Rabbis W. Gunther Plaut and Bernard Bamberger and Professor William Halo, which appeared in 1981.

One other sign of the new "traditionalism" of Reform has been its new emphases in Jewish education. Hebrew language texts are being produced constantly and a survey by Rabbi Hillel Gamoran done in 1976 indicated that over three-quarters of Reform temples teach Hebrew as a language, 48 percent require 4 years of study prior to Bar or Bat Mitzvah, 18 percent more schools now offer a 2-day program of education as compared to 15 years ago and 125 percent more insist on a 3-day program each week than was the case 15 years ago. Today, one-third of the prayer services is in Hebrew and two-thirds of the temples offer adult Hebrew courses. One other remarkable fact: the CCAR passed a resolution favoring the establishment of Day Schools under Reform auspices and there were six schools operating in 1979.

## The Land of Israel

Reform has moved even more solidly into the Zionist, pro-Israel camp in the last decade. The Centenary Perspective was extraordinarily positive in affirming support for Israel and even calling for *aliyah*. Borowitz writes that Israel provides our people "unique opportunities for Jewish self-expression" and he agrees that "only in Israel can one live naturally as a Jew." In a lengthy statement on Israel adopted in 1983, the CCAR affirmed its commitment to the sovereignty of the State, expressed opposition to a division of Jerusalem, called for dialogue between Diaspora Jewry and Israel, and emphasized Israel's centrality in world Jewry. At the same time, it underscored the need for the moral use of power by Israel, it urged reconciliation between Arabs and Jews, it insisted on the protection of the dignity, rights and self-determination of Palestinian Arabs and the cessation of further colonization on the West Bank. The statement further commended to Israel the notion of religious pluralism for Arabs and non-Orthodox Jews of all persuasions and it closed with a plea for support of UJA, Israel Bonds, and *aliyah*.[11]

In a variety of resolutions, the CCAR expressed its opposition to the ultranationalist Gush Emunim group who are colonizing in Judea and Samaria. A resolution adopted in 1981 urged the abolition of the office of Chief Rabbi and several joint pronouncements with non-Orthodox groups demanded that Reform clergy have the same ecclesiastical rights in Israel as the Orthodox. Several Reform spokesmen have endeavored to infuse the nationalism of the State of Israel with prophetic morality. For example, Rabbi Roland Gittelsohn, in a speech to the CCAR convention of 1981 in Jerusalem, expounded his view that Israel must not be just a "normal" state for "its end is the liberation and continued creativity of the whole Jewish people." He suggested that Judaism is more than nationalism or religion; that Israel needs liberal Judaism to teach that religion is more than ritual; that law in Israel must not be static or moribund. And Rabbi David Polish suggested, "Our objective should be to help restore those prophetic and rabbinic commitments to social ethics which once distinguished Zionism . . . Reform must release Zionism from the limits of traditional nationalism which can injure us." Rabbi Levi Olan has gone even further in summoning Reform to influence Israel to fashion a "religious socialist society."[12]

Reform Jewry has made headway in marshaling support for Israel through its new Zionist organizations ARZA in America and KADIMA in Canada. There were fifteen Reform congregations in Israel by 1982 and two *kibbutzim* have been founded under Reform auspices: Yahel, begun in 1976, and Lotan, established in 1983. The Reform movement is now ordaining rabbis in Israel, its Leo Baeck High School in Haifa is flourishing, and its Hebrew Union College in Jerusalem is expanding. Additionally, Rabbi Richard Hirsch, head of Israel's Reform group, has proved to be an effective and articulate spokesman for the movement.

*Social Action*

On the whole, Reform has remained true to its prophetic notion of social justice and its pronouncements have followed a basically liberal path. The ethical drive continues to be a powerful leavening in Reform's social thrust. To be sure, the old, unbounded faith in humanity has been shattered by the Holocaust and the optimism of classical Reform has been jettisoned. Moreover, the classical Reform stress on the mission of Israel has been viewed lately with greater suspicion: some have described it as presumptuous and pompous, as too great a claim on our part and rendering too little appreciation of others. Other Reform leaders have concluded that the movement had been too preoccupied with saving the world to the exclusion of Jewry, too universalistic in its passion while ignoring particularistic needs. Consequently, the social action concerns of Reform have taken a more parochial and less worldly turn in the past decade; greater stress has been laid on Jewish rather than general needs.

Still, the liberal drive is far from spent in Reform, as is evident in recent social-action pronouncements of the movement. The CCAR and the UAHC have unanimously favored liberal abortion and opposed an amendment that would constrict a woman's rights in this area. The movement has consistently opposed breaches in the wall of separation between church and state; it has battled constitutional amendments allowing prayer in public schools; it has led the fight to cut military spending while insisting on increased funding of social welfare; it has helped spearhead boycotts of grape and lettuce growers in California who use nonunion laborers; it has argued for the decriminalization of homosexuality; it has consistently opposed capital punishment under all circumstances. On an international level, the Reform movement has gone on record several times as favoring a bilateral nuclear freeze and has endorsed the ratification of the SALT II disarmament treaty. It has championed the cause of Soviet Jewry and Ethiopian Jewry and has been vocal in defending Israel's needs.[13]

In recent years, as the tensions between blacks and Jews have mounted, Reform has urged a restructuring of that old partnership, summoning a "coalition of conscience" aimed at "building together a just society." A 1984 resolution of the UAHC called on the temples to "initiate a program of dialogue with black churches and other representative black officials . . .

to assert our common concerns and interpret our differences in an atmosphere of friendship and understanding."[14]

While the Reform movement has shifted the direction of its social actions to more specifically Jewish concerns, it is obvious that the customary liberal drive is hardly extinct.

## Women's Rights

Reform Judaism has long been a leader in championing the equal role of women in ritual and in affording them equal opportunity. It was only recently, however, that Reform has actually implemented those proposals. Today, Reform has elevated women to the highest posts including the rabbinate, the cantorate, and presidencies of synagogues. By 1984, 72 female rabbis had been ordained by the Hebrew Union College and 28 women had been invested as cantors. Dozens of women serve as temple presidents and the number of women students in the Reform seminary has been rising steadily.

On a broader scale, Reform has fought for the ERA amendment to give women equal treatment and equal pay with men in comparable jobs. It has called for removal of sexist language in prayer and an end to stereotypic treatment of women in textbooks and curricula, in media and advertising, in synagogue life and organization, and it has insisted that women be elevated to high executive posts in Jewish and communal agencies.

## Critique and Prognosis

Reform Judaism has undergone many changes and mutations during the past decade or two. But this is in keeping with its stress on change as the only really constant factor in Jewish life. It has returned to many traditional practices; its synagogue services are more Hebraic than ever; its social justice concerns have shifted to a more particularistic stream; its passion for the State of Israel has become more pronounced. At the same time, it has remained committed to autonomy and the right of the individual to choose freely which pattern of Jewish living to follow. This has made for tensions and stresses and Reform leaders and theologians are split over basic issues such as autonomy versus authority, particularism versus universalism, the worldly versus the Jewish. These tensions are at the root of Reform's current polarization.

Rabbi Daniel Jeremy Silver, for example, has suggested: "By and large, our congregations have been strengthened, not weakened, by this pattern of diversity . . . The danger of *hefkerut* [anarchy] is implicit in this lack of order, and in many ways we stand convicted." Silver insisted that "Prophetic Judaism" is too simple a notion; we need the warmth of poetry and Torah to guide us and we can no longer accept today's wisdom as superior to yesterday's because it is today's. Finally, Silver urged that the new synagogue must not be "a bastion of liberal politics" but "the source of Jewish spirit.[15]

Rabbi Richard Hirsch, speaking at the same convention with Rabbi Silver, called for an end to blithe ignoring of Halakhah so as to resolve the plight of those viewed as inauthentic, a view passionately held, as we have noted, by Rabbi W. Gunther Plaut. In the same vein, Rabbi William Braude cautioned against playing "fast and loose with the tradition." This plea for greater traditionalism and reliance on some kind of guidelines or norms or Halakhah has been gaining ascendancy in Reform ranks, and the critics who decry unbridled autonomy have been winning supporters.[16]

Still, there are those who denigrate these new trends and who yearn for the good old days of autonomy and liberalism. Rabbi David Polish, for example, decries the prayer books with their varied services and antithetical texts which he sees as sowing confusion and displaying a lack of confidence and sense of direction. He agrees that Reform might *consult* Halakhah but not as a constitutional system, for that is theocracy. He also has suggested that Reform has been neglecting social concerns as it becomes preoccupied with Jewish problems. Rabbi Levi Olan criticized the loss of the thrust for social justice: "The social justice resolutions of Reform Judaism have a hollow ring today," he concluded. Olan has urged Reform to speak again in the name of Prophetic faith to the sleek "fat cats" and preach "religious socialism" and "liberation theology."[17]

Despite these internal tensions and dialectics, Reform has been experiencing a sense of success in the last decade. Rabbi Alexander Schindler, in noting the new growth of the movement (which he estimates to be 5 percent annually), stated in a speech before the CCAR in 1982 that Orthodoxy's mass strength was in the first generation, Conservative Judaism's strength was in the second generation, while Reform is a third-generational phenomenon. He added triumphantly, "The future clearly belongs to us." In more modest tones, Rabbi Solomon B. Freehof wrote: "Therefore when we can re-win our people to regular Jewish self-study, our future will be as bright as our past was heroic." Eugene Borowitz maintains that Reform has convinced most American Jews and movements to accept four basic Reform theses:

1. *Judaism interacts with modern culture*;
2. *Jews express themselves in contemporary esthetic form*;
3. *Modern critical scholarship is essential*;
4. *Change is a fundamental reality.*

Reform has displayed, he suggests, more limited success in projecting ethics as the essence of Judaism, in promoting the equal role of women in Jewish life and in convincing Jews that Judaism depends on the *will* of informed individuals and *individual choice.*[18]

From a different perspective, sociologist Bernard Lazerwitz (professor of sociology at Israel's Bar-Ilan University) predicts that Orthodoxy will shrink to 3 percent of American Jewry while Conservatism will continue to decline. He concludes that Reform will become the largest denomination in American Jewry. Many sociologists agree with Lazerwitz' projections of future trends.[19]

In sum, Reform feels more hopeful and confident about its future than it has in several decades and its growth cannot be gainsaid. Still, it must resolve its basic philosphical problem of autonomy versus authority for that is at the heart of so many of its problems including mixed marriage, patrilineal descent, ritual observances, and the like. Can a movement that leaves critical decisions to the individual conscience of each rabbi or layperson survive as a movement? Can it grip the loyalty of its followers without norms or discipline? Can it reproduce itself without even the loosest form of disciplines or parameters? The future of Reform Judaism boils down to the resolution of this vital issue.

# Conservative Judaism

The last decade has not been an easy one for the Conservative movement. The phenomenal growth that had marked the movement in the 1950s and 1960s slowed down perceptibly by the end of the 1970s and 1980s. There was a mood of discontent, of self-criticism, of malaise that seemed to afflict leaders and laypersons alike and a sense of futility or frustration gripped the rabbis and ideologues. The issue of women's role in synagogue life coupled with the question of ordination of women as rabbis ripped the fragile fabric of the coalition that comprised the Conservative movement. Coming on the heels of the secession of the Reconstructionist wing, the women's question added yet another note of divisiveness and despair to an already faltering movement.

While the number of rabbis in the Rabbinical Assembly soared to an unprecedented 1,130 by 1984, the number of congregations stabilized at just over 800. Twenty-six new ones entered the United Synagogue at its 1983 Convention but uncounted congregations merged with neighboring ones or simply closed their doors. The United Synagogue Youth and its Kadimah junior division grew somewhat to 35,000 members, but the Atid college organization went out of business and a new one, Ometz, was recently set up in an attempt to replace it. The Ramah Camps have remained crowded and popular with the children of Conservative synagogues, but the membership of the United Synagogue (roughly estimated at 300,000 families) has been noticeably aging and the movement in general seems to be "graying" along with much of American Jewry.

The internal squabbles between MERCAZ, the World Council for Synagogues, the United Synagogue, the Movement for Mesorati (Traditional) Judaism in Israel, and other wings of the Conservative superstructure have bordered on a fiasco and strong central leadership has been markedly absent. All of these factors seem to point to a movement that has, in the words of Rabbi Mordecai Waxman, entered a period of stasis.

There has also been an ideological shift in the last 20 years and a realignment of forces. Twenty years ago, the left wing was the odd-man-out; it complained that the movement was *too* traditional and inexorably bound to Halakhah. Today, the left wing is gone, having broken off into the Reconstructionist movement so that the right wing feels isolated and complains that Conservative Jewry has gone radical and has flouted halakhic norms.

## Redefinition of Ideals and Goals

For some time now, Conservative leaders have urged that Conservative Judaism could advance its programs and capture the hearts and souls of Jews in North America and elsewhere if it would state its ideological platform and ritual demands in a clear and unequivocable fashion. Indeed, years ago Rabbis Max Arzt and Robert Gordis had called for the publication of guides to ideology, ethical behavior, and religious practices. The late Rabbi Isaac Klein published an impressive *Guide to Religious Practice* in 1979 and it is a veritable *Shulhan Arukh* or Codebook for Conservative Jews. While no similar theological or ethical guides have yet been issued, a number of the older as well as younger ideologues of the movement have been wrestling with new formulations of the principles of Conservative Judaism.

Professor Elliot N. Dorff, for example, has called for the movement to drop the name "Conservative" and replace it with "Traditional Judaism." Dorff, who teaches philosophy at the

University of Judaism in California, argues that the term "Conservative" is too defensive and that the slogan, "tradition and change" is misleading since it causes the people to perceive of the movement as championing "change" as the all-important aspect of Conservative Jewry.[1]

Professor David Lieber, president at the University of Judaism, has offered a long-term program for the movement and has urged that it present a clear and persuasive definition of Conservative Judaism in order to project its ideals.

> *As I see it, this would include among others: articulating a definition of Conservative Judaism which is intelligible and unambiguous; taking theology seriously in an effort to satisfy the religious hungers which are becoming more pressing; developing a theory of Halakhah which maintains its centrality in Jewish life and yet allows for change and growth; fashioning a genuine Conservative laity which is moved not only by institutional or personal loyalties but by deep commitment to a way of life; and strengthening Conservative institutions.*[2]

Professor Neil Gillman of the Jewish Theological Seminary, in seeking to formulate a theology of Conservative Judaism, has written that three characteristics mark the movement: 1) praiseworthy pluralism of theology and halakhic opinions; 2) a critically open or positive attitude to the entire non-Jewish world making for mutual enrichment and synthesis of the best in the world and Judaism; 3) commitment via the process of study rather than from a higher authority, a rabbi, or a text.[3]

In a speech to the 1984 Convention of the Rabbinical Assembly, Rabbi Gilbert S. Rosenthal sought to outline the elements that unite the members of the Conservative movement. He noted (in an obvious borrowing from Maimonides' theory of negative attributes) that Conservative Jews are *not* Orthodox because they do not believe that every word of the Bible is God's, nor do they view their approach to Judaism as the only legitimate one. Nor are they Reform because Conservative Jews accept Halakhah as their *governance*, not merely their *guidance*, and autonomy of choice and popular vote do not determine whether to retain or discard rituals. Conservative Judaism exposes a positive program that includes: a protean, organismic notion of God; a belief in the Divine origin of Torah that is subject to human interpretation and development; an understanding of ritual as a means to a higher end including improvement of human character and society; the mission of Israel to spread God's word; the notion of Israel as the sacred land worthy of our support; the importance of never-ending Jewish education; a view of prayer as man's response to God; and the positive *mitzvah* of social action to improve society.[4]

## The Women's Issue

Unquestionably, the most explosive and divisive dilemma confronting the Conservative movement in the past decade has been the women's issue which encompasses items ranging from the degree of female participation in ritual services to the ultimate question: the ordination of a woman as a rabbi. The matter of female role in ritual goes back 30 years or so. In 1955, the Law Committee of the Rabbinical Assembly had sanctioned *aliyot* for women and in 1973 it voted to count them for the *minyan* or prayer quorum. The 1975 Rabbinical Assembly Convention tabled a formal resolution urging the Seminary to admit women to the Rabbinical School, but in 1977 a resolution was passed petitioning the Seminary's chancellor, Rabbi Gerson D. Cohen, to establish an interdisciplinary commission to study the possiblity of women rabbis in the Conservative movement with a target date of 1979 for its final report. Dr. Cohen responded affirmatively by setting up a 14-member commission headed by himself and consisting of rabbis and laypersons.

Meanwhile, pressure for acceptance of women rabbis began to mount. Liberals such as Rabbi Aaron Blumenthal argued that "Jewish men must recognize the fact that the Halakhah often has been unfair, ungracious and discriminatory toward our women" and while we cannot undo the past, "we can measure up to the needs of the present by granting full equality to Jewish women under the Halakhah."[5] Dr. Robert Gordis reasoned that there are no halakhic objections to ordaining women rabbis and that it would be wrong to deny the talents and dedication of 50 percent of American Jewry who happen to be females.[6]

The opposition was not sleeping through all of this and a loose coalition named the Committee for Preservation of Tradition led by Rabbis I. Usher Kirshblum, Wilfred Shuchat, David Feldman, and David Novak and others began to rally the more traditional rabbis in an attempt to forestall favorable actions that would result in ordination of women.

The Commission's Report was submitted in 1979 and recommended by 11 to 3 to admit female students into the Rabbinical School.[7] The Chancellor submitted his favorable recommendations to the Seminary faculty, which proceeded to table his proposal, much to his chagrin and the disappointment of a clear majority of the Rabbinical Assembly. The Assembly sought to force the issue in two ways: at its 1980 Convention it urged that the faculty vote to admit women and it sought to accept non-Seminary trained female rabbis into its membership. Dr. Cohen resubmitted the proposal and on October 24, 1983, it passed, although five senior Talmud professors boycotted the final vote and impugned its validity. The incoming class of September 1984, numbering 41 students, counted 20 women, several of whom had been studying for years and biding their time to enroll formally in the Rabbinical School.

With the ball back in its court, the Rabbinical Assembly took up once more the admission of females into the Rabbinical Assembly. This time there was a specific candidate, Rabbi Beverly Magidson, who had been ordained at the Hebrew Union College. At a stormy session of the Assembly in Dallas in 1983, the champions of admission argued that justice required favorable action. The opponents were equally vehement in insisting that Judaism is *not* an egalitarian religion, that Halakhah does not permit a woman to serve as a witness to a divorce or marriage, that a female may not officiate at a wedding, serve as a cantor or read the Torah, and that such a step would link Conservatism with Reform. Two votes were finally taken with 210 in favor of admission and 75 opposed. Rabbi Magidson garnered 74 percent but needed 75 percent; she had lost by four votes. The matter was resubmitted to the 1984 Convention and this time the vote was 230 to 99 or 22 votes short of the necessary 75 percent. Many opponents indicated, however, that once the Seminary would ordain a female they would vote for her admission. The first such candidate, Amy Eilberg, was ordained by the Seminary in 1985 and, along with Rabbi Magidson and Rabbi Jan Kaufman, was admitted to the Rabbinical Assembly at its 1985 Convention.[8]

The right-wing group of rabbis, with the assistance of some laypersons, was not sitting idly by during all of this turmoil. The old Committee for Preservation of Tradition gave way to the Union for Traditional Conservative Judaism. Claiming a membership of 200 rabbis and laypersons, it emphasized its belief in distinct roles for men and women in ritual life and its opposition to ordination of women. It has set up its own halakhic panel to answer legal queries and has taken out ads impugning the faculty vote to admit women and seeking to thwart admission of women to the Rabbinical Assembly.

While this storm over ordination has been raging, women have made significant strides in ritual roles in the Conservative movement. Many women serve as presidents of congregations and some Conservative synagogues have engaged female rabbis trained either at the Hebrew Union College or at the Reconstructionist Rabbinical College. Unquestionably, they are playing a greater role in the ritual life of the synagogue as a 1983 survey done by Rabbi Stephen C. Lerner demonstrated. Many more congregations grant *aliyot* and count women in a *minyan* than did so in 1975. The trend is unmistakably for *greater* female participation in ritual. Whether that includes acceptance of female rabbis is yet to be determined.

*Halakhah and Jewish Law*

The Conservative movement has been deeply involved in halakhic matters and has been actively dealing with legal problems and the search for a philosophy of Jewish law. The quest for halakhic principles had been hampered by procedural squabbles and organizational factionalism. For example, some RA members have urged the dissolution of the Committee on Jewish Law and Standards and its replacement with a panel on Jewish law that would meet from time to time to study legal problems. Many have criticized the procedure by which both majority and minority opinions of the Committee are viewed as equally valid so that only a *unanimous* decision is binding on all members of the Assembly. Despite these squabbles, the Committee has rendered important decisions ranging across the spectrum of Jewish life and its responsa have grown into a literary body. Some of its distinguished members, including Professor Seymour Siegel, Rabbis David Feldman, and David Novak have issued important studies on critical biomedical problems that have only recently come to the attention of modern Jews.

Additionally, this has been a particularly fruitful decade or two for the development of Conservative liturgy. The Rabbinical Assembly, under the editorship of Rabbi Jules Harlow, has produced a number of impressive volumes including a new High Holiday *Mahzor* (1972), a prayerbook for the house of mourning, the *Bond of Life* (1975), as well as some lesser works. The other major liturgical creation is a complete prayer book for Sabbaths, Festivals, and daily use, *Siddur Sim Shalom*, slated for publication in 1985. There are, additionally, plans to author and publish a new Torah Commentary that would reflect the ideology and philosophy of Conservative Judaism.

Many of the best minds in the movement have been intensely involved in seeking to formulate a philosophy of Halakhah to guide Conservative Jews and set the course for the movement. Rabbi Jacob Agus, for example, has criticized the workings of the Committee on Jewish Law and Standards as inadequate since it is merely a "law-interpreting body" rather than a "law-making body." He has urged the creation of a Jewish Academy that would pass far-reaching *takkanot* (ordinances.) Agus is convinced that Halakhah always reacted to contemporary pressures and needs and must continue to do so. He is of the opinion that revelation of God's will is ongoing; that successive covenants in Jewish history have constituted that religious experience; and that *takkanah* legislation is, in effect, the periodic reenactment of this covenant in regard to specific problems. He has called for a new, American Talmud and "fresh traditions" emerging from conclaves of rabbis and knowledgeable laypersons.[9]

Professor Robert Gordis, in a lengthy essay on the dynamism of Halakhah, has demonstrated that Jewish law was *not* in conflict with the contemporary age; that sociology has not been anathema to the law but, in fact, "is an integral element in it." Gordis writes that Jewish law has always responded to new conditions and that new ethical insights and attitudes have shaped legal decisions in a host of areas while the law has adjusted to the needs of the survival of the Jewish people. Consequently, the Rabbinical Assembly's Law Committee has been within the mainstream of classical Halakhah in taking positions on various issues.[10]

Professor Seymour Siegel suggests that specific laws are *responses* to revelation, not the *content* of revelation. "If specific laws no longer express the ethical values which tradition teaches . . . we have the responsibility to revise the laws," he argues. In evaluating halakhic changes, Siegel posits five principles: 1) the needs of the time; 2) history and development of law as guides; 3) consideration of the whole of Jewish law; 4) Aggadah and ethical demands must control Halakhah; 5) pluralism of practices of the law is legitimate. Siegel has also urged that the movement campaign to strengthen Jewish observance, publish literature on Halakhah, and revamp the Law Committee, creating in its stead an Academy of Jewish law whose decisions will be final.[11]

Several profound symposia and conferences have been convened by the Rabbinical Assembly and the resulting papers have enriched the discussion of the role and nature of Halakhah. In one such symposium, Rabbis Kassel Abelson and Phillip Sigal urged that the Assembly train men to write responsa to deal with new areas of concern such as biomedical problems, environmental issues, and political and international problems. Rabbi David Feldman agreed but insisted that first we must immerse ourselves in more intensive study.[12] The Rabbinical Assembly summoned a full-day Conference (*Kallah*) on Halakhah in 1980 at which many viewpoints were expressed in the various papers. Rabbi Gilbert S. Rosenthal, for example, underscored the human element in halakhic decisions and he urged that the *telos* or goal of the *mitzvot* must be decisive because Halakhah concretizes the value-concepts of Judaism and "translates theological norms into concrete deeds." On the other hand, Rabbi David Novak, while conceding the element of change in Halakhah, challenged the thesis that Halakhah must express norms of Aggadah for if Aggadah is primary, what distinguishes Conservative from Reform Jews?[13]

Critical evaluations of the halakhic stance of the movement have been offered by two of its top leaders. Rabbi Benjamin Z. Kreitman, executive vice president of the United Synagogue and a past chairman of the Law Committee, stated that the movement's failure to define authority, revelation, and Halakhah has led to "tensions that have made us theologically neurotic and religiously timid" and has permitted us to be "polarized on the left and on the right." Because of these tensions, we have developed egregious contradictions in our ritual patterns (for example, in the area of female participation in ritual). Kreitman insisted on the need to issue statements on core problems such as revelation and he urged the creation of supportive fellowships of observers if Halakhah is to be truly binding.[14]

Rabbi Gerson D. Cohen, who heads the Seminary, is equally concerned about the need for cadres of learned and committed laypersons. While he has been liberal in his halakhic views, he exhorted:

> *I suggest that we stop speaking of change in Jewish law. Authentic Halakhah does not require change. It develops through a process of usage, exegesis, and interpretation. The rules and mechanisms for its development are built into the law itself . . .*

Consequently, Cohen suggested, we must accept adaptations of Halakhah if they are grounded in history and the wording of the law itself. The development of law must be undertaken for the enhancement of the law and for the sake of human dignity.[15]

Obviously, there are many fertile approaches to Halakhah within the Conservative movement and the range of opinions is widely spread. But all agree that Halakhah is binding on Conservative Jews and the number one challenge is to develop a committed and observant laity if the movement is to grow and prosper.

## Conversion and Mixed Marriage

Confronted by the fearsome problem of mixed marriages that affects so many families from Conservative homes, the movement has followed some of the lead set by the Reform movement, especially in the area of outreach to the mixed married. At its 1976 Convention, the Rabbinical Assembly passed several resolutions dealing with the question of how to handle mixed-married couples and the problem of out-marriages. The rabbis authorized a multi-pronged campaign to combat out-marriages, to reach out to intermarried couples and to those contemplating a mixed marriage. They approved a plan to prepare curricula of studies for potential converts and to open schools for such candidates; they also called for the development of standards for converts and proper publicity for such outreach programs. Every rabbi was, furthermore, urged to speak to mixed-married couples and to discuss the possibility of conversion to Judaism. The United Synagogue followed suit the next year at its biennial Convention by endorsing this plan.

The pages of *Conservative Judaism* magazine contain quite a few articles on the *mitzvah* of *keruv*, of bringing non-Jewish partners in marriage or potential non-Jewish spouses close to Judaism, Torah, and the Jewish way of life. In a word, proselytizing among non-Jews who have married or plan to marry Jews has been endorsed by a host of rabbis and Conservative leaders including Rabbis Jacob Agus, Seymour Siegel, Joel Roth, Kassel Abelson, Stephen Lerner, and many more. The logic of the proponents of outreach is simple: we must replenish our depleted ranks; we must save Jewish families and Jewish children for our People; we must add new blood to our anemic stock.[16]

Reform and Reconstructionist Jews have opted to accept patrilineal descent as a way to insure the Jewish connection of mixed-married couples. This proposal has found some echoes in Conservative ranks, too. The late Rabbi Solomon D. Goldfarb (himself a very traditional, right-wing rabbi) endorsed the idea in a controversial article that was published posthumously in *Conservative Judaism* magazine. Rabbi Phillip Sigal seconded his suggestion, calling the present halakhic position that follows the mother's religion "a grave injustice." The Rabbinical Assembly's executive vice president has also come out for a patrilineal ruling. But the then president of the Assembly, Rabbi Arnold Goodman, sustained the traditional view in speeches and articles, and he elicited a voice vote of support for his stance at the 1984 Rabbinical Assembly. For the time being, the Conservative movement is maintaining the traditional matrilineal position on Jewishness while moving more aggressively into an outreach, proselytizing campaign.[17]

*Israel and the Zionist Movement*

Two issues have exercised the Conservative movement in its relationship to Israel and Zionism in the past years. The first was the issue of affiliation with the World Zionist Organization via the instrumentality of a Conservative Zionist group. The second and more complex problem is the recognition of non-Orthodox rabbis by the State of Israel whose religious establishment is controlled by the Orthodox rabbinate.

Actually, the matter of the creation of a Conservative Zionist organization had been debated for some time. The issue came to a head in the 1970s when more and more leaders expressed concern that Conservative Jews would not make a sufficient impact on Israel and would not get their "fair share" unless there were a Conservative political presence in the Zionist decision-making bodies. The Rabbinical Assembly passed a resolution at its 1975 Convention urging full participation in the World Zionist Organization "as a regular Zionist organization" and Rabbis Simon Greenberg and Mordecai Waxman articulated this position most passionately. The establishment of a Zionist organization to be called MERCAZ was hotly debated at the 1977 United Synagogue Convention with Rabbis Greenberg and Gordis espousing the new group while United Synagogue President Jacob Stein opposed it. Finally, MERCAZ was born and the Conservative movement was accepted into the Zionist superstructure alongside of the Reform's group, ARZA. However, membership has languished and both the Rabbinical Assembly and United Synagogue were constrained to pass resolutions urging mass enrollment in MERCAZ in order to increase leverage in the World Zionist Organization.[18]

The second great debate focused on the role of Conservative Judaism in Israel and the legitimacy of Conservative rabbis in Israel. This issue had been brewing for a long time and periodically the Conservative and Reform groups have publicized joint statements. In 1984, the two religious bodies joined with B'nai B'rith, the American Jewish Committee, and several other secular bodies in denouncing attempts at amending the Law of Return that would call into question non-Orthodox conversions and marriages.

Increasingly, the Conservative group has been losing patience over this problem. Rabbi Judah Nadich, in his presidential address to the 1973 RA Convention, called for the State of Israel to help set up non-Orthodox synagogues in parity with Orthodox ones and to end harassment of and extend full rights and privileges to non-Orthodox rabbis. In his presidential address before the RA in 1978, Rabbi Stanley Rabinowitz defended joint campaigns with Reform colleagues to gain legitimacy in Israel despite the theological and ritualistic differences, and he suggested that collaboration between the two groups would enable them to secure important resolutions within the World Zionist Organization to foster religious pluralism and gain equal treatment for non-Orthodox groups.

Although these tensions have not yet been resolved, Conser-

vative Judaism remains as firmly committed to the State of Israel as ever. It has spearheaded fund-raising efforts via the
United Jewish Appeal, Israel Bonds, the Jewish National Fund,
and a host of other charities and investments, and its political
action in the legislatures, Congress, and White House are
fervent. The Conservative movment in Israel is now called
the Movement for Traditional Judaism (Mesorati). There are
about 120 Conservative rabbis living and working in Israel;
some 40 Conservative synagogues are functioning; and there is
a youth group in operation in the country. The first Conservative kibbutz, Hanaton, has been launched near Nazareth; a
school for the study of Judaism is active in Jerusalem (*Midreshet
Yerushalayim*); and a rabbinical school for Israeli students
opened its doors in 1984. *Aliyah* campaigns, however, have met
only limited success.

Conservative ideologues and theologians have been busily
articulating a theology of Zionism and a platform for Conservative Jews. Dr. Robert Gordis, for example, formulated a plan of
Zionist action for Conservative Jews that would include the creation of synagogues for Israelis, tours of duty by RA rabbis in
Israel to service cities, schools, *kibbutzim*, etc., an adult education
program, the formation of schools and *kibbutzim* to reflect Conservative ideology, building co-op housing for Conservative
families, and a fight for freedom for all religious groups.[19]

Rabbi Hertzel Fishman, who has represented the Conservative movement in the World Zionist Organization, sees the
movement's role in a different light. He urges the movement
champion *klal Yisrael*, the ideal of one family with fellow Jews;
he suggests it must teach a relevant and updated approach to
Halakhah; he counsels the movement to reach out to the Sephardim who need a religious revival in the modern sense; and
he admonishes the movement to disseminate the ideals of democratic pluralism and Jewish peoplehood while increasing its
presence through *aliyah* of young and old.[20]

The scholarly English Rabbi Louis Jacobs has set forth his
view of what Zionism and Israel ought to mean to Conservative
Jews. He suggests that we are not literal in accepting the view

that Eretz Yisrael is a divinely promised land in a direct sense but rather by association and historical experiences. He pleads for "enriched universalism" rather than total subordination to the group; that the state is *not* the highest end of all. Additionally, Jacobs cautions against the danger of using messianic terminology in referring to Zion.[21]

Obviously, Conservative Jewry's involvement with Zionism and Israel remains passionate and deeply felt.

## Social Action

After deep involvement in social action in the 1960s, especially in the civil rights movement, the Conservative movement has been detached from many of the social issues of the day, confining itself to statements and convention resolutions. The Joint Commission for Social Action that represented all arms of the movement has been defunct for several years and scant public activities have been directed to non-Jewish causes. This may be a reflection of the inward turn of the movement to strictly Jewish problems (e.g., Soviet, Syrian and Ethiopian Jewry, Israel, Jewish poverty, etc.). It may also represent the movement's disillusionment with general social issues in the light of anti-Semitism (and more specifically black anti-Semitism), as well as its all-consuming concern for the fate of the State of Israel, to the exclusion of other causes.

To be sure, both the Rabbinical Assembly and United Synagogue have issued periodic statements and resolutions on social issues of the day, generally following a more liberal course. In domestic affairs, for example, the movement has been sharply condemnatory of the Reagan Administration for having cut social welfare programs, food stamps, college loans, and entitlements to help the poor. It has urged a restoration of those services, called for greater employment opportunities, a national health plan, antipoverty efforts, and federal involvement in alleviating the needs of the homeless through rehabilitation of old housing and the construction of new dwellings. The Rabbinical Assembly and United Synagogue have gone on record in favor of the Equal Rights Amendment; they have endorsed gun control legislation; they have supported the United Farm Workers' drive for unionization of workers; and they have expressed deep concern over the erosion of separation between church and state and opposition to prayer in public schools. At the same time, the Rabbinical Assembly has retreated somewhat from its opposition to Federal aid to parochial schools and it has endorsed the Packwood-Moynihan Bill that would give tax credits to parents of children attending private and parochial schools. The Rabbinical Assembly took a strong stand against smoking at its 1982 Convention and advocated the banning of smoking in public places. The Assembly has given modified support to the right of a woman to an abortion when the mother's life is endangered or her health jeopardized. At the same time, it opposed abortion as a birth-control technique and it urged larger Jewish families to stem the population decline.

Concerned over the rupture of Black-Jewish relations, Rabbis Arnold Goodman and Alexander Shapiro, both presidents of the Rabbinical Assembly, have urged that the two groups repair their old coalition and open up new dialogue. Rabbi Goodman reminded his colleagues at the 1984 RA Convention that "we were in the forefront of working with black leaders in the 1960s" and he urged that we reconstitute that historic coalition in dealing with common problems. Simultaneously, he insisted that black leaders disavow racist and anti-Semitic sentiments expressed by the Rev. Jesse Jackson and Louis Farrakhan.

On the international scene, the Conservative movement has been outspoken in its concern over nuclear proliferation and the threat of nuclear war. Several conventions of both the Rabbinical Assembly and United Synagogue have called for nonproliferation treaties, the implementation of a bilateral, mutually verifiable freeze on nuclear weapons followed by a reduction of nuclear arsenals. The movement has championed the cause of human rights and has been deeply involved in fighting for Soviet, Syrian, and Ethiopian Jews. With the revitalization of the Rabbinical Assembly's Committee on Social Action, a series of national days of social concern were organized in Washington, New York, and Philadelphia. It appears that the Conservative movement is determined to place social action concerns high on the priority list once again.

## Critique and Prognosis

Evaluations of the future of Conservative Judaism range from extreme optimism to dire pessimism and predictions of the end of the movement in a generation or two. Rabbi Wolfe Kelman, executive vice president of the Rabbinical Assembly, remains an inveterate optimist who believes that the Conservative movement has done extraordinarily well, has grown phenomenally, and will yet increase in size and influence in North American Jewish life and possibly elsewhere. But sociologist Marshall Sklare sees a serious decline in the Conservative group as evidenced by the drop in religious observance, the loss of youth, and defection of the less committed to Reform or to nonaffiliation. Sociologist Charles Liebman and Dr. Saul Shapiro agree with Sklare and in a survey of the movement they detect an aging body whose membership seems to range from fifty-one to fifty-five years of age, whose children go either to Reform Judaism or nowhere, or even to Orthodoxy, and whose halakhic commitment and ritual observance are minimal. They suggest that without an upgrading of Jewish education and *mitzvot* observance the movement is doomed. The true situation surely lies between these two extremes.[22]

Some critics within and without the movement view it as shifting to the Reform camp; others are equally positive that it is moving towards the Orthodox. Some underscore Conservative Judaism's inability to produce great religious personalities such as Rabbi Joseph B. Soloveitchik or Rabbi Moshe Feinstein; others decry the lack of passion and religious fervor among partisans of a movement whose chief virtue, they assert, is in loyalty to institutions. There are critics who accuse Conservatives of elitism to the neglect of the masses; others assail it for bowing to sociological trends and the *Zietgeist* in emulation of

Reform Judaism's pattern.[23] All critics seem to concur that the chief failing of Conservatism is its inability to develop a cadre of committed laymen who study Torah and take observance of *mitzvot* seriously. And many are of the opinion that too many laypersons view Conservative Judaism as a movement that, in the words of Rabbi Myron M. Fenster, makes changes but demands little in the way of traditional observances.[24]

Rabbi Mordecai Waxman suggests that Conservative Judaism's "very success may in itself be a cause of failure." He adds:

*The Americanization of Orthodoxy and the traditionalization of Reform mean that both of them offer a greater competition to Conservative Judaism than they did in the past, since they provide something of the same values and approach that characterized the Conservative movement under other titles and names.*

Waxman notes that since the movement flourished spontaneously after the second World War, there was no need or time to rethink its position and point to new directions. As a result, some of the internal dynamism has been lost and there is a need to change strategy and add "a pinch of missionary zeal and a conviction that it battles for the Lord."[25]

The late Rabbi Ben Zion Bokser observed that the movement's stress on the historical has led to a failure to stress "ethical and moral dimensions of Judaism" so that personal religion has declined in favor of institutional loyalty.[26]

What is to be done to regenerate the movement and rediscover the lost élan of Conservative Jewry? Dr. Gerson D. Cohen has urged the creation of an independent apparatus of functionaries including ritual slaughterers and circumcisors, ritual baths, Day Schools, etc., so as not to depend on the Orthodox. Above all, he calls for the development of a learned laity who will be as sophisticated as the rabbis. Rabbi Benjamin Kreitman agrees that the solution of the problems in the movement will come by the organization of "a supportive fellowship or community of observers" of Jewish law plus the definition of key concepts such as revelation and the articulation of an ideology. Dr. Robert Gordis writes in much the same vein: he urges the crystallization and articulation of a philosophy of Jewish faith and practice and the building of a committed laity who will embody in their personal lives ideals, insights, and practices to which the movement is dedicated.[27]

There may be a temporary crisis of confidence in Conservative Judaism and the growth of the past has slowed. But comparing the movement in the 1980s to what existed at the birth of the United Synagogue in 1913 or at the inauguration of the Jewish Theological Seminary in 1886 is an inspirational experience and hopeful exhilaration. If the surveys are correct, half of American Jews who belong to synagogues are affiliated with Conservative congregations and the total of American Jews who identify with Conservative Judaism equals Reform and Orthodoxy combined. Nor may we overlook the centripetal force the movement has exerted on its sister movements to the right and left. It clearly has pulled modern Orthodoxy and Reform to the center ideologically and in practice; it has shaped the face of American Judaism incalculably. It has had its failures; but it would be egregiously shortsighted to overlook its successes.

# Reconstructionism

Two phenomena have marked the development of Reconstructionism in the past decade. The first is its solidification into a formal movement in Jewish life and the fourth religious philosophical school. The second is the change of faces and personalities in the movement so that few of the founding fathers and their followers are still in the limelight.

Recontructionism has crystallized into a movement of its own since the mid-1970s. The Reconstructionist Rabbinical College in Philadelphia, founded in 1968, has grown and developed and ordained men and women rabbis. The Fellowship of Reconstructionist Congregations and Havurot numbered 54 members by 1984—double the 1980 membership. The Reconstructionist Rabbinical Association was founded in 1975 and by 1984 counted over 110 men and women. But the total of Reconstructionist members has not climbed appreciably as evidenced by the number of subscribers to the *Reconstructionist* magazine which has remained fairly constant at around 6,600 to 7,000.

The leadership has changed, too. The old familiar leaders are gone; new faces have replaced them. Mordecai M. Kaplan, founding father of Reconstructionism, died in November 1983, at the remarkable age of 102. Rabbi Eugene Kohn, his longtime associate, had previously passed away. Kaplan's son-in-law Rabbi Ira Eisenstein retired as president of the Reconstructionist Rabbinical College and editor of the *Reconstructionist* magazine, and Rabbi Ludwig Nadelmann retired as executive vice president of the Reconstructionist Foundation. Ira Silverman was installed as president of the College; Rabbi Arthur Green became its new dean of the faculties. Rabbi David Teutsch was selected to the post of executive vice president of the Foundation. A female president, Lillian Kaplan of Maryland, was elected as president of the Fellowship of Reconstructionist Congregations and Havurot at the 1984 Convention and a host of young rabbis began to rise to leadership in the movement. In sum, the old order had passed from the scene; a new one had emerged.

*Reevaluation of Principles*

Reconstructionism has always preached the doctrine that Jews must constantly reevaluate and reinterpret Jewish ideas and values. True to that concept, the leaders of the movement have designated 1985 to reevaluate Reconstructionism with the hope of formulating a new platform to be voted on in June 1985. As the editorial in the *Reconstructionist* magazine put it (in an obvious attempt to cut the umbilical cord to Mordecai Kaplan):

> *The rise of a new generation of Reconstructionist leaders and thinkers, including graduates of the Reconstructionist Rabbinical College, has enriched and broadened the base of our leadership, with the inevitable result that one can no longer turn to a single figure for the authoritative Reconstructionist response to a question.*[1]

The editorial continues by noting that people want direction and it suggests that reevaluation is needed to transform "our democratic *philosophy* into a truly democratic *movement*."

The reevaluation has begun with a fresh look at the liturgy of the prayer book and a liturgical commission has started working on an updated version of the Reconstructionist *Sidur* which was published in 1945 and has not been overhauled since.

Rabbi Joseph D. Herzog, for example, has urged that Reconstructionists avoid the "trendy" both in language and ideology. We must learn "to eschew the total identification of Jewish civilization with democratic forms and practices (no matter how admirable these latter may be), to recognize the *evolutionary* character of Jewish worship, and to be unafraid to stand for tradition when such a stand seems desirable and/or defensible." Rabbi Sidney H. Schwarz has cautioned that "*how* we pray is at least as important as *what* we pray." Accordingly, he has underscored the value of a proper atmosphere for prayer, utilization of more, not less Hebrew, and flexibility and change from week to week in order to make prayer a fresher experience.[2]

Little is said, however, about reevaluating Reconstructionism's stance towards Halakhah. In addressing himself to the question, Rabbi Ira Eisenstein seems to reiterate the older views of the movement on the subject. He writes:

> *Let those who have criticized Reconstructionists concede that, by entering the field as a full-fledged movement, they have not, as so often asserted, contributed to divisiveness in Jewish life but have added a fourth option to those now available. As we have said again and again, while we have our doubts about the dynamism of the Halakhah, we contend that Jewish life cannot endure without a Halakhah.*[3]

Eisenstein adds that this means communities and people must legislate and amend the "constitution" and it includes stripping Israel's rabbinate of theocratic privileges. "We do not propose anarchy," he argues, "we propose democracy." The basic Reconstructionist posture on Jewish law seems to remain firm in this period of reevaluation.

There have been some new positions staked out in the realm of Jewish education, however. The *Reconstructionist* magazine has deplored the spread of cults in the ranks of Jewish youth but it has, at the same time, criticized the failure of Jewish spiritual leaders to offer wise and intelligible Torah and it assailed the ineffectiveness of Jewish educators and teachers who are repeating mistakes of the past. Rabbi Sidney H. Schwarz suggested guidelines for more effective teaching of God, Bible, prayers, holidays, and chosenness in a nonsupernatural, non-dogmatic fashion in order to prepare youngsters to meet the challenges of cults and missionaries as well as of other religions and secular ideologies. And several articles and editorials in the *Reconstructionist* have urged the establishment of Reconstructionist Day Schools—a sharp reversal of the long-standing opposition of the movement to such schools as being undemocratic, divisive, and destructive of the public school system.[4]

Thus far, there has been little reevaluation of the God idea in Reconstructionism. There have been many articles in the *Reconstructionist* on the transnatural nature of Divinity, on religious humanism in theology, and on Kaplan's God concept. Still, it is possible that the young generation of reevaluators might yet revise the old Kaplanesque notion of God.[5]

However, the Reconstructionist rejection of the idea of Israel as God's chosen people has been subjected to sharp criticism. Kaplan had abandoned the traditional notion that God had chosen Israel from among all the peoples as an invidious and racist notion. With very few exceptions, his disciples had endorsed his view and the liturgy of the movement reflects that position.

Today, however, the new generation has been reassessing that rejection of the concept of chosen people and some are actually calling for its restoration to the theology and liturgy of the movement. Rabbi Richard A. Hirsch of the Reconstructionist Rabbinical College, for example, has argued:

> *In sum, we can affirm the nuance of chosenness which indicates the uniqueness of Jewish identity based on our relationship to Torah, but we must reject the dimension of chosenness which negates the possibility of other equally unique, sacred and meaningful ways of living in the world.*[6]

Rabbi David Brusin has gone even further and has written that chosenness does not imply invidious comparisons or racist superiority. "To be chosen," he suggests, "is not to be *better* but to be *different* . . . This is not a question of racism, though it may be

a matter of Jewish survival." He adds that there is nothing arbitrary in our chosenness and that it is "both a reason to persist
and a promise of a better world in which all will share."
Whereas some participants in this symposium on the chosen
people merely rehashed Kaplan's views, others among the
younger rabbis urged that a new Reconstructionist Prayer Book
ought to restore the concept to the prayers.[7]

At the same time that the other movements are evaluating
their stances vis-à-vis women, Reconstructionists have but little
to say on the matter, primarily because the movement had
equalized the role of females in Judaism long ago by creating
the Bat Mitzvah ceremony, by giving women a fully equal
participatory role in the worship services, and by accepting
women for ordination as rabbis at the Reconstructionist Rabbinical College from the outset. The *Reconstructionist* magazine
applauded the Jewish Theological Seminary for its vote to admit women to the Rabbinical school. At the same time, it challenged the Seminary faculty and the Rabbinical Assembly to resolve the normative opposition to women participating in a
Beth Din (rabbinical court) and serving as witnesses on sacred
documents such as marriages or divorces. The same editorial
called on the Conservative movement to now realize that normal halakhic channels are impossible to resolve such dilemmas
but "the earnest will of a majority of committed Jews can be de-
terminative." To further implement its ideal of equalization of
men and women in Judaism, the Reconstructionists instituted
an egalitarian *get* (religious divorce) in 1980 so that a woman
may now divorce her husband if she chooses and not be subject
to his whim. In the light of the egalitarian strivings and wom-
en's liberation tendencies in the other wings of Judaism,
Reconstructionism views its position on equality of the sexes as
vindicated.[8]

## Mixed Marriage

The painful problem of mixed marriage has, naturally, affected the Reconstructionist movement as well. A series of con-

ferences and sessions sponsored by both the rabbis and laity of
the movement have grappled with the issue. Already in 1968,
the Reconstructionist movement affirmed the practice of regarding as a Jew a child whose father *or* mother is Jewish provided that the child is raised and educated as a Jew. Such a
child, ruled the group, has all the privileges and full status as a
Jew. In other words, the Reconstructionists espoused the cause
of patrilineal descent a dozen years before the Reform created
such a public stir and so much ill-will by their decision. Curiously, almost no publicity accompanied the Reconstructionist
proposal and little vituperation from Orthodox quarters was
heard. Indeed, when the Reform movement promulgated its
1980 decision to favor patrilineal descent, the *Reconstructionist*
magazine took note of the occasion, congratulated the Reform
group and urged the Conservative group to follow suit, while
at the same time it reminded its readers that the Reconstructionists had led the way in 1968.[9]

Subsequently, the Reconstructionist Rabbinical Association
and the Federation of Reconstructionist Congregations and Havurot sought to clarify the movement's stance on the matter.
The Rabbinical Association, while opposed to conversion activities, has gone on record as favoring conversion for marriage
and urged a program of outreach to non-Jewish spouses. The
Rabbinical Association issued *Guidelines on Inter-Marriage* in
1983 spelling out in detail its approach to the problem. The
*Guidelines* reiterate the belief that Jewish marriage is the best
way of preserving Jewish values and that intermarriage between a Jew and a non-Jew in which no conversion has taken
place is "a matter of serious concern" that can only be com-
batted by "strengthening of Jewish life as a whole." The *Guidelines* urge that rabbis counsel mixed couples contemplating
marriage and seek to win over the non-Jew to conversion since
"conversionary marriages" enrich the Jewish People qualita-
tively and quantitatively. The *Guidelines* suggest that synagogues be receptive to intermarried couples, recognize the children as fully Jewish, but leave it up to the individual
congregation to decide about accepting non-Jewish spouses

into membership. The *Guidelines* summon the rabbi to maximize communication with the couple in order to save the children for Judaism. They believe that a Jewish wedding ceremony (*kiddushin*) "should be reserved for the marriage of a Jew to a Jew." The rabbi may, if he deems it fruitful, attend a civil marriage of a couple where the non-Jew has not converted and "offer appropriate remarks welcoming the couple into the Jewish community and encouraging their continued involvement in the life of the Jewish people." Only if the couple plans to identify as Jews should he join in the civil ceremony. The *Guidelines* conclude by suggesting that since intermarriage will surely rise as integration of Jews continues, rabbis cannot afford to turn away mixed couples. Indeed, "if we are more receptive to those already intermarried as well as to those contemplating intermarriage, this challenge may yet be turned into a promising opportunity for Jewish renewal." The Appendix to the *Guidelines* spells out the process of conversion, endorses ritual immersion and circumcision, but leaves the matter of symbolic circumcision of already circumcised males to the discretion of the rabbi.[10]

The Fellowship of Reconstructionist Congregations and Havurot adopted a Resolution on Intermarriage at its 1984 convention that endorsed the *Guidelines* and went further by inviting the Reconstructionist Rabbinic Fellowship to prepare guidelines for a "non-*kiddushin* ceremony of marriage." It also opposed rabbinic participation with non-Jewish clergy in weddings and it suggested that a rabbi who refuses to serve a mixed couple refer them to another rabbi.[11]

These Guidelines and Resolutions provoked sharp controversy in the pages of the *Reconstructionist* magazine. Veteran Reconstructionist leader Rabbi Jack J. Cohen was highly critical of them. He deplored the notion of a rabbi "saying a few words at the civil ceremony"; he wondered how a synagogue can accept unconverted Jews as members; he described out-marriage as a dead-end for Jews and depicted the *Guidelines* as hypocritical. Conservative Rabbi Stephen Lerner, writing in the *Reconstructionist*, viewed the *Guidelines* as "ingenuous in the extreme" and suggested that the idea of a rabbi lending his presence to a c ̇ l wedding "would subvert the revitalization of American Jewish life." Rabbi Albert Axelrod of Brandeis University urged that rabbis officiate selectively at mixed marriages when we have a chance for conversion. Rabbi Richard A. Hirsh suggested we require *ab initio* conversion of babies but not *fait accompli* conversions for adults who have lived as Jews. Rabbi Ronald M. Brauner offered a novel suggestion: he would revive the ancient biblical status of a *ger toshav* or resident alien, have a rabbi *devise* a ceremony to create such a category of semi-Jew, and then invite a "sensitive, committed Jewish representative of the state" (preferably a judge) to perform the marriage with a rabbi assisting. Other equally ingenious solutions to the mixed-marriage dilemma have been offered by Reconstructionist rabbis and laypersons.[12]

## The State of Israel

Reconstructionism has remained a firm and passionate partisan of the State of Israel and the Zionist movement. At the same time, it has not remained an uncritical lover. For example, several editorials in the *Reconstructionist* magazine took Prime Minister Begin to task for establishing settlements at a time when they are calculated to irritate the president of the United States and the administration. At the same time, it concurred that no part of Eretz Yisrael should be declared forever *Judenrein*.[13]

Several editorials denounced the marriage of religion to politics in Israel and the favoring of Orthodoxy to the exclusion of other forms of religious expression. One editorial assailed Mr. Begin for dealing with the Agudat Israel Party in seeking to change the Law of Return that would delegitimatize non-Orthodox conversions. Another found it inconceivable that the State should grant religious liberties to Christians and Moslems but not to Jews. Yet another editorial called for the disestablishment of the religious parties lest Israel become an Iranian-style theocracy. Several editorials denounced Jewish terrorists and "militant theocracy" and cited the need to reconstitute the Jewish spirit and Zionist visions of old predicated on social justice, religious pluralism, contemporary culture, economic equality, and peace. "We must lend support with yet greater vigor to those struggling to create a democratic and spiritually open Jewish State." Yet another editorial queried:

> *How long must we wait for the emergence in Israel of a cogent voice which advocates a progressive spiritual movement, which takes the Jewish tradition seriously and grapples with its meaningful reinterpretation in a contemporary Israeli society?*

The same editorial urged the emergence of Israeli discussions of the relevance of Jewish tradition to contemporary problems and the development of a religion of ethical nationhood that will protest against Orthodox hegemony.[14]

In other recent editorials on Israel, the *Reconstructionist* magazine assailed Zionist leaders in Israel and officials of the Jewish Agency for failing to be aware of the complexities of Jewish life the world over. The editors suggested that only by forging a greater partnership with Diaspora Jewry can Israel encourage *aliyah*. In an even more controversial editorial, the journal called for acts of mutual recognition between Israel and the PLO as the only way to peace.[15]

## Social Action

Reconstructionism has remained committed to progressive social action as in the past. Generally, its stand on social problems has been liberal, compassionate, committed to human and civil rights, and devoted to the ideal of separation of church and state.

The Reconstructionists have been sharply critical of attempts to erode the separation of church and state and the Reagan Administration and the Rev. Jerry Falwell and his fundamentalist Christian colleagues have come under fire in numerous editorials in the *Reconstructionist* magazine. The editorials have deplored the introduction of a Constitutional amendment to allow prayer in the public schools since that merely distracts us from the really crucial issues of the day, namely unemployment, bankruptcies, suspension of social programs, drug abuse, social unrest, and crime. Another editorial supported the Supreme Court ruling banning the display of the Ten Commandments in classrooms. A long editorial expressed strong opposition to the Supreme Court's ruling allowing the placing of a crèche on public property arguing that it is *not* an American symbol and urging the mobilization of Jewish political resources to defend America from this action that "lays the groundwork for the further legitimization of religious beliefs and values which are not comparable to Christian ones." The editorial argues that nondenominational prayer is equally dangerous to our freedoms, for who will compose such prayers? And what of the plight of the children forced to listen? "We deplore totalitarian attempts to enforce social and religious values by legislation which deprives the individual of freedom of choice," adds the editorial, and it urges that disestablishment of religion and pluralism are needed in America.[16] Interestingly, the movement has abandoned Dr. Kaplan's old proposal to create a civic religion that could be introduced into public life and public schools. Clearly, events have doomed his proposal to failure as sectarianism has gripped much of public affairs in recent years.

Several editorials and public statements denouncing policies of the Reagan Administration were fired off by the movement. The Reagan policies of cutting social services, aid to the poor, and cultural and educational programs have been decried. The approach of the government in handling poverty is wrong, suggest the magazine's editors, because it blames the poor for poverty, relinquishes government responsibility to the corporations and voluntary sector, and focuses distressingly on statistics. Additionally, various editorials and resolutions have called for federal gun-control legislation, tighter accountability of the CIA, and the ratification of the SALT II arms control treaty while at the same time deploring the continued faith in the validity of détente in the face of continued Communist expansion.[17]

In 1981, the Reconstructionist Rabbinical Association took a stand on the controversial abortion question. It affirmed the right of women to choose abortion; it denounced limiting of federal and state funding for abortions; it opposed hospital policies that would harass women or curtail their access to abortions; and it opposed legislation or Constitutional amendments restricting women's rights to abortion.[18] As to the matter of declining Jewish population, the *Reconstructionist* editorial staff suggest that the trend to declining population will not be reversed by exhorting couples to have more children but by the establishment of a community "which offers as much esteem to full-time parents (mothers or fathers) as to successful professionals." The editors exhort, "Only if the commitments of Jews are cultivated do we have reason to expect that the traditional Jewish values of family life will achieve renewed popularity."[19]

Among other significant social and political pronouncements of Reconstructionists are: an attack on the politicization of UNESCO and the suggestion that America withhold funds; a statement of support for the Polish Solidarity movements; endorsement of "living wills" to avoid heroic efforts to prolong life; and approval of conscientious and selective conscientious objectors who refuse to serve in the armed forces.[20] In a word, Reconstructionists deal with the entire gamut of social and political concerns and follow a basically liberal line.

*Critique and Prognosis*

Until recently, Reconstructionists have engaged in little self-criticism or analysis of the basic tenets of the movement. The late Rabbi Milton Steinberg was a notable exception: he challenged both Kaplan's concept of God as well as his rejection of the chosen people idea. But the rest of Kaplan's disciples accepted the master's views almost uncritically and their writings can best be described as "warmed-over Kaplan."

This is no longer the case among the new generation of Reconstructionists, many of whom neither knew nor studied with Dr. Kaplan and are therefore not emotionally committed to his views by virtue of personal contact with him. A symposium on *The Future of Reconstructionism*, edited by Rabbi Sidney H. Schwarz, appeared in the March 1982 *Reconstructionist* magazine and offers glimpses into the new thinking of the young rabbis and leaders. All agree that Reconstructionism has made a great contribution by defining Judaism as a religious civilization; all concur that its naturalistic conception of God is most meaningful to modern Jews; all are attracted to its emphasis on Jewish peoplehood, its pragmatism, its pluralistic approach to Judaism, and its rigorous and rationalistic examination of past principles. Most of the participants believe that a new approach is needed in the area of liturgy, and several urge the restoration of the chosen people concept.[21]

Rabbi Ron Aigen, for example, calls for the creation of new liturgy which speaks to post-Holocaust Jews. Reconstructionist liturgy no longer applies because it is too rational and unresponsive to the emotional upheavals of the Holocaust, the State of Israel, and the nuclear age. Rabbi Rachel Alpert, while applauding Kaplan's notion that "the past must have a vote, not a veto," urges that a new *Sidur* must be produced offering a choice of the "traditional Reconstructionist text" plus alternative forms of prayers. Rabbi Ronald Brauner agrees with Rabbi Alpert on the need for alternatives in prayer texts but he insists on restoring the chosen people concept since he believes Kaplan's critique is no longer relevant. Rabbi David Brusin suggests that future editions of the prayer books contain traditional prayers at the same time that we must continue searching for better, more meaningful prayers. Rabbi Ira Eisenstein tries to defend the old views of naturalism-humanism, and while he concedes that flexibility is needed in liturgical reform, he insists that a new prayer book must be true to naturalism. Rabbis David Klatzker and Dennis C. Sasso see no need for a new prayer book or updated liturgy and they second Eisenstein's insistence on naturalism-humanism in worship. Ira Silverman, however, writes that Kaplan went too far in deleting supernaturalism from his theology and liturgy and he suggests a synthesis of naturalism and supernaturalism. Rabbis David Teutsch and Neal R. Weinberg want a new *Sidur* with varieties and options of English and Hebrew prayers, and while Rabbi Elliot Skidell agrees with Rabbi Brauner that it is time to restore the concept of chosenness to the prayers, he maintains that Kaplan's transnatural God idea must be preserved. Obviously, the younger rabbis of the movement are not prepared to accept older views on God, prayer, chosenness of Israel, and other basic concepts simply because Mordecai M. Kaplan articulated them.

The future of Reconstructionism is, however, unclear. The founding father is gone; the cult of personality that developed around the incomparable Rabbi Kaplan is over. Can the movement carry on without him? Does it have enough impetus and substance to continue to grow and develop? And is the program of Reconstructionism uniquely attractive and able to draw new members to its ranks?

Much of the answer depends on the directions taken by Reform Judaism. Reform has veered unmistakably to greater respect for tradition. It is reinstituting many discarded ritual practices; it is deeply committed to the State of Israel; its liturgy and religious education are stressing Hebrew; its commitment to Jewish peoplehood is passionate. The older aspects of "classical" Reform so severly criticized by Dr. Kaplan have all but been discarded; the new version of Reform is virtually indistinguishable from Reconstructionism. Even its stand on mixed marriage and patrilineal descent is identical with that of Reconstructionism. In a word, the two movements seem to have arrived at an almost identical position in issues of theology and practice. Why, therefore, should Reconstructionism continue to go its own way and compose and march to its own tune? Would not a coalition with Reform make sense, especially in light of Reconstructionism's success in influencing Reform's ideology and orientation? However, people and institutions being as they are, it is unlikely that the Reconstructionists will dismantle their College, their organization structure, their rabbinic and lay groups, their magazine and press, even if the raison d'être for a fourth grouping in Jewish religious life seems to have evaporated. For the foreseeable future, therefore, it appears likely that Reconstructionism will proceed to expand and implement its programs.

# Notes to the Second Edition

Notes on Orthodoxy

1. See George Gershon Kranzler, "The Changing Orthodox Jewish Community," *Tradition*, 16, 2 (Fall 1976), pp. 61–72.
2. See David Ellenson, "A Response by Modern Orthodoxy to Jewish Religious Pluralism: The Case of Esriel Hildesheimer," *Tradition*, 17, 4 (Spring 1979), pp. 74–89. Cf. Allan Nadler, "Piety and Politics: The Case of the Satmar Rebbe," *Judaism*, 3, 2 (Spring 1982), pp. 135–152.
3. See the reports in *The Jewish Week* of June 1, 1984, p. 8. Cf. "The State of Orthodoxy" in *Tradition*, 20, 1 (Spring 1982). Also Cf. Rabbi Klaperman's letter to *The Jewish Week* of June 1, 1984, p. 24, explaining the RCA's position on participation in the Synagogue Council of America.
4. Rackman's views are expressed in *Tradition*, 20, 1 (Spring 1982), pp. 58 ff.
5. See Alster's letter to *The Jewish Week* of June 15, 1984.
6. See Eliezer Berkovits, *Not in Heaven* (New York, 1983), *passim*; cf. his *Crisis and Faith* (New York, 1976).
7. See J.D. Bleich, *Contemporary Halakhic Problems*, 2 vols. (New York, 1977 & 1983), *passim*. Cf. my review in *Conservative Judaism*, XXXIII, 1 (Fall 1979), pp. 83–89.
8. The Agudat Harabanim, for example, issued a statement in 1982 prohibiting a woman from participating in women's worship services as "worthless ceremonies that are totally contrary to Halacha." Such women's prayer

groups "are a product of pure ignorance and illiteracy," continues the statement, and it admonishes these Orthodox rabbis: "Do not make a comedy out of Torah." See Jeffrey S. Gurock, "Resisters and Accommodators: Varieties of Orthodox Rabbis in America, 1886–1983," *American Jewish Archives*, XXXV, 2 (November 1983), p. 158. Even a leader of the liberal wing, Dr. Norman Lamm, President of Yeshiva University, has assailed the Reform movement's patrilineal decision as a "fig leaf" that is "too thin to cover the nakedness of a movement which has countenanced intermarriage, even without the benefit of conversion Reform-style." See *The Jewish Week* of May 13, 1983, p. 27.

9. Cf. articles by Avraham Weiss, Saul J. Berman, Chava K. Poupko, Devora L. Wohlgelernter, Arthur M. Silver, and Reuven P. Bulka in *Tradition*, 20, 2 (Summer 1982), pp. 106–118; 14, 2 (Fall 1973), pp. 5–28; 15, 4 (Spring 1976), pp. 45–67; 17, 3 (Summer 1978), pp. 74–85; 17, 4 (Spring 1979), pp. 27–40, etc.

10. Cf. her *On Women and Judaism* (Philadelphia, 1981), pp. 3, 6, 10, 95–97, 138, 143, 174, and *passim*.

11. Cf. Moshe Meiselman, *Jewish Woman in Jewish Law* (New York, 1978), pp. 145, 146, 150, 154, 169, and *passim*.

12. Cf. *Tradition*, 14, 2 (Fall 1973), pp. 113–117. Klaperman's speech is quoted in *The Jewish Week* of June 15, 1984, p. 8.

13. For Rackman's and Greenberg's view see the symposium on women in the Rabbinate in *Judaism*, 33, 1 (Winter 1984), pp. 23–32 and 63–69.

14. Cf. Eliezer Don-Yehiya, "Jewish Orthodoxy, Zionism, and the State of Israel," *The Jerusalem Quarterly*, 31 (Spring 1984), pp. 10–30.

15. See Lawrence Kaplan, "Rabbi Isaac Hutner's 'Daat Torah Perspective' On the Holocaust: A Critical Analysis," *Tradition*, 18, 3 (Fall 1980), pp. 235–248.

16. See Immanuel Jakobovits, "Religious Responses to Jewish Statehood," *Tradition*, 20, 3 (Fall 1982), pp. 188–204.

17. See Jakobovits' statement in *Tradition*, 20, 1 (Spring 1982), pp. 42 f. Cf. Rabbi Soloveitchik's view in his *Be-Sod Hayahad Ve-Hayahid* (Jerusalem, 5736), pp. 431 f.

18. Hecht is quoted in the editorial of the *Jerusalem Post*, June 17–24, 1984 (international edition), p. 23. The statement of the 25 American rabbis was published as an ad in the *Jerusalem Post* of June 8, 1984, daily edition. Professor Tendler's paper was sent out in a private mailing to garner support for the defense fund for the accused Jewish terrorists.

19. The counterstatement of 13 rabbis was published as a letter to the *Jerusalem Post* of June 13, 1984, daily edition, p. 2.

20. Cf. Jerry Hochbaum, "American Orthodoxy," *Tradition*, 14, 3 (Spring 1974), pp. 5–14; Joshua Berkowitz, "The Challenge to Modern Orthodoxy," *Judaism*, 33, 1 (Winter 1984), pp. 100–106.

21. See the "Symposium—The State of Orthodoxy," *Tradition*, 20, 1 (Spring

1982), consisting of essays by 22 participants, most of whom are or have been pulpit rabbis.

22. Cf. Aharon Lichtenstein, *ibid.*, pp. 49–50.

23. Cf. Michael Wyshograd, *ibid.*, pp. 80–83.

### Notes on Reform

1. For the text of the Centenary Perspective see Eugene Borowitz, *Reform Judaism Today* (New York, 1977–78), I, pp. XIX–XXV.

2. *Ibid.* The three volumes by Borowitz, *Reform Judaism Today*, are in reality a careful commentary on and analysis of the Perspective. The reader should contrast this latest document with Reform's previously articulated Pittsburgh and Columbus Platforms in the Supplement to Vol. III of Borowitz's book.

3. See Borowitz, *Reform Judaism Today*, Vol. I, pp. 12 f., 37 ff., etc. Cf. W. Gunther Plaut, "Religious Discipline and Liberal Judaism," CCAR *Yearbook*, 85 (1975), pp. 163–173. See Eugene Lipman, "Change and Authority: The Continuum of Jewish Experience," CCAR *Yearbook*, 93 (1983), pp. 21 ff.; Norman Mirsky, "Constructing a Reform Jewish Identity," *Journal of Reform Judaism*, XXXI, 2 (Spring 1984), pp. 3–19; Dan Cohn-Sherbok, "Law and Freedom in Reform Judaism," *ibid.*, XXX, 1 (Winter 1983), pp. 88–97.

4. See Plaut's speech cited in Note 3 above as well as his other writings.

5. Cf. Mordecai Podet in CCAR *Yearbook*, 93 (1983), pp. 33 f.; Walter Jacob and Mark N. Staitman, "Law and Freedom in Reform Judaism—a Rejoinder," *Journal of Reform Judaism*, XXX, 1 (Winter 1983), pp. 98–104; Solomon B. Freehof in his Introduction to *Reform Responsa for Our Time* (Cincinnati, 1977), p. 6; Daniel J. Silver, "Liberal Judaism Today," CCAR *Yearbook*, 84 (1974), pp. 84–92; William Braude, "An Outline for Theological Discourse in Reform," *Journal of Reform Judaism*, XXIX, 1 (Winter 1982), p. 14.

6. See the CCAR *Yearbook*, 93 (1983), pp. 157–160.

7. For divergent views, cf. David Polish, "Jewish Proselytizing—Another Opinion," *Journal of Reform Judaism*, XXVI, 3 (Summer 1979), pp. 1–9; articles in *ibid.*, XXX, 1 (Winter 1983), pp. 1–56 & XXX, 4 (Fall 1983), pp. 17–28.

8. See Freehof, *op. cit.* in Note 5, pp. 1–7; Walter Jacob, *ibid.*, pp. IX–XXVII and his Introduction to *American Reform Responsa* (New York, 1983), pp. XIV–XVIII. Cf. Robert N. Levine and David Ellenson, "Jewish Tradition, Contemporary Sensibility and Halacha," *Journal of Reform Judaism*, XXX, 1 (Winter 1983), pp. 54 ff.; Plaut, *op. cit.* in Note 3; Peter J. Haas, "Responsa Reconsidered," *Journal of Reform Judaism*, XXX, 3, pp. 31–37; Bernard H. Mehlman, "A Reform *Get*: A Proposal," *ibid.*, pp. 31–36.

9. See Mihaly's speech assailing Plaut and the traditionalists in CCAR *Yearbook*, 85 (1975), pp. 176–181; Leon I. Feuer, "The Condition of Reform Judaism," *Journal of Reform Judaism*, XXVII, 3 (1980), pp. 26 ff.

10. See Borowitz, *Reform Judaism Today*, Vol. II, pp. 131–135; Vol. III, pp. 6, 17, and *passim*.

11. Borowitz, *op. cit.*, Vol. I, pp. 64, 84, 97 and *passim*; CCAR *Yearbook*, 93 (1983), pp. 186–188.

12. See CCAR *Yearbook*, 91 (1981), pp. 119–124; David Polish, "An Outline for Theological Discourse in Reform," *Journal of Reform Judaism*, XXIX, 1 (Winter 1982), pp. 12–13; Levi Olan, "Reform Judaism in a Post-Modern World," *ibid.*, XXVIII, 1 (Winter 1981), pp. 1–14.

13. See the Social Actions statement in the CCAR *Yearbook*, 93 (1983), pp. 186–193. Cf. Borowitz, *op. cit.*, Vol. III, pp. 125–136.

14. See the *Jewish Week* of May 24, 1984, p. 4.

15. See Daniel J. Silver, "Liberal Judaism Today," CCAR *Yearbook*, 84 (1974), pp. 84–92.

16. See Richard G. Hirsch, "New Directions in Liberal Judaism in the World Today," *ibid.*, pp. 104 f. Cf. the views of Plaut and Braude cited in Notes 3 and 5.

17. See David Polish, "An Outline for Theological Discourse in Reform," *Journal of Reform Judaism*, XXIX, 1 (Winter 1982), pp. 1–13; Levi Olan, "Reform Judaism in a Post-Modern World," *Journal of Reform Judaism*, XXVIII, 1 (Winter 1981), pp. 1–14.

18. See Schindler's speech in the CCAR *Yearbook*, 92 (1982), p. 63. Cf. Freehof's brief note in the Symposium, "The Conditions of Reform Judaism" in the *Journal of Reform Judaism*, XXVII, 3 (Summer 1980), p. 21. Cf. Borowitz, *Reform Judaism Today*, Vol. I, pp. 15–26. Plaut has suggested that the Rabbinical Assembly will join the Central Conference of American Rabbis on some issues but split later on along different lines. See the *Journal of Reform Judaism*, XXVII, 3 (Summer 1980), pp. 10 f.

19. Cf. Bernard Lazerwitz, "Past and Future Trends in the Size of American Jewish Denominations," *Journal of Reform Judaism*, XXVI, 3 (Summer 1979), pp. 77–82.

Notes on Conservatism

1. See Elliot N. Dorff, "Traditional Judaism," *Conservative Judaism*, XXXIV, 2 (Nov./Dec. 1980), pp. 34–38.

2. See David Lieber, "Staking out the Conservative Position," *ibid.*, XXXII, 1 (Fall 1978), pp. 33–37.

3. See Neil Gillman, "Towards a Theology for Conservative Judaism," *ibid.*, XXXVII, 1 (Fall 1983), pp. 4–22.

4. See Gilbert S. Rosenthal, "The Elements that Unite Us," Rabbinical Assembly *Proceedings*, XLVI (1984), pp. 22–28.

5. See Aaron H. Blumenthal, "The Status of Women in Jewish Law," *Conservative Judaism*, XXXI, 3 (Spring 1977), pp. 24–40.

6. See Robert Gordis, "The Ordination of Women," *Midstream*, XXVI, 7 (August/September 1980), pp. 25–32. Cf. the Symposium, "Women As Rabbis," *Judaism*, 33, 1 (1984), pp. 6–90.

7. For the text of the Report cf. *Conservative Judaism*, XXXII, 3 (Summer 1979), pp. 56–80.

8. For the debate and votes, cf. RA *Proceedings*, XLV (1983), pp. 218–251.

9. See Jacob Agus, "Halakhah in the Conservative Movement," RA *Proceedings*, XXXVII (1975), pp. 102–117.

10. See Robert Gordis, "A Dynamic Halakhah: Principles and Procedures of Jewish Law," *Judaism*, 28, 3 (Spring 1979), pp. 263–282. Cf. the Symposium on Jewish Law in response to his essay with eighteen participants in *ibid.*, 29, 1 (Winter 1980), pp. 5–109.

11. Cf. Seymour Siegel, *Conservative Judaism and Jewish Law* (New York, 1977), Introduction, pp. XIII–XXVI; "Ethics and the Halakhah," *Conservative Judaism*, XXV, 3 (Spring 1971), pp. 33–40; "Conservative Judaism and Jewish Law," RA *Proceedings*, XXXVII (1975), pp. 118–126.

12. Cf. the papers of Kassel Abelson, David Feldman, and Phillip Sigal in RA *Proceedings*, XLV (1983), pp. 77–104.

13. The papers of the Conference are appended to the RA *Proceedings*, XLII (1980), pp. 335–419.

14. See Benjamin Z. Kreitman, "What Does Halakhah Mean to Us?", RA *Proceedings*, XL (1978), pp. 15–19.

15. See Gerson D. Cohen, "What is Conservative Judaism and What Isn't It—In Retrospect, 1922–1977," United Synagogue *Proceedings*, 1977, p. 9.

16. Cf. the Symposium on *Keruv* in *Conservative Judaism*, XXXV, 4 (Summer 1982), pp. 33–62; "*Gerut* and the Conservative Movement," *ibid.*, XXXIII, 1 (Fall 1979), pp. 28–62.

17. See Solomon D. Goldfarb, "Who Is a Jewish Child?", *ibid.*, XXX, 4 (Summer 1976), pp. 3–9. Cf. Phillip Sigal, *op. cit.* in note 12, p. 100.

18. For debates on MERCAZ and a Conservative Zionist organization see United Synagogue *Proceedings*, 1977, pp. 25–34; "A Conservative Zionist Party," *Conservative Judaism*, XXXI, 3 (Spring 1977), pp. 3–14 and XXXI, 4 (Summer 1977), pp. 13–20.

19. See Robert Gordis, "Israel and the Diaspora: A Reassessment," RA *Proceedings*, XXXVIII (1976), pp. 324–345.

20. See Hertzel Fishman, "The Role of Conservative Judaism in Forging Israel's Ethical Nationalism," RA *Proceedings*, XLIII (1981), pp. 64–78.

21. See Louis Jacobs, "Zionism After One-Hundred Years," RA *Proceedings*, XLIII (1981), pp. 56–63.

22. Cf. Wolfe Kelman, "The American Synagogue," RA *Proceedings*, XXXVII (1975), pp. 14–29; "Defeatism, Triumphism or *Gevurah*?", RA *Proceedings*, XLII (1980), pp. 13–24; Marshall Sklare, "Recent Developments in Conservative Judaism," *Midstream*, XVIII, 1 (January 1972), pp. 3–19 and subsequently incorporated in his revised volume, *Conservative Judaism*; Charles

Liebman and Saul Shapiro, "A Survey of the Conservative Movement," unpublished study, September 1979, United Synagogue.
23. Cf. the critical essays of Joseph Lookstein, David S. Shapiro, Ira Eisenstein, Roland Gittelsohn, and others in the Symposium, "Conservative Judaism on its Ninetieth Birthday," *Judaism*, 26, 3 (Summer 1977), pp. 261–357.
24. See Myron M. Fenster, "The Halakhah and Beyond," Supplement to the RA *Proceedings*, XLII (1980), p. 361.
25. Cf. Waxman's paper, "The Basic Issues—An Analysis," in the Symposium in *Judaism* cited in Note 23, pp. 279–285.
26. Cf. Bokser's paper, "The Interaction of History and Theology," *ibid.*, pp. 324 f.
27. Cf. Gerson D. Cohen, "The Conservative Jewish Mission in our Tenth Decade," RA *Proceedings*, XXXIX (1977), pp. 40–43; Benjamin Z. Kreitman, "What Does Halakhah Mean to Us?", *ibid.*, XL (1978), pp. 18 f.; Robert Gordis, *Understanding Conservative Judaism* (New York, 1978), Introduction, p. XI.

Notes on Reconstructionism

1. See the *Reconstructionist*, L, 2 (Oct.–Nov. 1984), pp. 6–7.
2. *Ibid.*, XLVIII, 3 (May 1982), pp. 7–10 & 11–16.
3. *Ibid.*, XLV, 10 (February 1980), pp. 5–6.
4. See Sidney H. Schwarz, "Reconstructionism in Our Hebrew Schools," the *Reconstructionist*, XLVII, 6 (October 1981), pp. 27–31. Cf. the editorial in the *Reconstructionist*, XLVII, 3 (May 1981), p. 4.
5. See William E. Kaufman, "The New Dimension in Kaplan's Religious Thought," the *Reconstructionist*, XLI, 7 (October 1975), pp. 7–13; "Mordecai M. Kaplan's Process Philosophy and the Problem of Evil," *ibid.*, XLVII, 5 (August 1981), pp. 26–31. Cf. Harold M. Schulweis, *Evil and the Morality of God* (Cincinnati, 1984), for a discussion of "predicate theology."
6. See the Symposium on, "The Chosen People Reconsidered," the *Reconstructionist*, L, 1 (September 1984), p. 11 and *passim*.
7. *Ibid.*, pp. 20 f.
8. See the Editorial in the *Reconstructionist*, XLIX, 3 (December 1983–January 1984), p. 5. The use of the egalitarian *get* was announced in May of 1980.
9. See the Editorial in the *Reconstructionist*, XLV, 9 (January 1980), pp. 3–5.
10. See "Guidelines on Intermarriage," published by the Reconstructionist Rabbinical Association. The "Guidelines" were approved on March 16, 1983 at the annual convention.
11. The Resolution was adopted at the 24th convention of the Fellowship of Reconstructionist Congregations and Havurot on June 16, 1984.
12. See Jack J. Cohen, "The Rabbinic Role: A Response to the RRA Guidelines," the *Reconstructionist*, XLIX, 3 (December 1983–January 1984), pp. 8–19. Cf. Stephen Lerner's critique, *ibid.*, p. 16; Richard A. Hirsh, the *Recon-*

*structionist*, XLIX, 5 (March 1984), pp. 25–28; Ronald M. Brauner, *ibid.*, XLVIII, 2 (April 1982), pp. 28–30.

13. See, e.g., the Editorials in the *Reconstructionist*, XLVII, 6 (October 1981), pp. 4–5; XLVI, 2 (April 1980), pp. 3–4, etc.

14. See the Editorials in the *Reconstructionist*, XLIX, 8 (July–August 1984), pp. 5–6; L, 1 (September 1984), pp. 6–7.

15. Editorial in the *Reconstructionist*, XLIX, 5 (March 1984), p. 6; XLVI, 4 (June 1980), pp. 4–6.

16. Editorials in the *Reconstructionist*, XLVIII, 4 (June 1982), pp. 3–4; *ibid.*, XLIX, 7 (June 1984), pp. 5–6. Kaplan had first proposed a "Nondenominational religion of democracy" in 1951 in his volume, *The Faith of America*.

17. See the Editorial in the *Reconstructionist*, XLIX, 5 (March 1984), pp. 5–6. Statements favoring gun-control legislation were made back in 1975 and have been repeated since. Criticism of the CIA and UNESCO were issued in 1975 and again in 1984.

18. The pronouncement of the RRA on abortion was published on January 13, 1981. Editorials in the *Reconstructionist* of June 1981 and February 1982 followed the same line.

19. Cf. Editorial in the *Reconstructionist*, L, 2 (October–November 1984), pp. 5–6.

20. See Editorials in the *Reconstructionist*, XLIX, 5 (March 1984), pp. 7 & 17; XLI, 9 (December 1975), p. 6.

21. See the Symposium, "The Future of Reconstructionism," the *Reconstructionist*, XLVIII, 1 (March 1982), pp. 7–23. Cf. the evaluations of Dr. Kaplan and Reconstructionism on the occasion of his hundredth birthday in *Judaism*, 30, 1 (Winter 1981), pp. 5–103 and the *Reconstructionist*, XLVII, 5 (July–August 1981).

# Supplementary Bibliography

*General**

Ahlstrom, Sidney, *A Religious History of the American People.* New Haven: Yale University Press, 1972.

Cohen, Steven M., *American Modernity and Jewish Identity.* New York: Travistock Publishers, 1983.

Cox, Harvey, *Religion in the Secular City.* New York: Simon and Schuster, 1984.

Howe, Irving, *World of Our Fathers.* New York: Harcourt, Brace, Jovanovich, 1976.

Jacobs, Louis, *A Jewish Theology.* New York: Behrman House, 1973.

Liebman, Charles, *The Ambivalent American Jew.* Philadelphia: The Jewish Publication Society, 1973.

Neuhaus, Richard John, *The Naked Public Square.* Grand Rapids, Mich.: Eerdmans Publishing Co., 1984.

*The reader should consult the *American Jewish Yearbook* published annually and *Judaism* magazine issued quarterly.

Rosenthal, Gilbert S., *Four Paths to One God*. New York: Bloch Publishing Co., 1975.

_____(Ed.), *The American Rabbi*. New York: Ktav, 1977.

_____, *The Many Faces of Judaism*. New York: Behrman House, 1978.

Rubenstein, Richard, *After Auschwitz*. Indianapolis: Bobbs-Merrill Co., 1966.

Sarna, Jonathan D. (Ed.), "The American Rabbinate: A Centennial View." Essays by Jeffrey S. Gurock, Abraham J. Karp, and David Polish. *American Jewish Archives*, XXXV, 2 (November 1983), pp. 91–341.

Silberman, Charles, *A Certain People*. New York: Summit Books, 1985.

Sklare, Marshall (Ed.), *The Jewish Community in America*. New York: Behrman House, 1974.

*Orthodoxy\**

Berkovits, Eliezer, *Crisis and Faith*. New York: Sanhedrin Publishing Co., 1976.

_____, *Not in Heaven*. New York: Ktav, 1983.

Bleich, J. David, *Contemporary Halakhic Problems*, (2 vols.). New York: Ktav, 1977, 1984.

Greenberg, Blu, *On Women and Judaism*. Philadelphia: Jewish Publication Society, 1981.

Rosenbloom, Noah, *Tradition in an Age of Reform*. Philadelphia: Jewish Publication Society, 1976.

Shapiro, David S., *Studies in Jewish Thought*. New York: Yeshiva University Press, 1975.

Soloveitchik, Joseph B., *Reflections of the Rav*. Edited by Abraham Besdin. Jerusalem: The World Zionist Organization, 1979.

_____, *Halakhic Man*. Philadelphia: The Jewish Publication Society, 1983.

*The reader should consult *Tradition* magazine issued twice yearly and *The Jewish Observer* published 10 times yearly.

————, *On Repentance.* Edited by Pinchas Peli. Ramsey, New Jersey: Paulist Press, 1984.

Spero, Shubert, *Morality, Halakha and the Jewish Tradition.* New York: Ktav, 1983.

*Reform*\*\*

Borowitz, Eugene B., *Reform Judaism Today,* (3 vols.). New York: Behrman House, 1977–78.

————, *The Mask Jews Wear.* Port Washington, N.Y.: Sh'ma Press, 1980.

Fackenheim, Emil L., *Quest for Past and Future.* Bloomington, Indiana: Indiana University Press, 1968.

————, *God's Presence in History.* New York: New York University Press, 1970.

————, *The Jewish Return into History.* New York: Schocken, 1978.

Freehof, Solomon B., *Reform Responsa for Our Time.* Cincinnati: Hebrew Union College Press, 1977.

Jacob, Walter (Ed.), *American Reform Responsa.* New York: Central Conference of American Rabbis Press, 1983.

Karff, Samuel (Ed.), *Hebrew Union College—Jewish Institute of Religion at One Hundred Years.* Cincinnati: Hebrew Union College Press, 1976.

Stevens, Elliot L. (Ed.), *Rabbinic Authority.* New York: Central Conference of American Rabbis Press, 1982.

*Conservatism*\*\*\*

Dorff, Elliot N., *Conservative Judaism: Our Ancestors to Our Descendants.* New York: The United Synagogue, 1977.

Gordis, Robert, *Understanding Conservative Judaism.* New York: The Rabbinical Assembly, 1978.

\*\*The reader should consult the *Journal of Reform Judaism* issued quarterly and the *Yearbook* of the Central Conference of American Rabbis published yearly.

\*\*\*The reader should consult *Conservative Judaism* magazine issued quarterly and the *Proceedings* of the Rabbinical Assembly published yearly.

Greenberg, Simon, *A Jewish Philosophy and Pattern of Life.* New York: The Jewish Theological Seminary, 1981.

Jacobs, Louis, *We Have Reason to Believe.* London: Vallentine, Mitchell, 1965.

———, *A Tree of Life.* Oxford: Oxford University Press, 1984.

Klein, Isaac, *A Guide to Jewish Religious Practice.* New York: The Jewish Theological Seminary, 1979.

Novak, David, *Law and Theology in Judaism,* (2 vols.). New York: Ktav, 1974, 1976.

Siegel, Seymour (Ed.), *Conservative Judaism and Jewish Law.* New York: The Rabbinical Assembly, 1977.

Siegel, Seymour and Elliot Gertel (Eds.), *God in the Teachings of Conservative Judaism.* New York: The Rabbinical Assembly, 1985.

*Reconstructionism**

Brauner, Ronald A. *Shiv'im: Essays and Studies in Honor of Ira Eisenstein.* New York: Ktav, 1977.

———, (Ed.), *Essays and Studies.* Philadelphia: The Reconstructionist Rabbinical College, 1979.

———, *Jewish Civilization: Essays and Studies.* New York: The Reconstructionist Rabbinical College, 1981.

Kaufman, William, *Contemporary Jewish Philosophies.* New York: The Reconstruction Press, 1976.

Kushner, Harold, *When Bad Things Happen to Good People.* New York: Schocken, 1981.

Schulweiss, Harold, *Evil and the Morality of God.* Cincinnati: Hebrew Union College Press, 1984.

*The reader should consult the *Reconstructionist* magazine issued 8 times yearly.

# Index